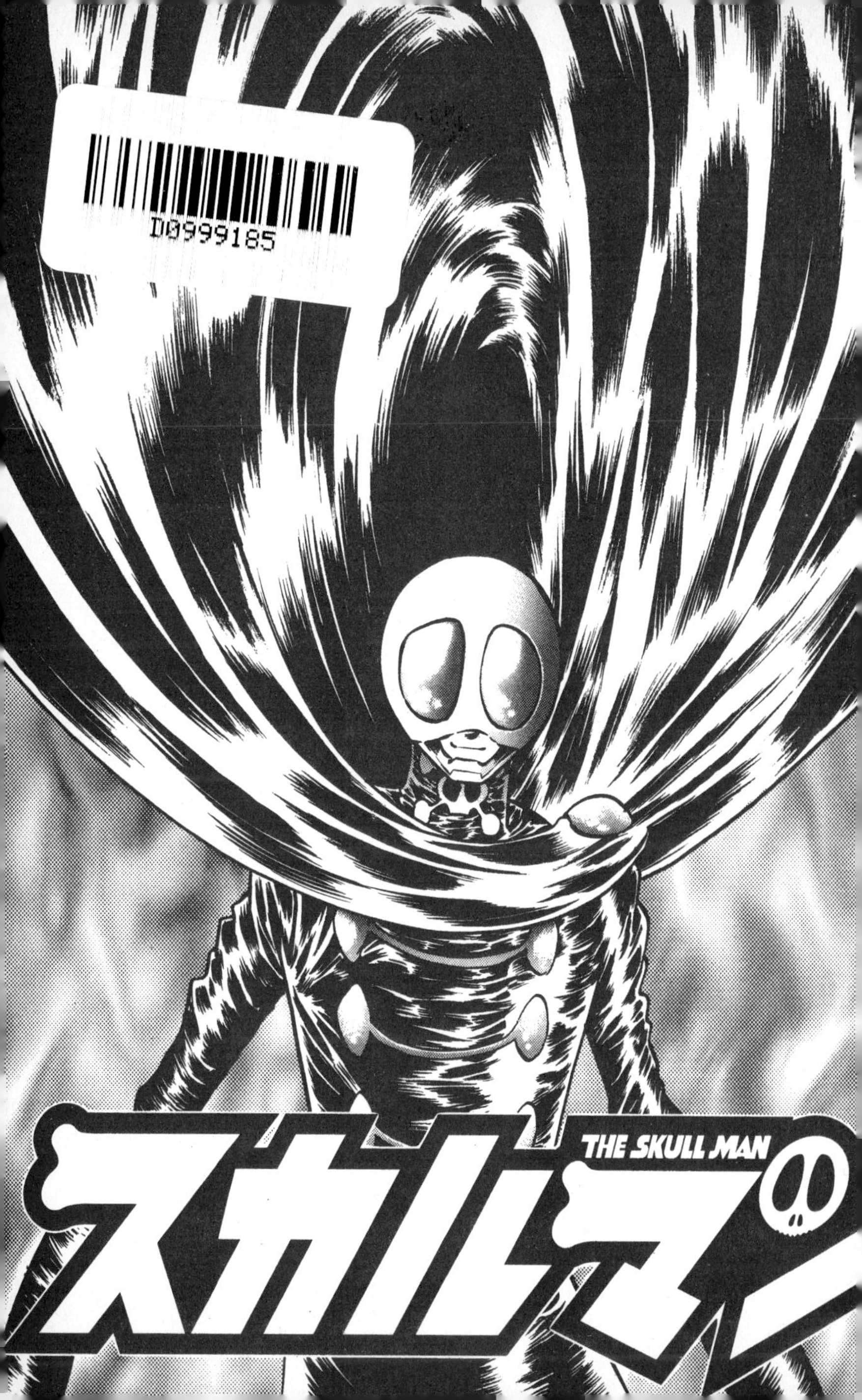
THE SKULL MAN
スカルマン

Other 100% Authentic Manga Available from TOKYOPOP®:

COWBOY BEBOP 1-3 (of 3)
All-new adventures of interstellar bounty hunting, based on the hit anime seen on Cartoon Network.

MARMALADE BOY 1-3 (of 8)
A tangled teen romance for the new millennium.

REAL BOUT HIGH SCHOOL 1-3 (of 4+)
At Daimon High, teachers don't break up fights…they grade them.

MARS 1-3 (of 15)
Biker Rei and artist Kira are as different as night and day, but fate binds them in this angst-filled romance.

GTO 1-4 (of 23+)
Biker gang member Onizuka is going back to school…as a teacher!

CHOBITS 1-2 (of 5+)
In the future, boys will be boys and girls will be…robots? The newest hit series from CLAMP!

SKULL MAN 1-3 (of 7+)
They took his family. They took his face. They took his soul. Now, he's going to take his revenge.

DRAGON KNIGHTS 1-3 (of 17)
Part dragon, part knight, ALL glam. The most inept knights on the block are out to kick some demon butt.

INITIAL D 1-3 (of 23+)
Delivery boy Tak has a gift for driving, but can he compete in the high-stakes world of street racing?

PARADISE KISS 1-2 (of 3+)
High fashion and deep passion collide in this hot new shojo series!

KODOCHA: Sana's Stage 1-2 (of 10)
There's a rumble in the jungle gym when child star Sana Kurata and bully Akito Hayama collide.

ANGELIC LAYER 1-2 (of 5)
In the future, the most popular game is Angelic Layer, where hand-raised robots battle for supremacy.

LOVE HINA 1-4 (of 14)
Can Keitaro handle living in a dorm with five cute girls…and still make it through school?

Coming Soon from TOKYOPOP®:

SHAOLIN SISTERS 1 (of 5)
The epic martial-arts/fantasy sequel to Juline, by the creator of Vampire Princess Miyu.

KARE KANO: He Says, She Says 1 (of 12+)
What happens when the smartest girl in school gets competition from the cutest guy?

Vol.3

Written and Illustrated by
Kazuhiko Shimamoto

Created by
Shotaro Ishinomori

Los Angeles - Tokyo

English Adaptation - Fred Patten
Translator – Ray Yoshimoto
Retouch and Lettering – Max Porter
Cover Designer – Rod Sampson

Editor – Luis Reyes
Production Manager – Joaquin Reyes
Art Director – Matt Alford
VP of Production – Ron Klamert
Publisher – Stuart Levy

Email: editor@TOKYOPOP.com
Come visit us at www.TOKYOPOP.com

A  manga

TOKYOPOP® Presents
The Skull Man Vol. 3 by Kazuhiko Shimamoto Shotaro Ishinomori
TOKYOPOP® is a registered trademark of Mixx Entertainment, Inc.

ISBN: 1-931514-67-4
First TOKYOPOP® Printing: August 2002

10 9 8 7 6 5 4 3 2 1

Printed in the USA

The Skull Man
Vol 3

The Mimic 7

The Wasps 33

The Wasp Hive Hotel 59

The Hum of the Wasps 89

The Queen 117

The Killer Wasp 143

The Drone 169

The Sting 193

The Story Thus Far ...

Fearing that the genetic experiments being conducted by his son and daughter-in-law would prove more harmful to humanity than good, Toratsuki Chisato had the couple murdered and vowed to raise his grandchildren, Maya and Tatsuo. When the children began demonstrating the same types of superhuman abilities manifest in their parents, Toratsuki decided to put an end to it all by locking himself and his brood in a burning house. The children survived, though. Decades later they long to discover the source of their powers.

Tatsuo emerged from obscurity as The Skull Man and now longs to crush the estate that his grandfather left behind ... but a larger organization born out of what remained of the Chisato estate may be aiming to continue the genetic experimentation that killed his parents. Torn between revenge and a growing sense of responsibility for mankind, Tatsuo continues to search for answers, even as his body continues to mutate. Only his sister Maya, a mystical, unseen presence in his life, has the ability to pacify his rage ... and only the complete destruction of that mysterious organization will quell his thirst for revenge.

CH.15 擬態 MIMIC

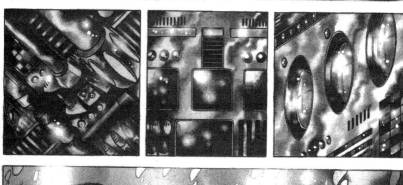

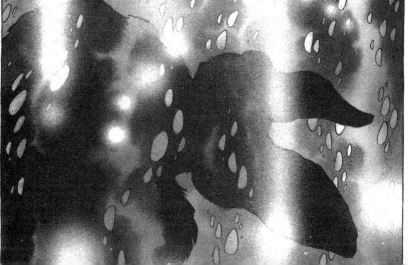

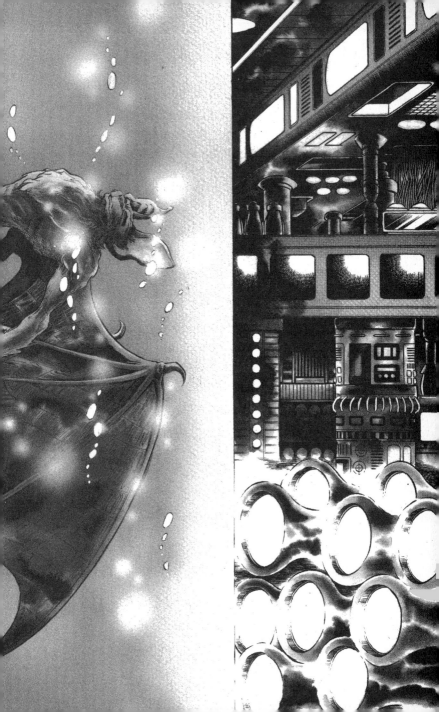

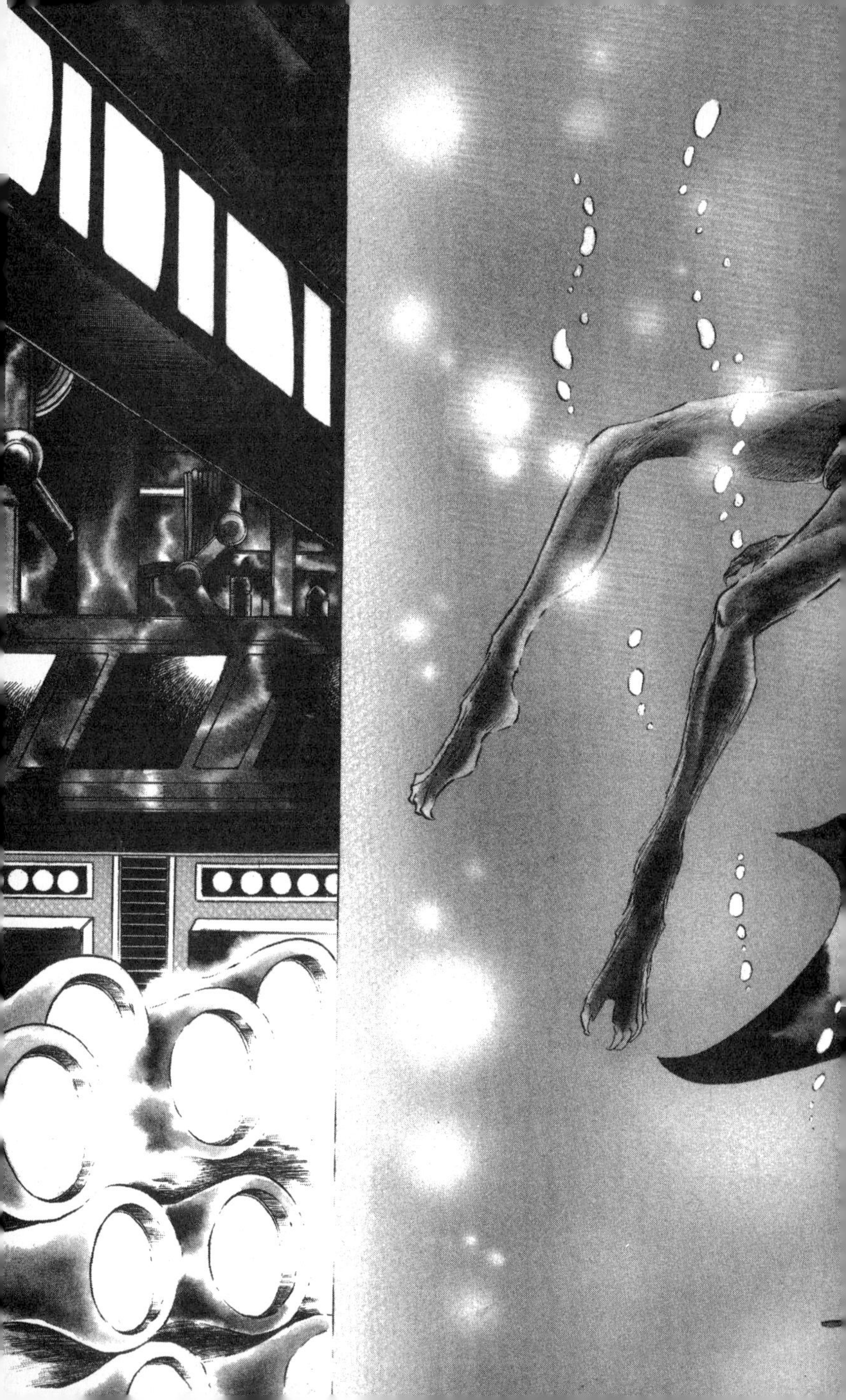

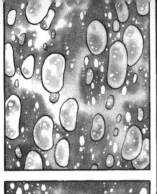
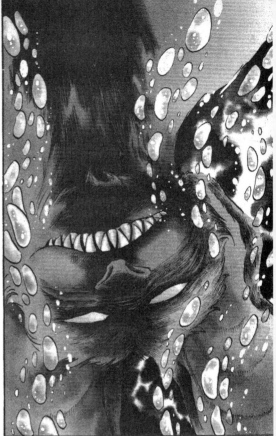
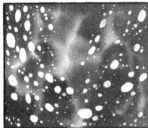

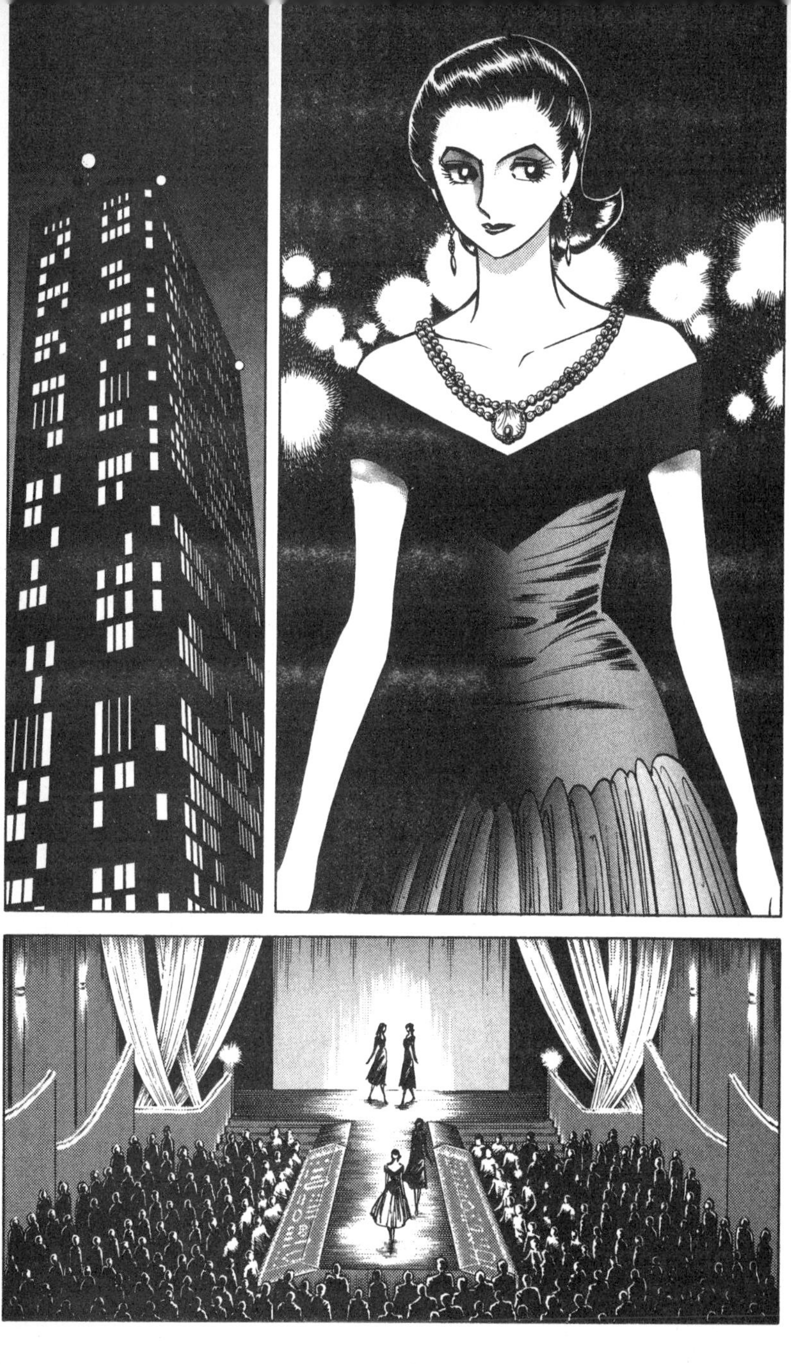

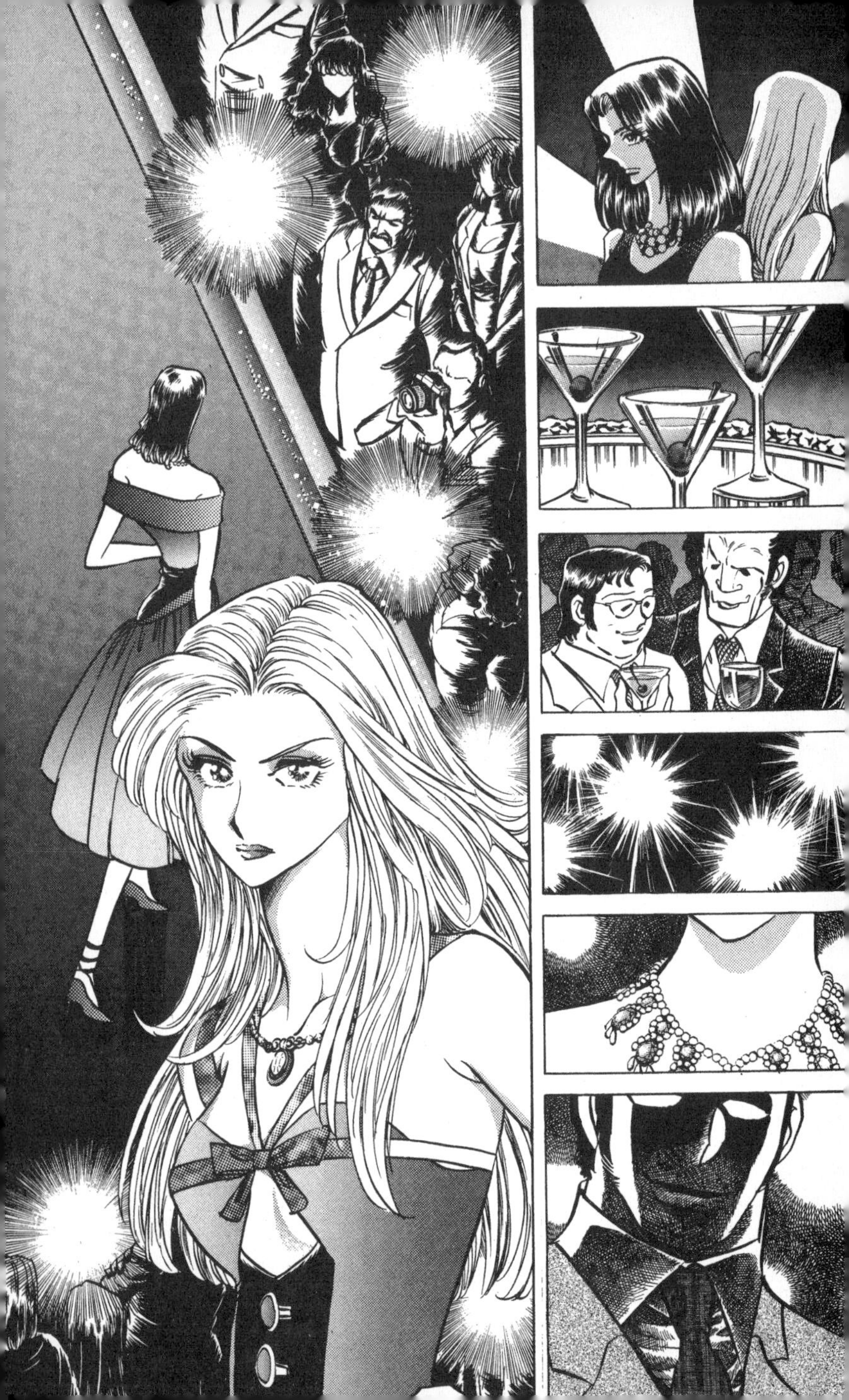

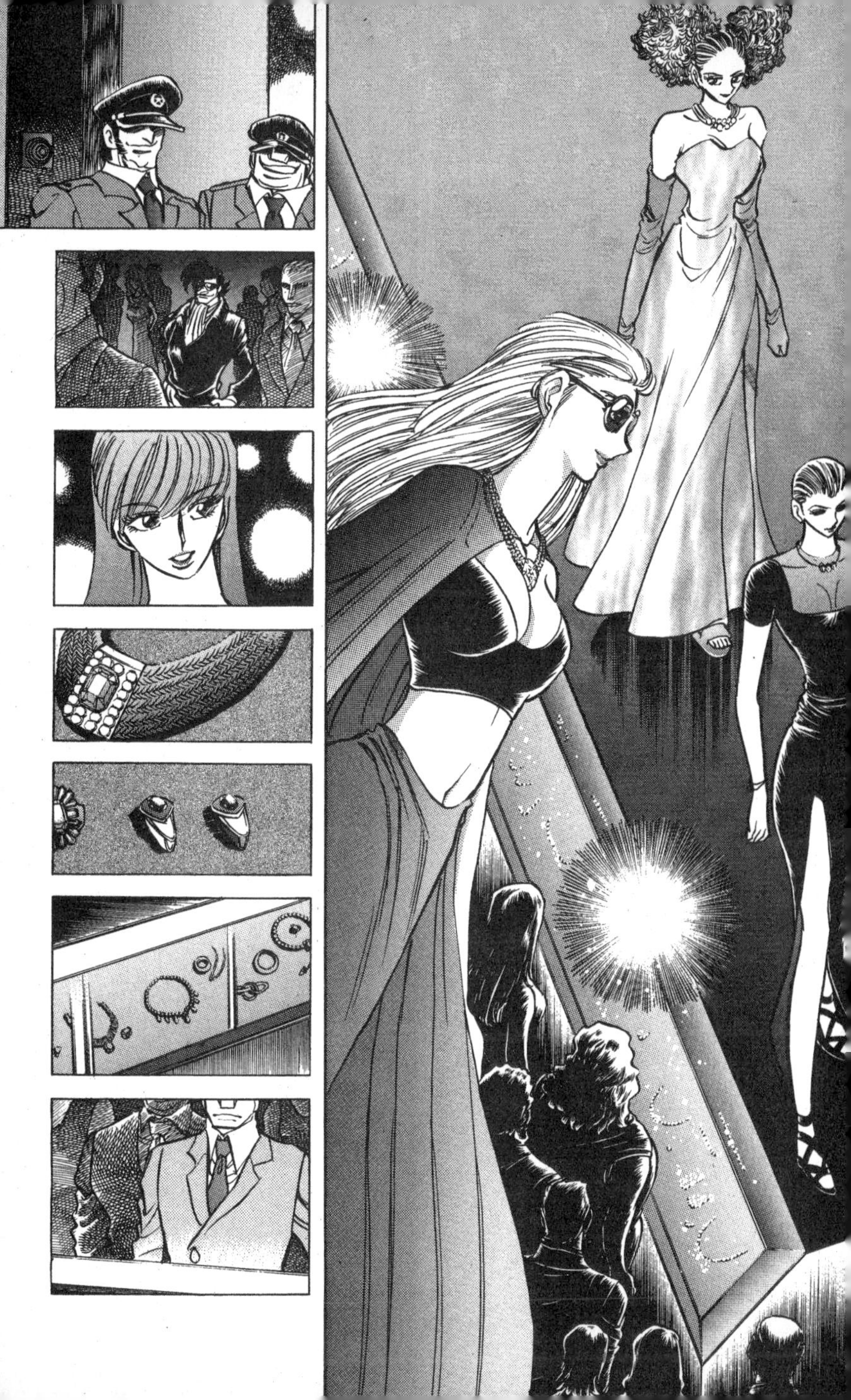

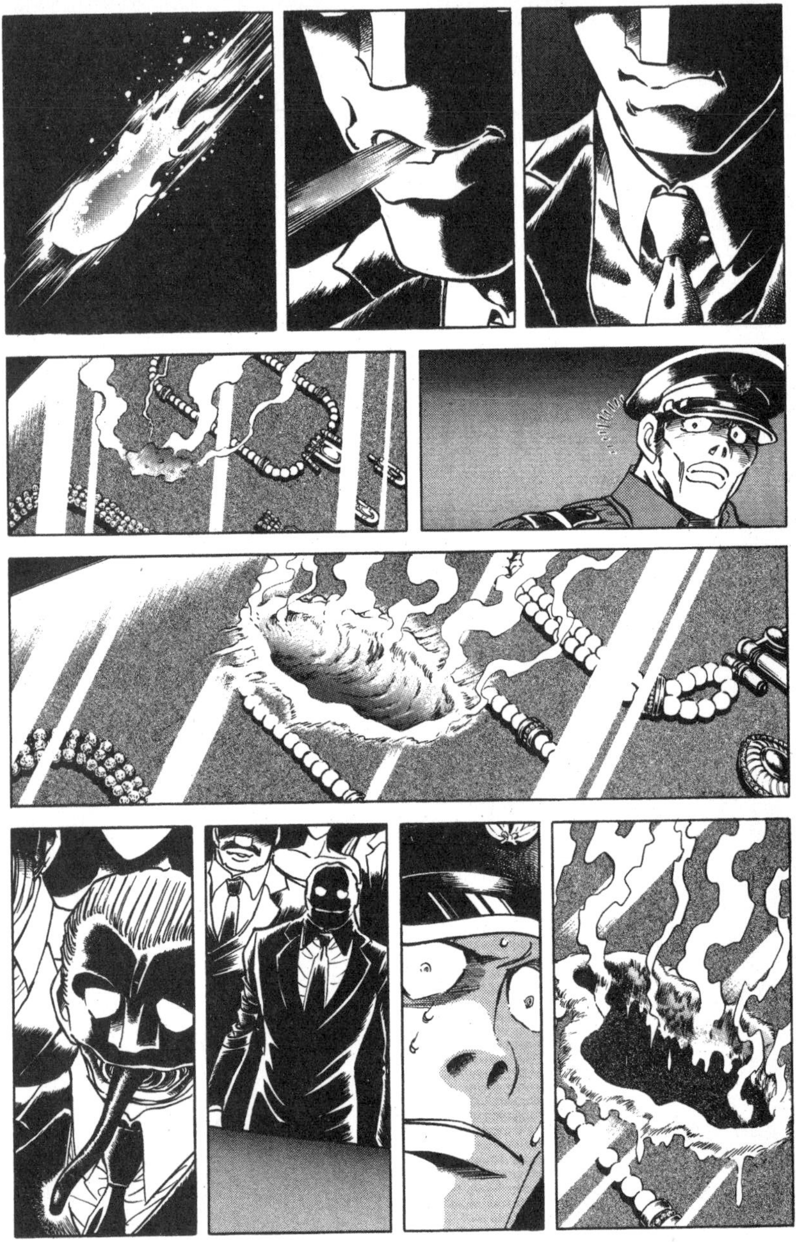

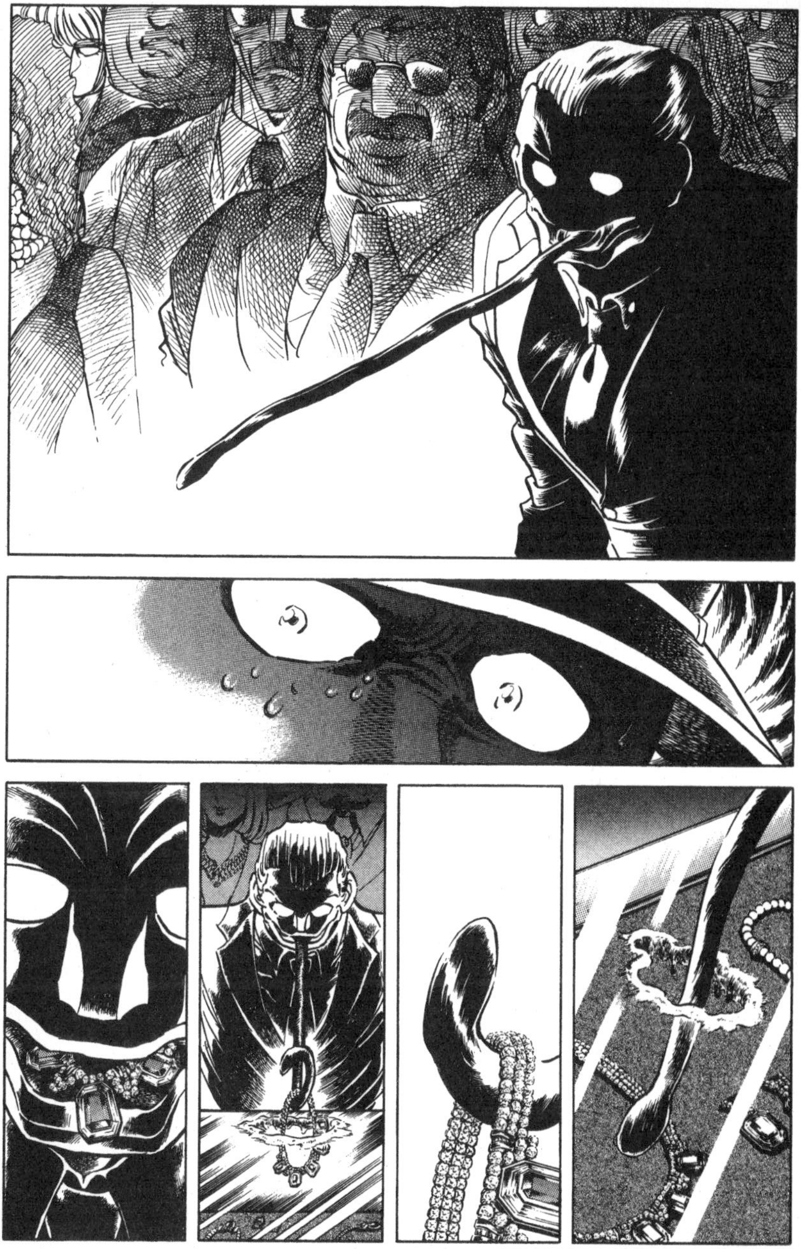

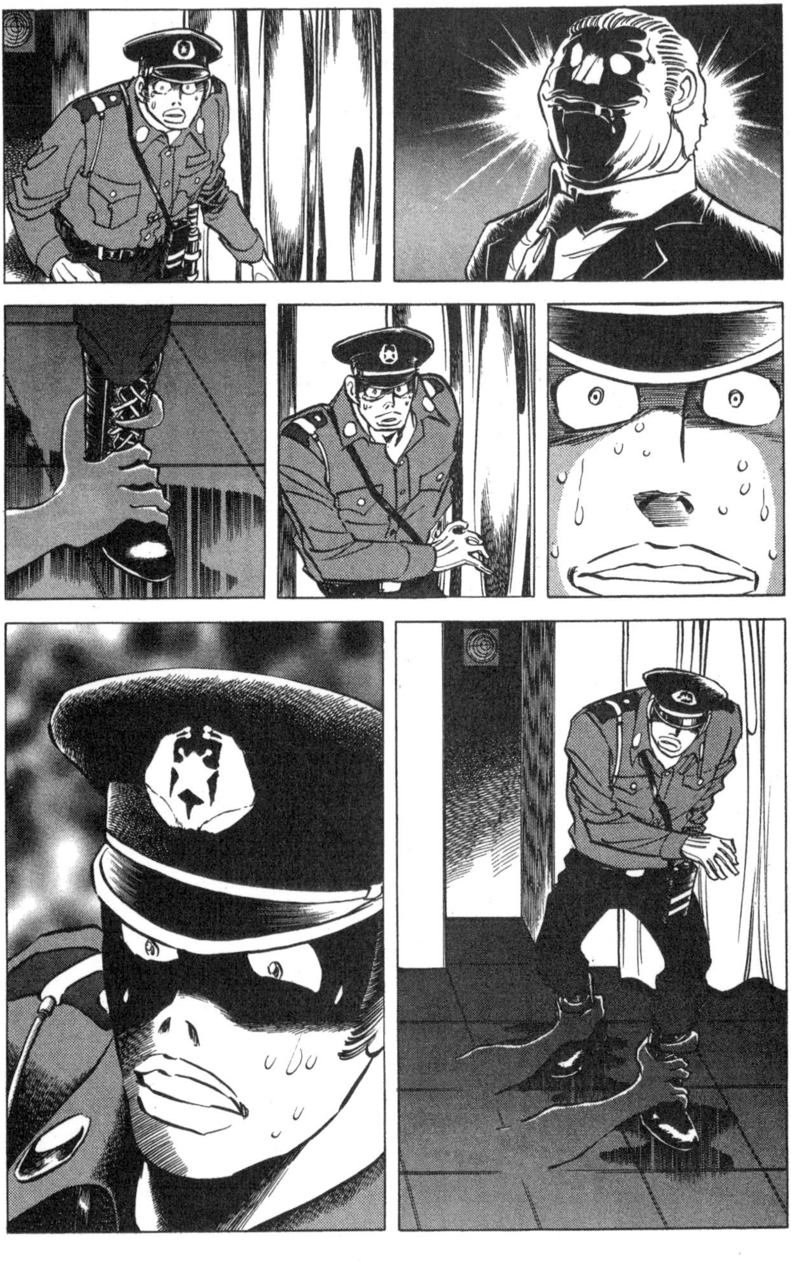

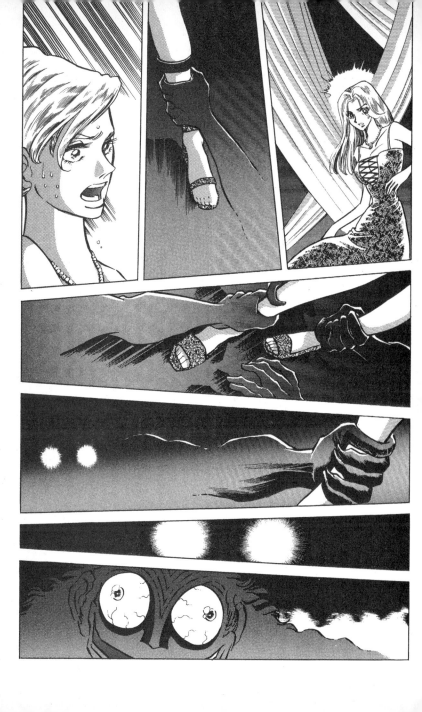

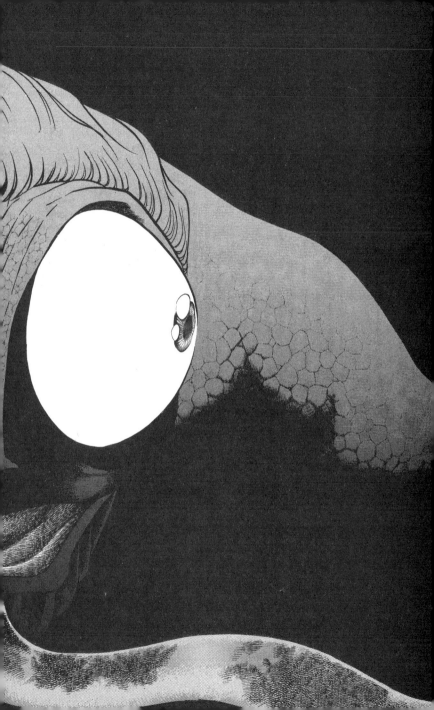

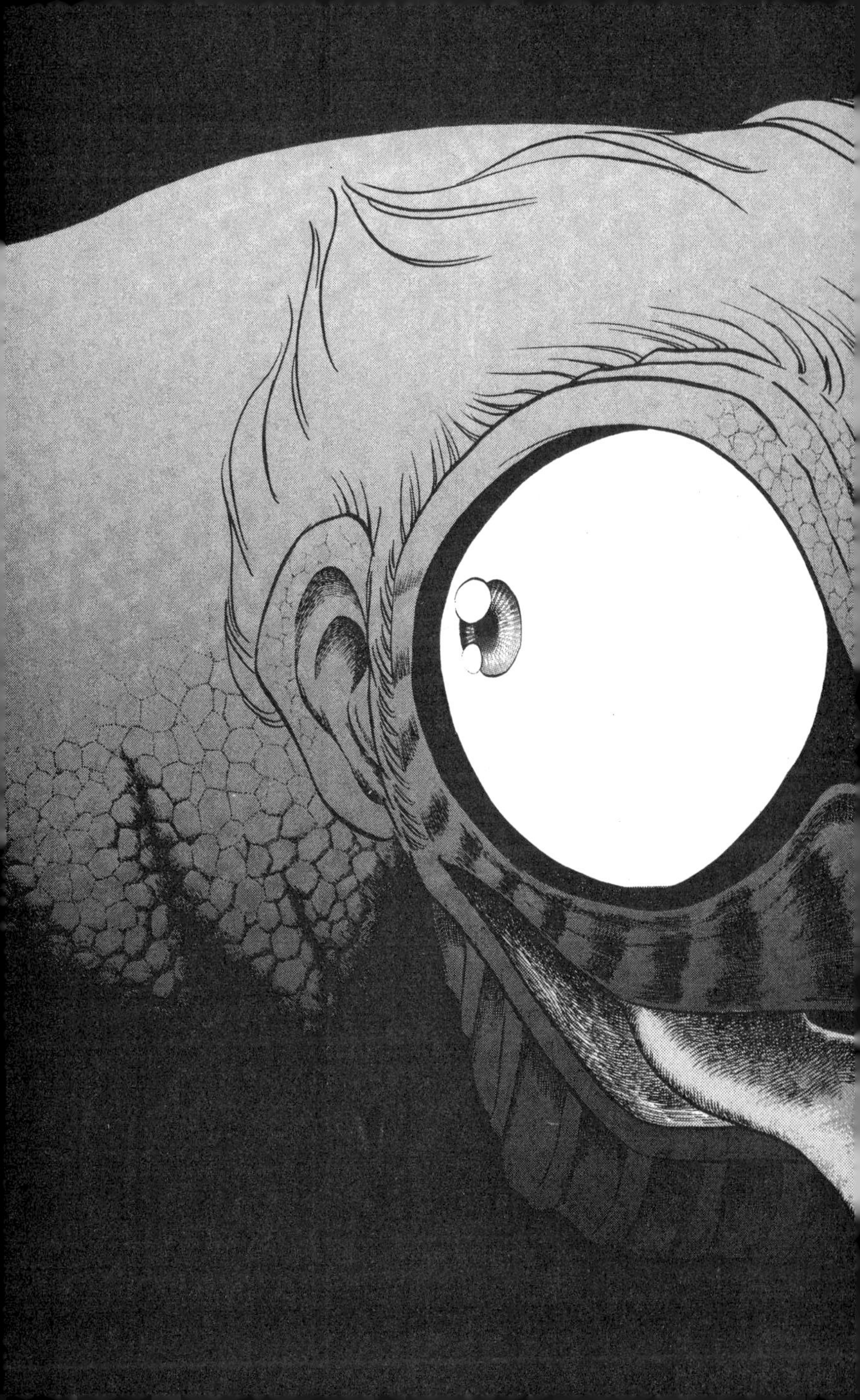

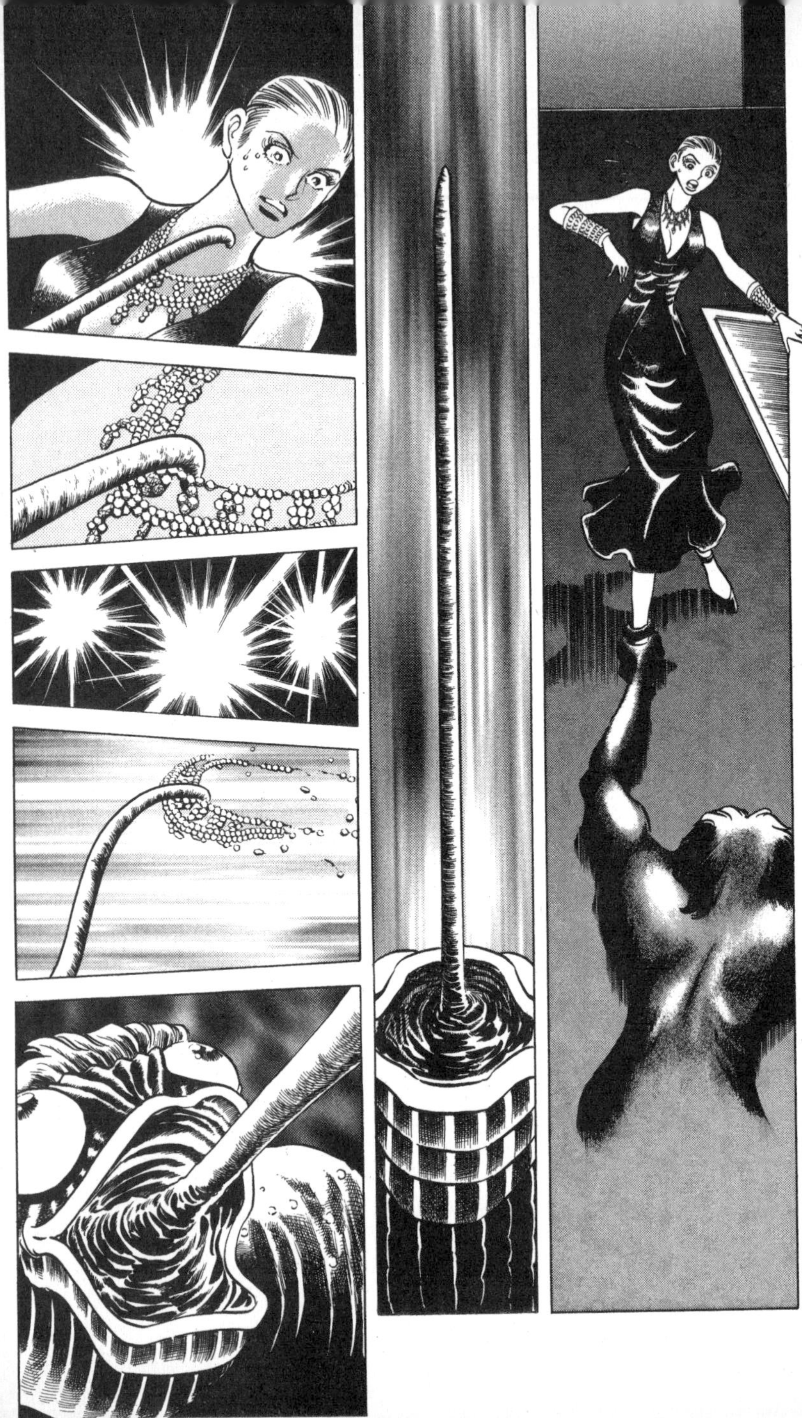

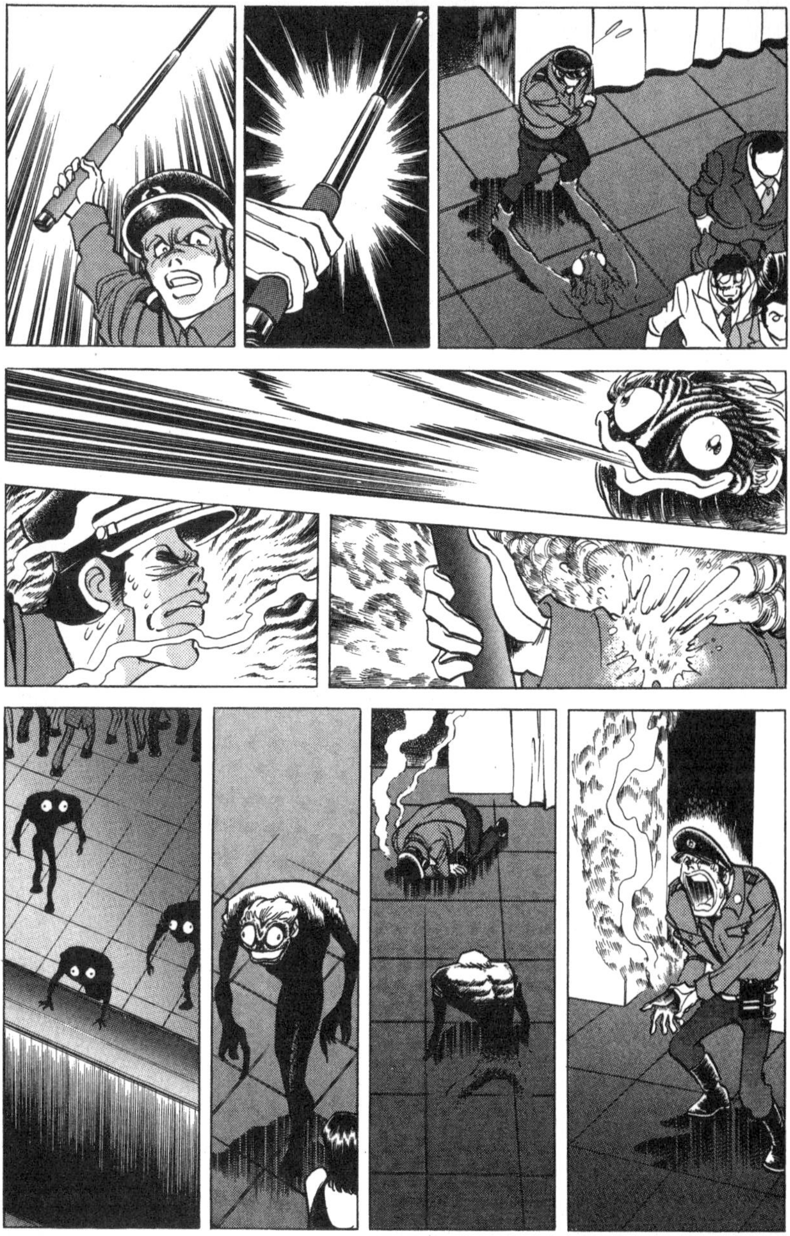

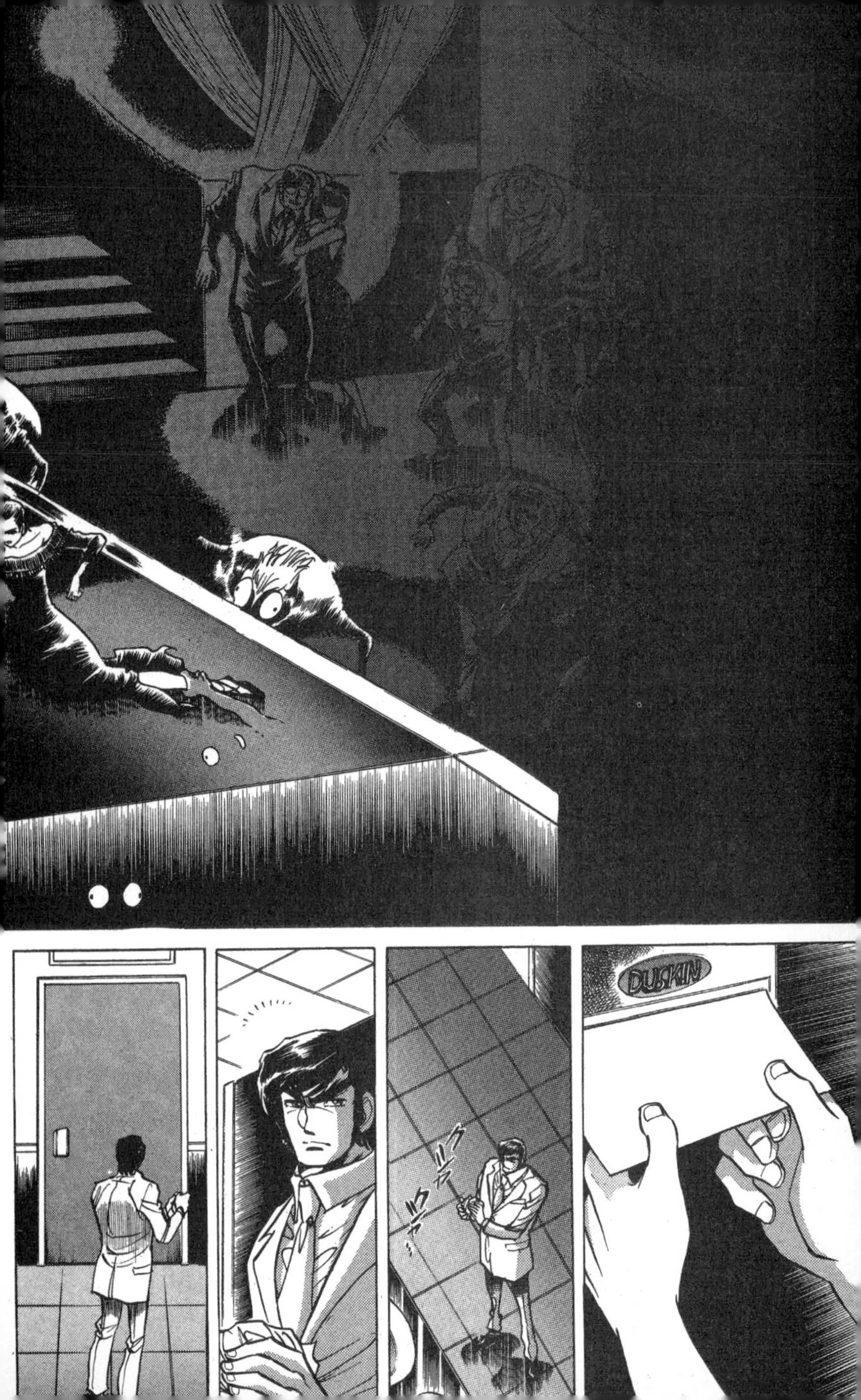
DUSKIN

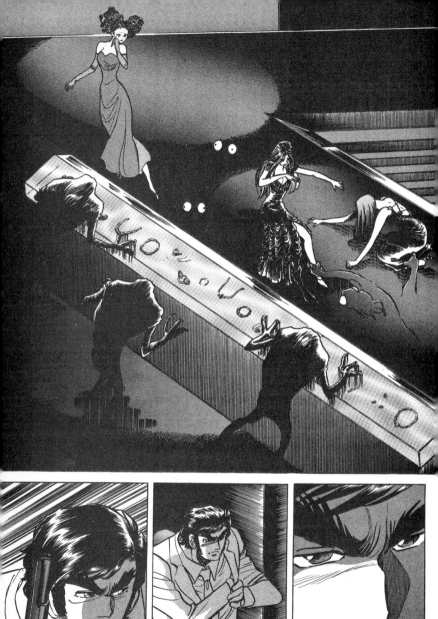

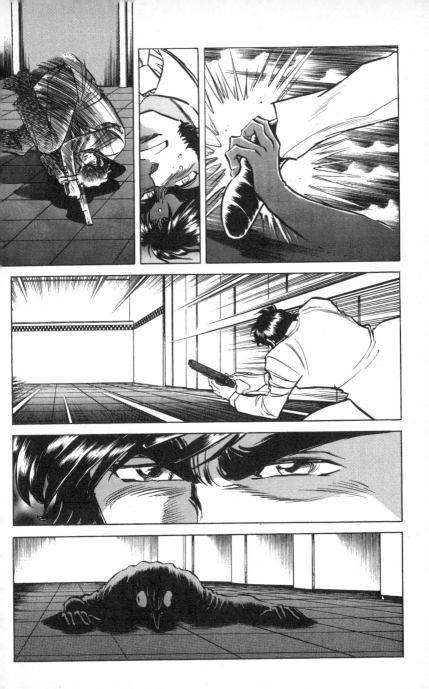

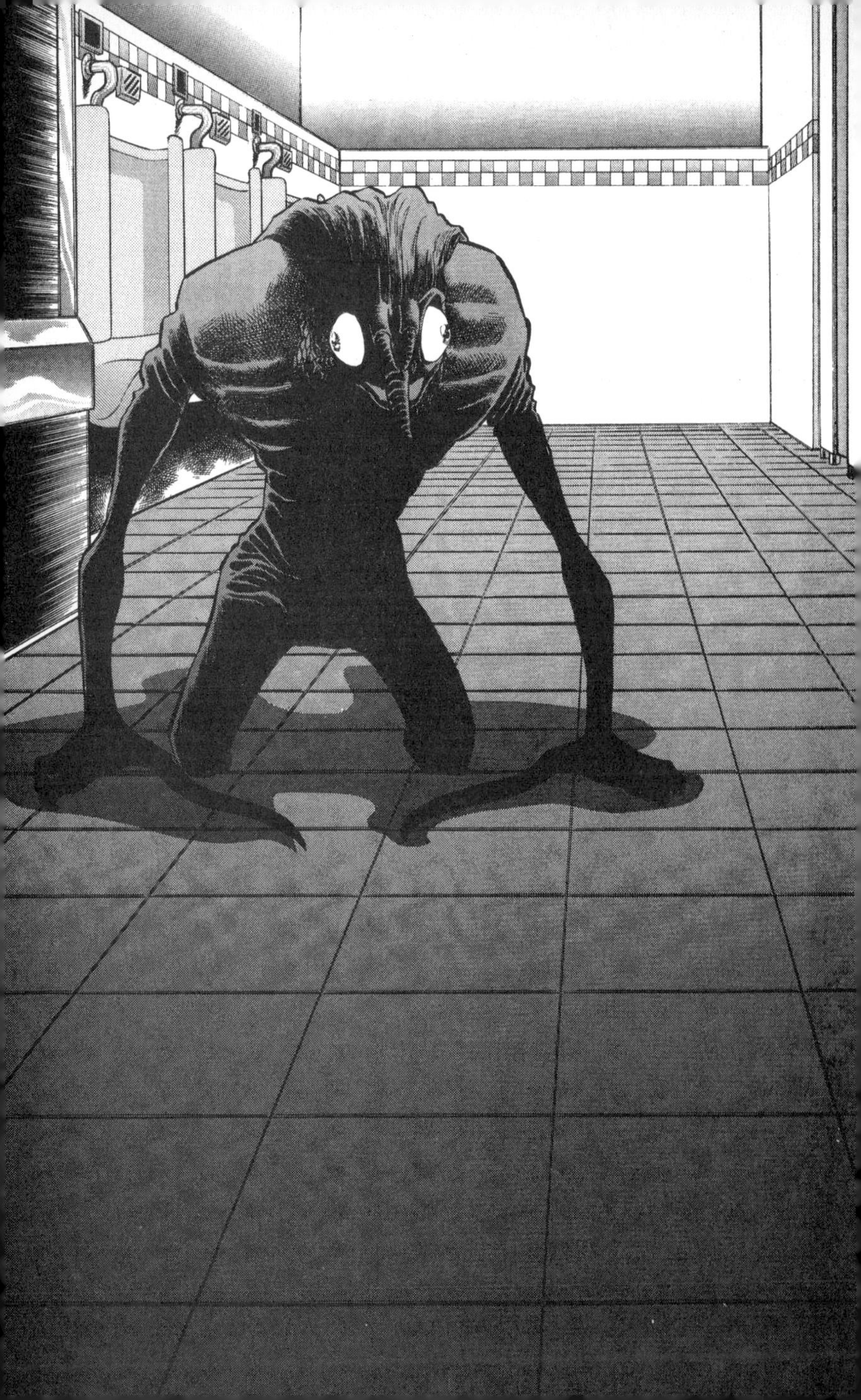

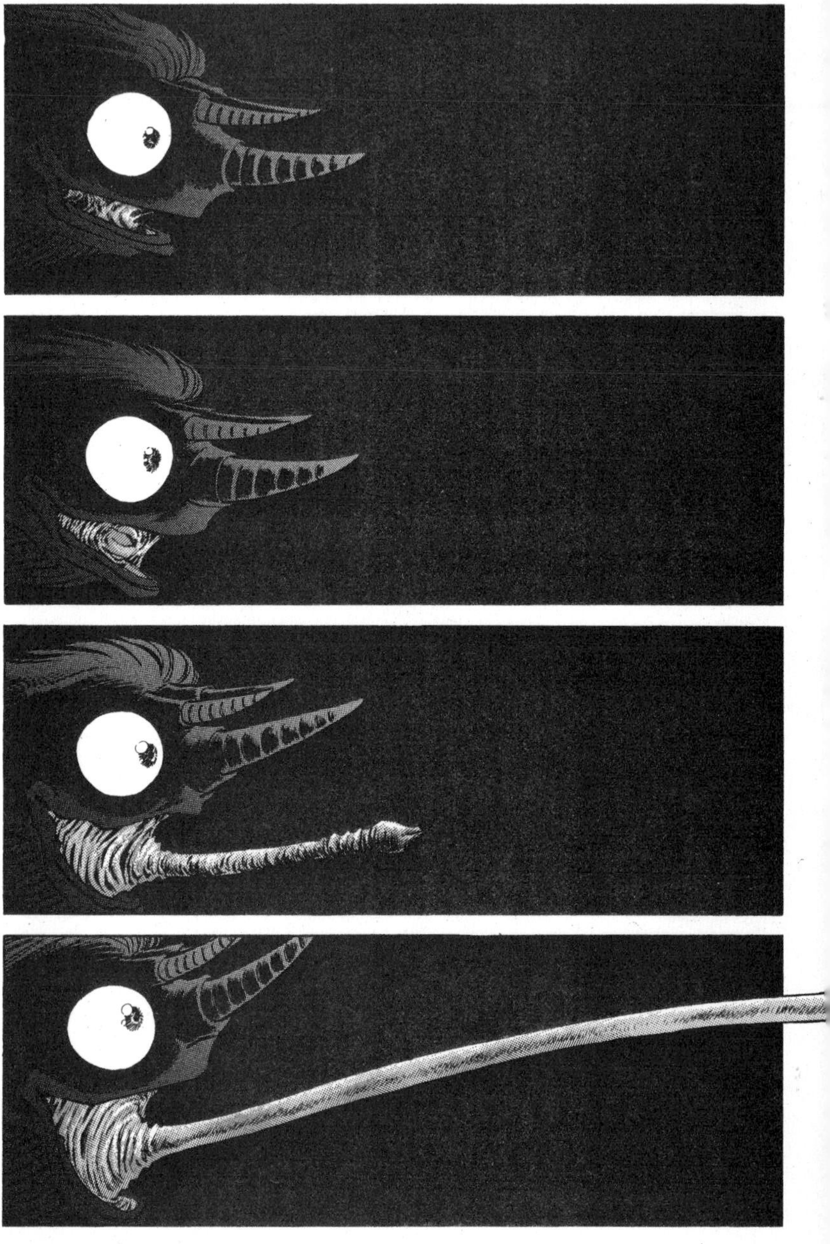

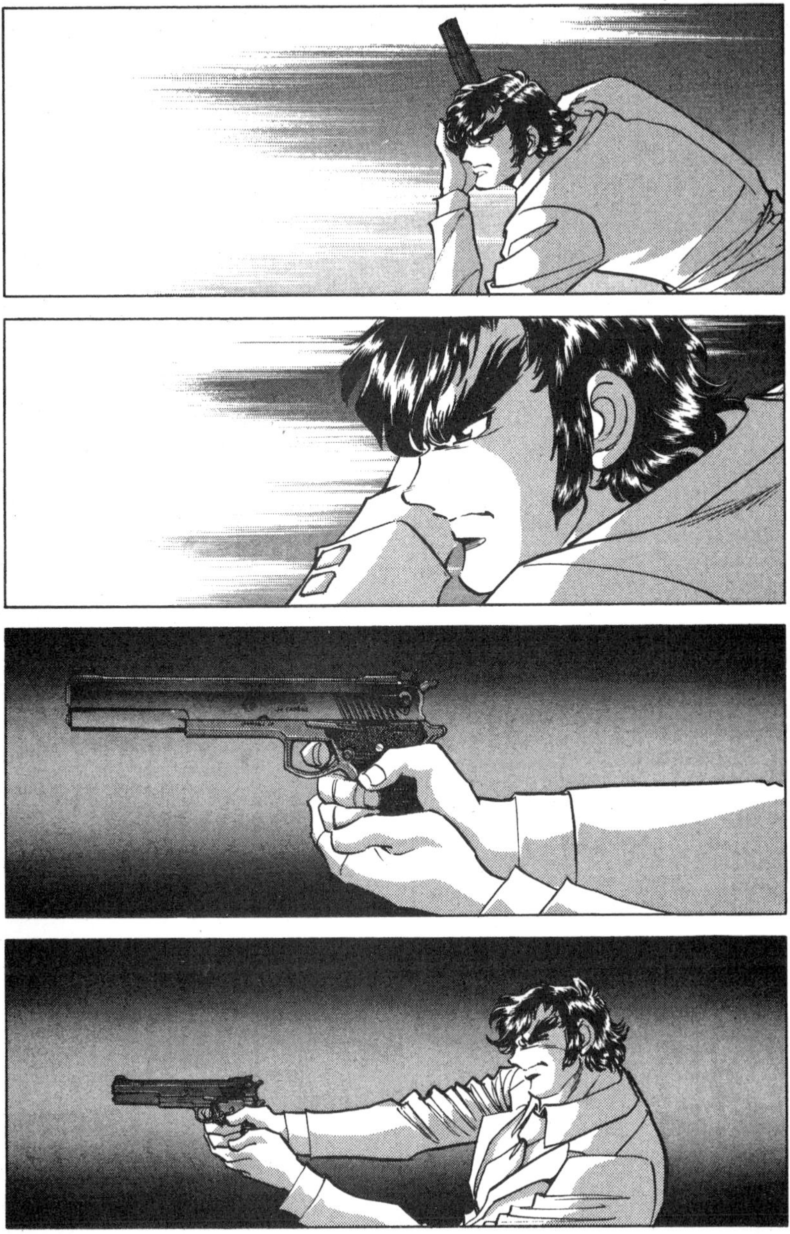

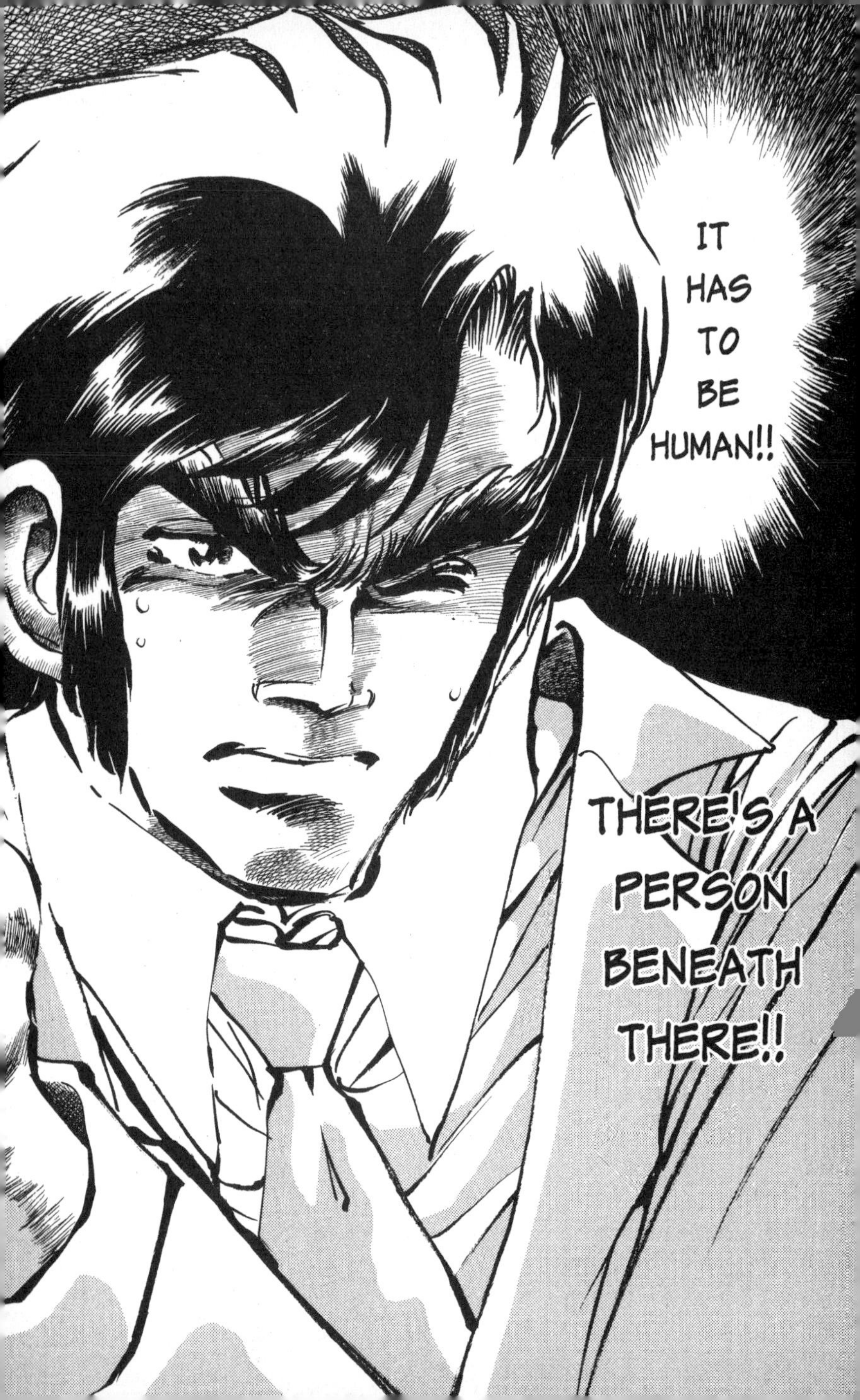
IT HAS TO BE HUMAN!!
THERE'S A PERSON BENEATH THERE!!

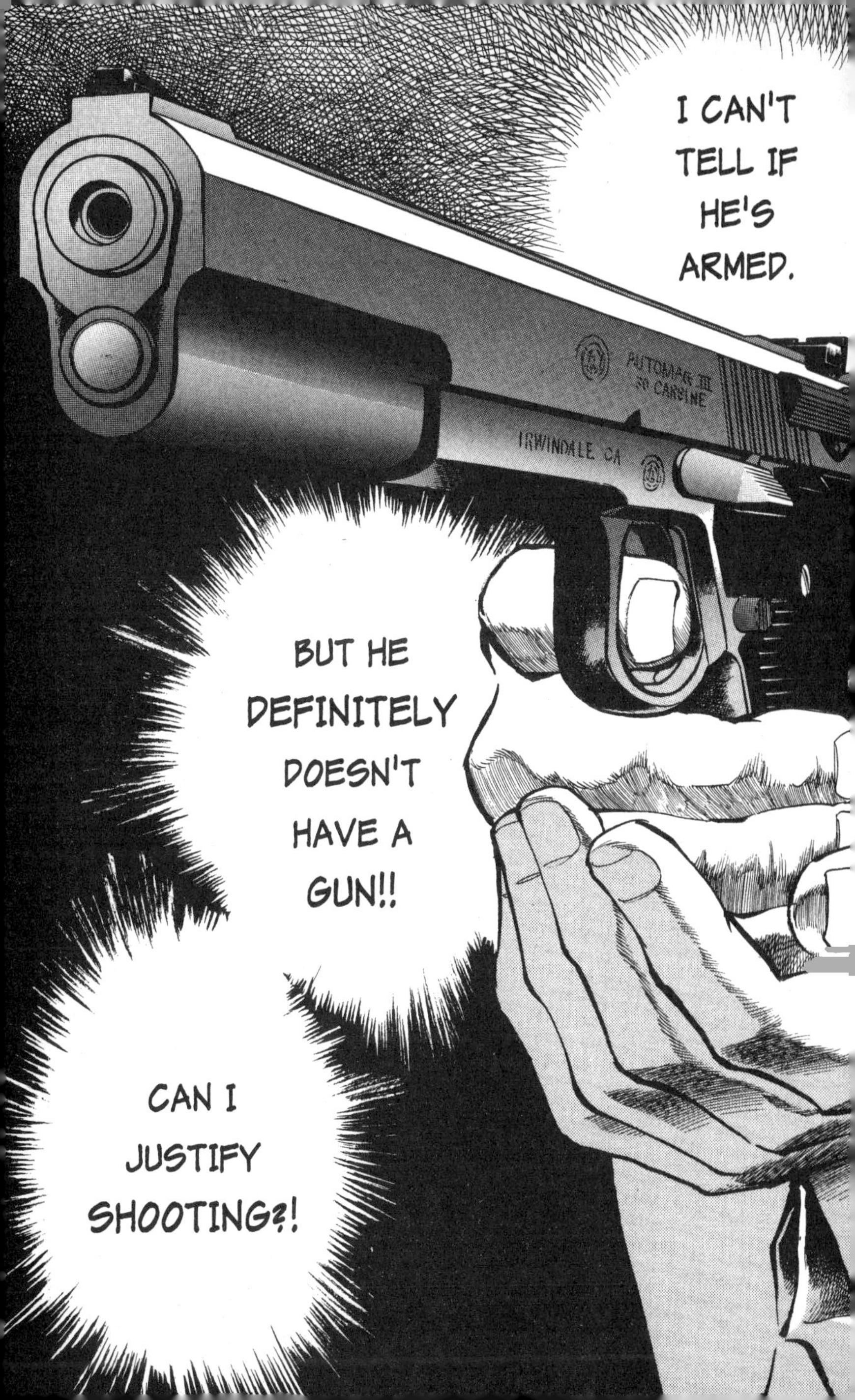
I CAN'T TELL IF HE'S ARMED.
AUTOMAG III
30 CARBINE
IRWINDALE CA
BUT HE DEFINITELY DOESN'T HAVE A GUN!!
CAN I JUSTIFY SHOOTING?!

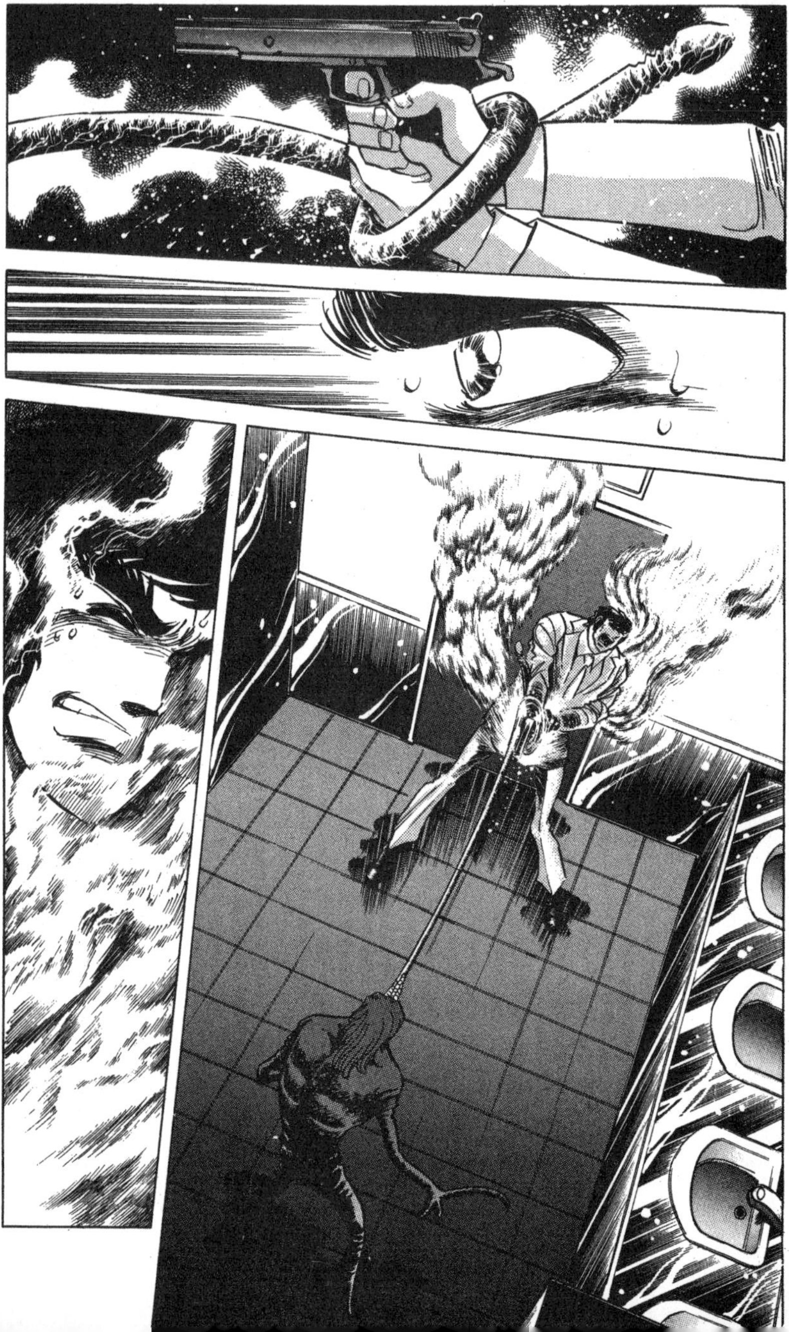

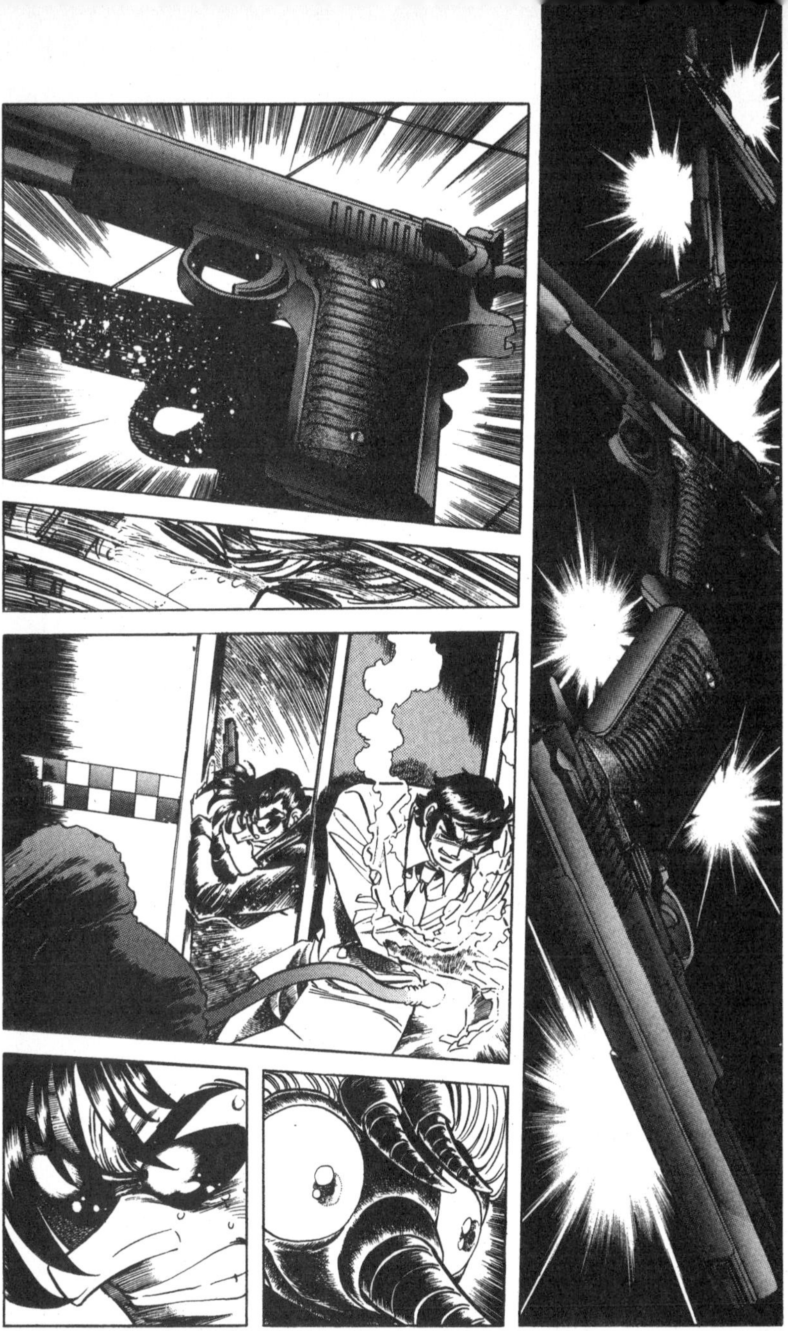

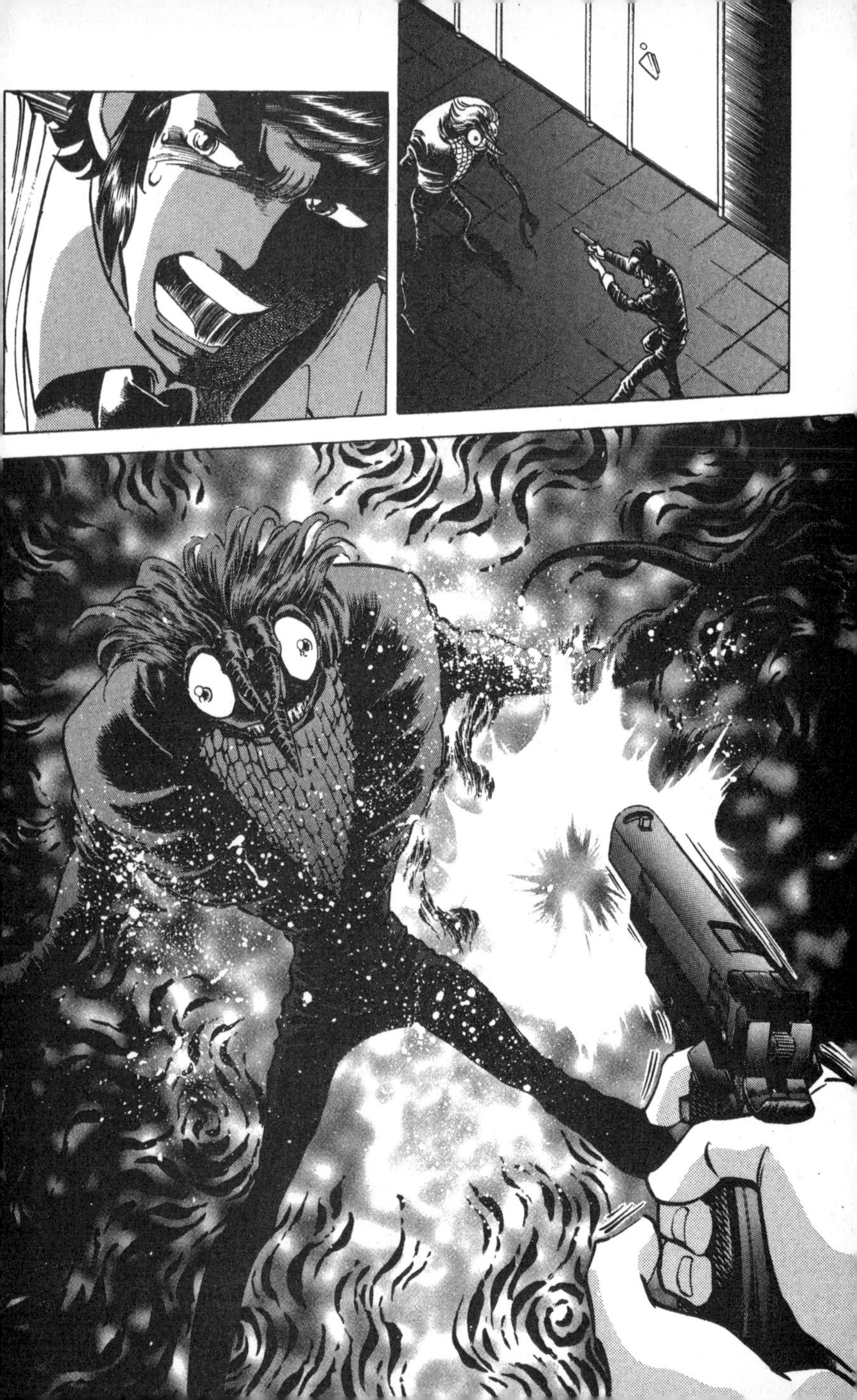

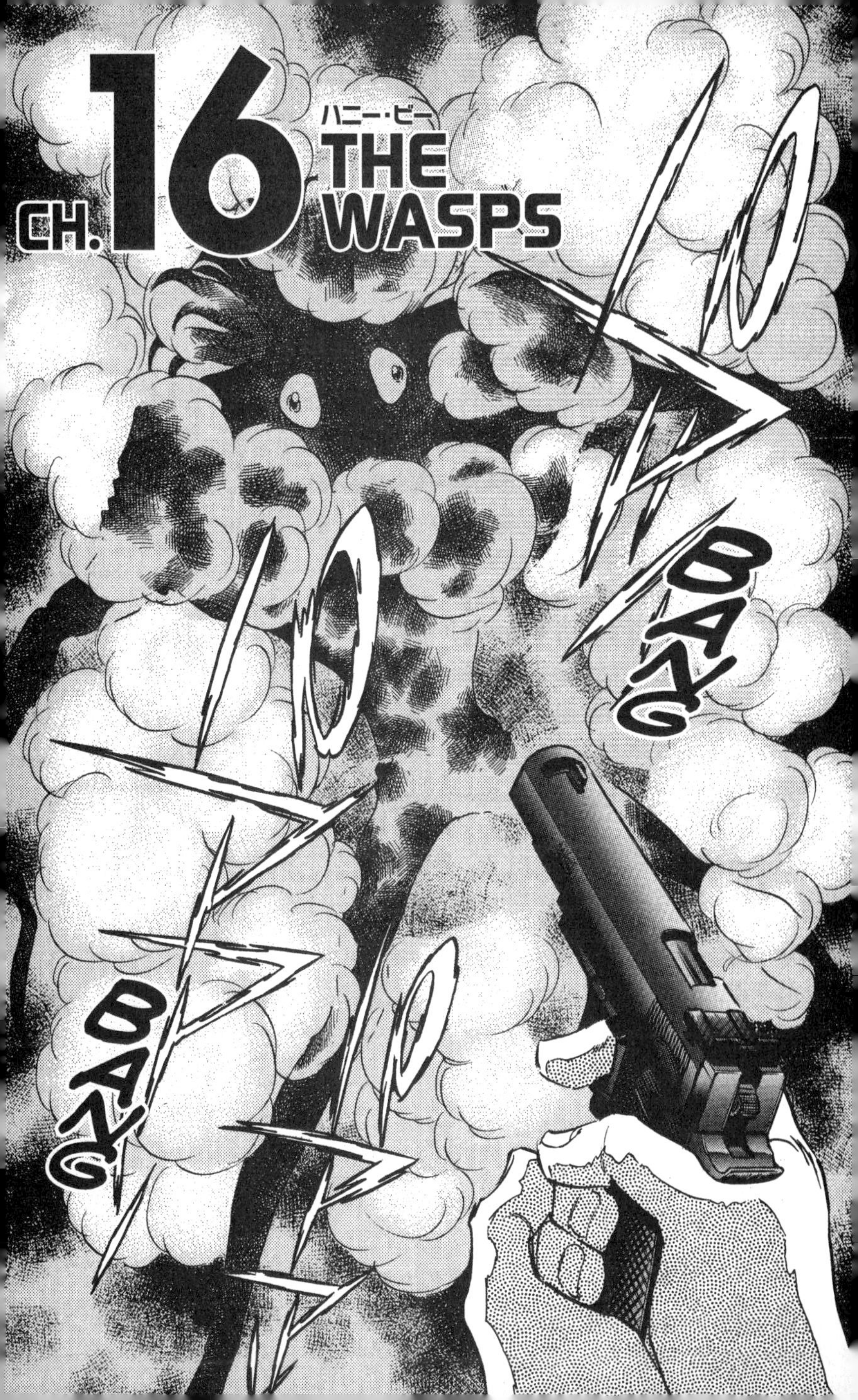
CH. 16
ハニー・ビー
THE WASPS
BANG
BANG

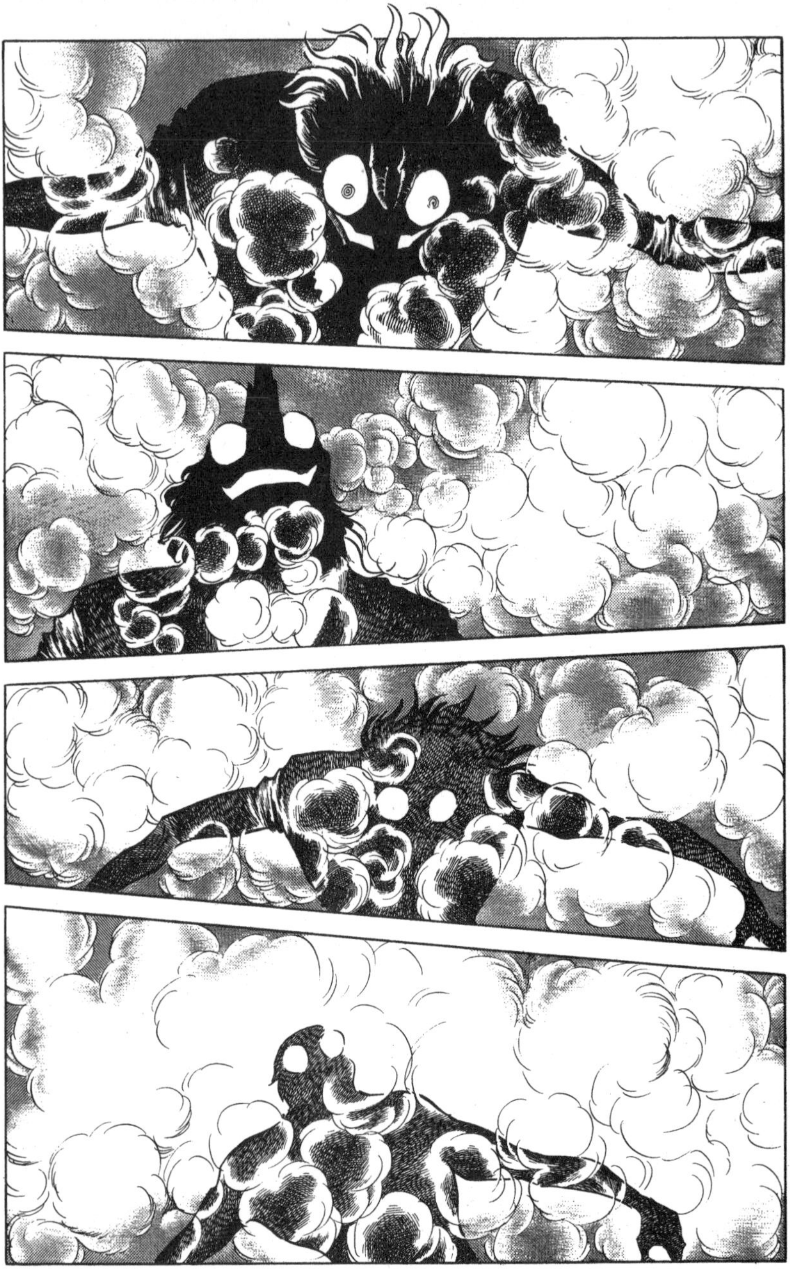

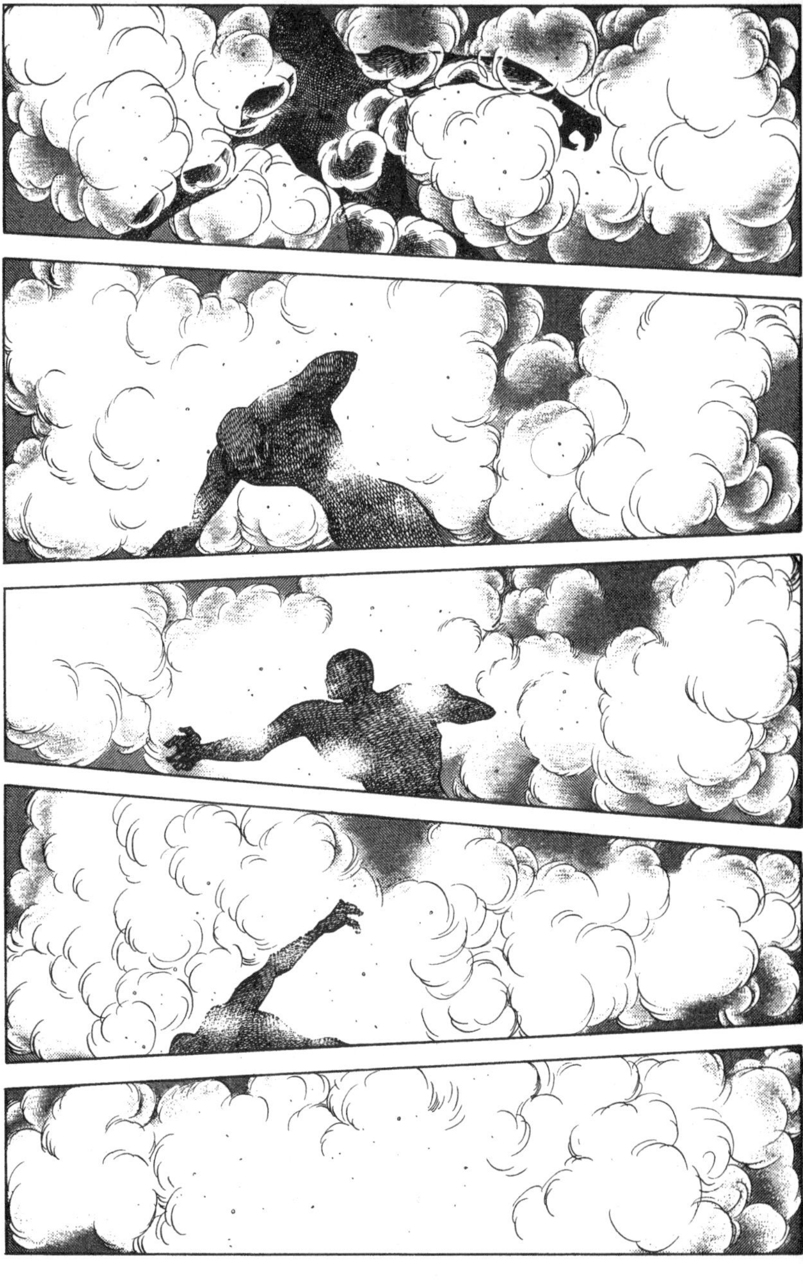

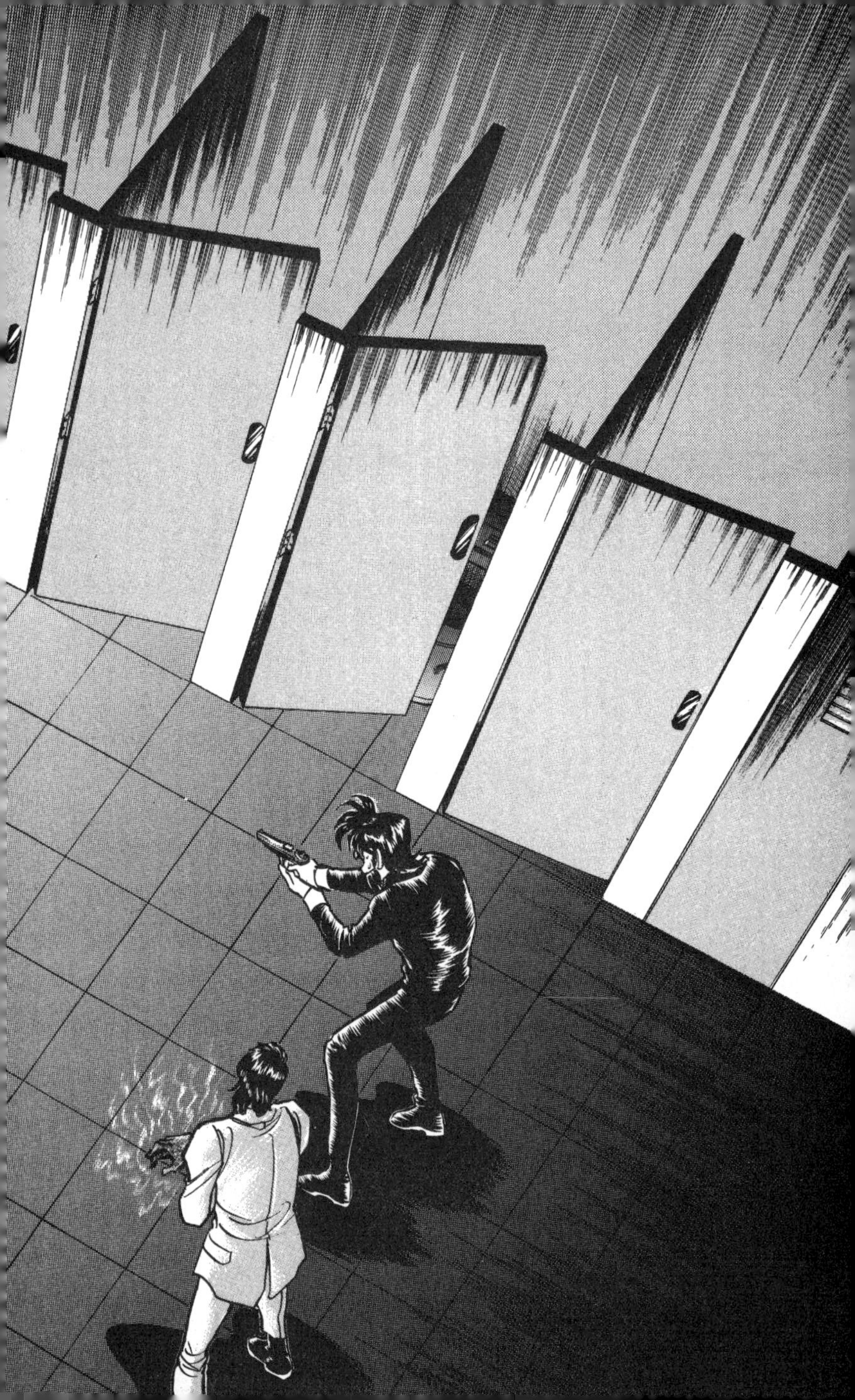

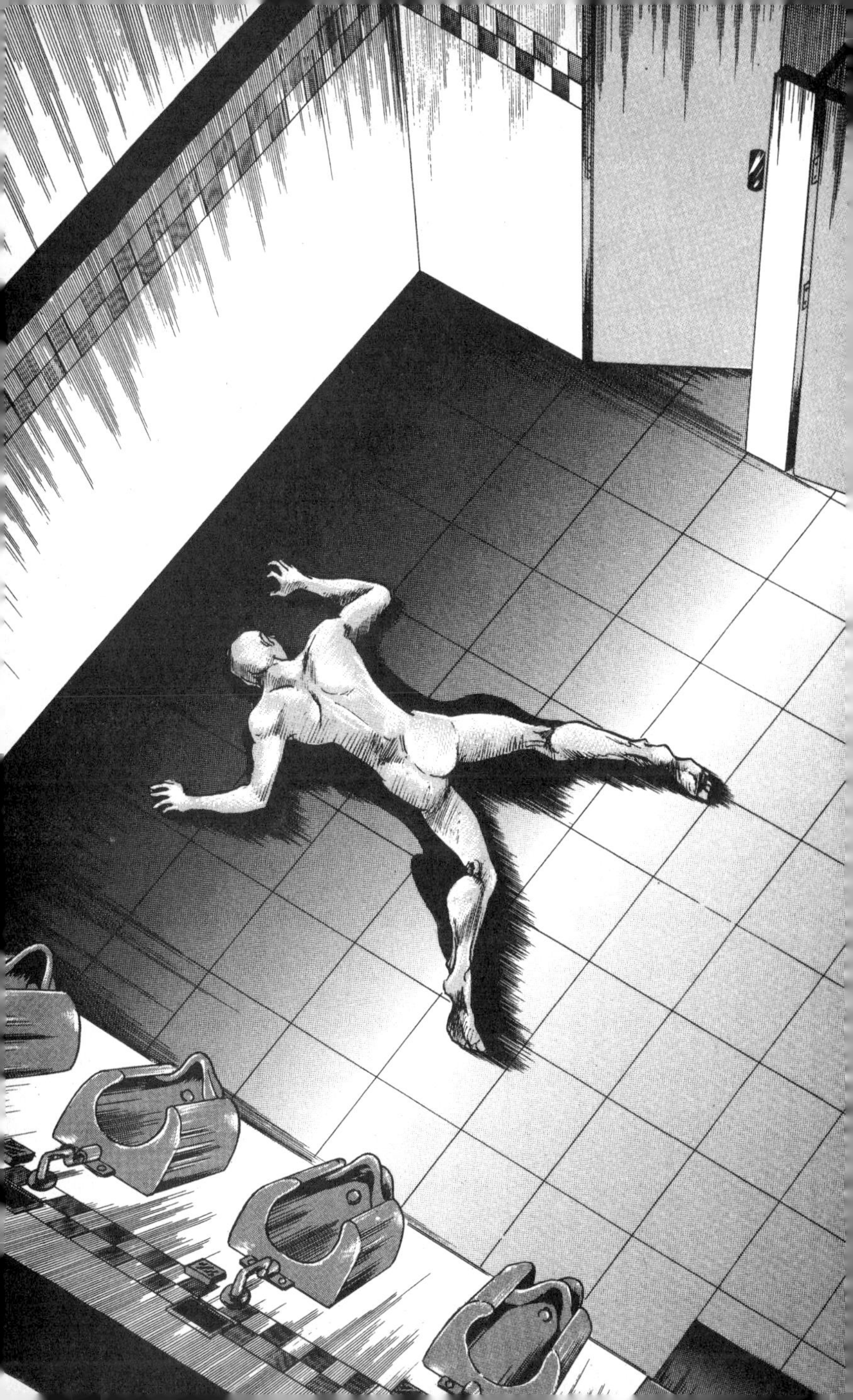

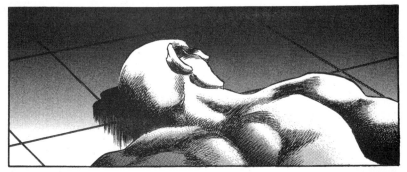

OTAKI, GET AN AMBULANCE!

NO!!

BU... BUT IT'S...

HUH?

... IT'S AN ORDINARY MAN!

AND NOW...

IT'S SOME KINDA MONSTER!!

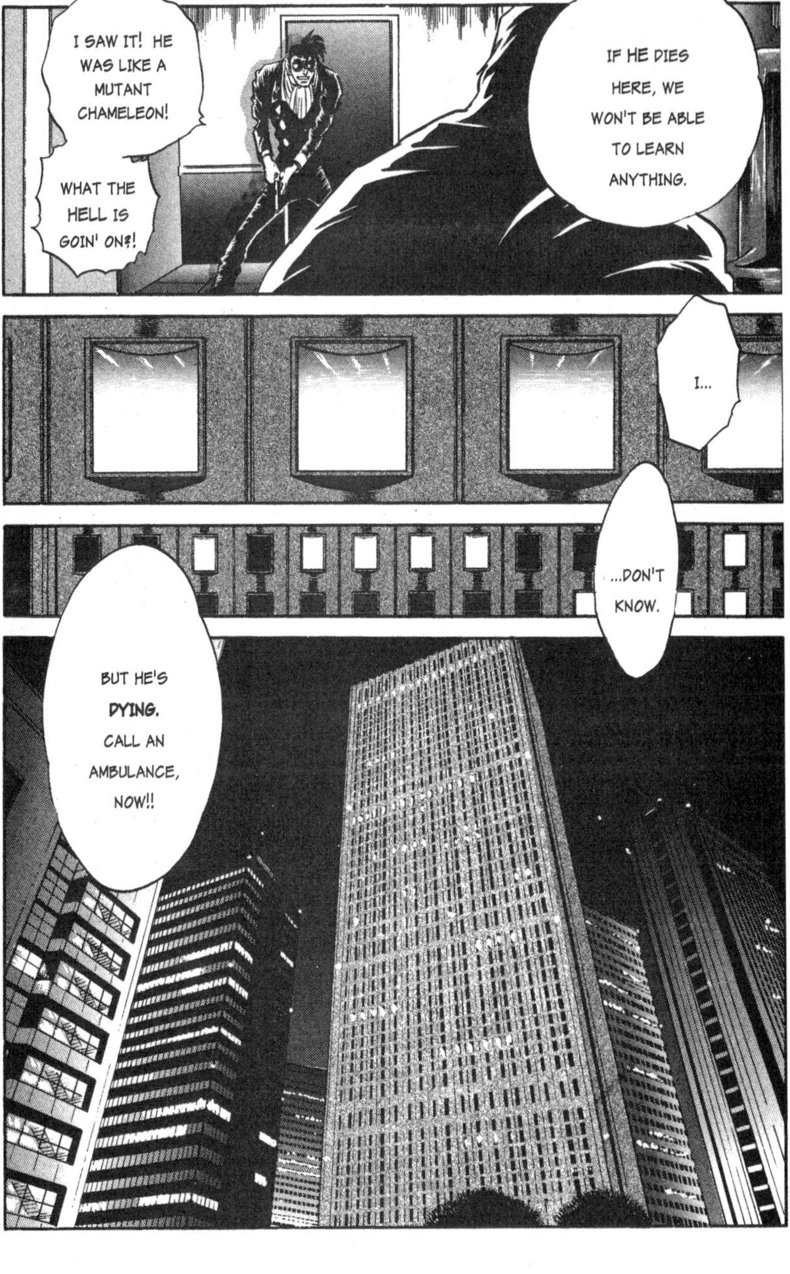
IF HE DIES HERE, WE WON'T BE ABLE TO LEARN ANYTHING.
I SAW IT! HE WAS LIKE A MUTANT CHAMELEON!
WHAT THE HELL IS GOIN' ON?!
I...
...DON'T KNOW.
BUT HE'S **DYING.** CALL AN AMBULANCE, NOW!!

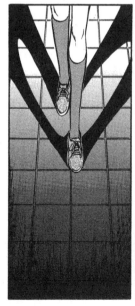

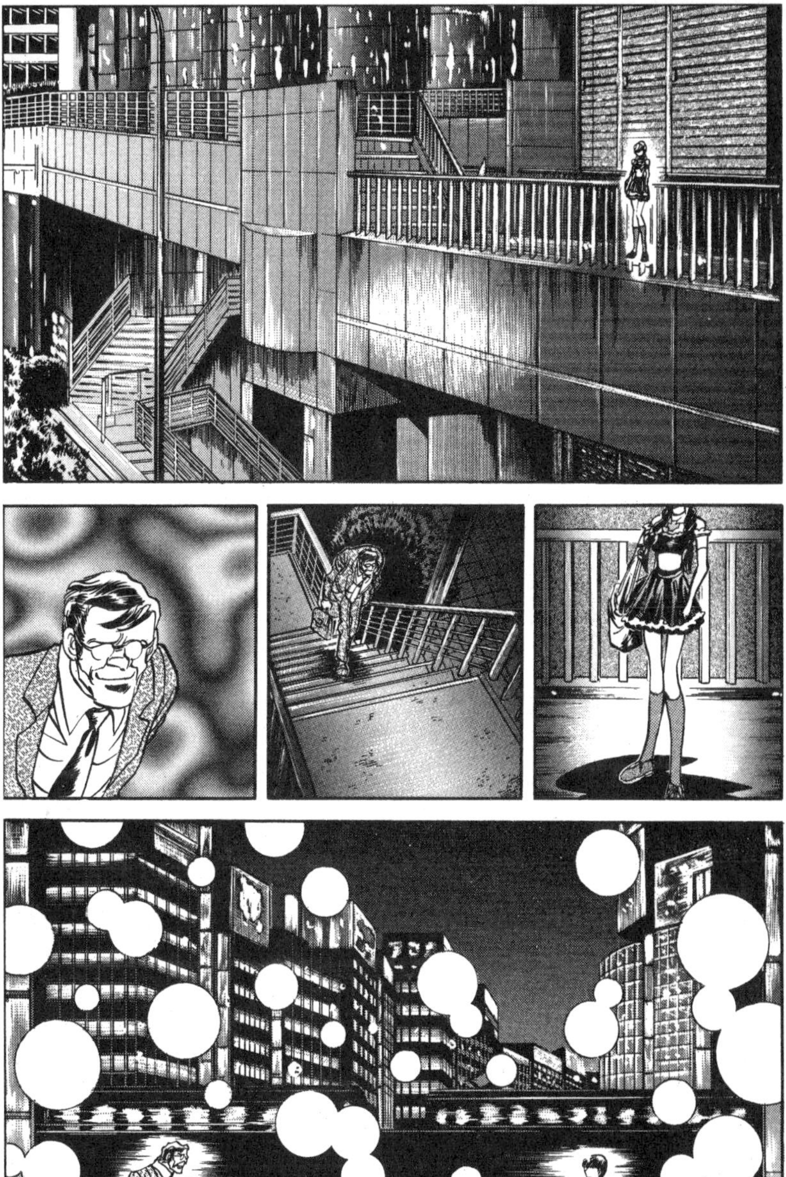

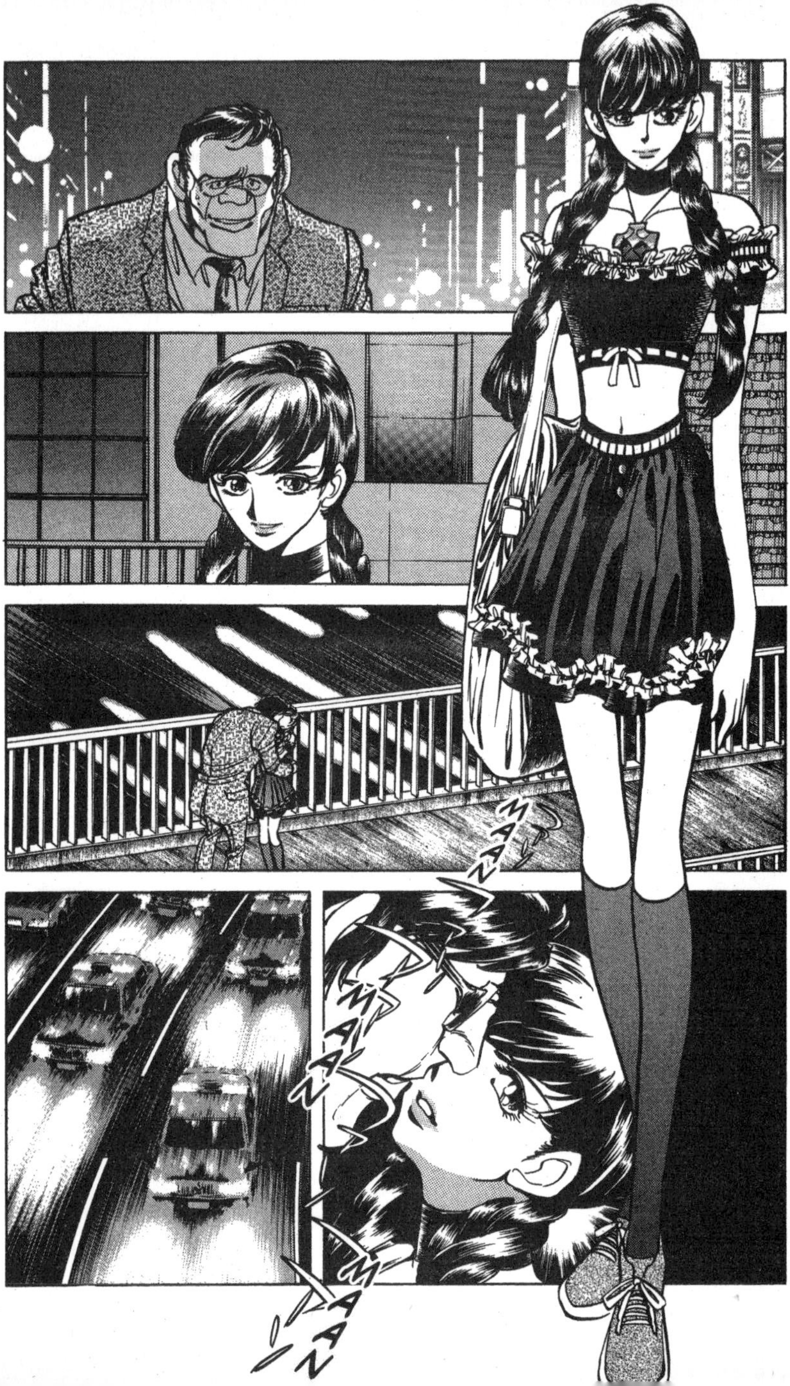
MAAN
MAAAN
MAAAN

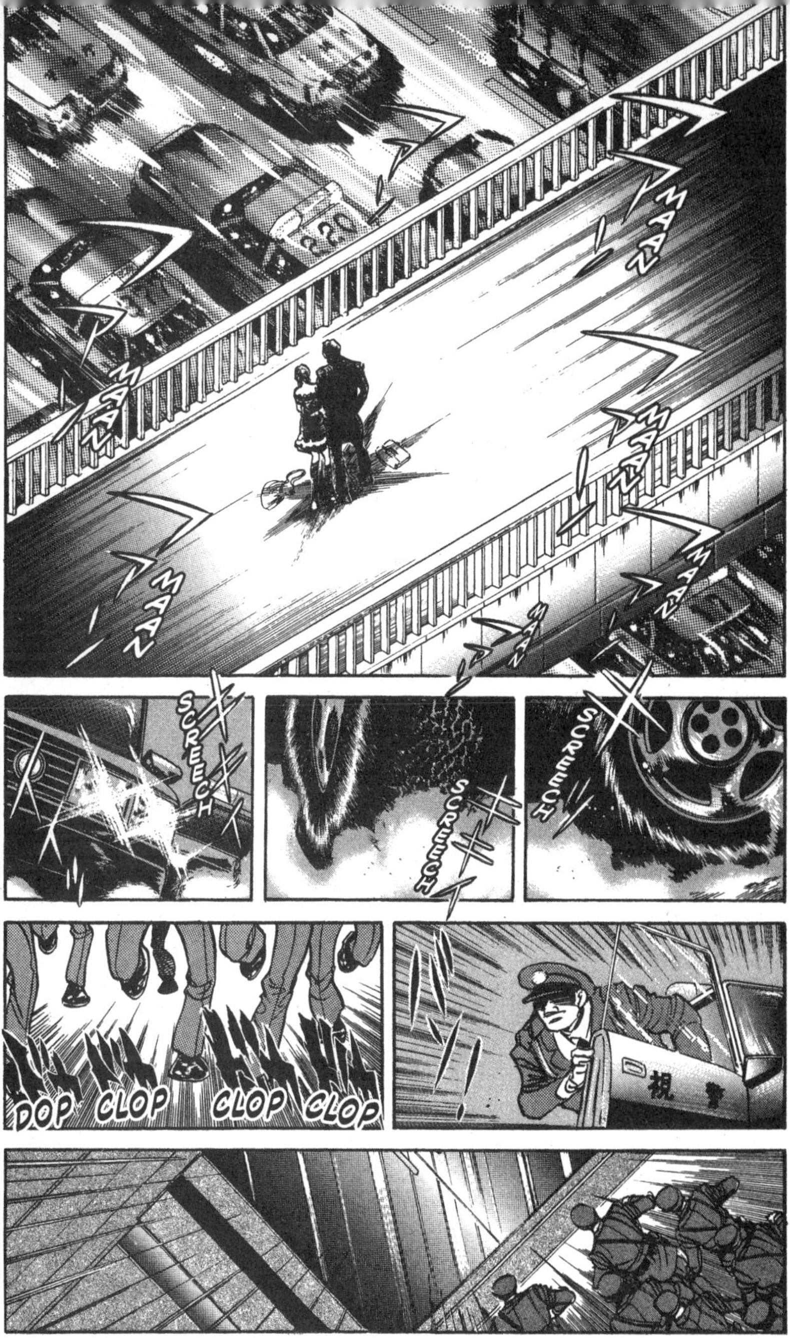
MAAN
MAAN
MAAN
MAAN
MAAN
MAAN
SCREECH
SCREECH
SCREECH
DOP CLOP CLOP CLOP

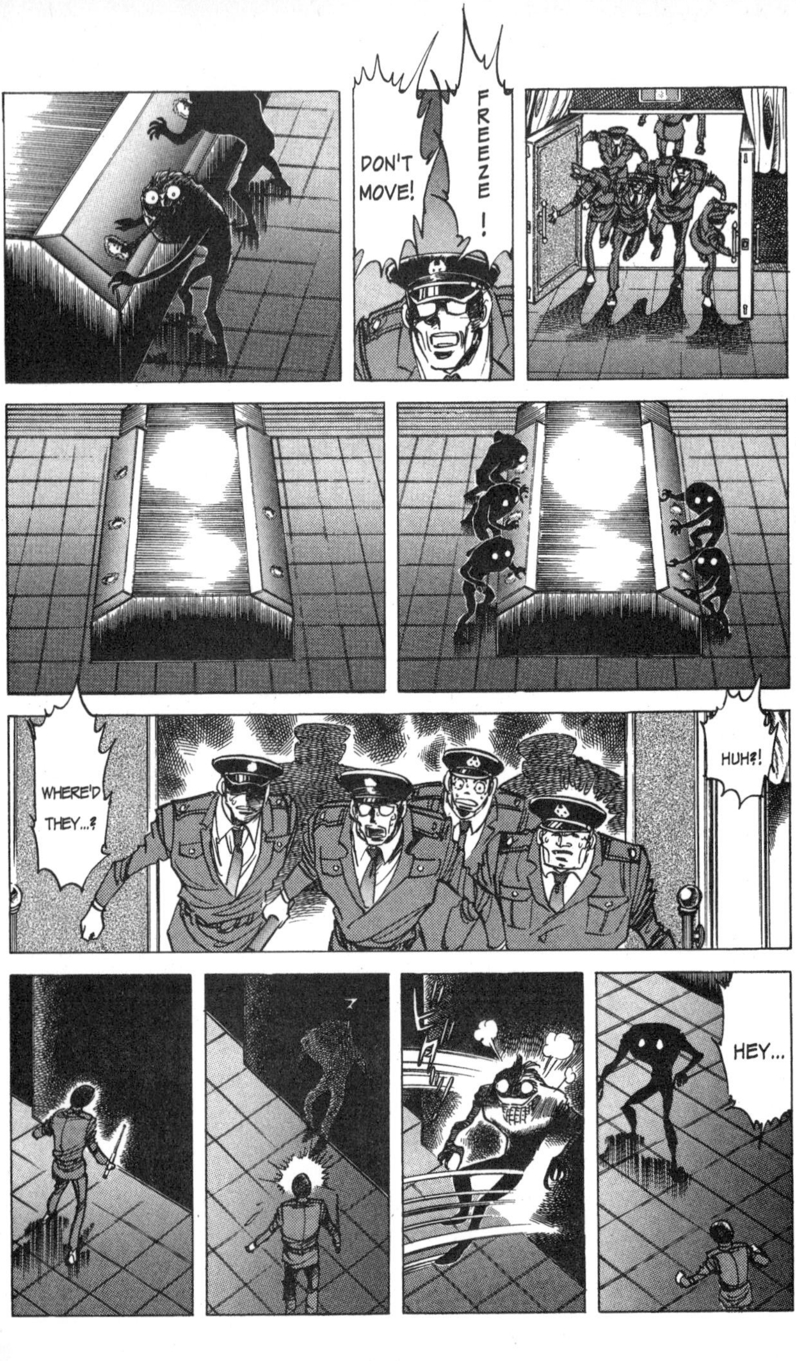
FREEZE !
DON'T MOVE!
HUH?!
WHERE'D THEY...?
HEY...

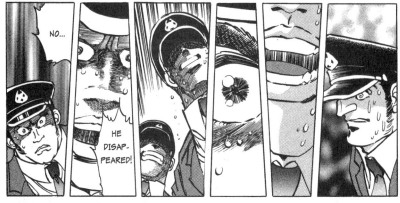

NO...

HE DISAP-PEARED!

IT'S CAMOU-FLAGE!!

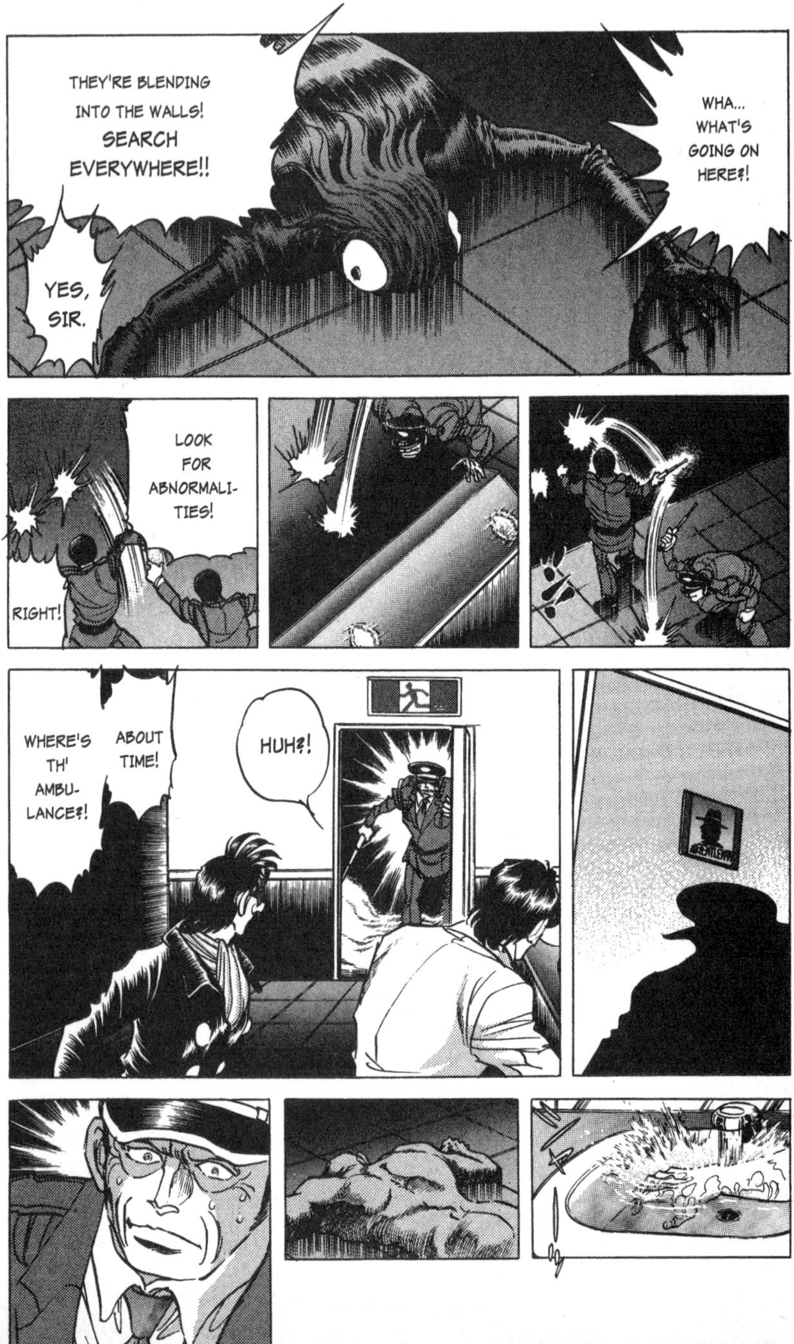
WHA... WHAT'S GOING ON HERE?!
THEY'RE BLENDING INTO THE WALLS! SEARCH EVERYWHERE!!
YES, SIR.
LOOK FOR ABNORMALI-TIES!
RIGHT!
HUH?!
ABOUT TIME!
WHERE'S TH' AMBU-LANCE?!

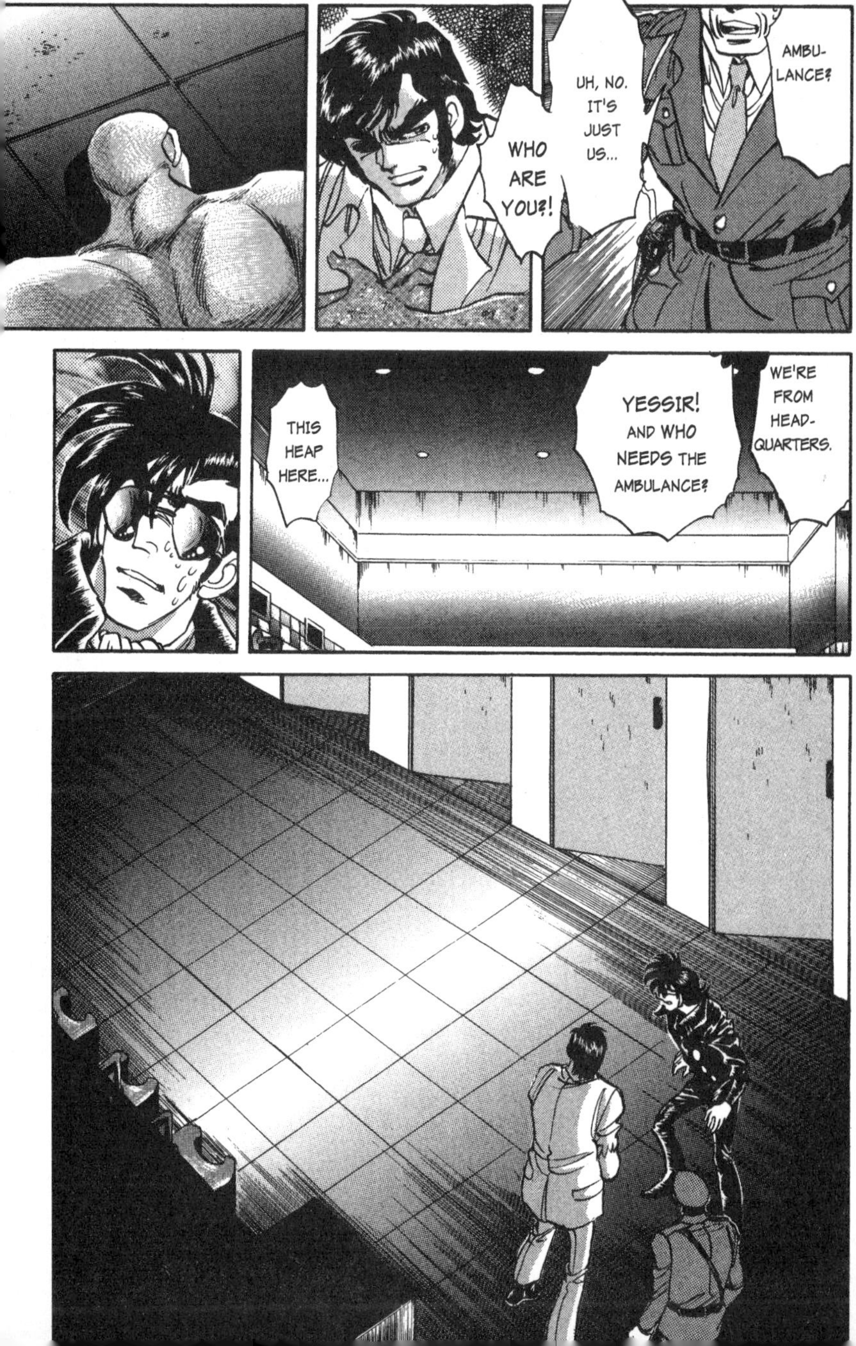
AMBU-LANCE?
UH, NO. IT'S JUST US...
WHO ARE YOU?!
WE'RE FROM HEAD-QUARTERS.
YESSIR! AND WHO NEEDS THE AMBULANCE?
THIS HEAP HERE...

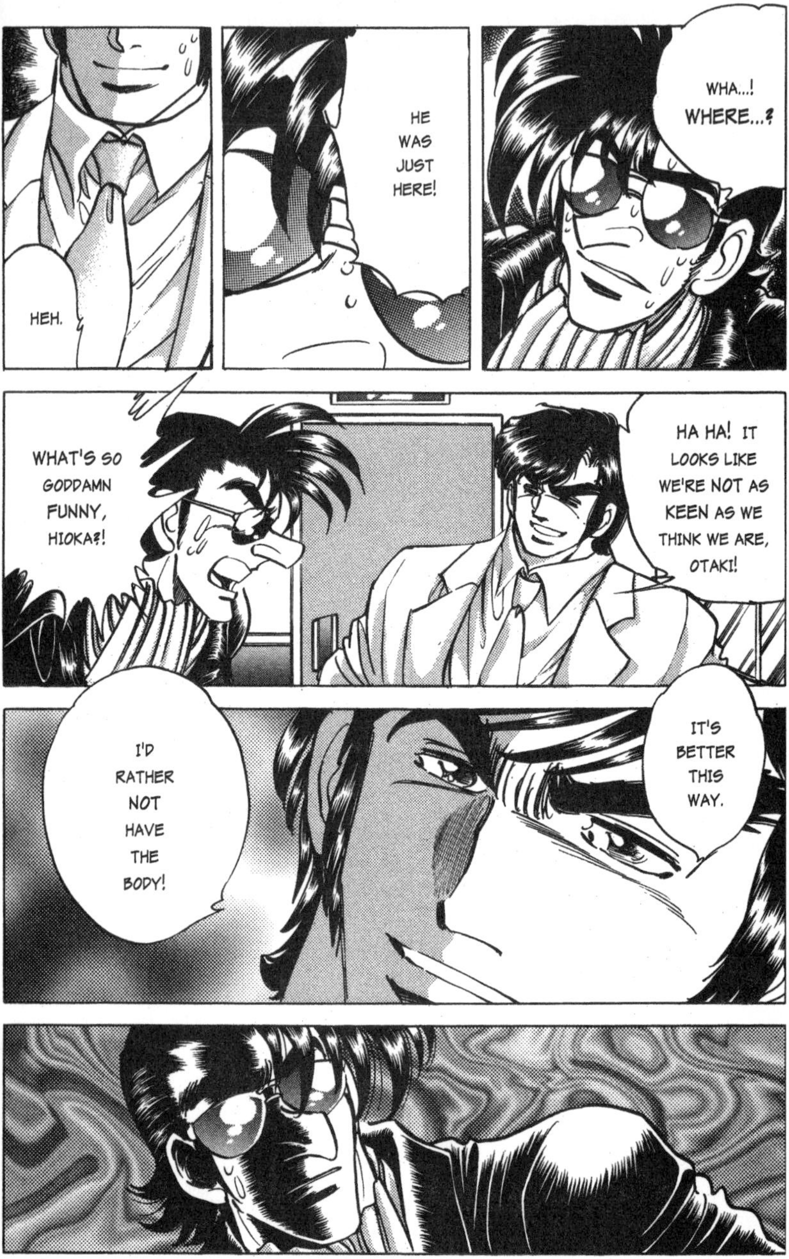
WHA...! WHERE...?!
HE WAS JUST HERE!
HEH.
HA HA! IT LOOKS LIKE WE'RE NOT AS KEEN AS WE THINK WE ARE, OTAKI!
WHAT'S SO GODDAMN FUNNY, HIOKA?!
IT'S BETTER THIS WAY.
I'D RATHER NOT HAVE THE BODY!

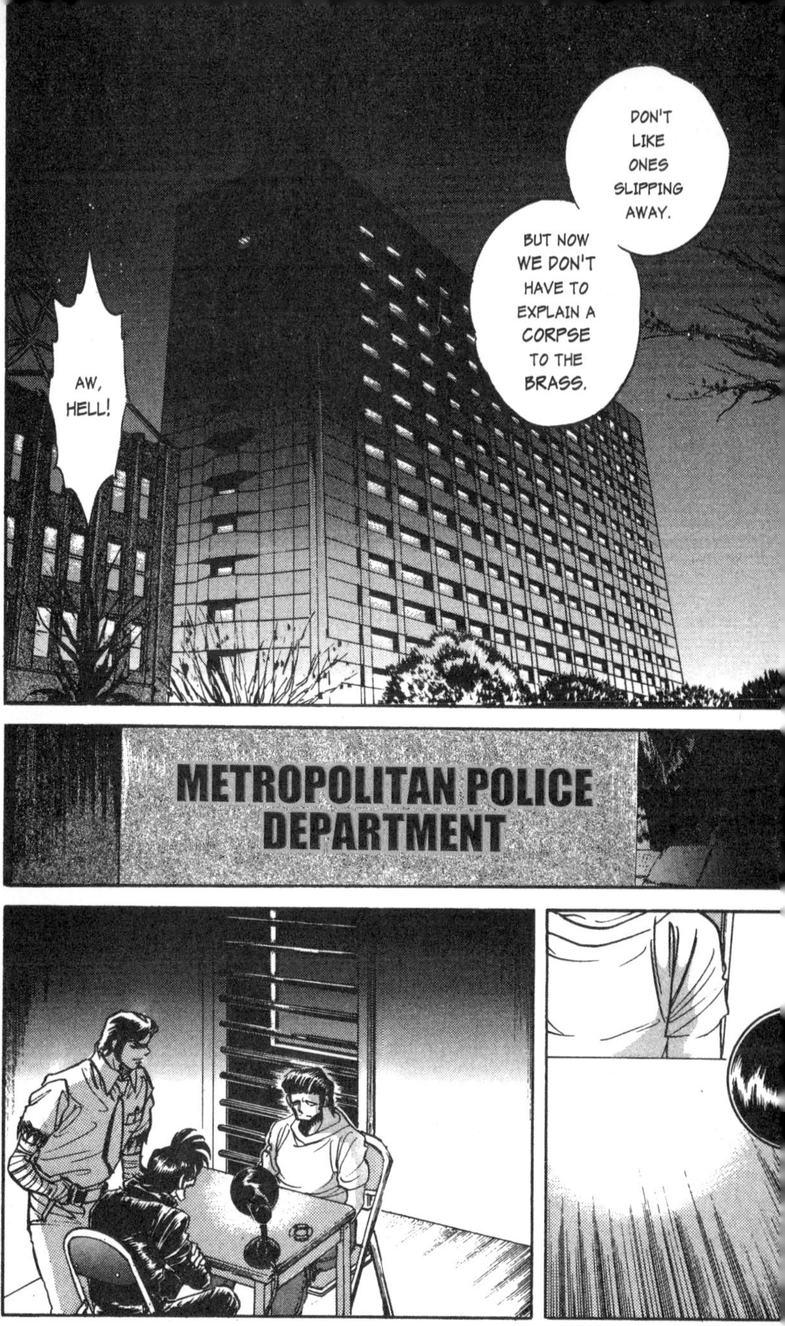
DON'T LIKE ONES SLIPPING AWAY.
BUT NOW WE DON'T HAVE TO EXPLAIN A CORPSE TO THE BRASS.
AW, HELL!
METROPOLITAN POLICE DEPARTMENT

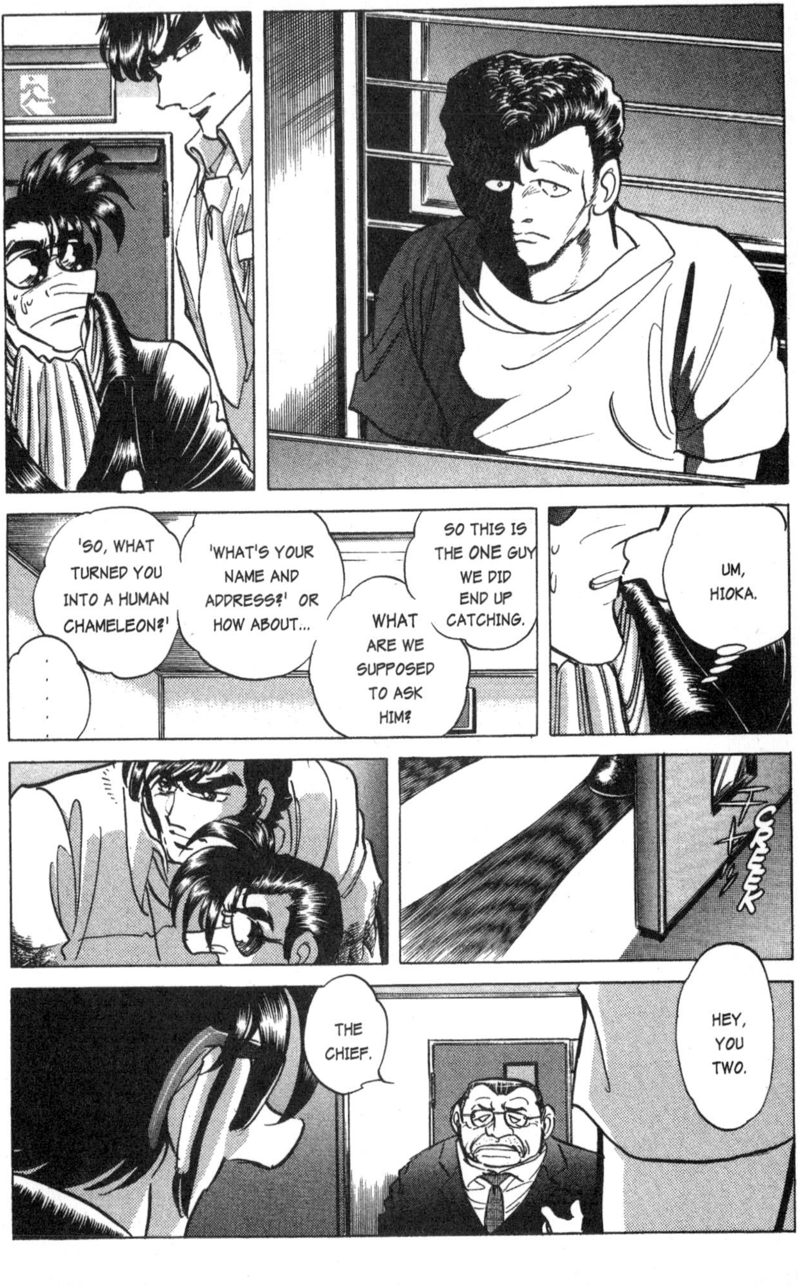
UM, HIOKA.
SO THIS IS THE ONE GUY WE DID END UP CATCHING.
WHAT ARE WE SUPPOSED TO ASK HIM?
'WHAT'S YOUR NAME AND ADDRESS?' OR HOW ABOUT...
'SO, WHAT TURNED YOU INTO A HUMAN CHAMELEON?'
CREEEK
HEY, YOU TWO.
THE CHIEF.

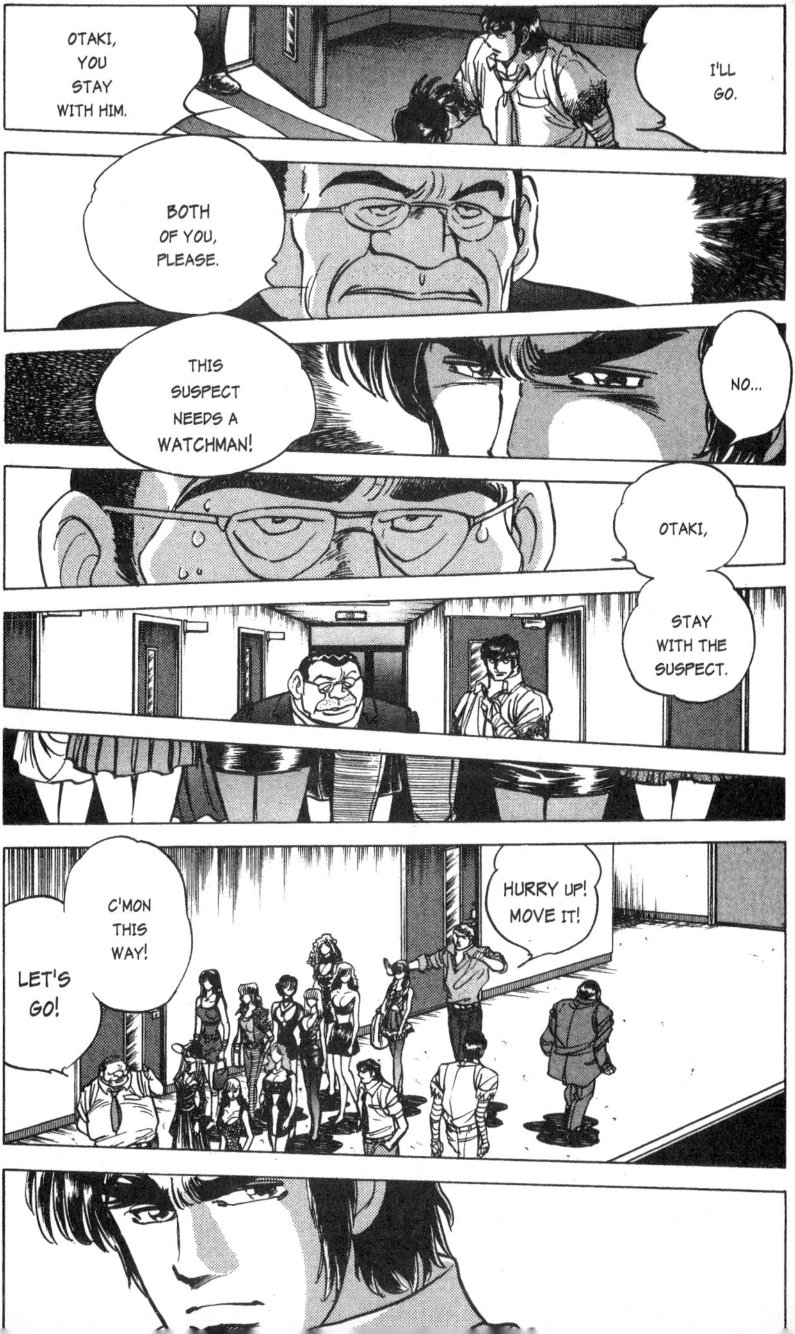
I'LL GO.
OTAKI, YOU STAY WITH HIM.
BOTH OF YOU, PLEASE.
NO...
THIS SUSPECT NEEDS A WATCHMAN!
OTAKI,
STAY WITH THE SUSPECT.
HURRY UP! MOVE IT!
C'MON THIS WAY!
LET'S GO!

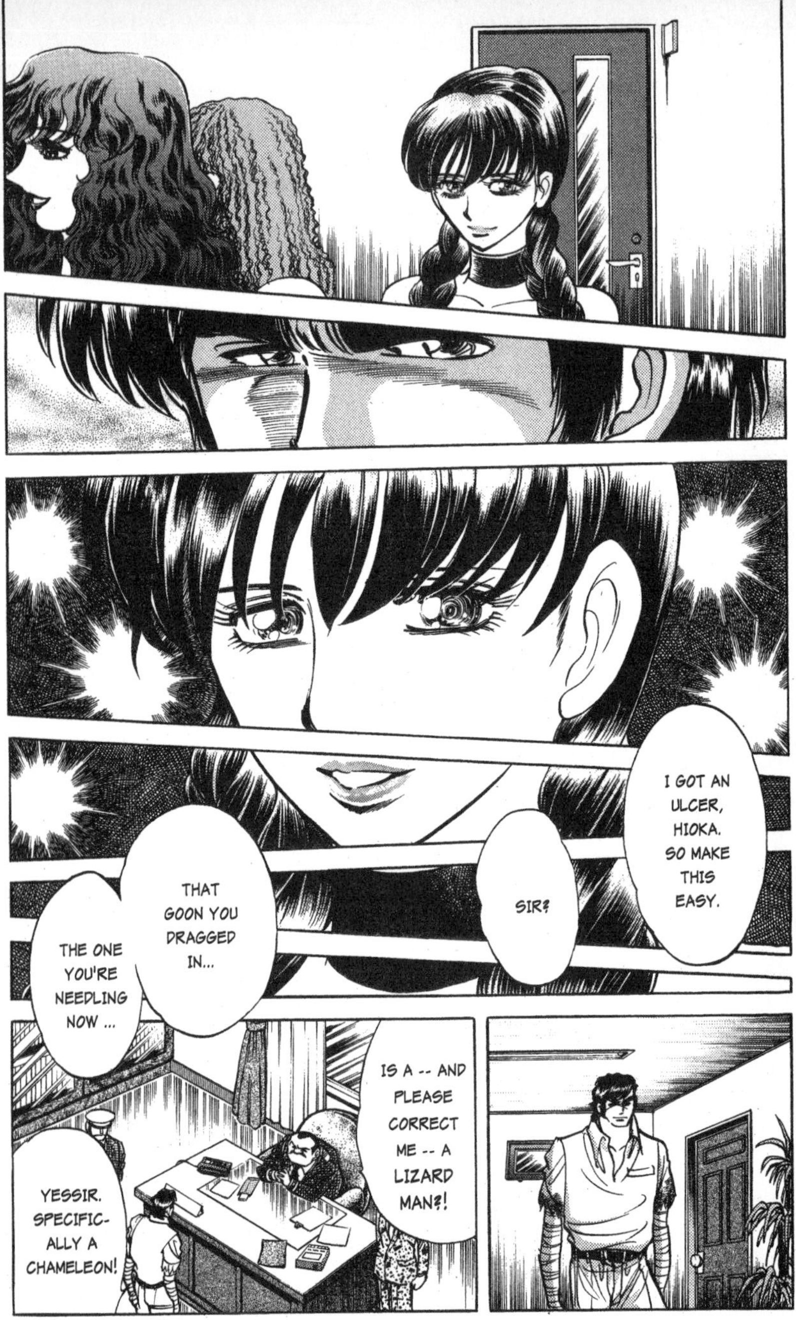
I GOT AN ULCER, HIOKA. SO MAKE THIS EASY.
SIR?
THAT GOON YOU DRAGGED IN...
THE ONE YOU'RE NEEDLING NOW ...
IS A -- AND PLEASE CORRECT ME -- A LIZARD MAN?!
YESSIR. SPECIFIC-ALLY A CHAMELEON!

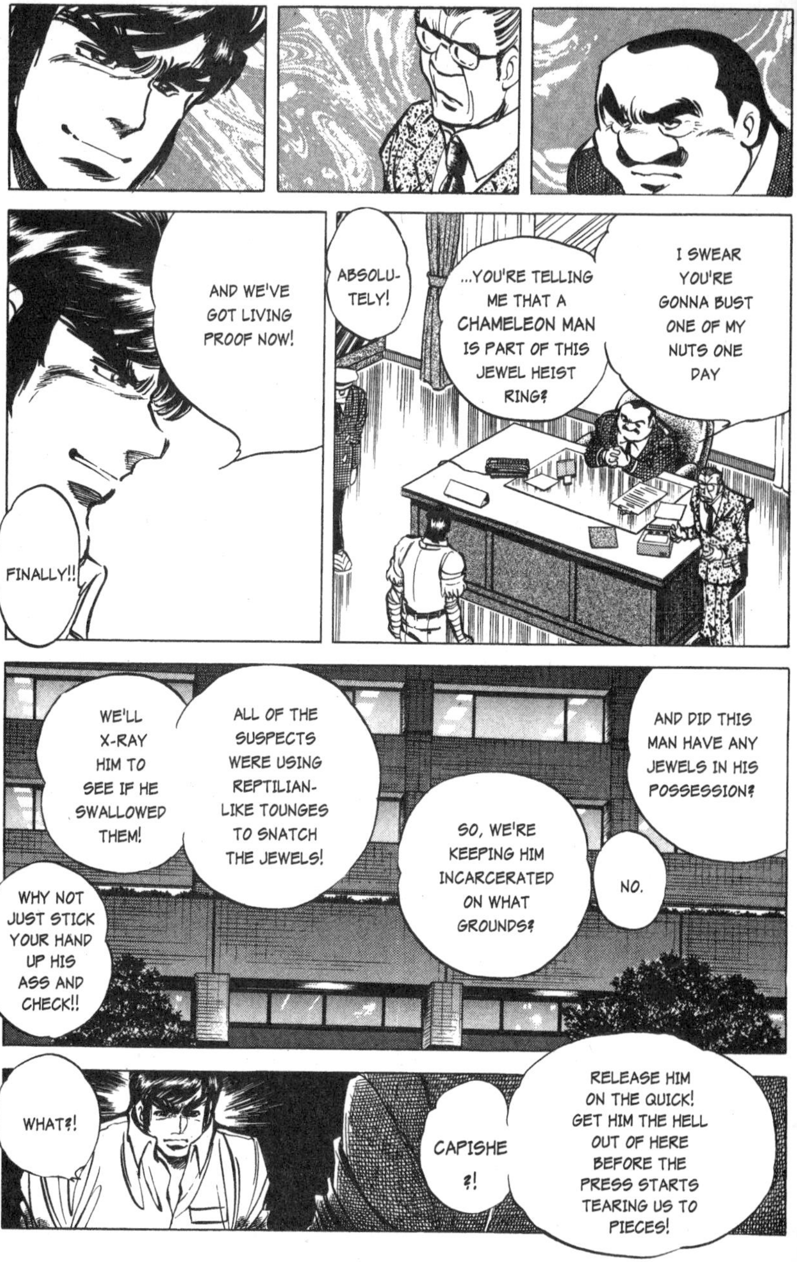
I SWEAR YOU'RE GONNA BUST ONE OF MY NUTS ONE DAY
...YOU'RE TELLING ME THAT A CHAMELEON MAN IS PART OF THIS JEWEL HEIST RING?
ABSOLU-TELY!
AND WE'VE GOT LIVING PROOF NOW!
FINALLY!!
AND DID THIS MAN HAVE ANY JEWELS IN HIS POSSESSION?
NO.
SO, WE'RE KEEPING HIM INCARCERATED ON WHAT GROUNDS?
ALL OF THE SUSPECTS WERE USING REPTILIAN-LIKE TOUNGES TO SNATCH THE JEWELS!
WE'LL X-RAY HIM TO SEE IF HE SWALLOWED THEM!
WHY NOT JUST STICK YOUR HAND UP HIS ASS AND CHECK!!
RELEASE HIM ON THE QUICK! GET HIM THE HELL OUT OF HERE BEFORE THE PRESS STARTS TEARING US TO PIECES!
CAPISHE?!
WHAT?!

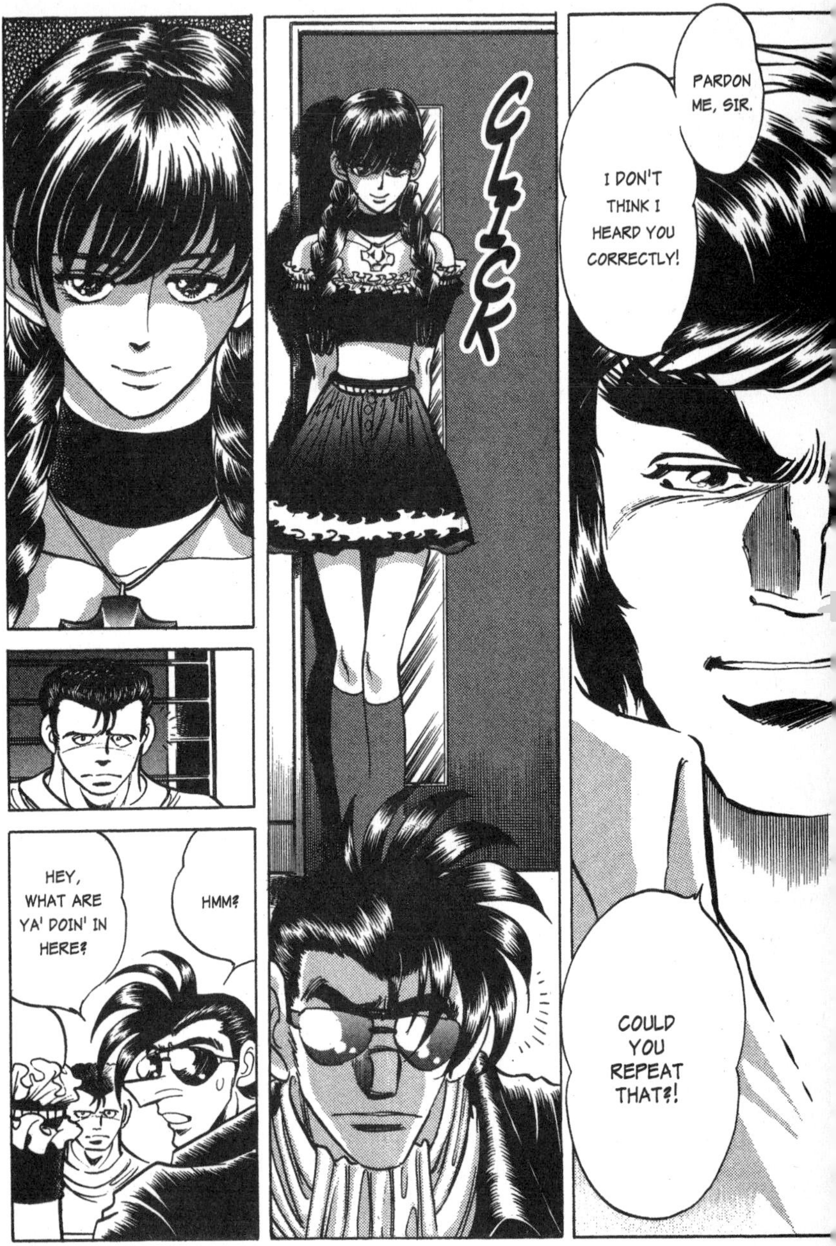
PARDON ME, SIR.
I DON'T THINK I HEARD YOU CORRECTLY!
COULD YOU REPEAT THAT?!
CLICK
HMM?
HEY, WHAT ARE YA' DOIN' IN HERE?

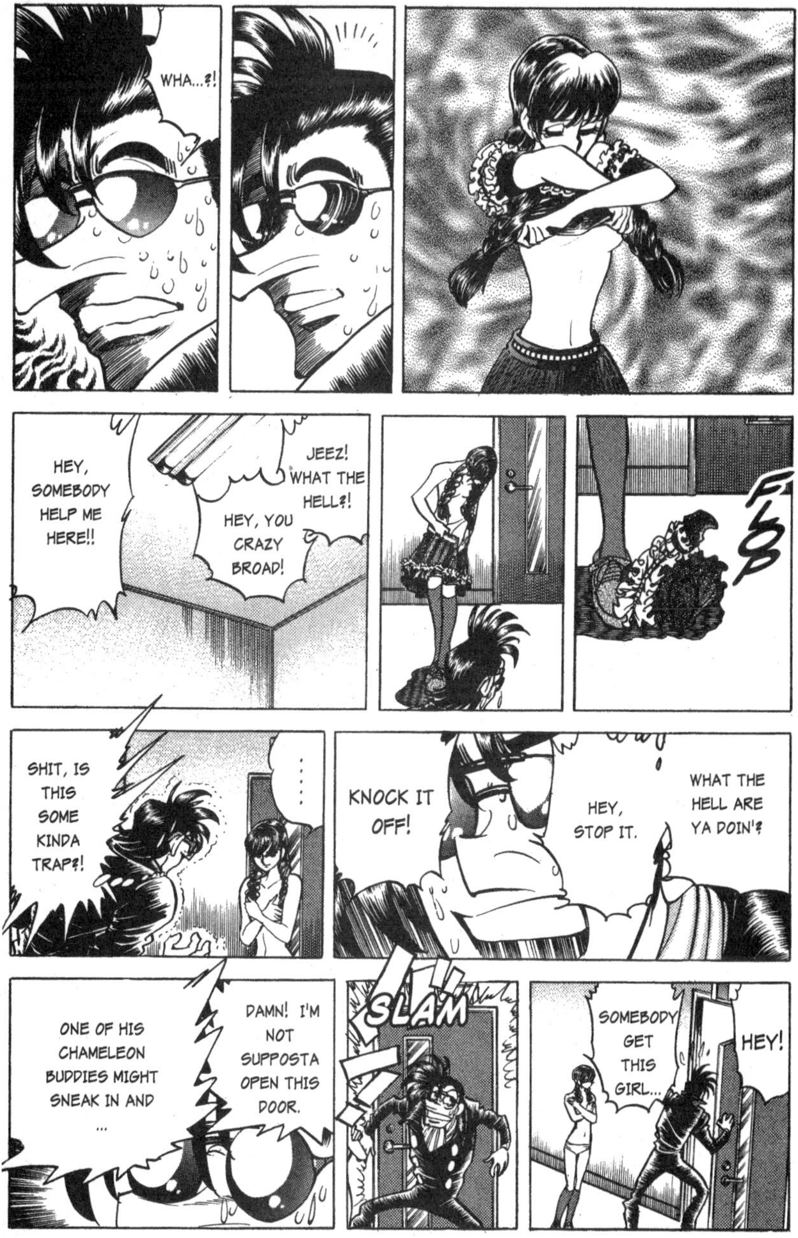
WHA...?!
FLOP
JEEZ! WHAT THE HELL?!
HEY, YOU CRAZY BROAD!
HEY, SOMEBODY HELP ME HERE!!
WHAT THE HELL ARE YA DOIN'?
HEY, STOP IT.
KNOCK IT OFF!
.....
SHIT, IS THIS SOME KINDA TRAP?!
HEY!
SOMEBODY GET THIS GIRL...
SLAM
DAMN! I'M NOT SUPPOSTA OPEN THIS DOOR.
ONE OF HIS CHAMELEON BUDDIES MIGHT SNEAK IN AND ...

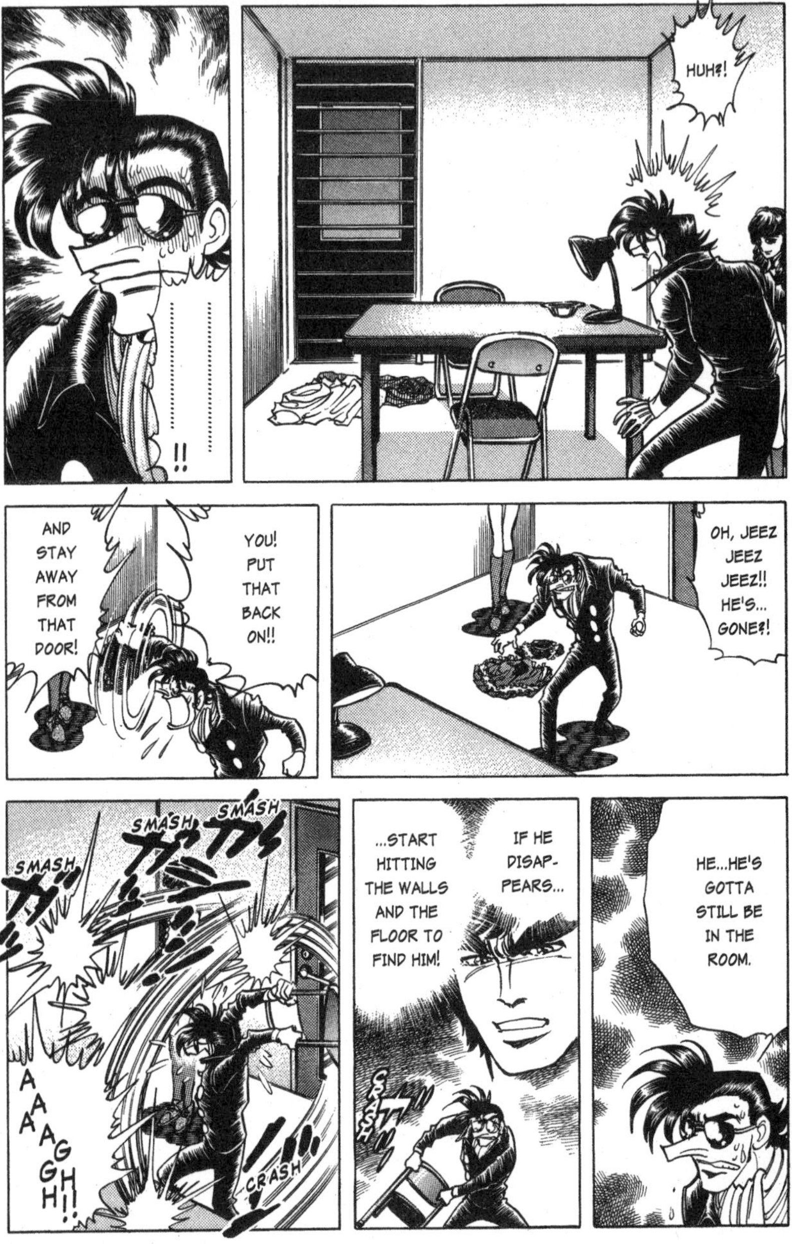
HUH?!
....
!!
OH, JEEZ JEEZ JEEZ!! HE'S... GONE?!
YOU! PUT THAT BACK ON!!
AND STAY AWAY FROM THAT DOOR!
HE...HE'S GOTTA STILL BE IN THE ROOM.
IF HE DISAP-PEARS...
...START HITTING THE WALLS AND THE FLOOR TO FIND HIM!
CRASH
SMASH
SMASH
SMASH
AAAAGHH!!
CRASH

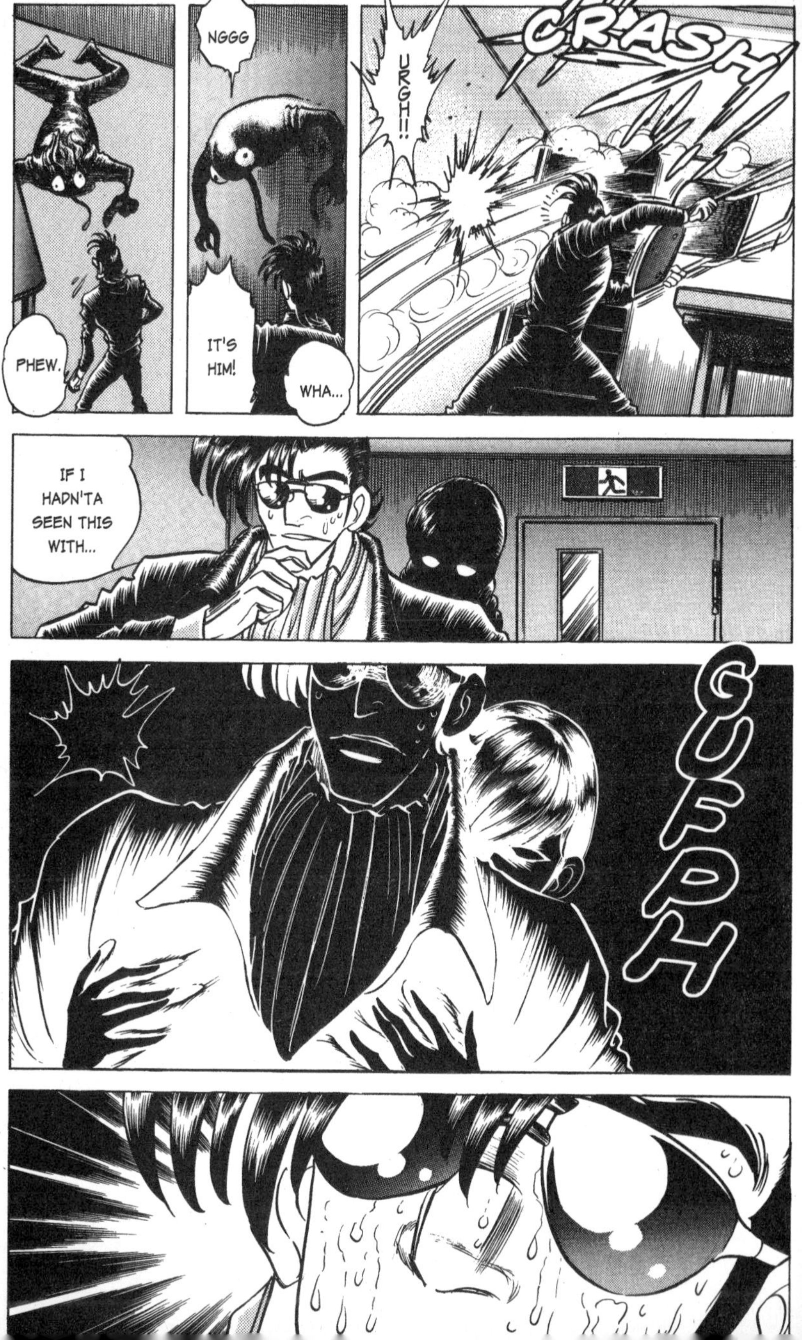
CRASH
URGH!!
NGGG
WHA...
IT'S HIM!
PHEW.
IF I HADN'TA SEEN THIS WITH...
GUFPH

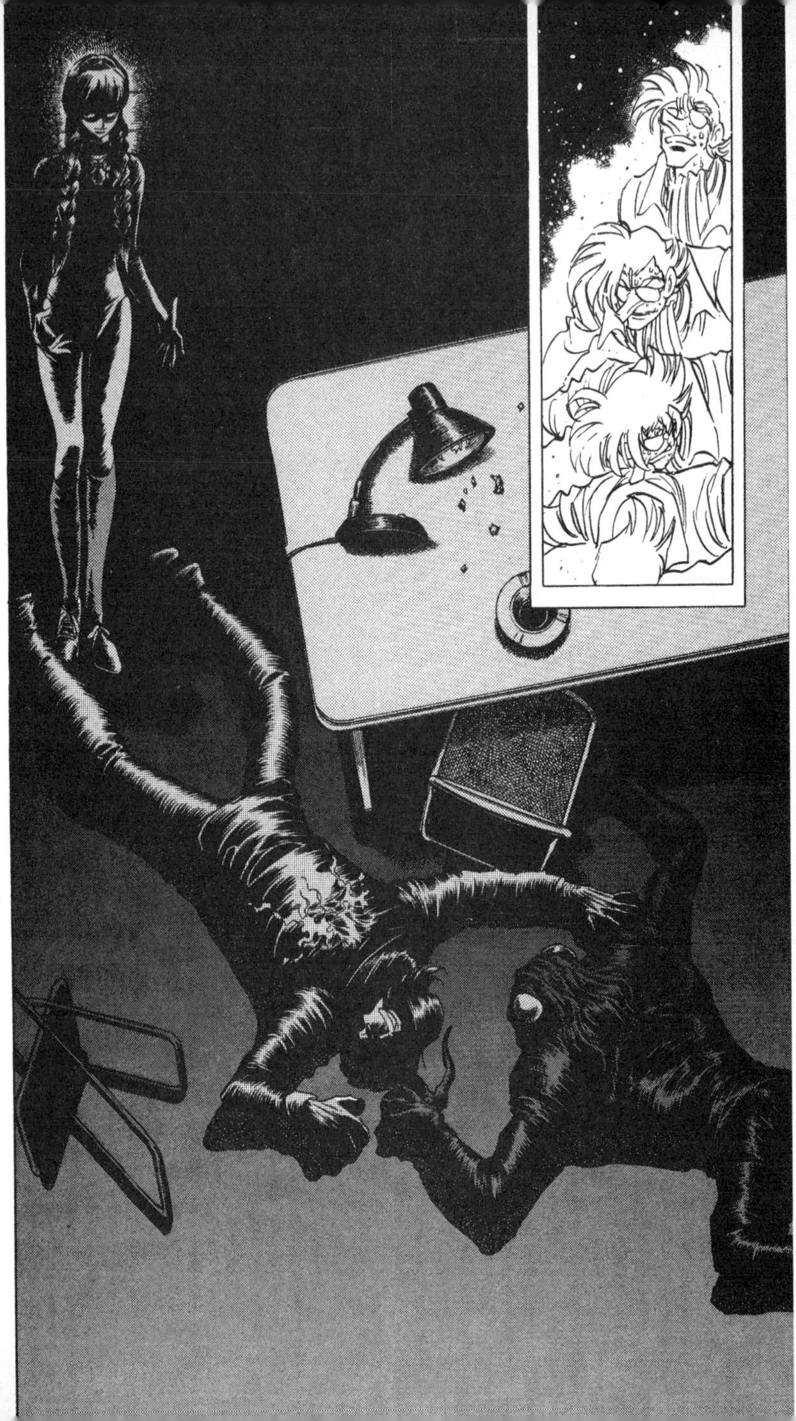

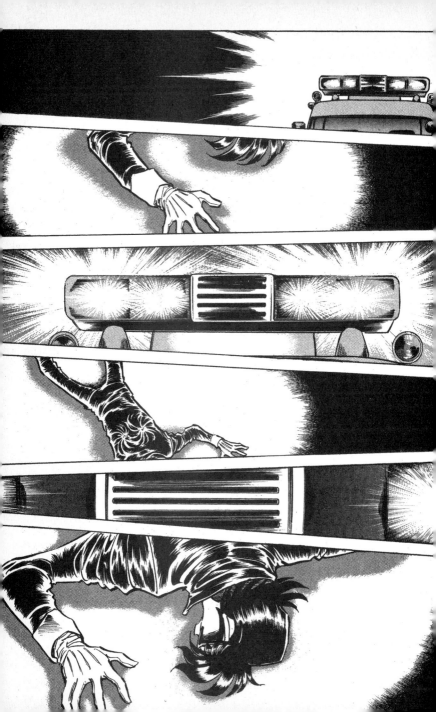

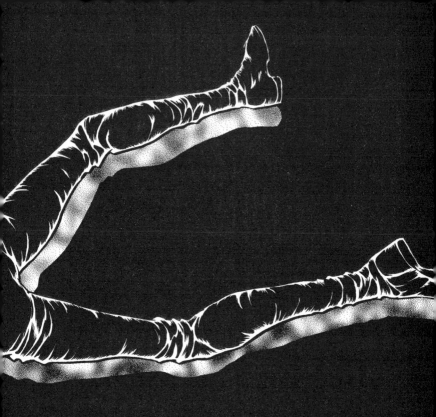

ホテル・ビーハイヴ

CH. 17 The Wasp
Hive Hotel

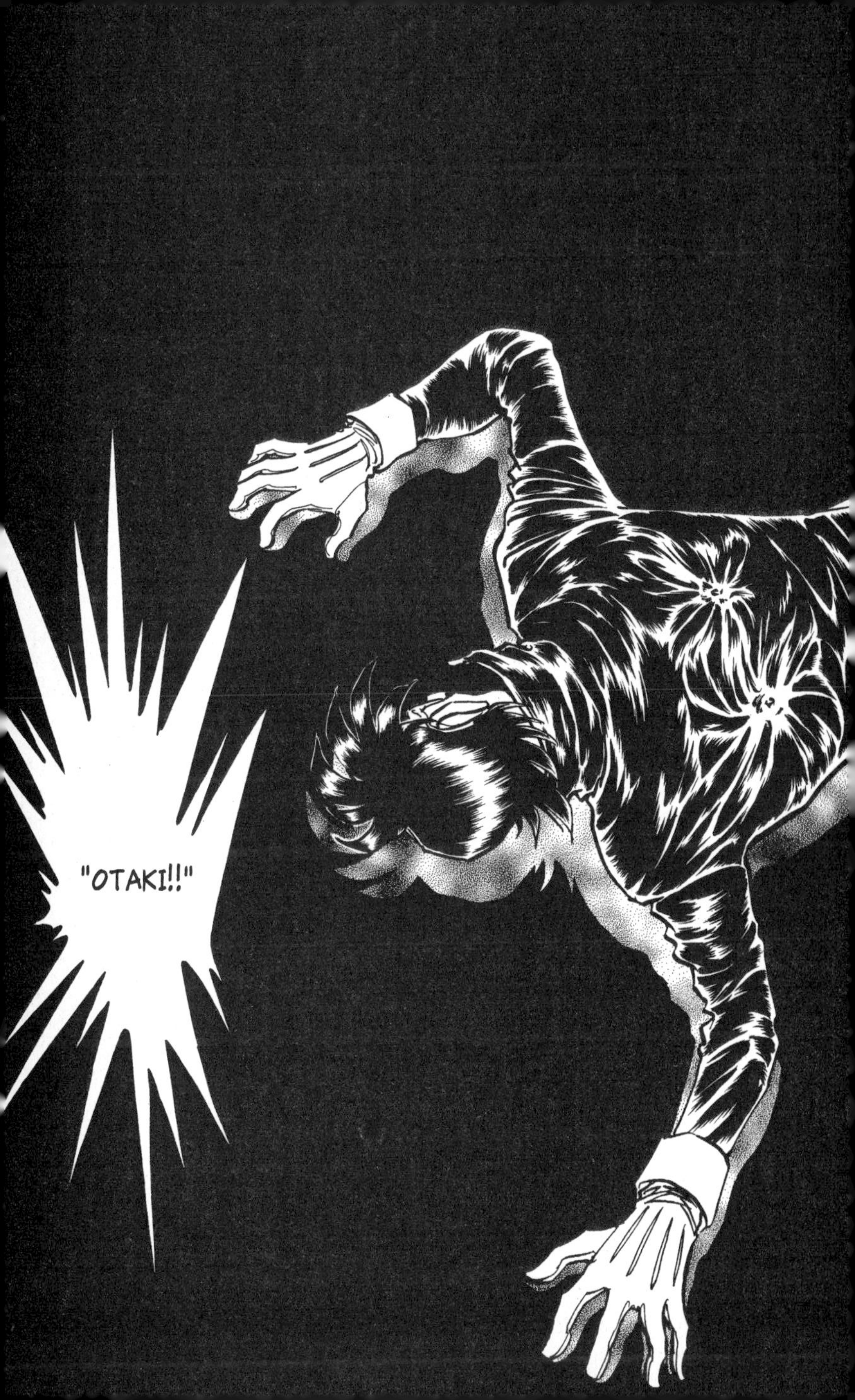
"OTAKI!!"

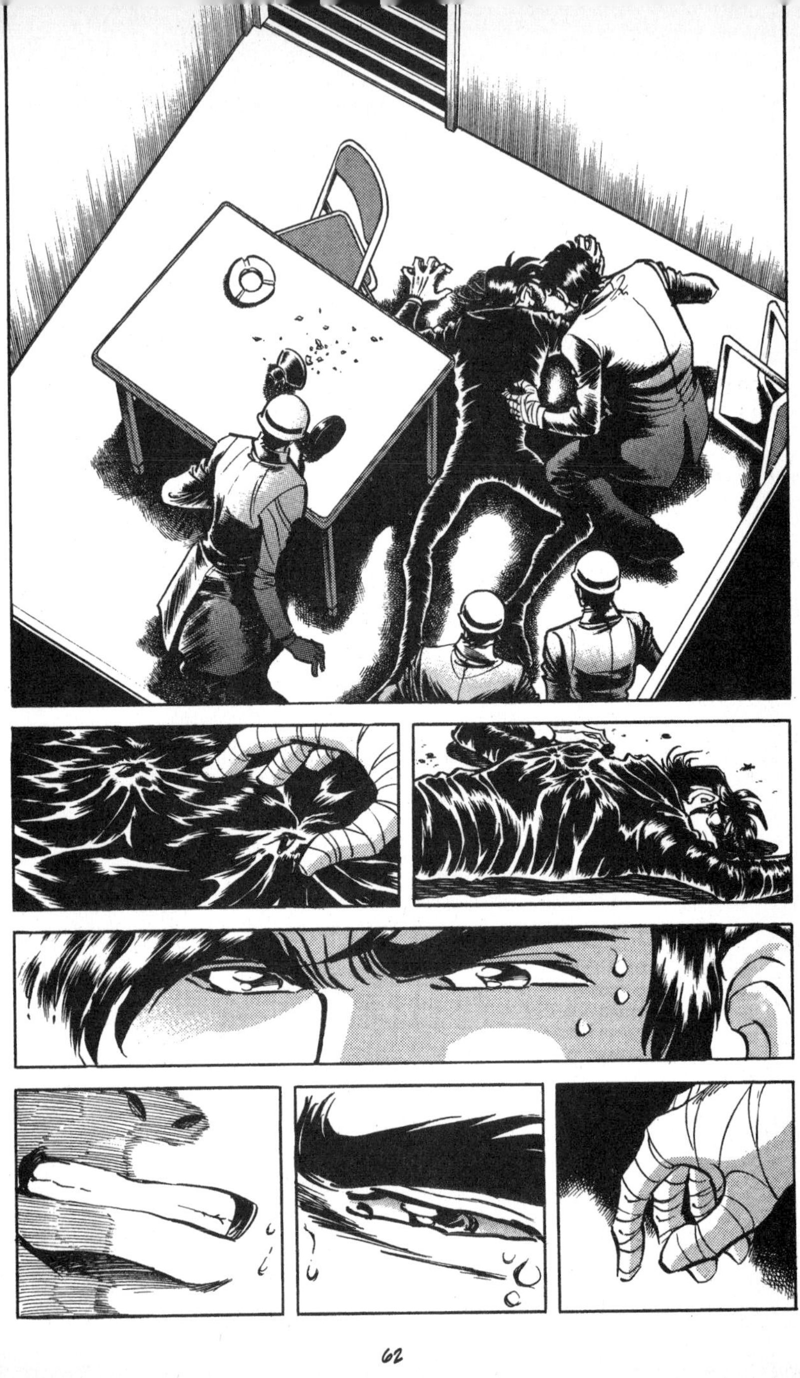

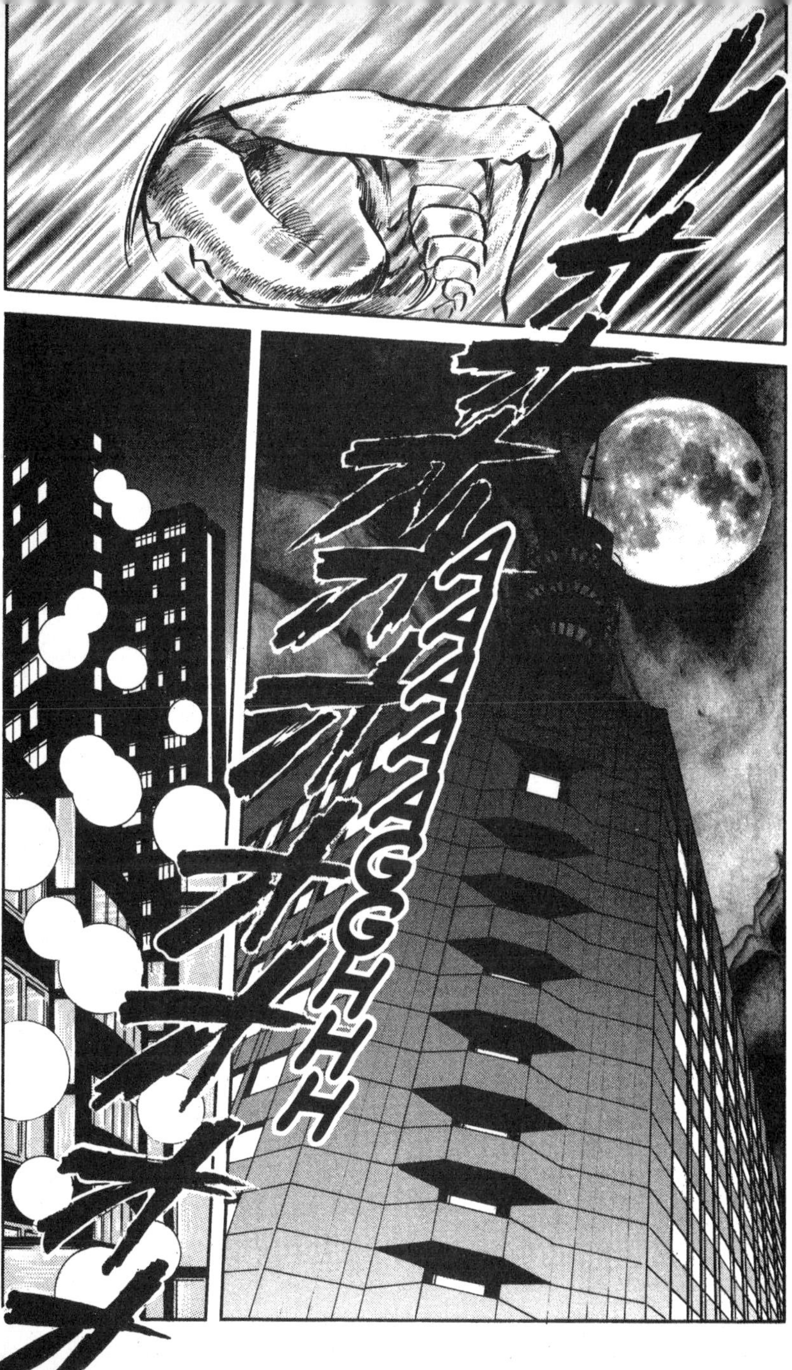
AAAAAGGGHHH

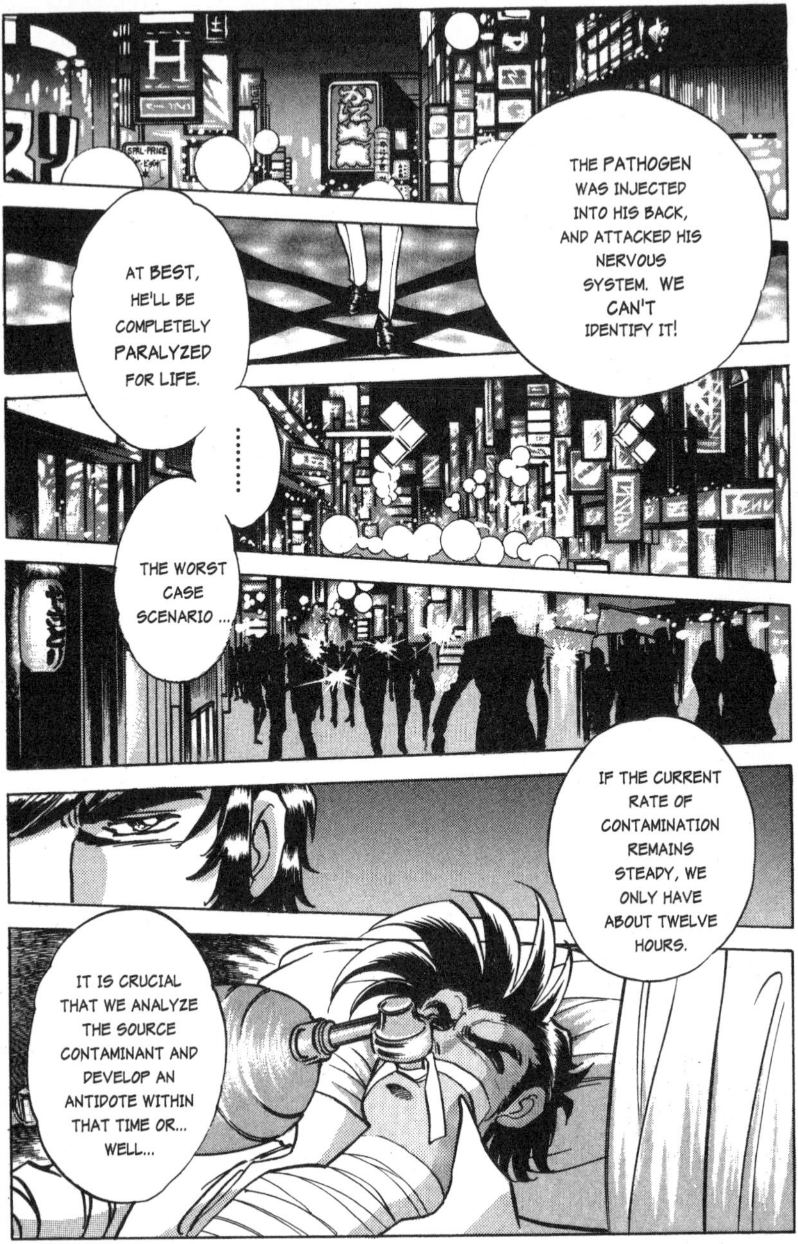
THE PATHOGEN WAS INJECTED INTO HIS BACK, AND ATTACKED HIS NERVOUS SYSTEM. WE CAN'T IDENTIFY IT!
AT BEST, HE'LL BE COMPLETELY PARALYZED FOR LIFE.
......
THE WORST CASE SCENARIO ...
IF THE CURRENT RATE OF CONTAMINATION REMAINS STEADY, WE ONLY HAVE ABOUT TWELVE HOURS.
IT IS CRUCIAL THAT WE ANALYZE THE SOURCE CONTAMINANT AND DEVELOP AN ANTIDOTE WITHIN THAT TIME OR... WELL...

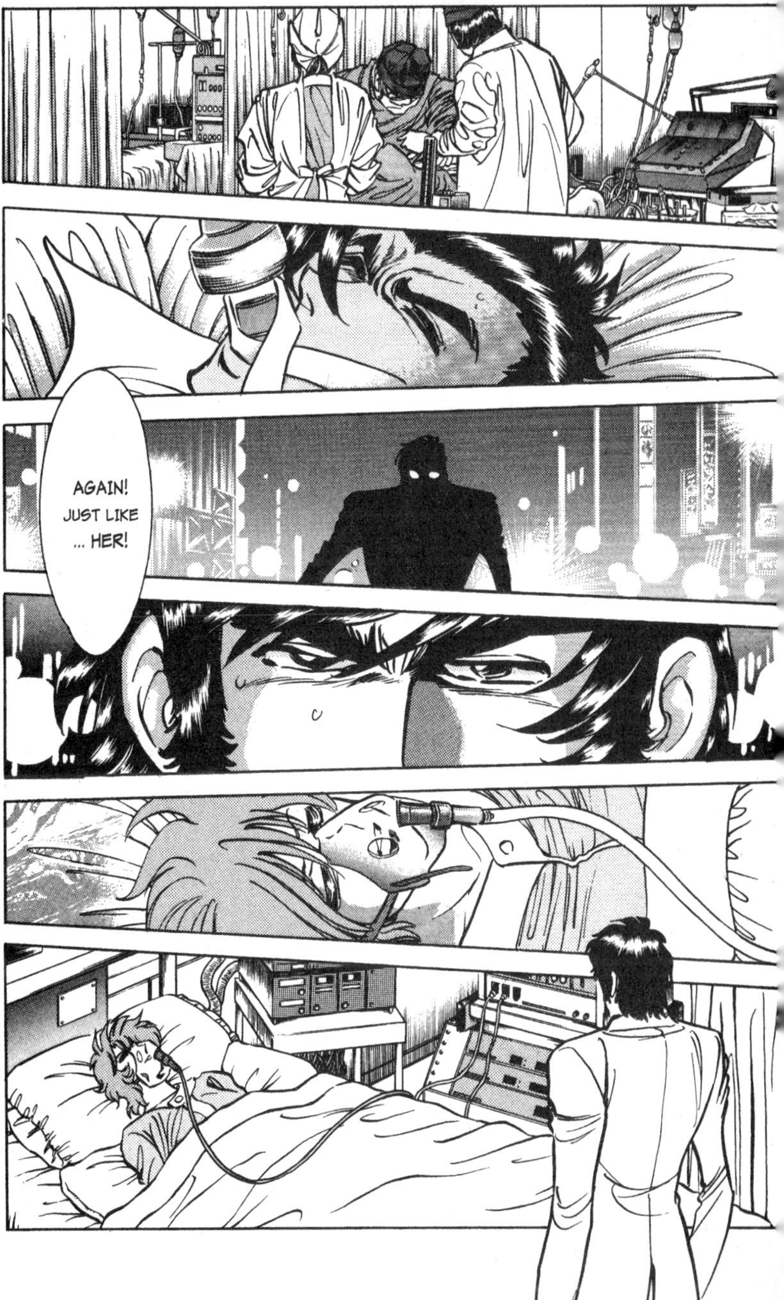
AGAIN! JUST LIKE ... HER!

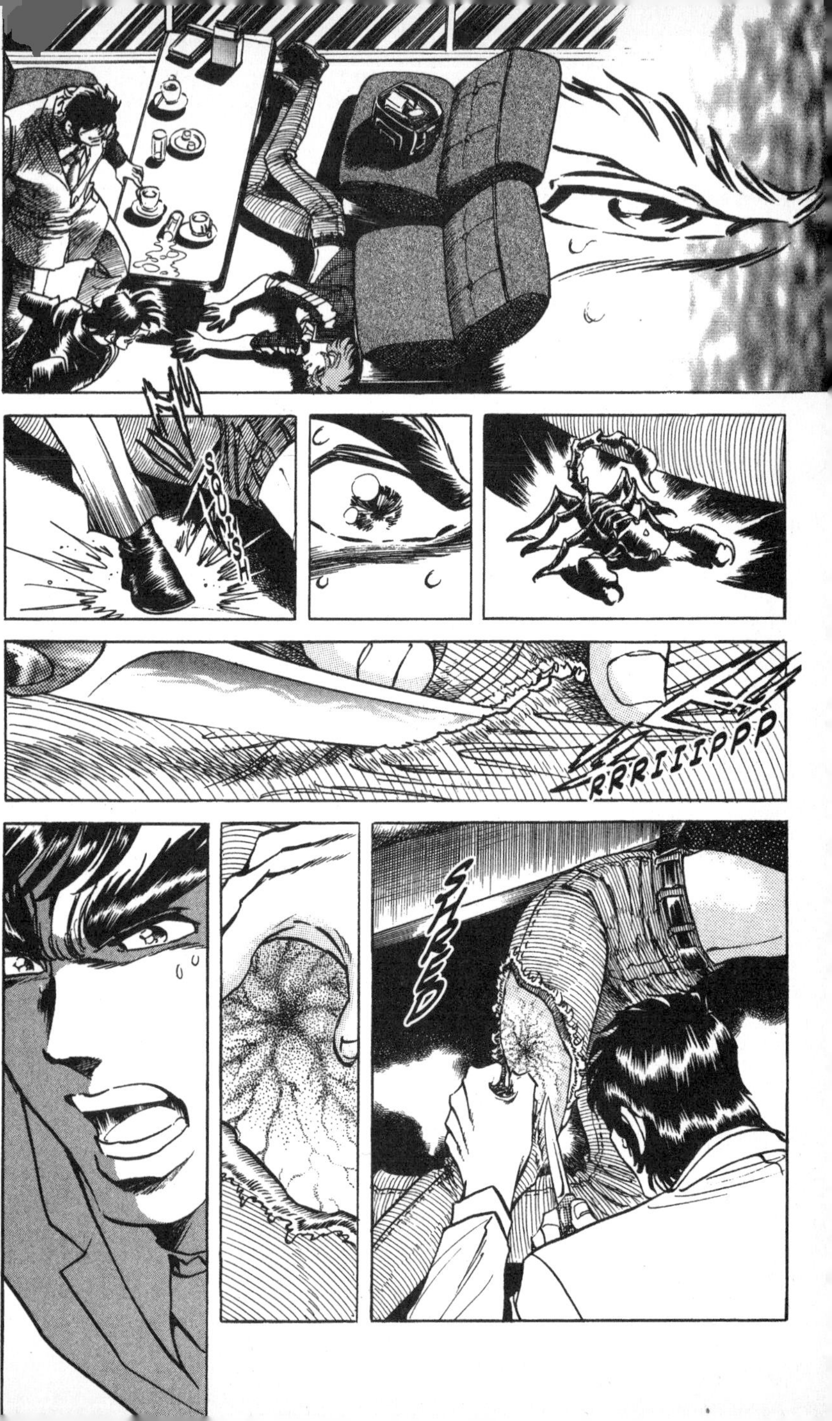
SQUISH
RRRIIIPPPP

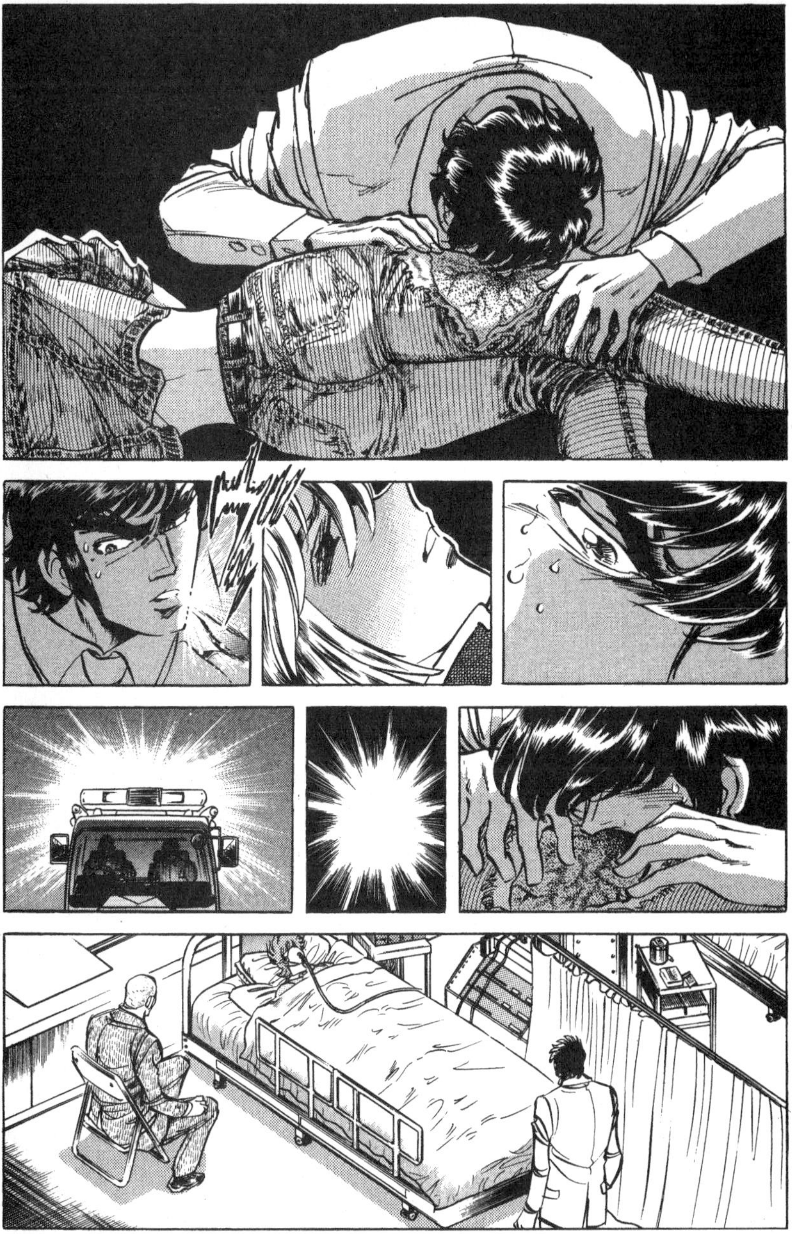

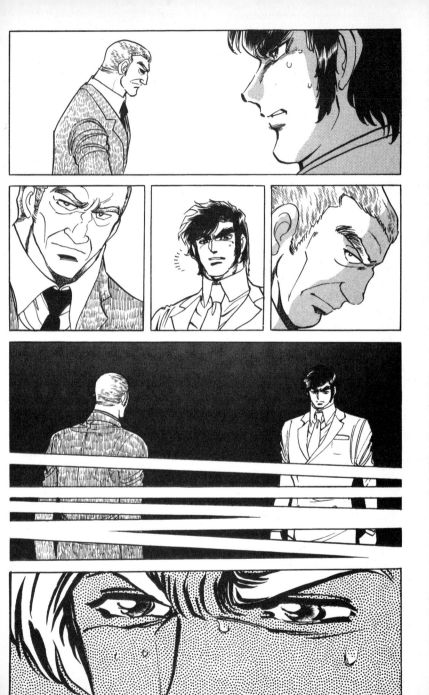

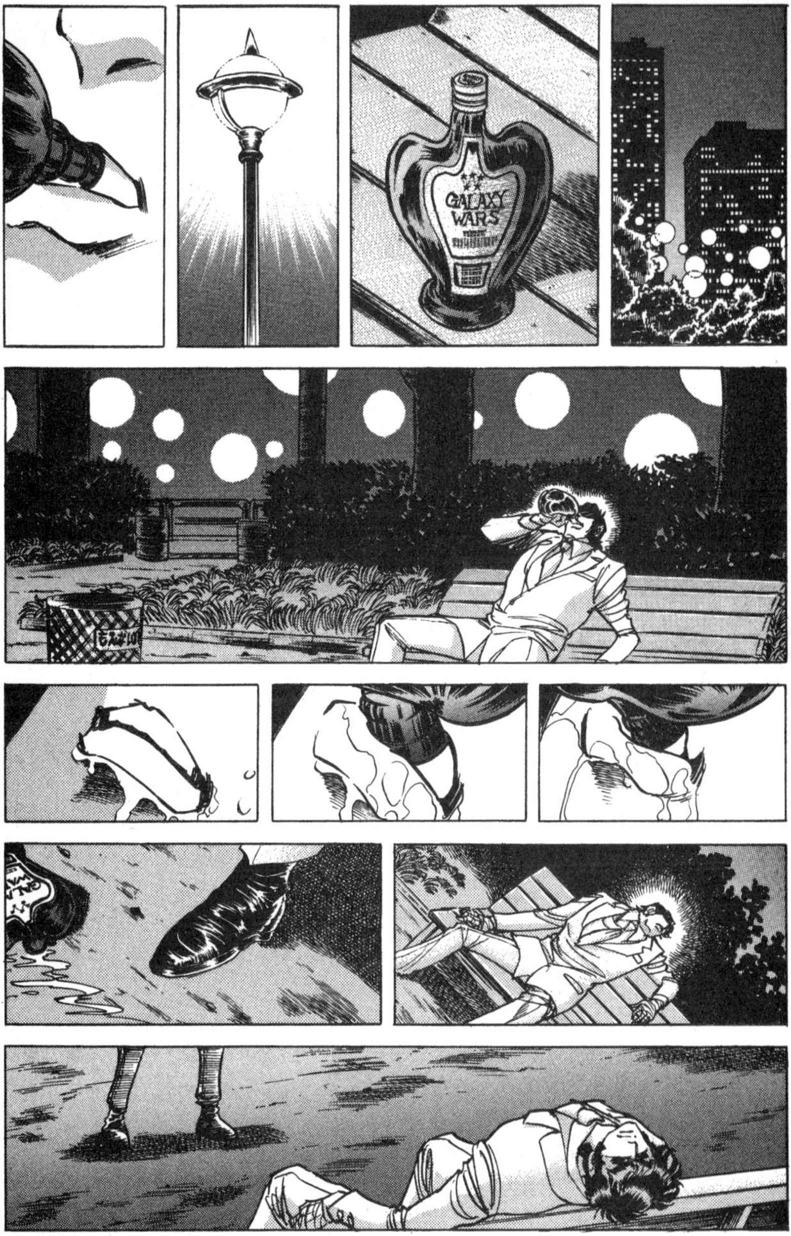
GALAXY
WARS

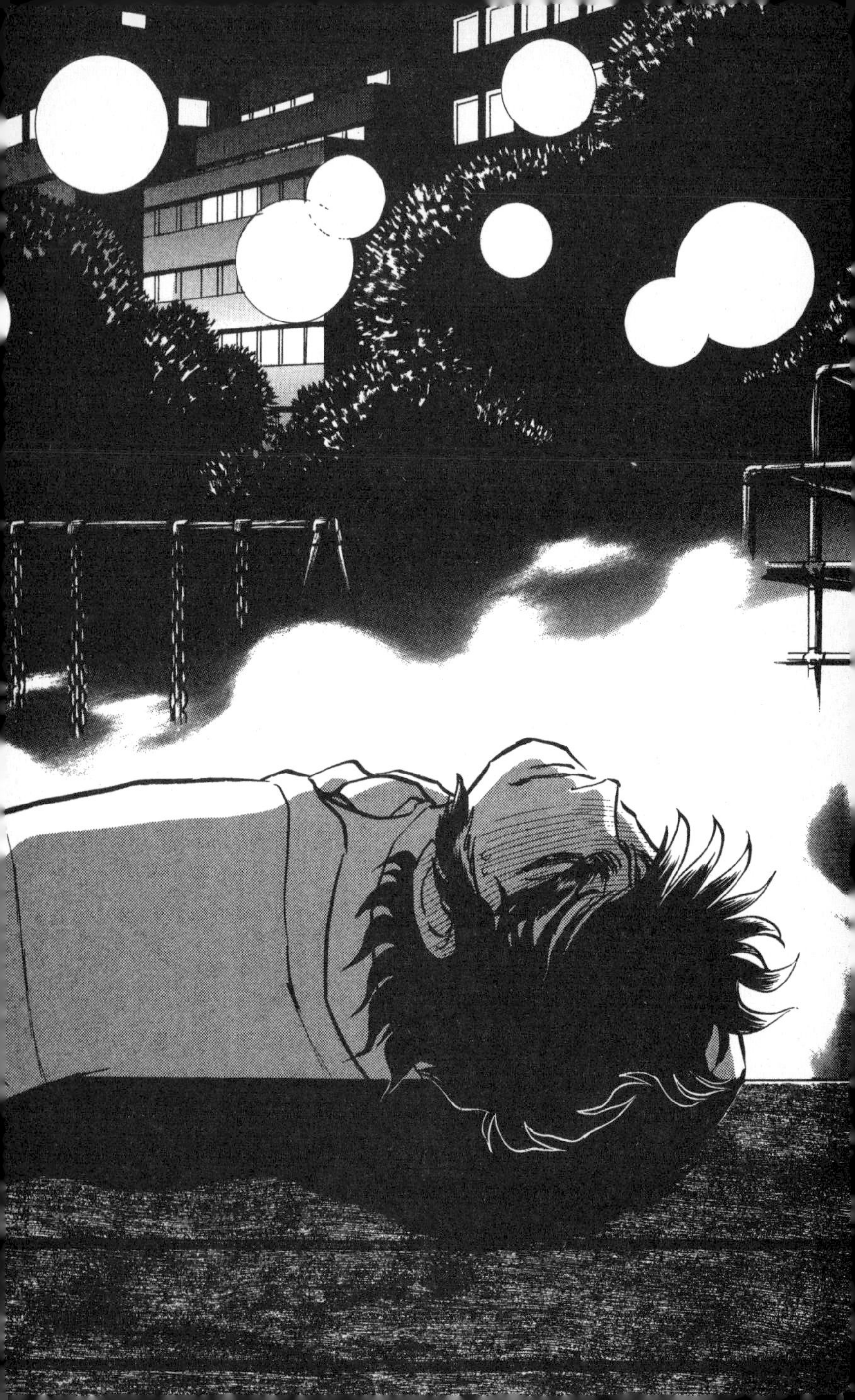

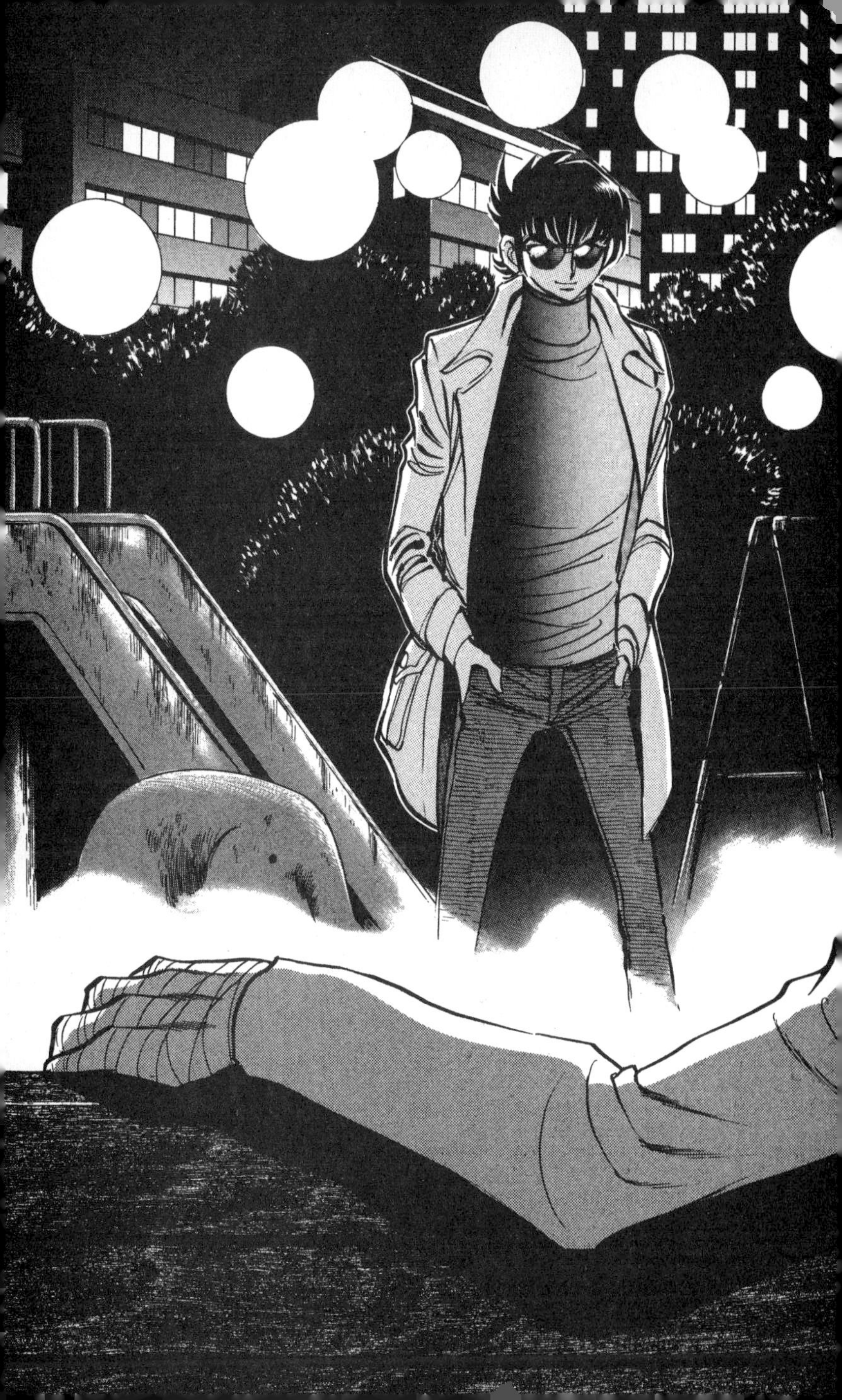

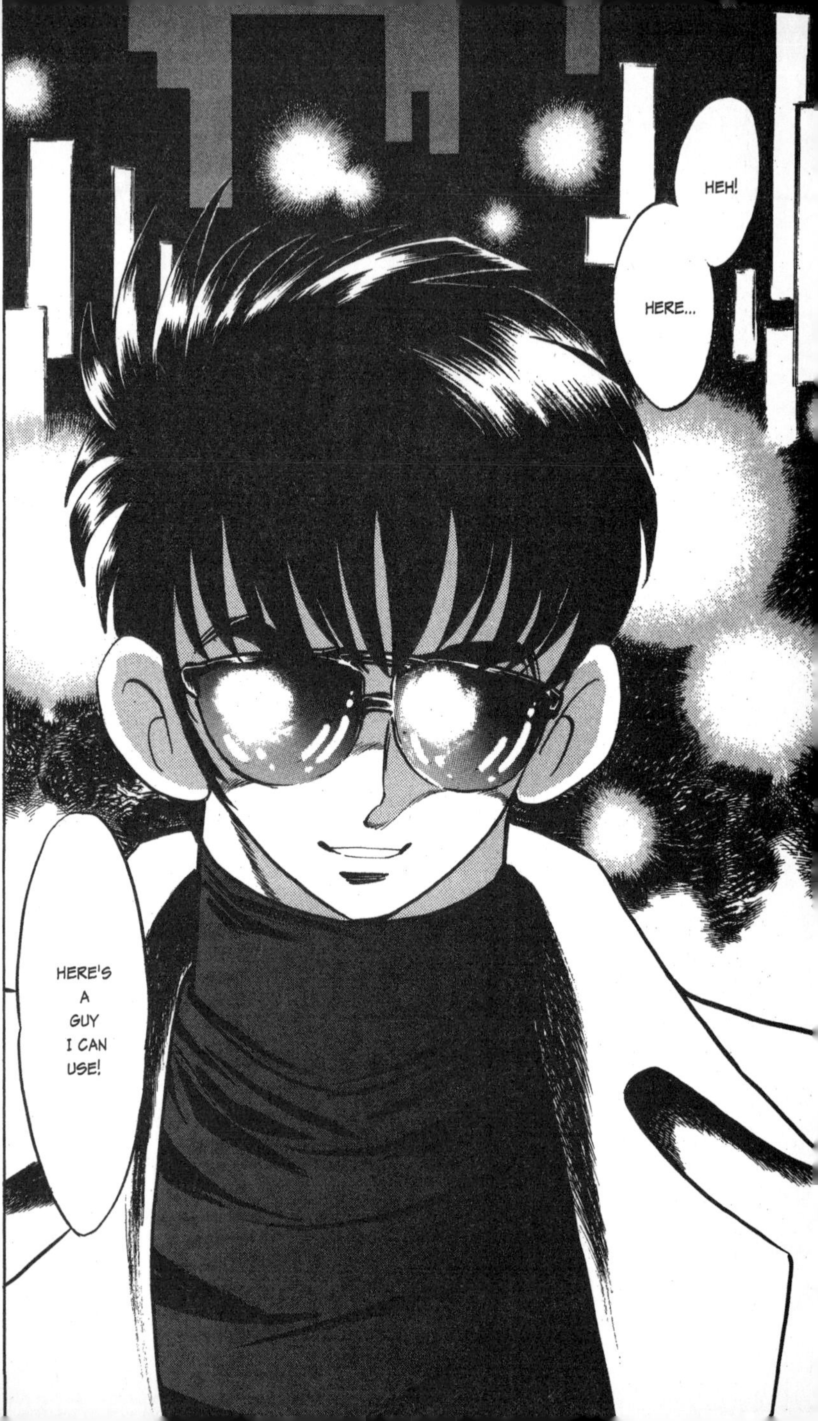
HEH!
HERE...
HERE'S A GUY I CAN USE!

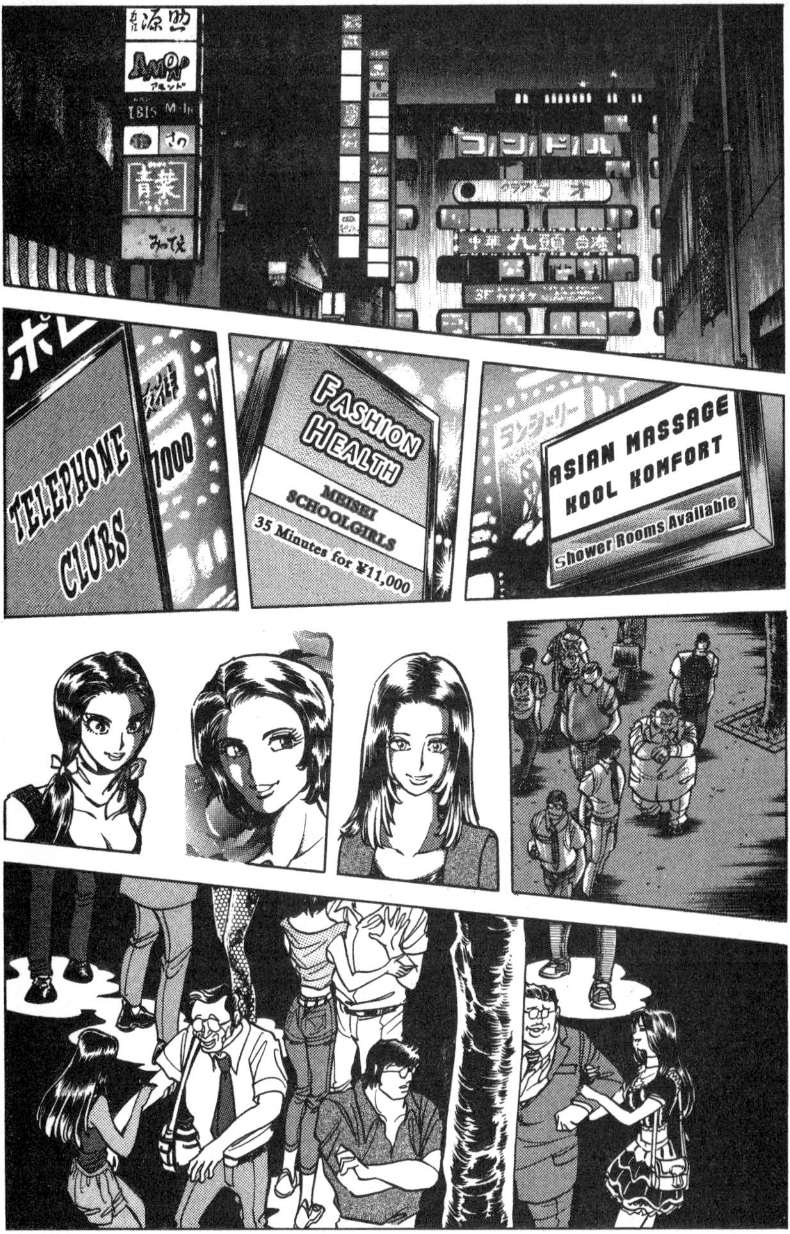
ASIAN MASSAGE
KOOL KOMFORT
Shower Rooms Available
FASHION HEALTH
MEISHI SCHOOLGIRLS
35 Minutes for ¥11,000
TELEPHONE CLUBS

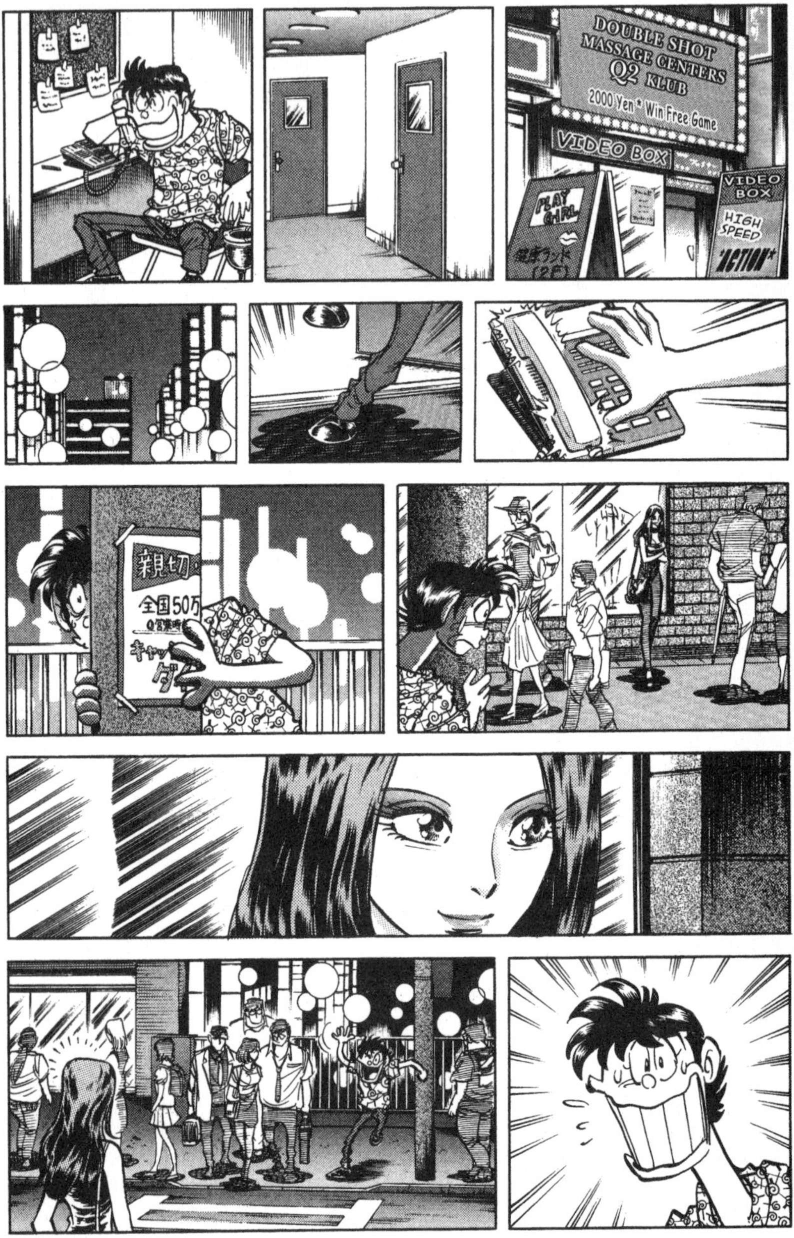
DOUBLE SHOT MASSAGE CENTERS Q2 KLUB
2000 Yen* Win Free Game
VIDEO BOX
VIDEO BOX
HIGH SPEED
"ACTION*"
PLAY GIRL
(2F)
親切
全国50万
キャッ
ダ

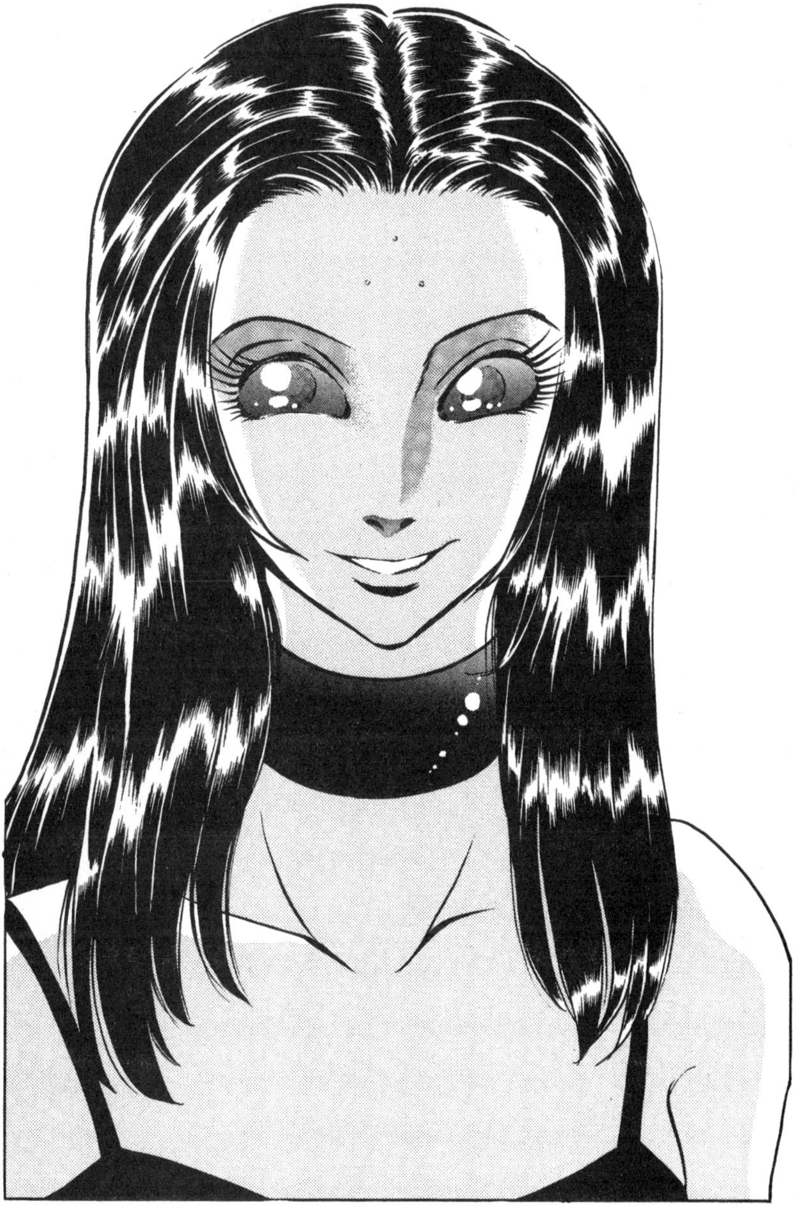

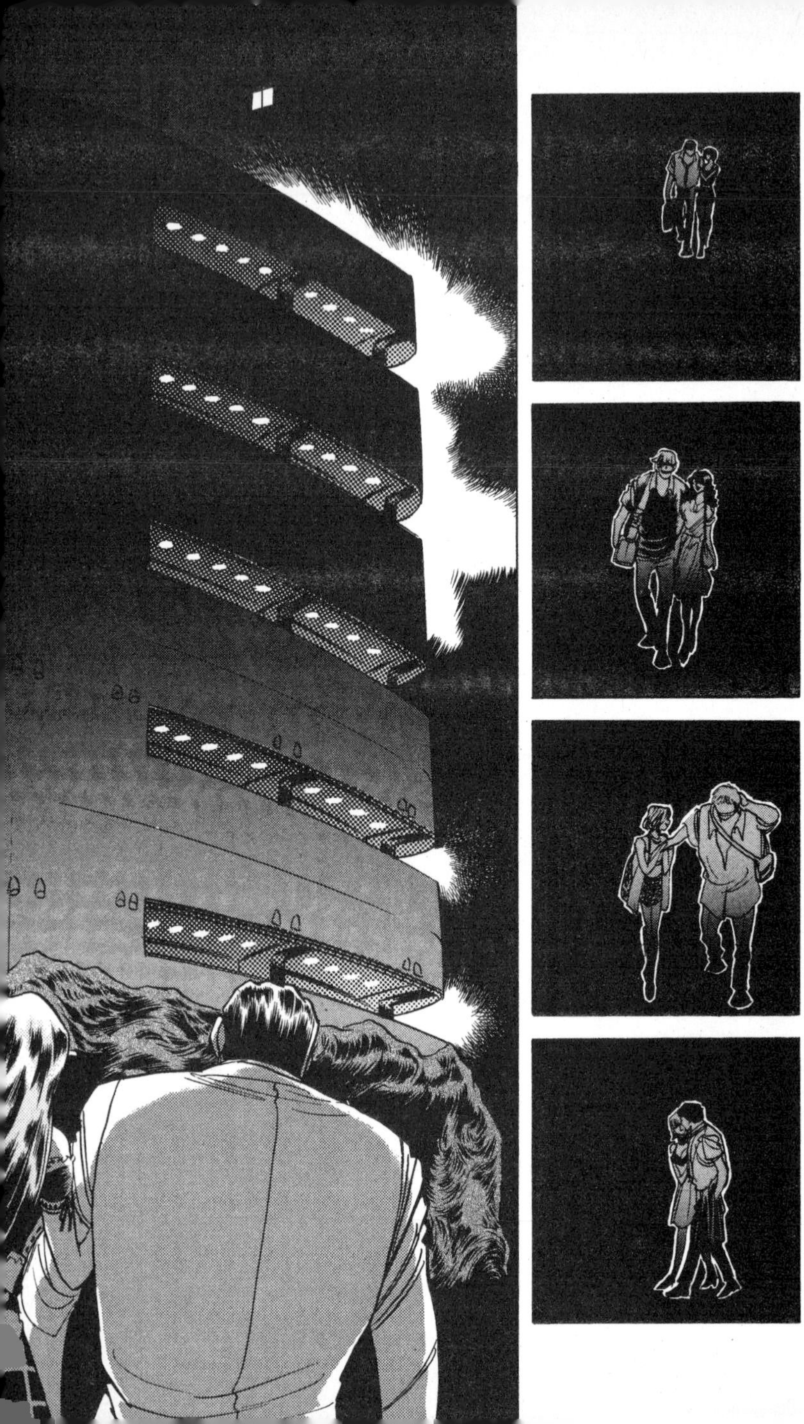

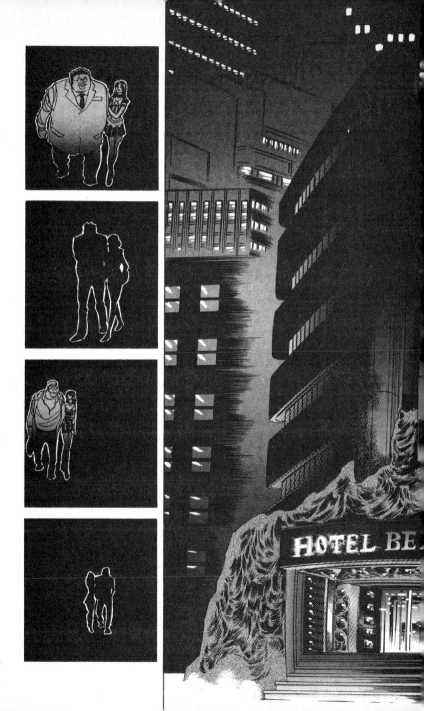

HOTEL BE

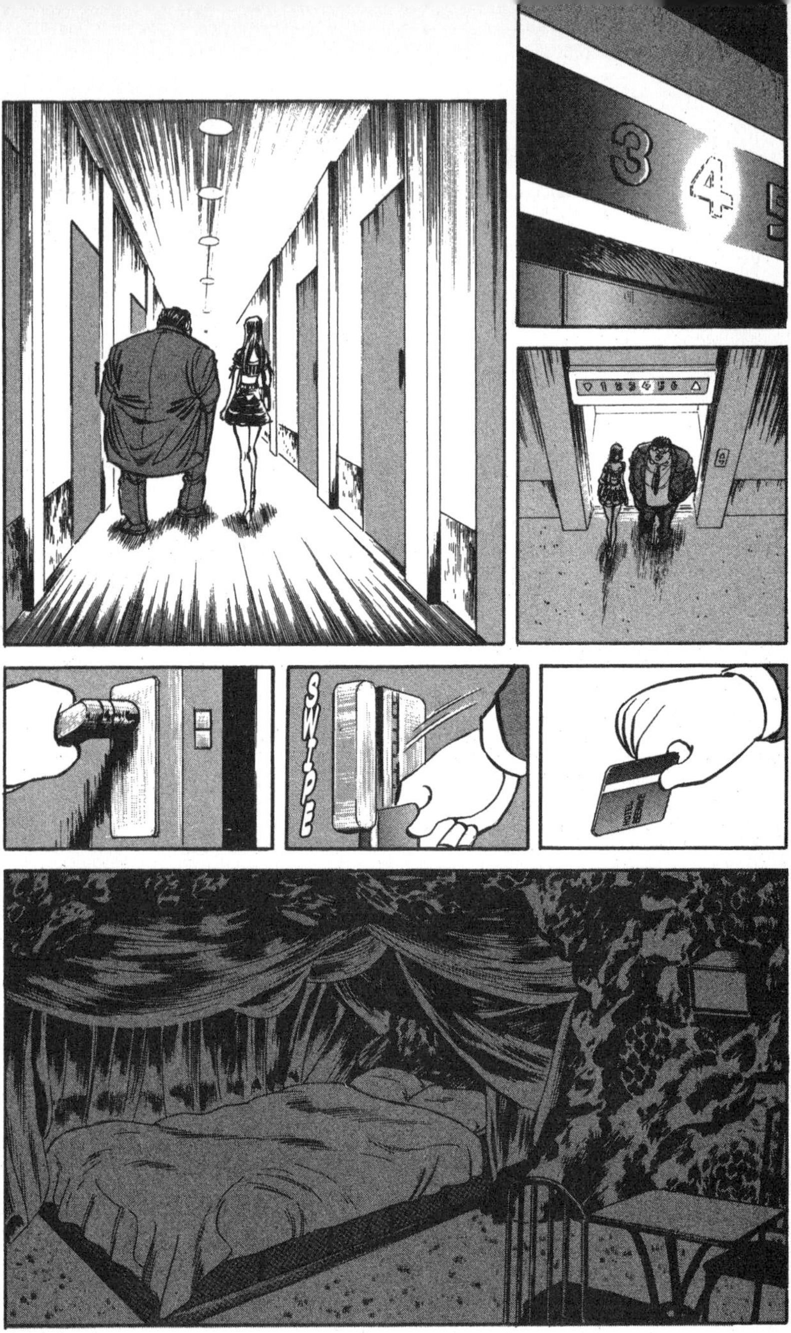
SWIPE

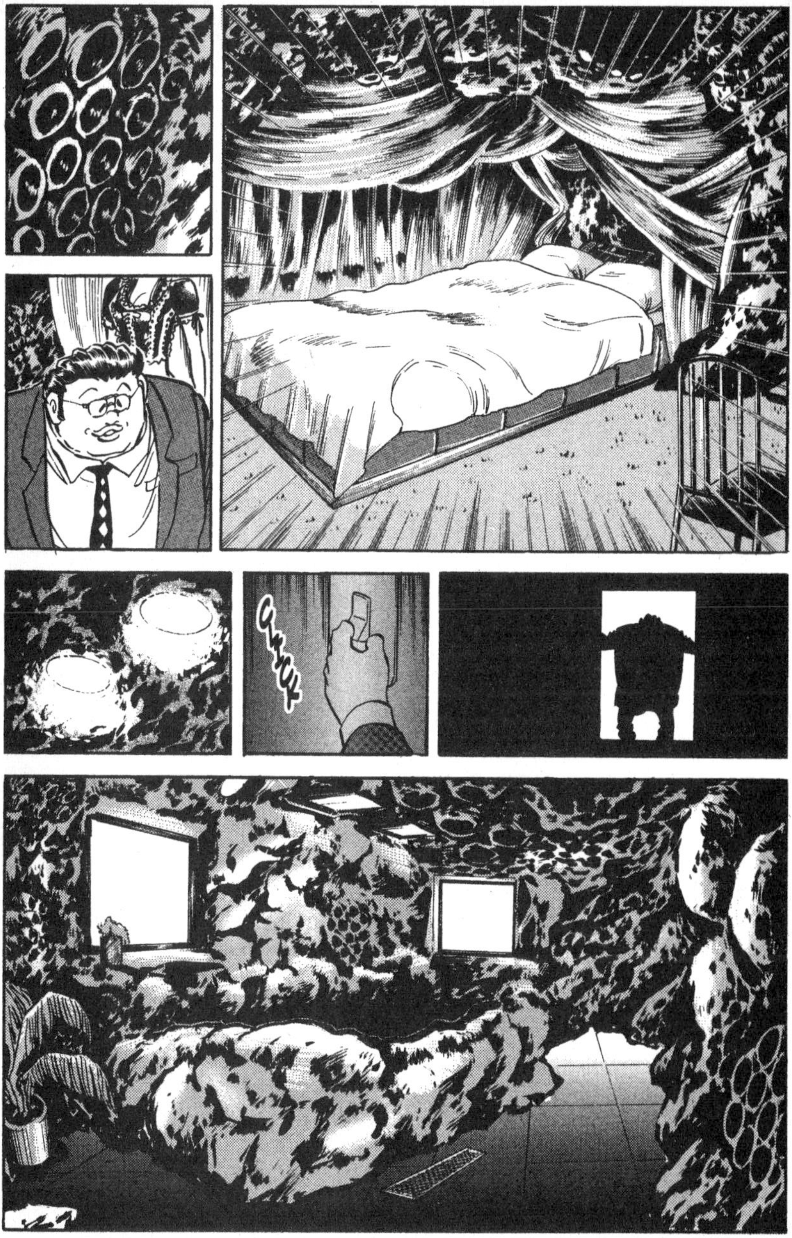
CLICK

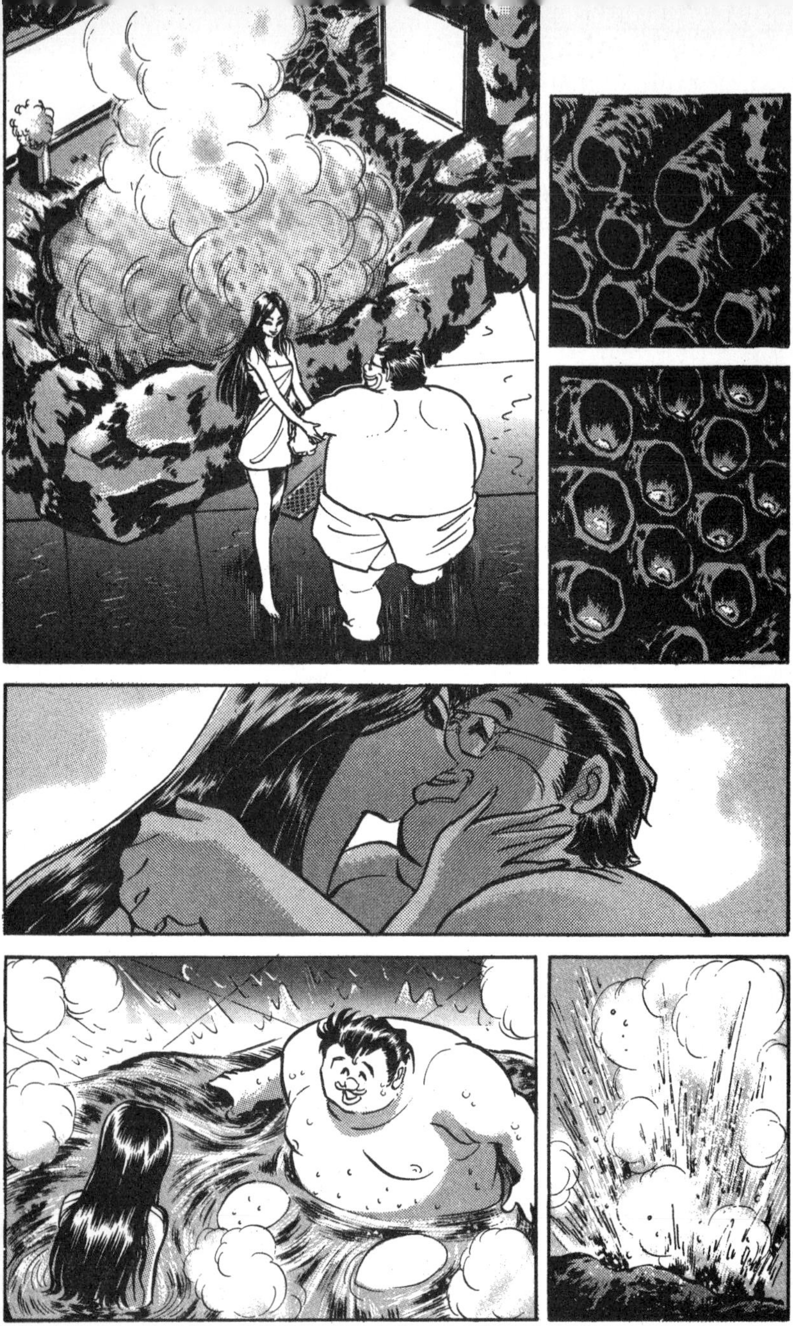

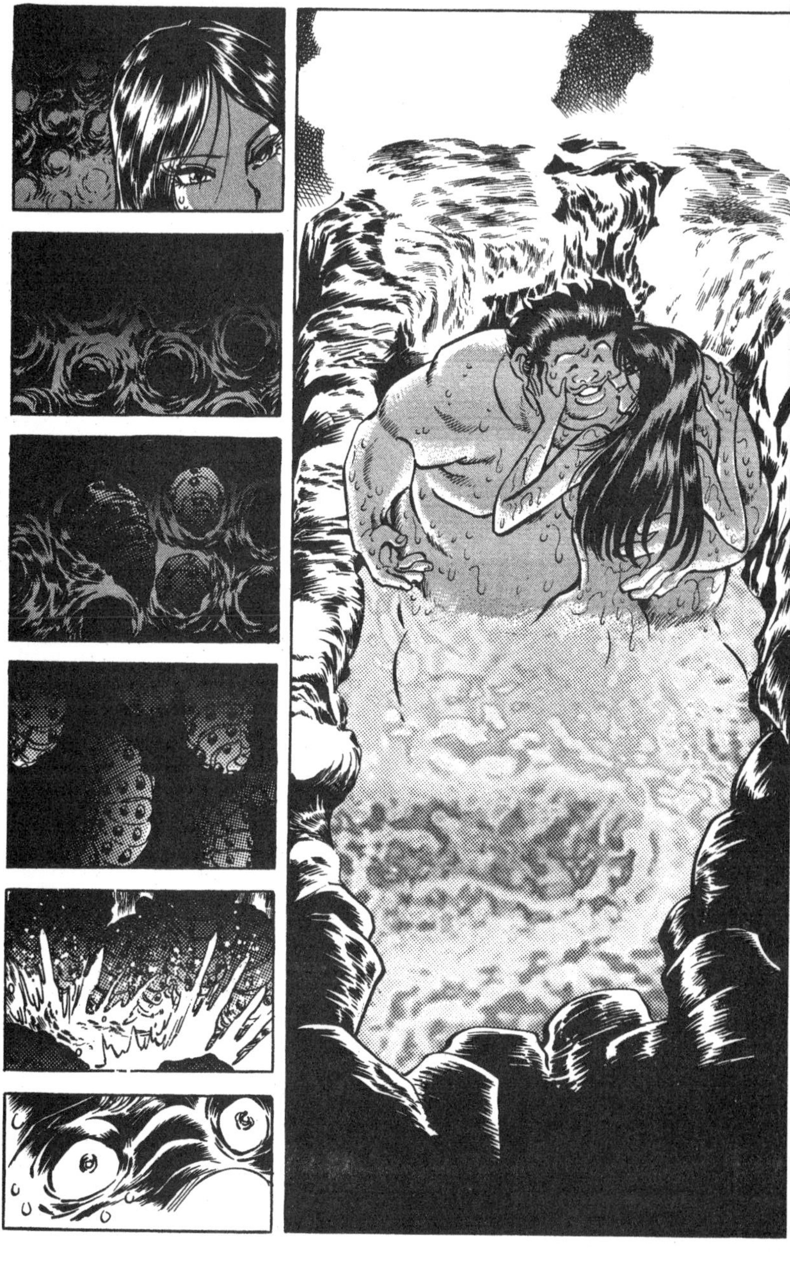

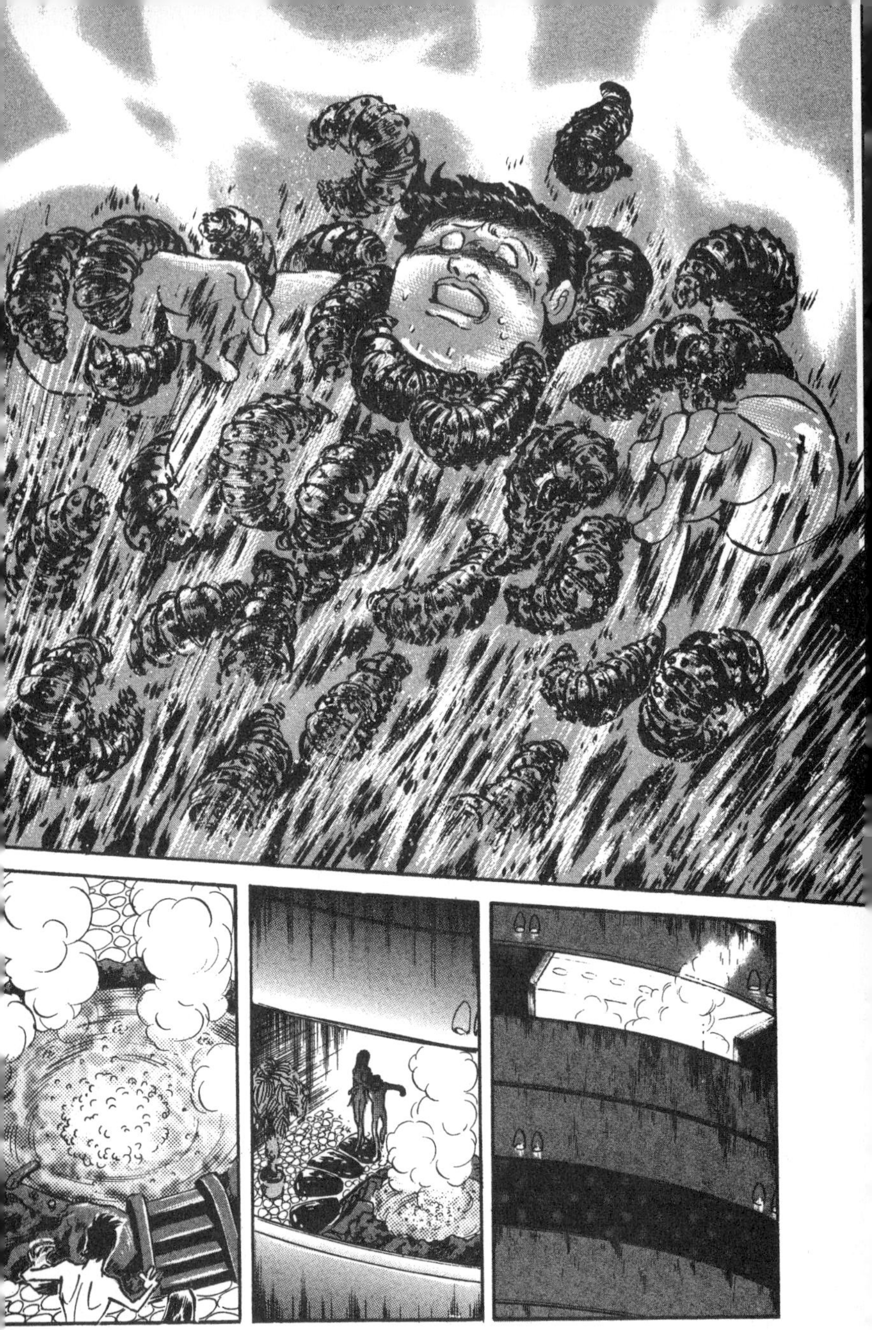

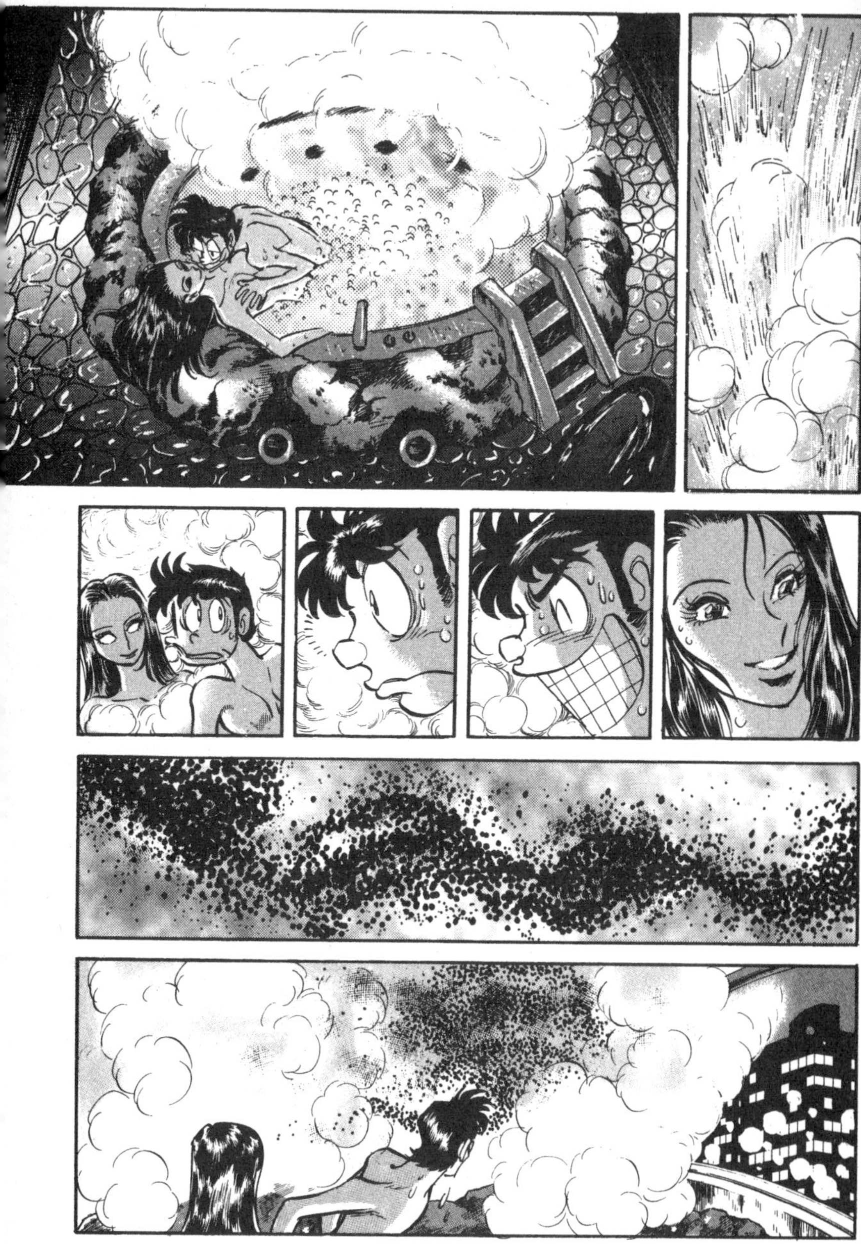

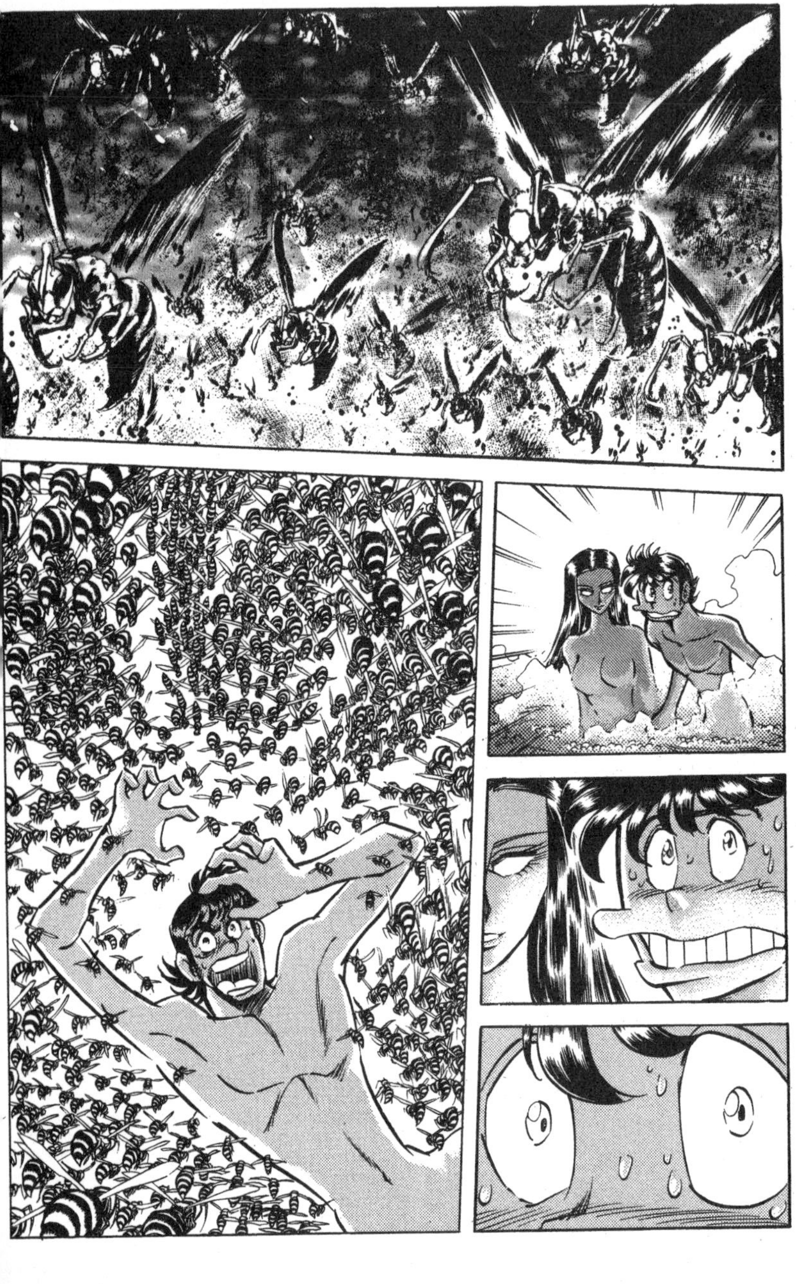

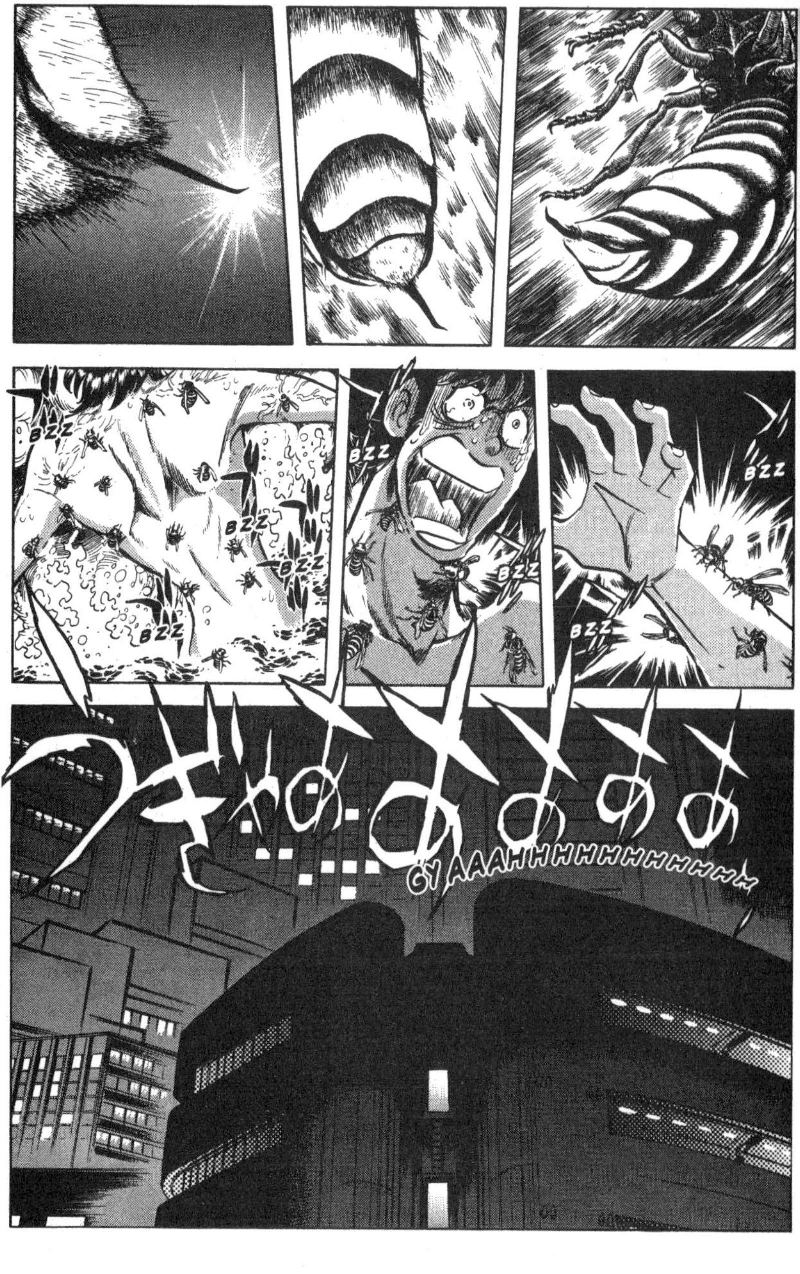
BZZ
BZZ
BZZ
BZZ
BZZ
BZZ
BZZ
BZZ
GYAAAHHHHHHHHHHHH

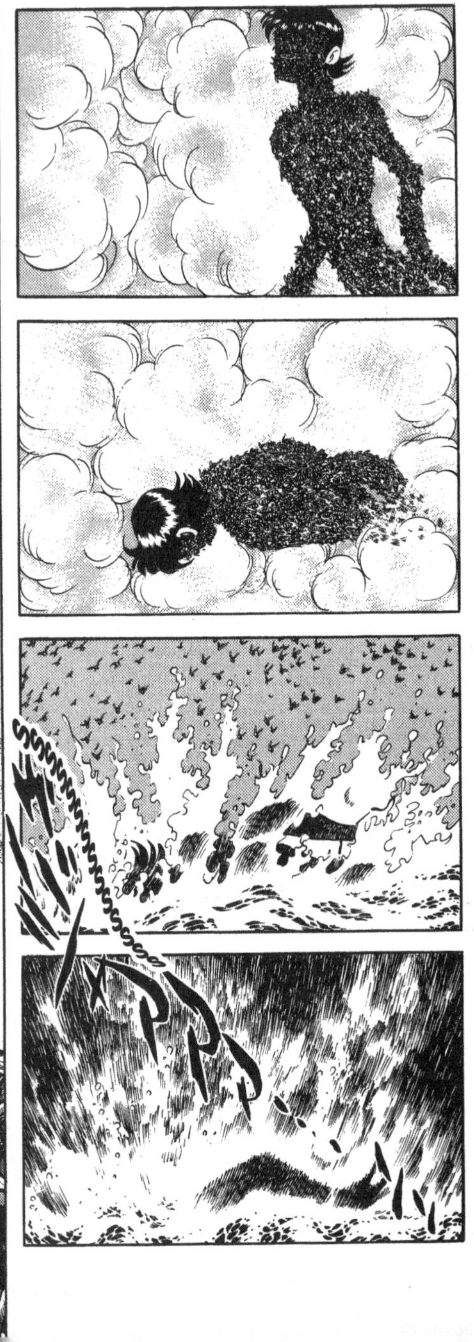

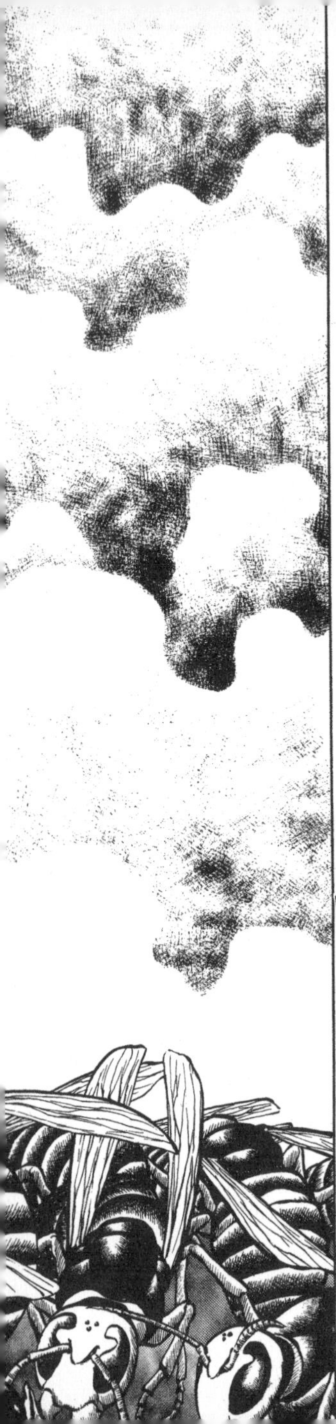

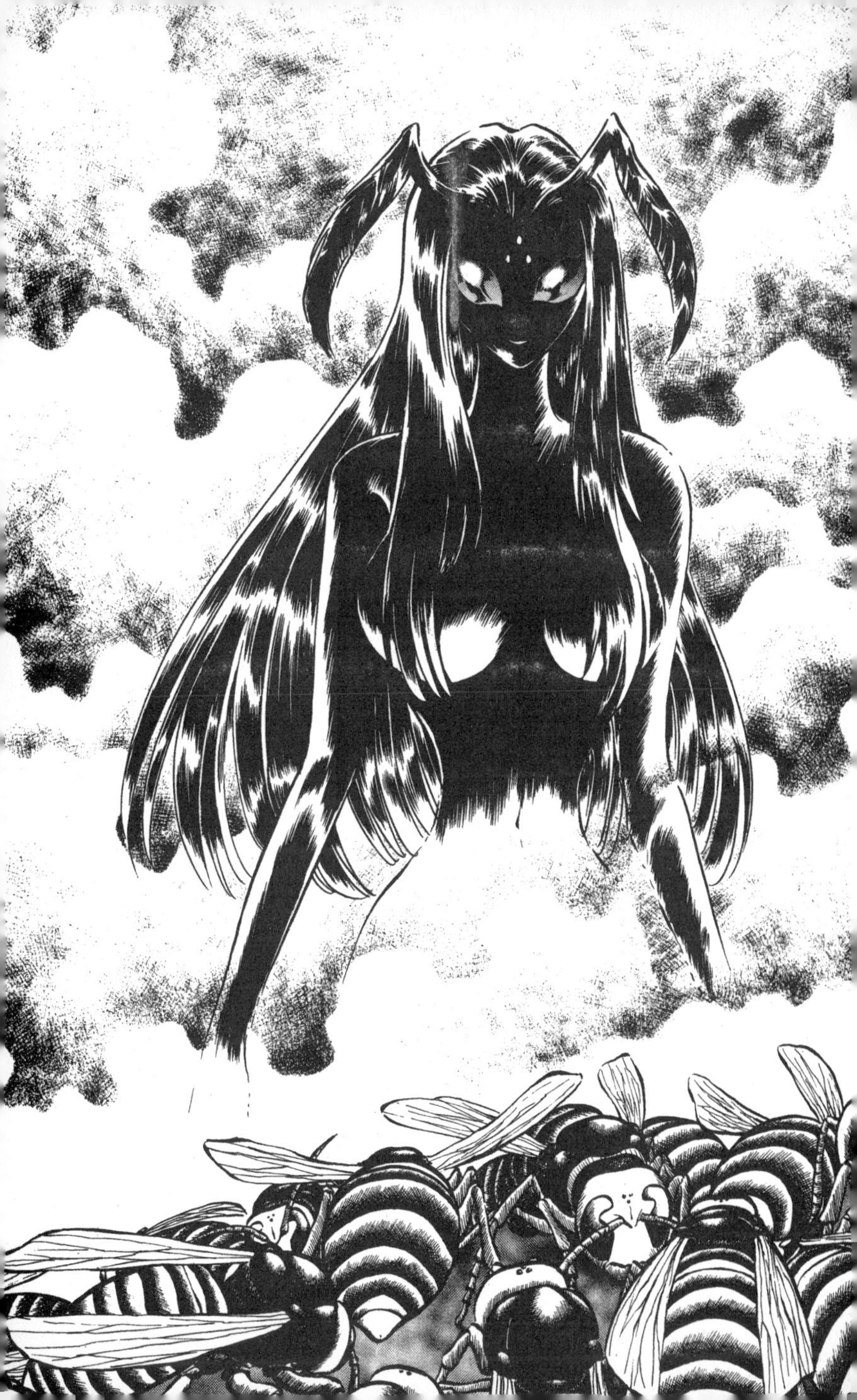

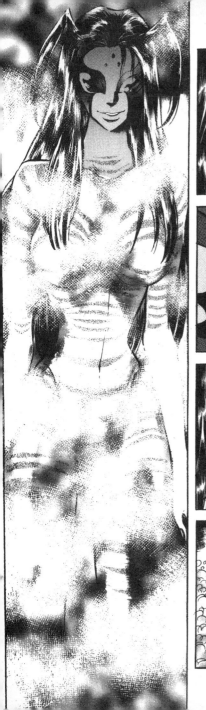

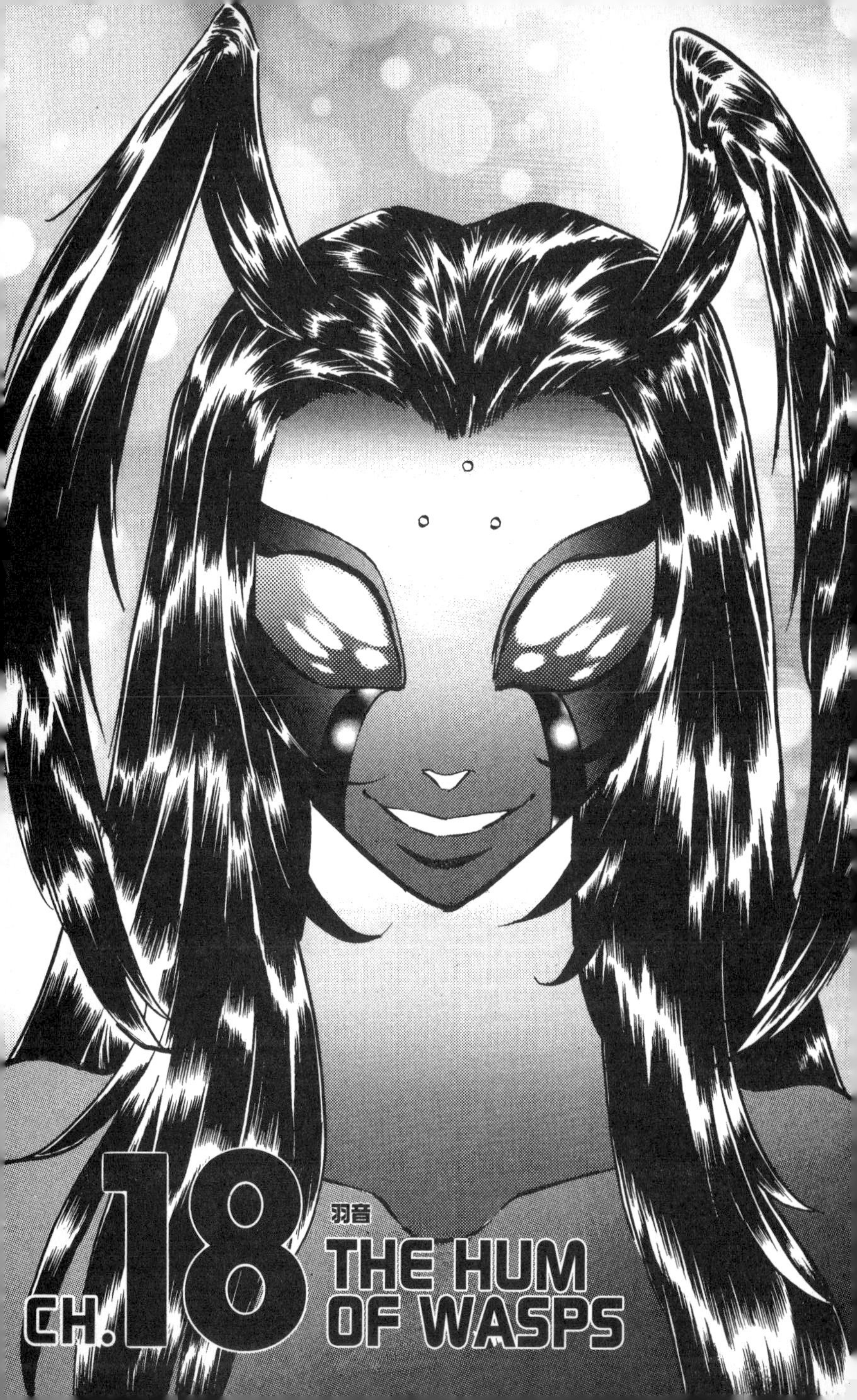
CH. 18
羽音
THE HUM OF WASPS

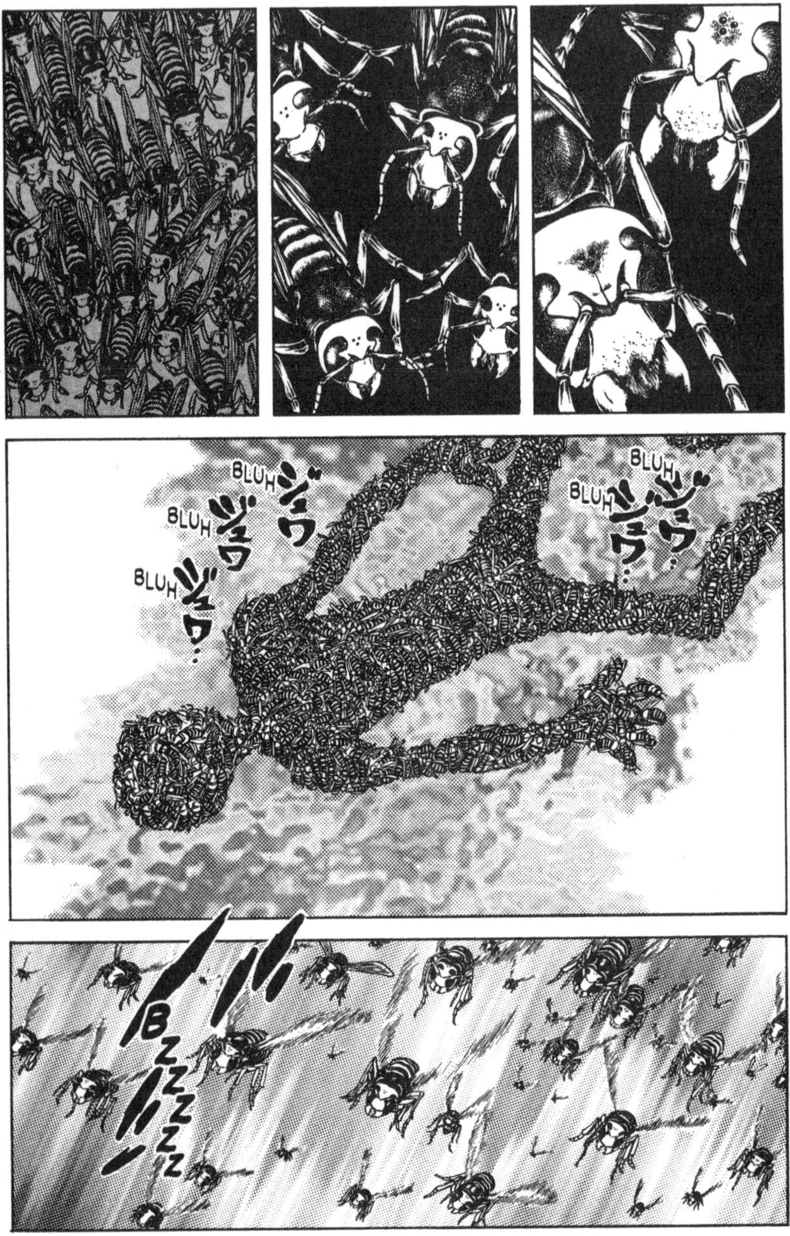
BLUH ジュワ
BLUH ジュワ…
BLUH ジュワ
BLUH ジュワ
BLUH ジュワ…
BZZZZZZ

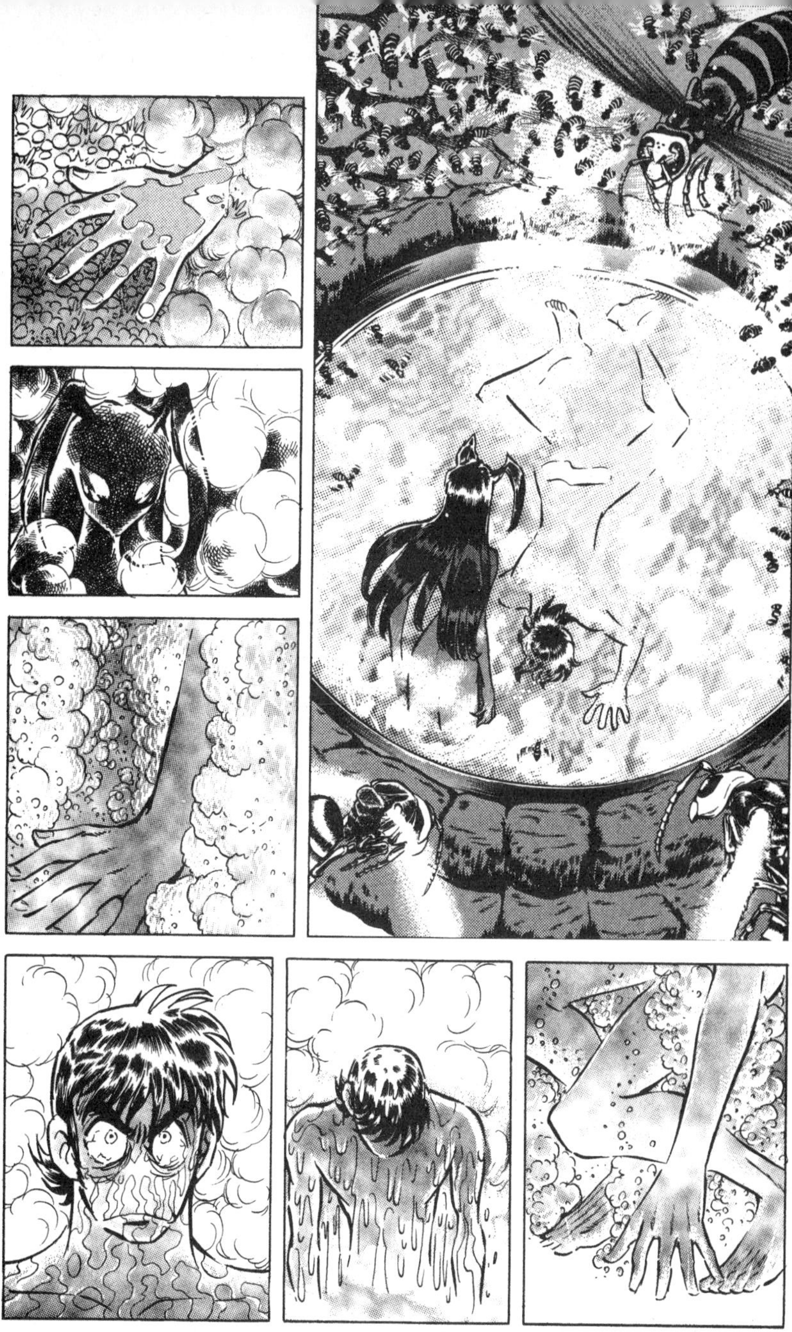

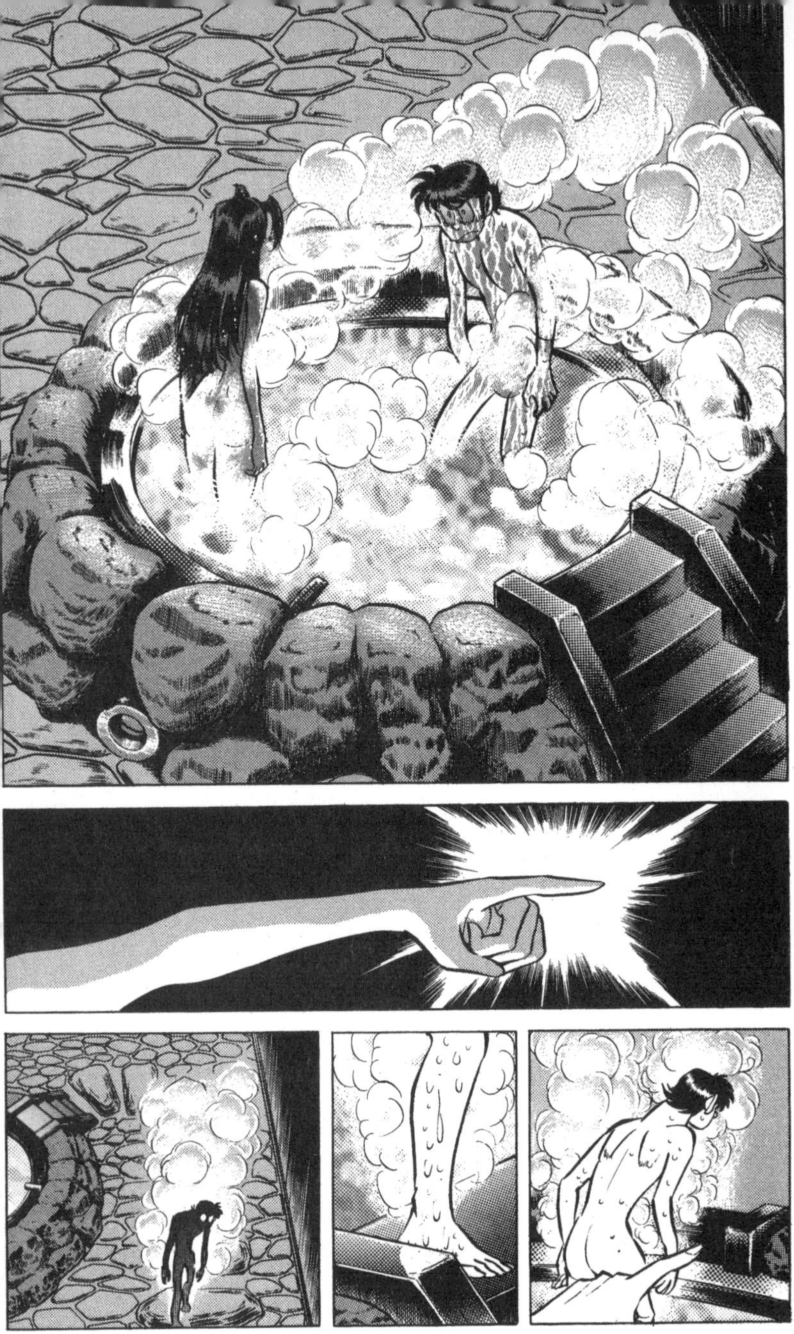

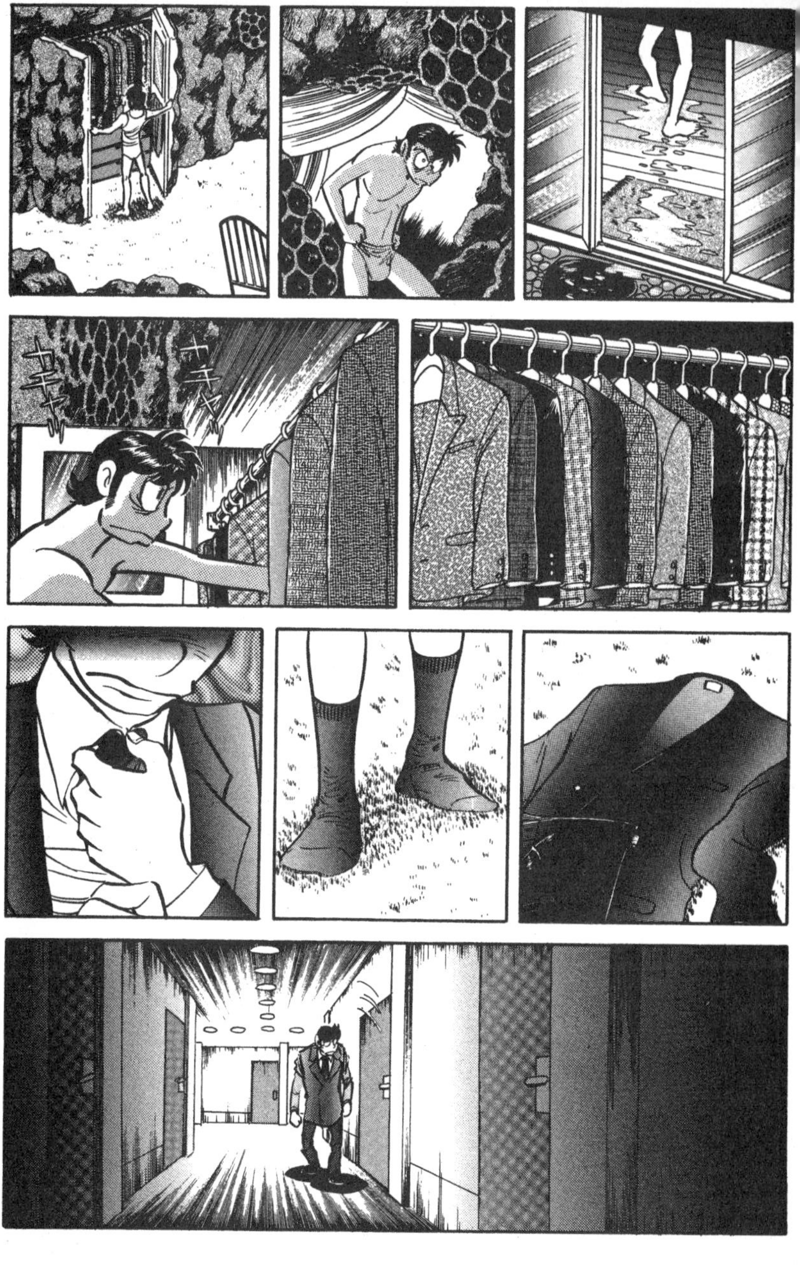
カチャッ
カチャッ

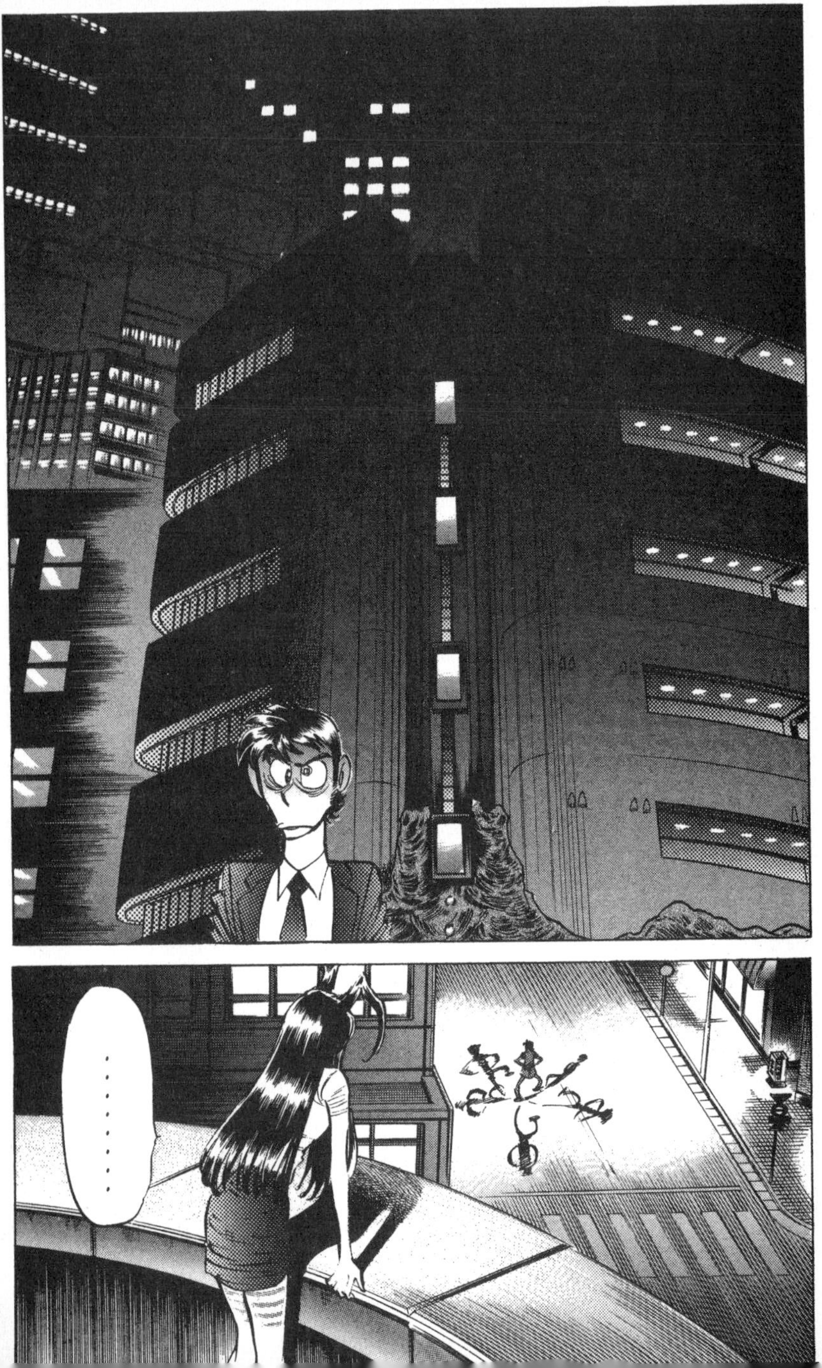
....

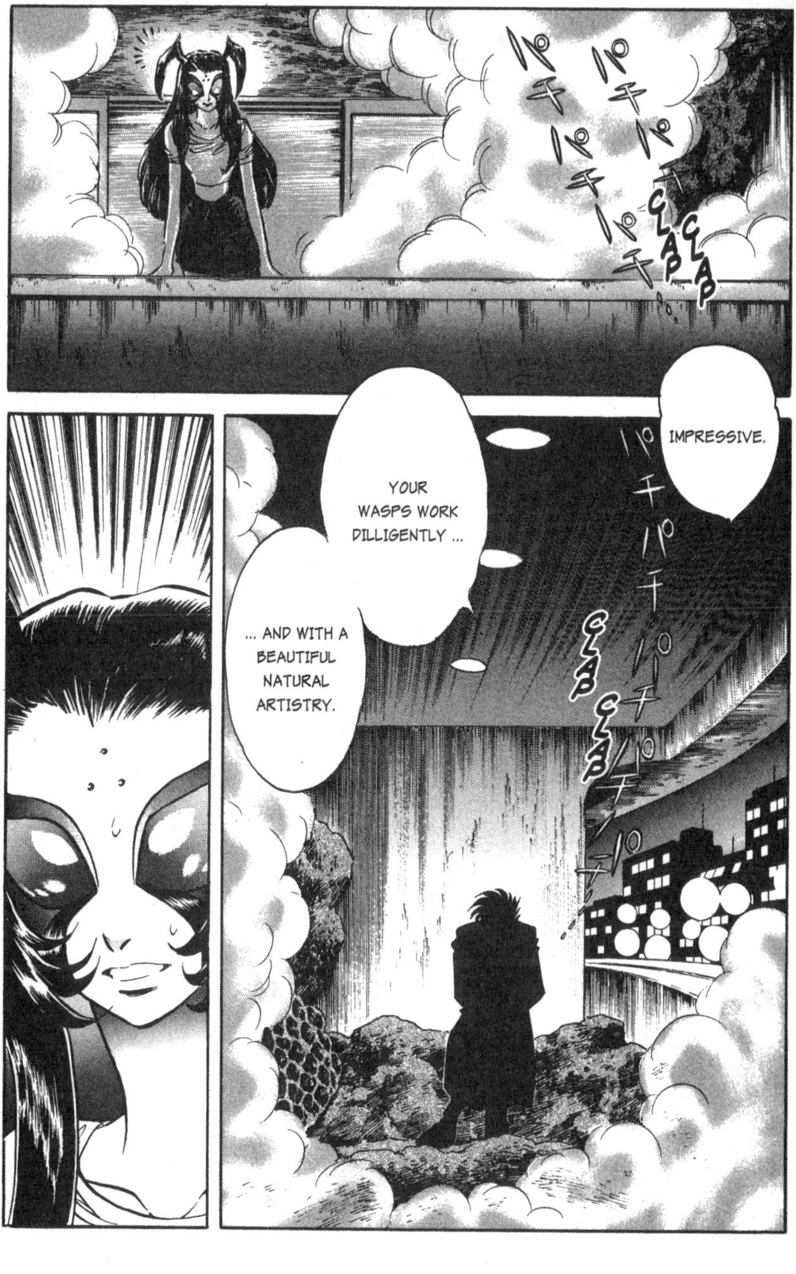
CLAP CLAP
CLAP
IMPRESSIVE.
YOUR WASPS WORK DILLIGENTLY ...
... AND WITH A BEAUTIFUL NATURAL ARTISTRY.
CLAP CLAP
CLAP

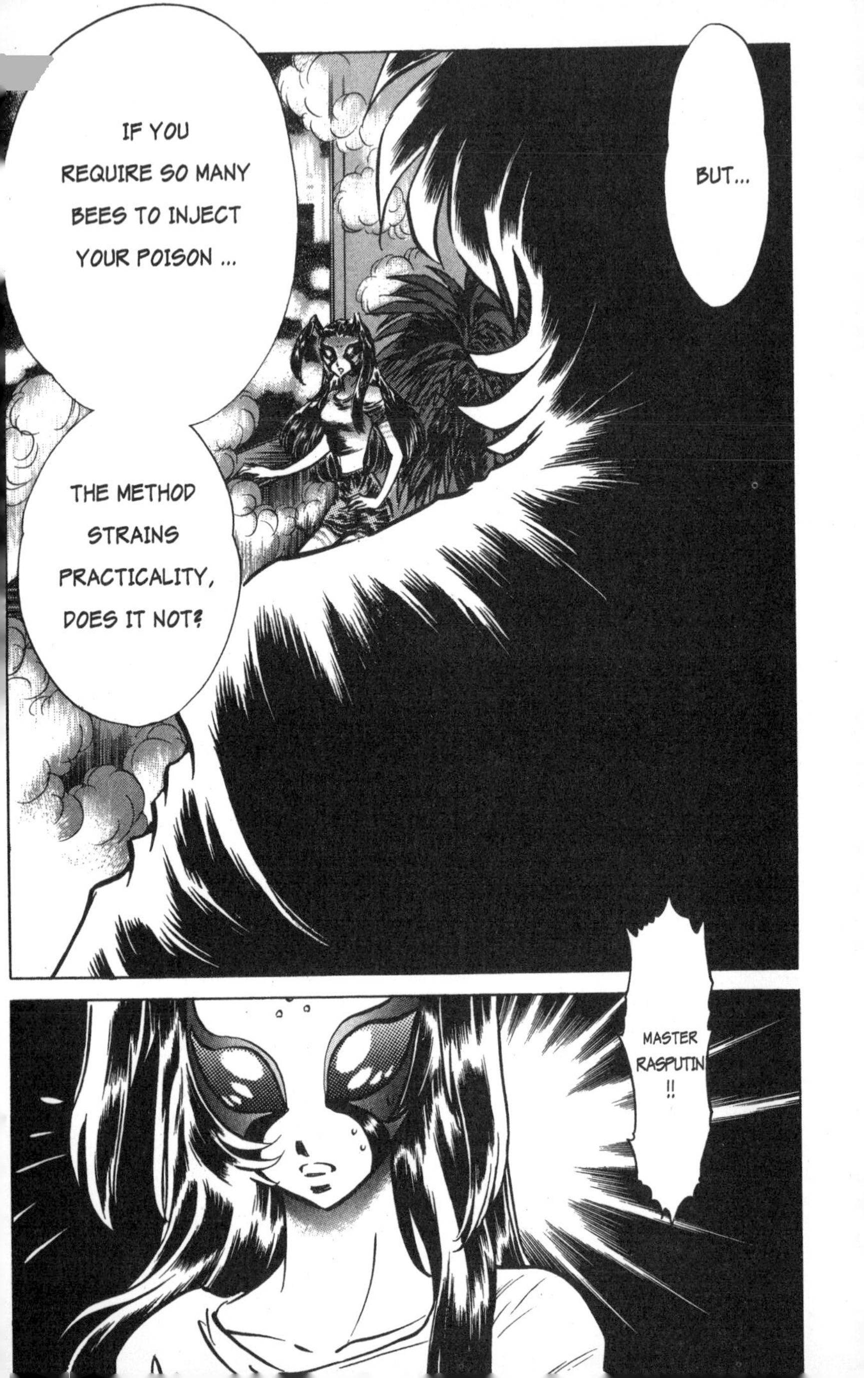
BUT...
IF YOU REQUIRE SO MANY BEES TO INJECT YOUR POISON ...
THE METHOD STRAINS PRACTICALITY, DOES IT NOT?
MASTER RASPUTIN !!

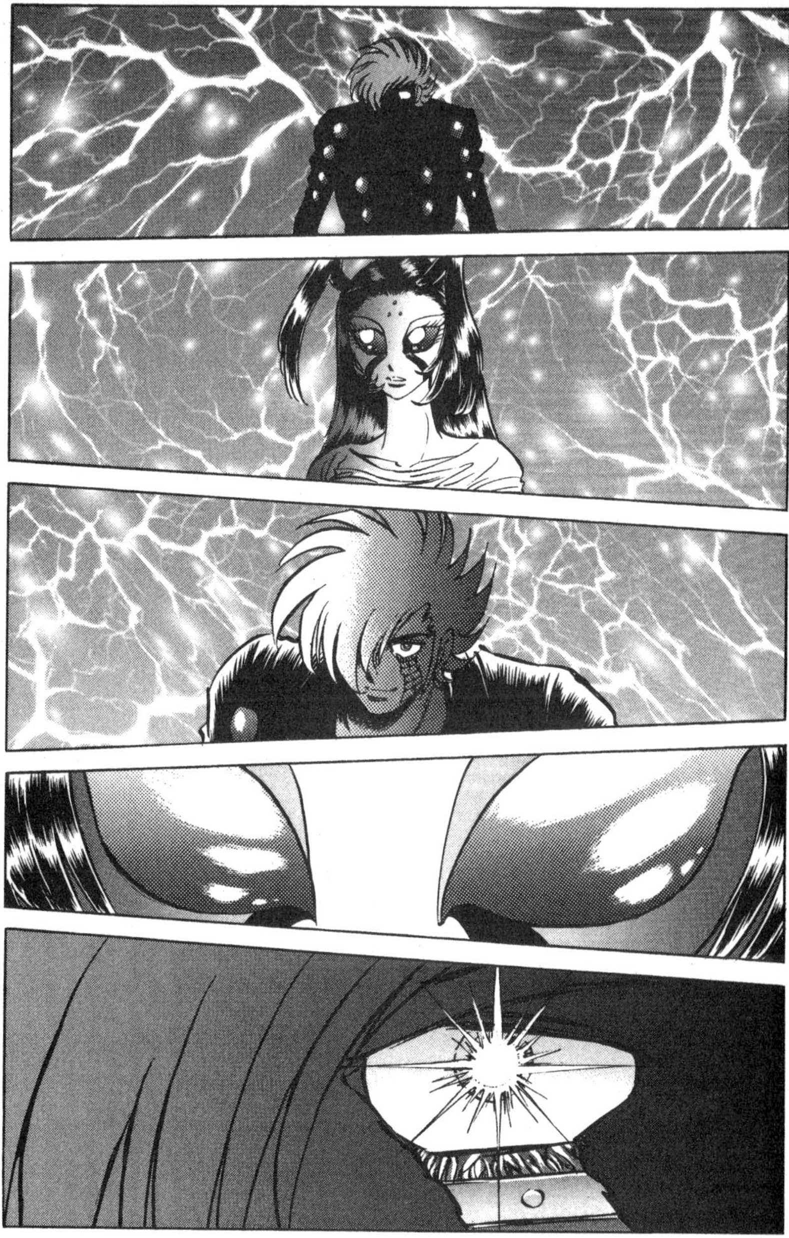

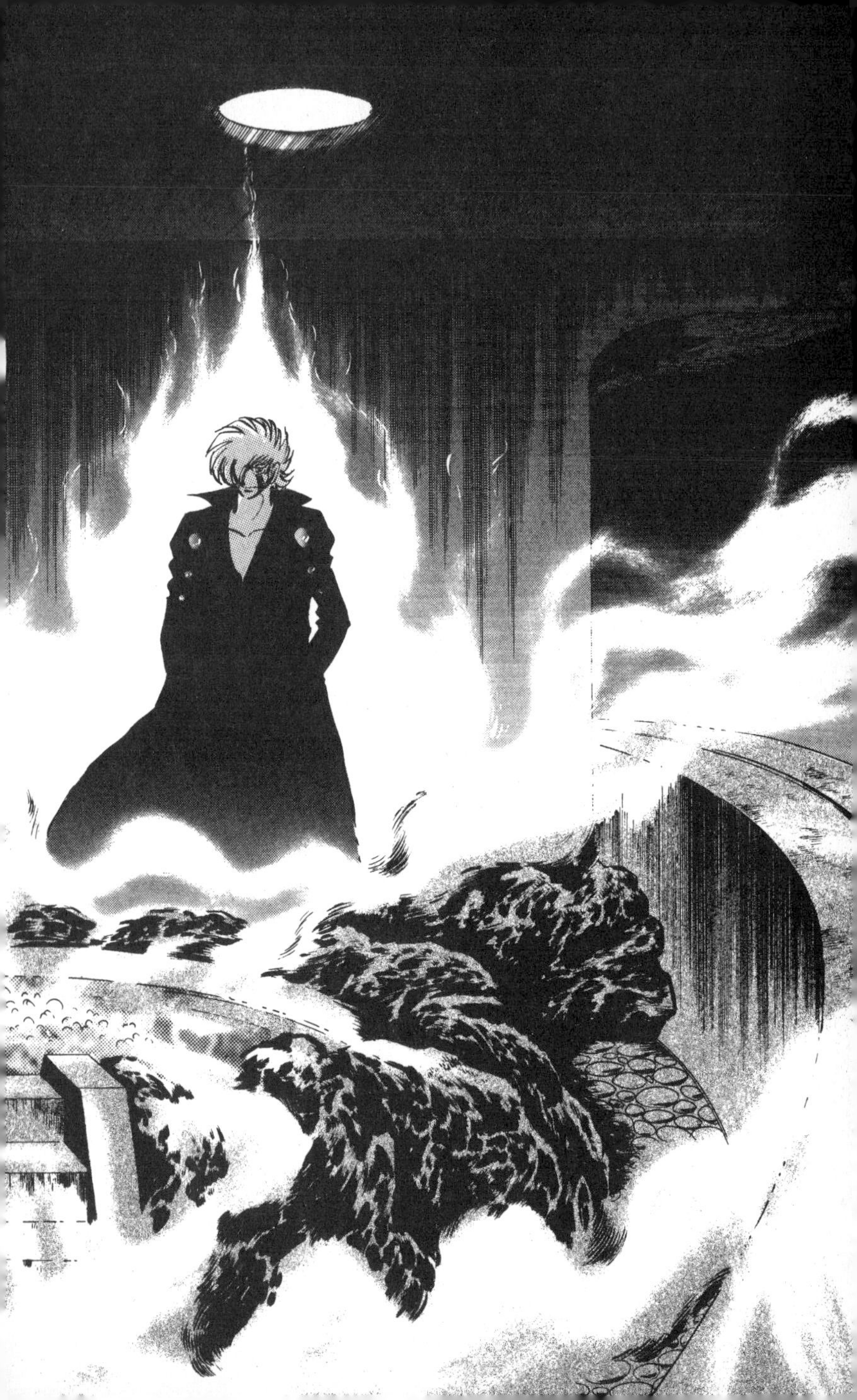

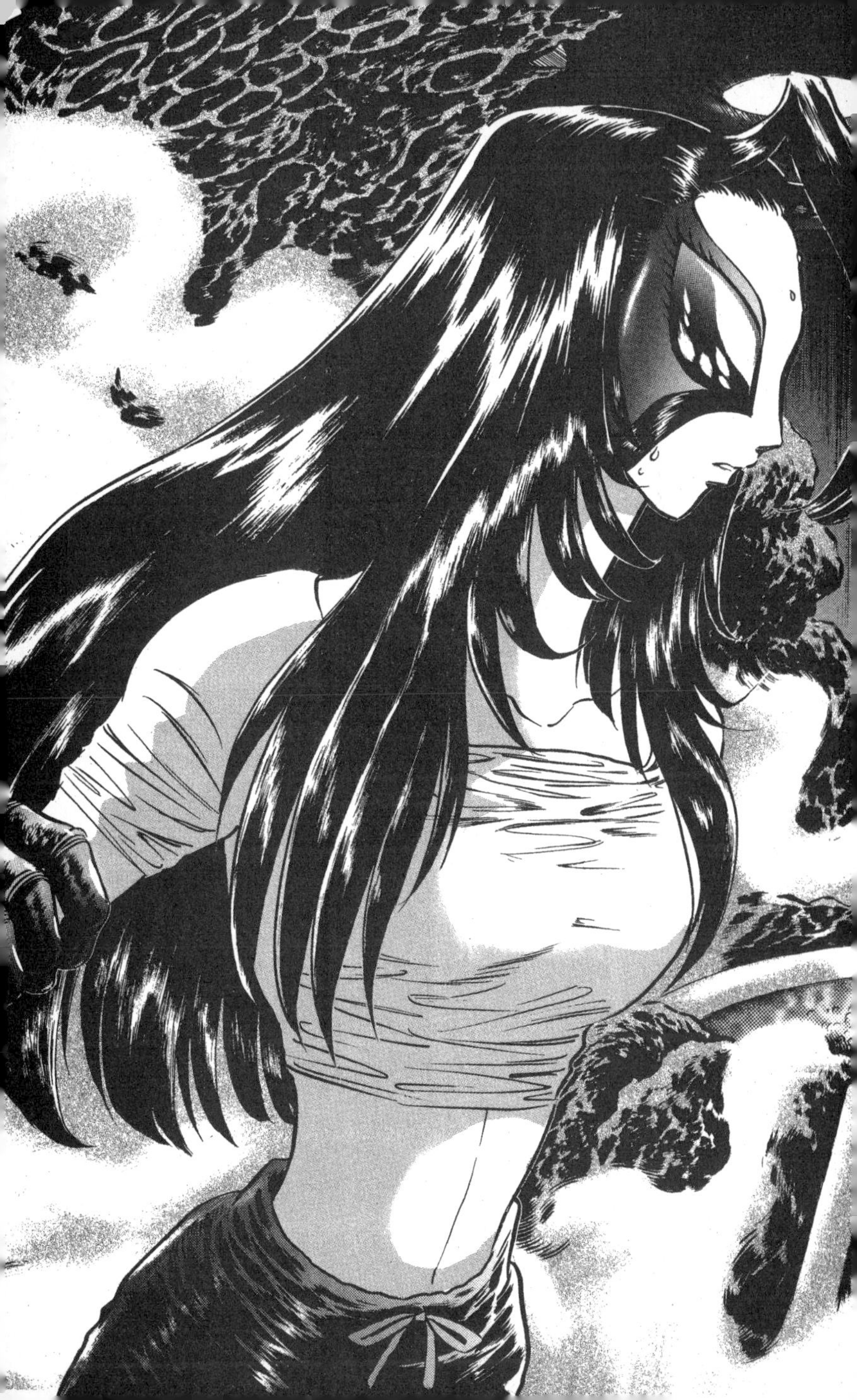

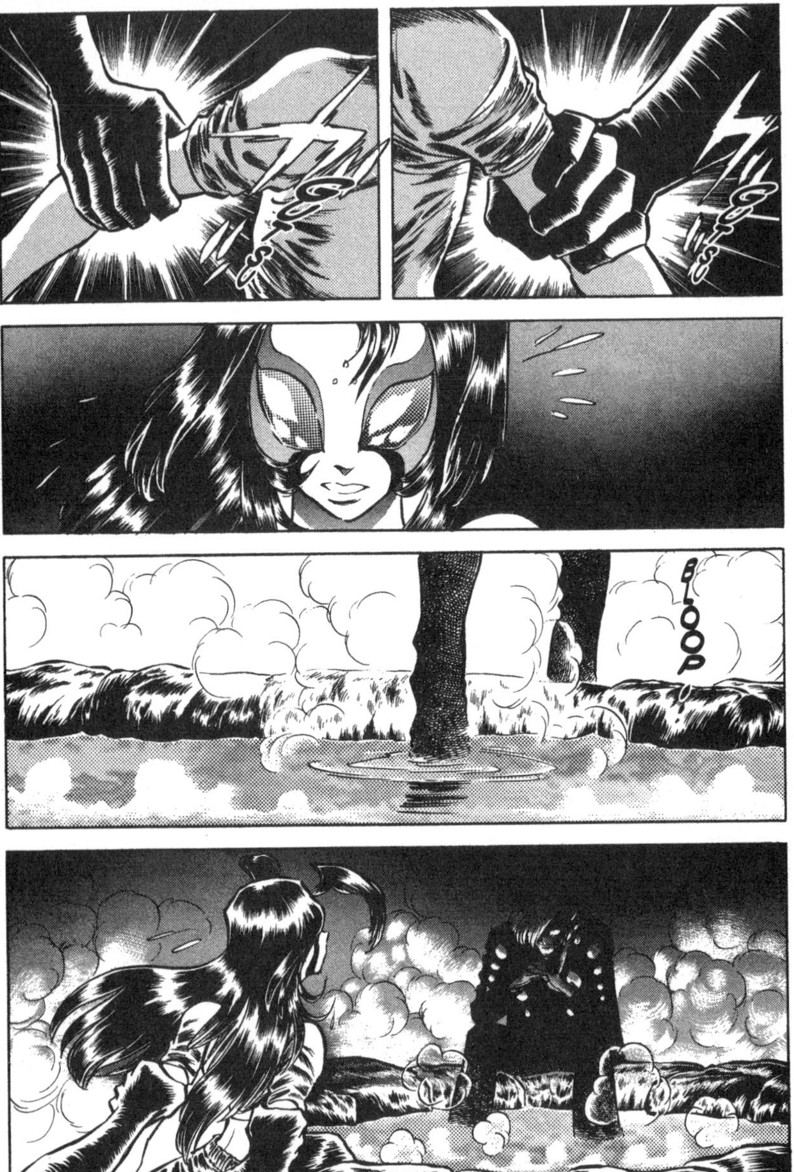
GUTSU
GUTSU
BLOOP

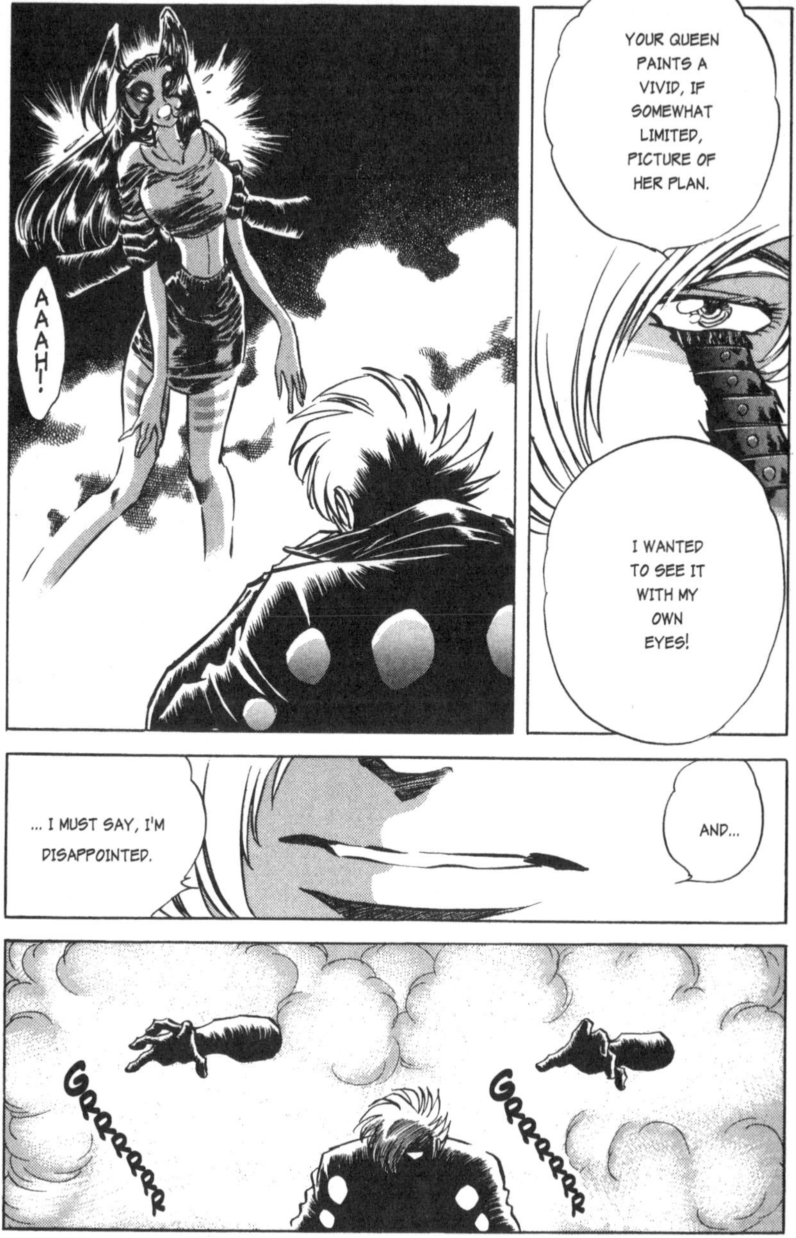
YOUR QUEEN PAINTS A VIVID, IF SOMEWHAT LIMITED, PICTURE OF HER PLAN.
I WANTED TO SEE IT WITH MY OWN EYES!
AAAH!
AND...
... I MUST SAY, I'M DISAPPOINTED.
GRRRRRRR
GRRRRRRR

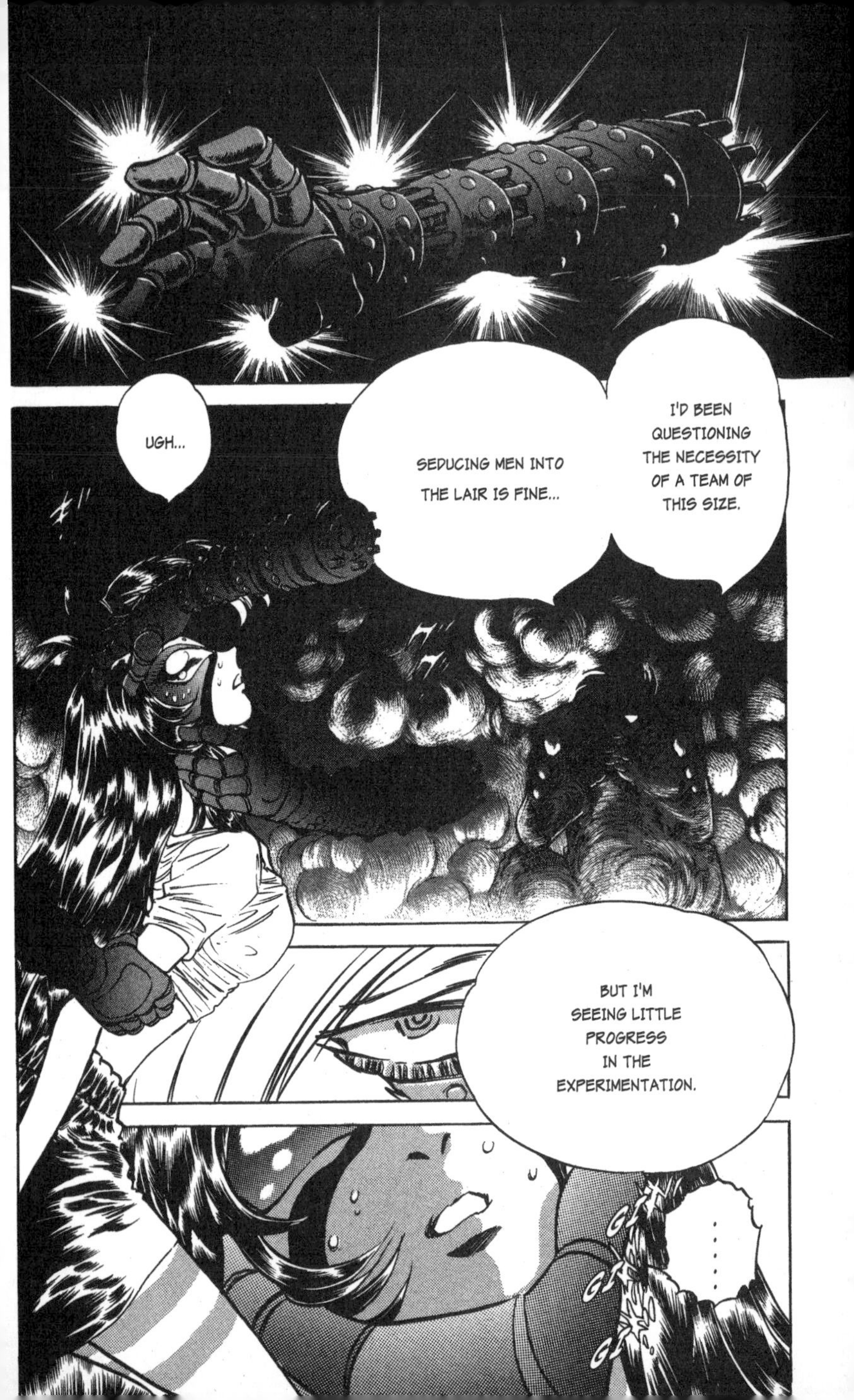

I'D BEEN QUESTIONING THE NECESSITY OF A TEAM OF THIS SIZE.
SEDUCING MEN INTO THE LAIR IS FINE...
UGH...
BUT I'M SEEING LITTLE PROGRESS IN THE EXPERIMENTATION.
......

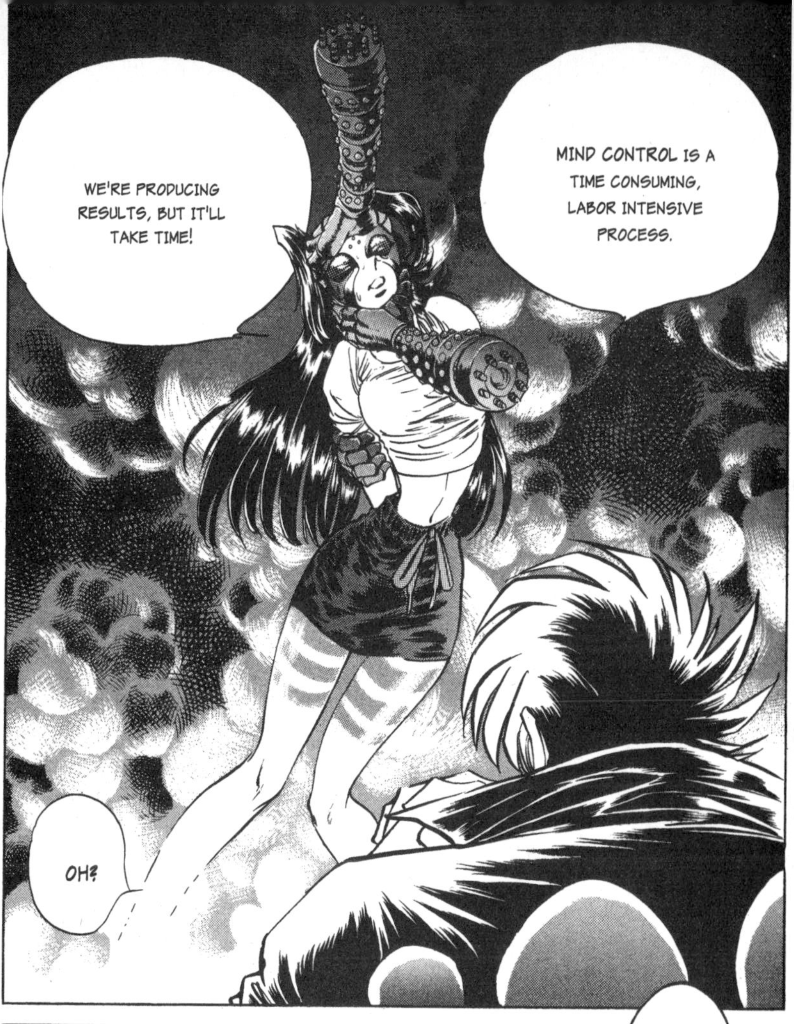
MIND CONTROL IS A TIME CONSUMING, LABOR INTENSIVE PROCESS.
WE'RE PRODUCING RESULTS, BUT IT'LL TAKE TIME!
OH?
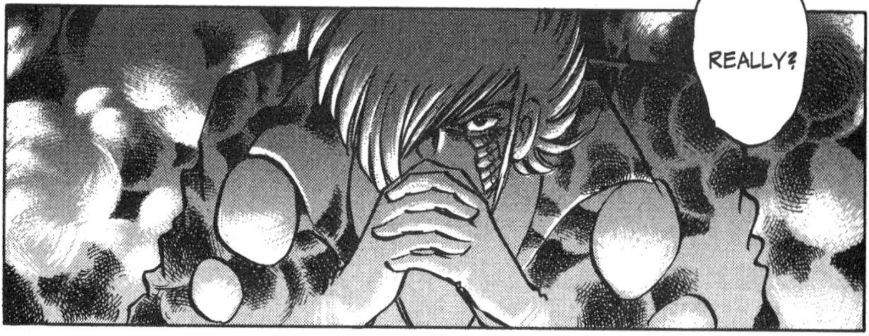
REALLY?

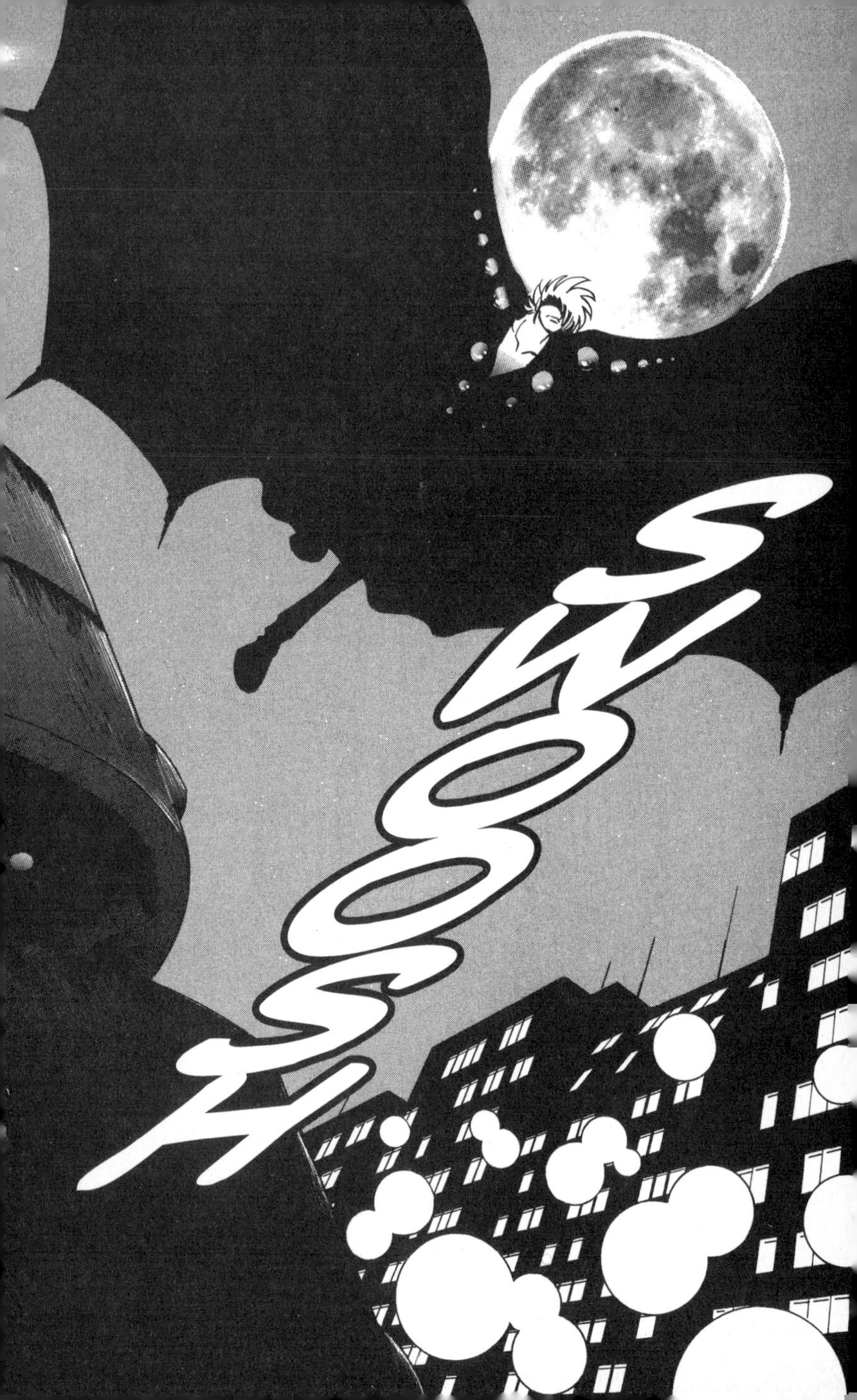
SWOOSH

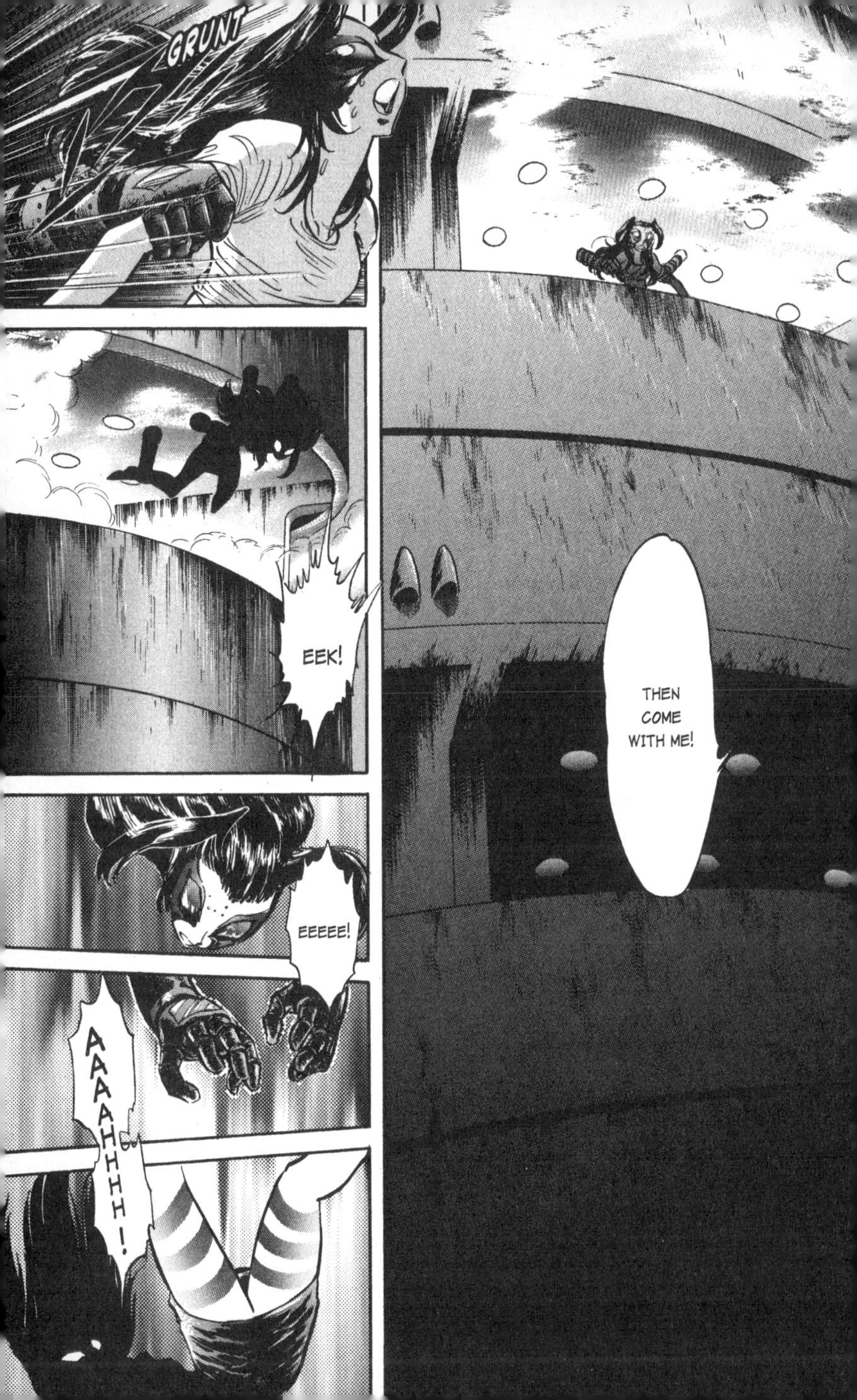
THEN COME WITH ME!
GRUNT
EEK!
EEEEE!
AAAAHHHH!

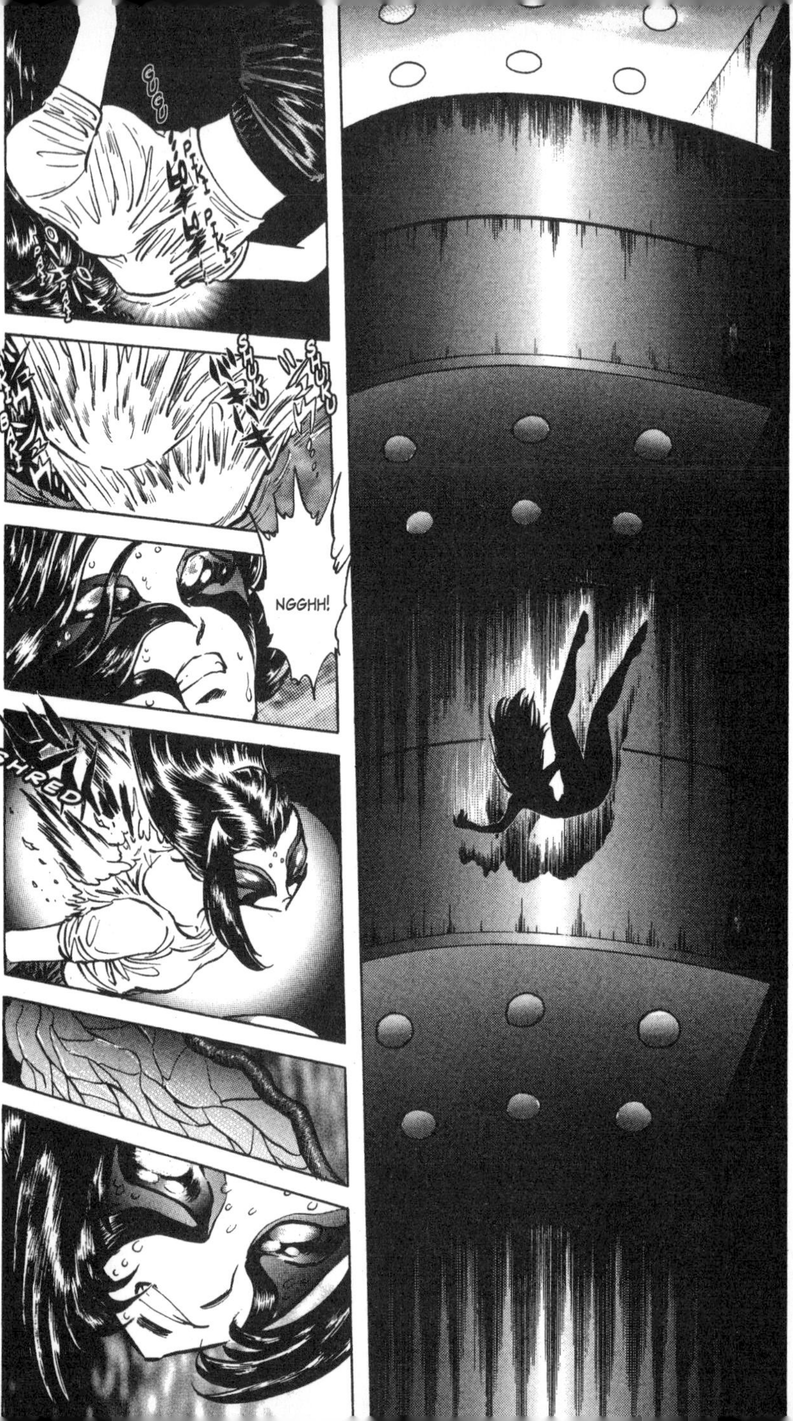
PIKI PIKI
GUGU
PAKI PAKI
SHUKU SHUKU
BAKI BAKI
NGGHH!
SHRED

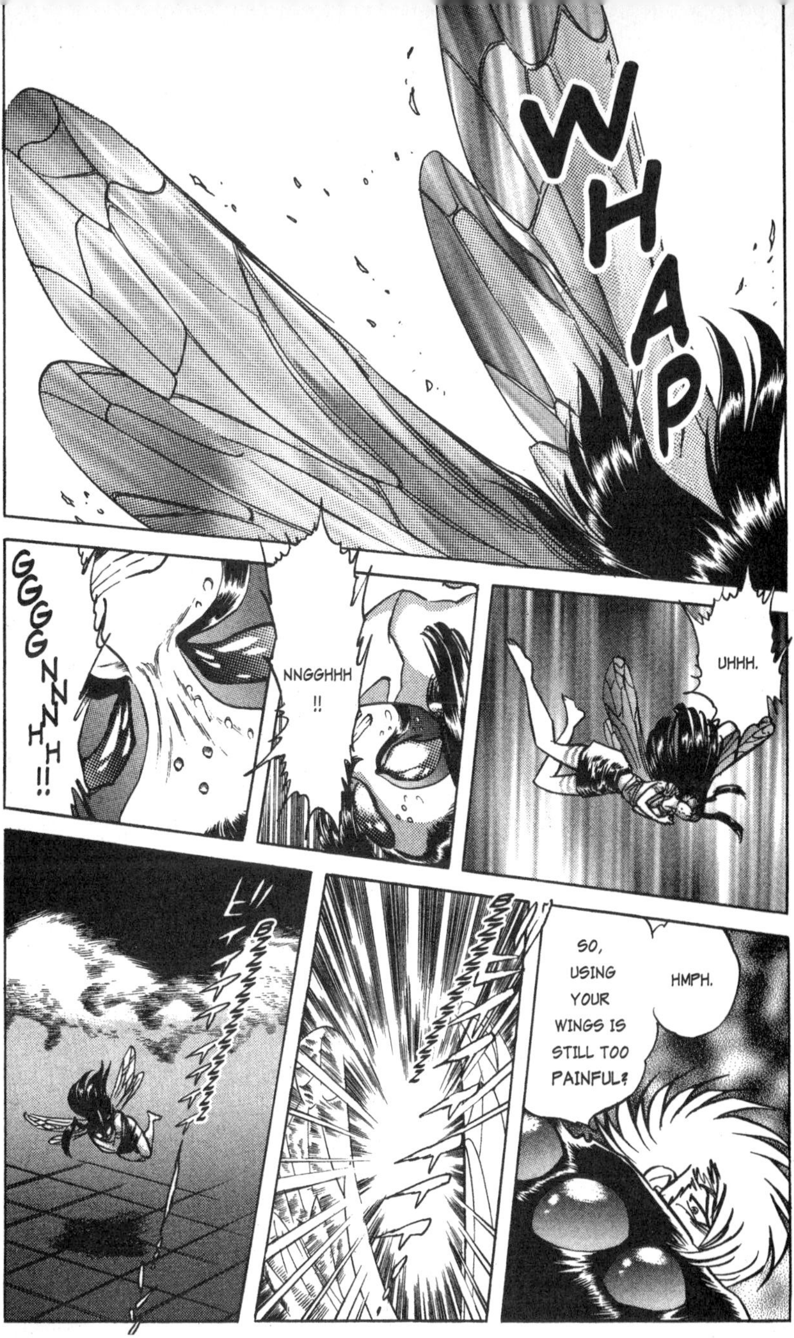
WHAP
UHHH.
NNGGHHH !!
GGGGNNNNHHH!!
SO, USING YOUR WINGS IS STILL TOO PAINFUL?
HMPH.

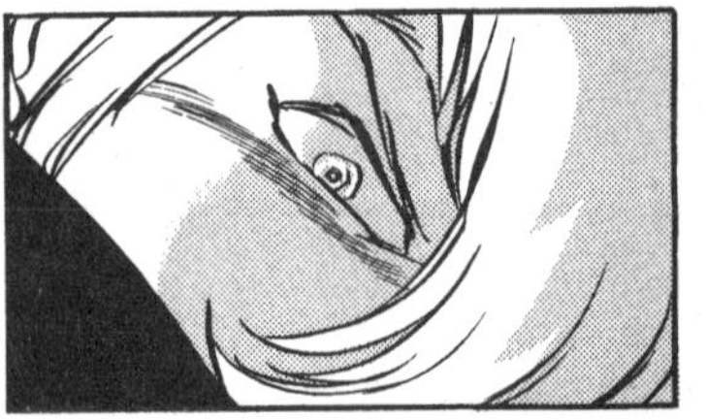
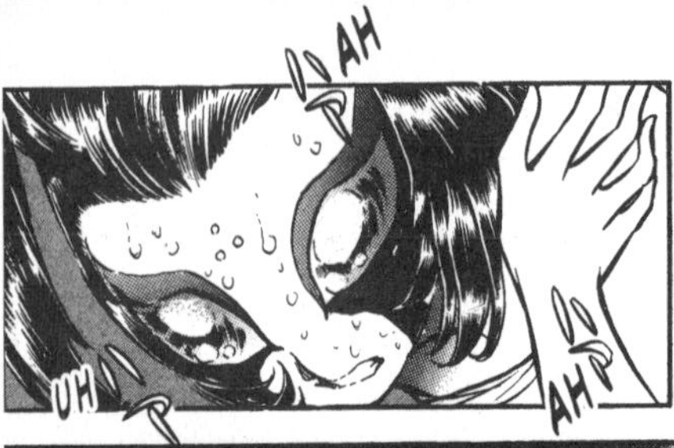
AH
UH
AH
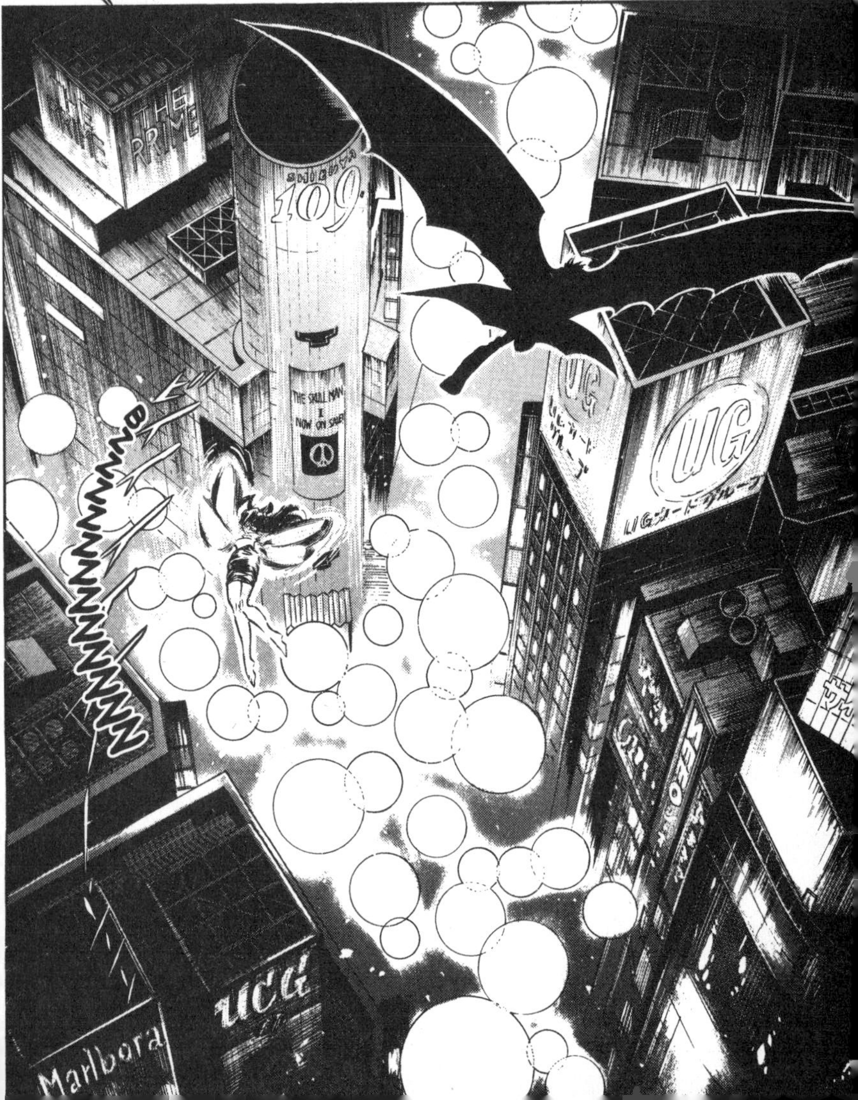
THE PRIME
THE PRIME
109
THE SKULL MAN I NOW ON SALE
BZZZZZZZZZZZZZZZZ
UG
UG
UCG
Marlbora

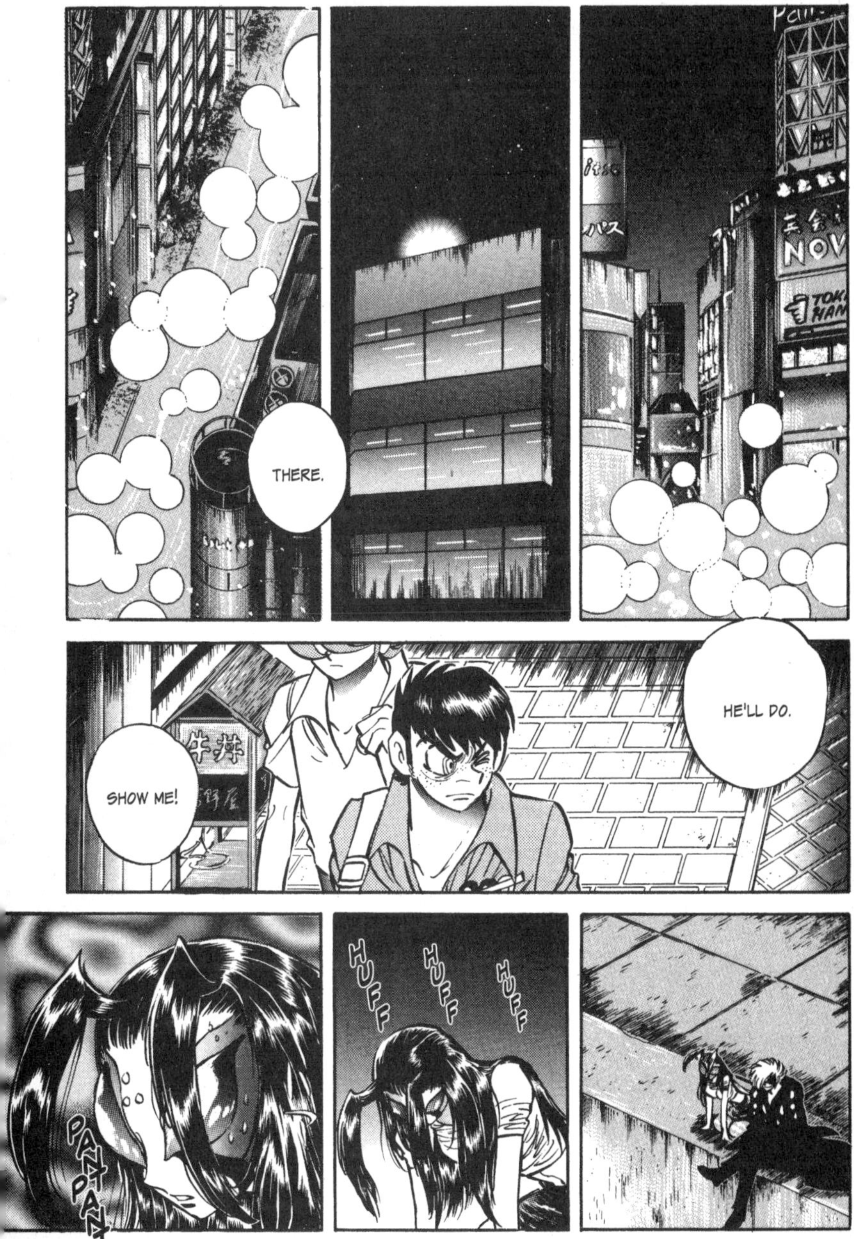
THERE.
HE'LL DO.
牛丼
SHOW ME!
HUFF HUFF HUFF
PANT PANT

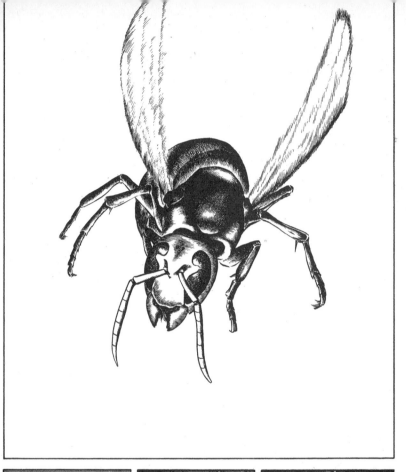

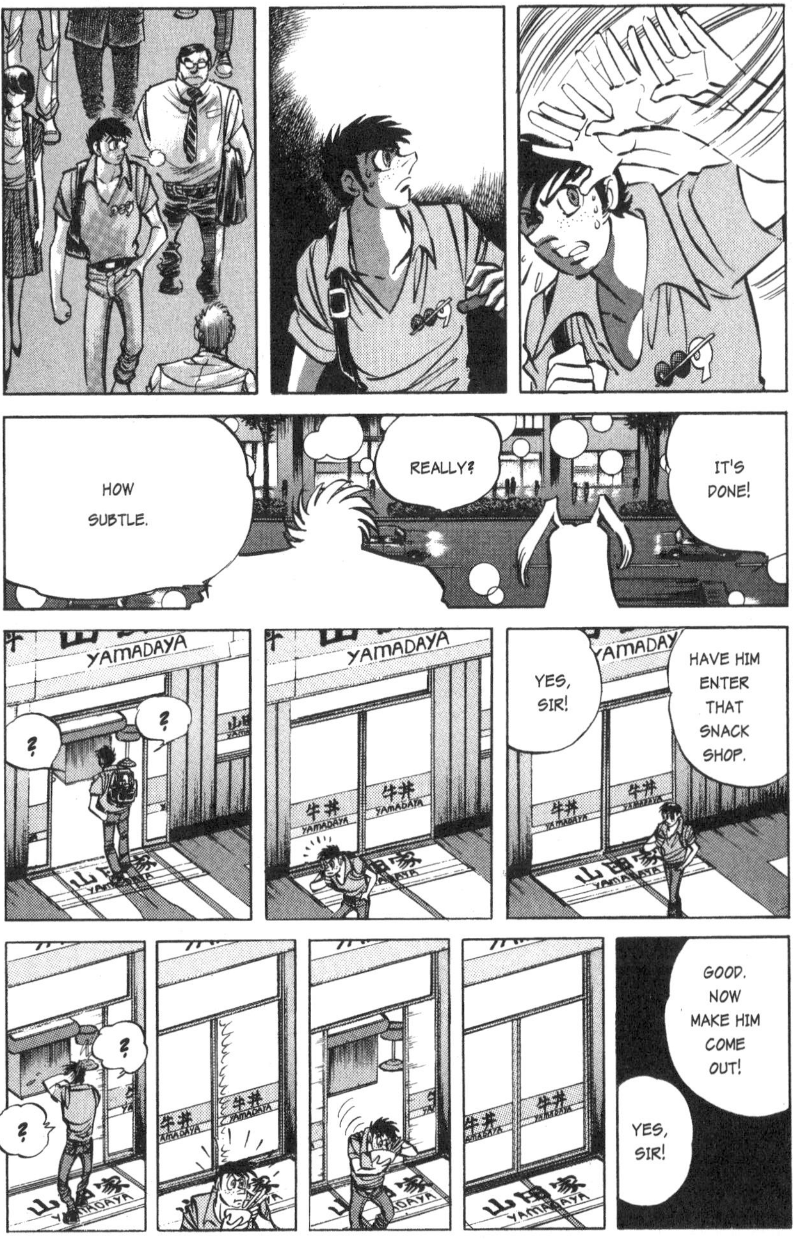
IT'S DONE!
REALLY?
HOW SUBTLE.
YAMADAYA
HAVE HIM ENTER THAT SNACK SHOP.
YES, SIR!
YAMADAYA
牛丼 YAMADAYA
山田家 YAMADAYA
YAMADAYA
?
?
GOOD. NOW MAKE HIM COME OUT!
YES, SIR!
牛丼 YAMADAYA
山田家 YAMADAYA
?
?

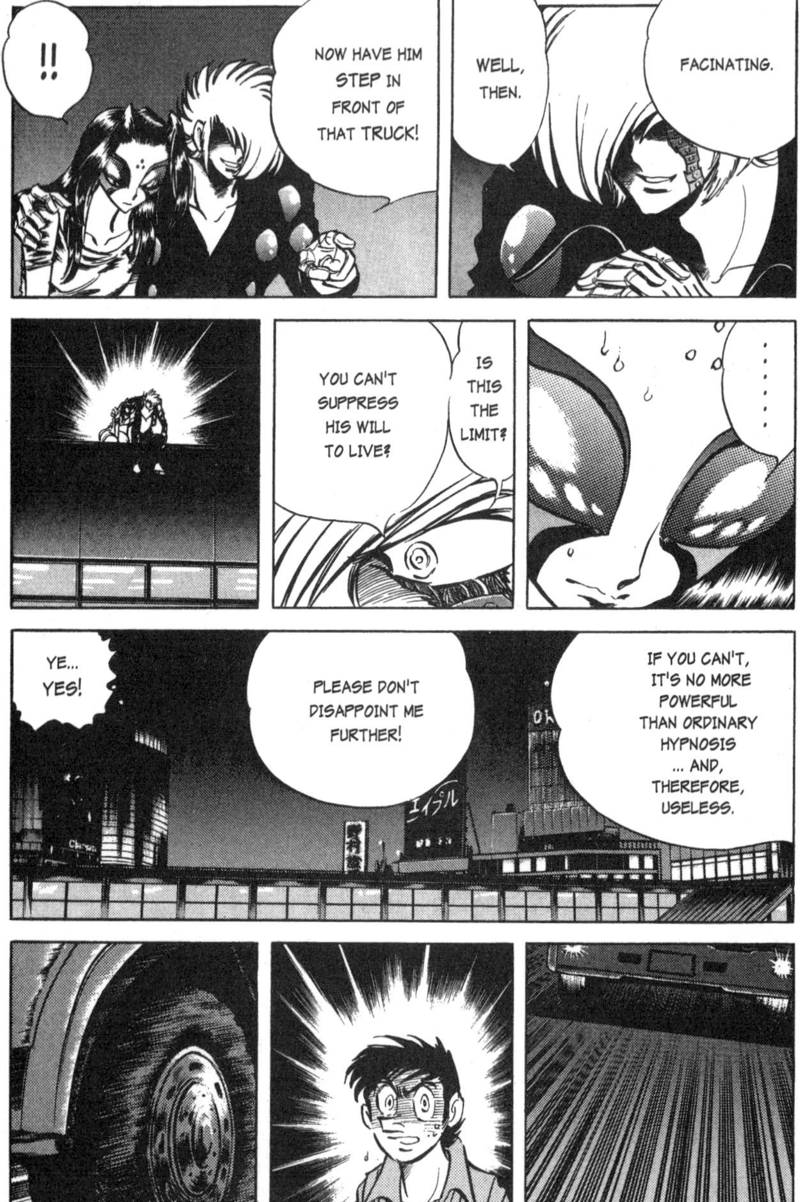
FACINATING.
WELL, THEN.
NOW HAVE HIM STEP IN FRONT OF THAT TRUCK!
!!
......
IS THIS THE LIMIT?
YOU CAN'T SUPPRESS HIS WILL TO LIVE?
IF YOU CAN'T, IT'S NO MORE POWERFUL THAN ORDINARY HYPNOSIS ... AND, THEREFORE, USELESS.
PLEASE DON'T DISAPPOINT ME FURTHER!
YE... YES!

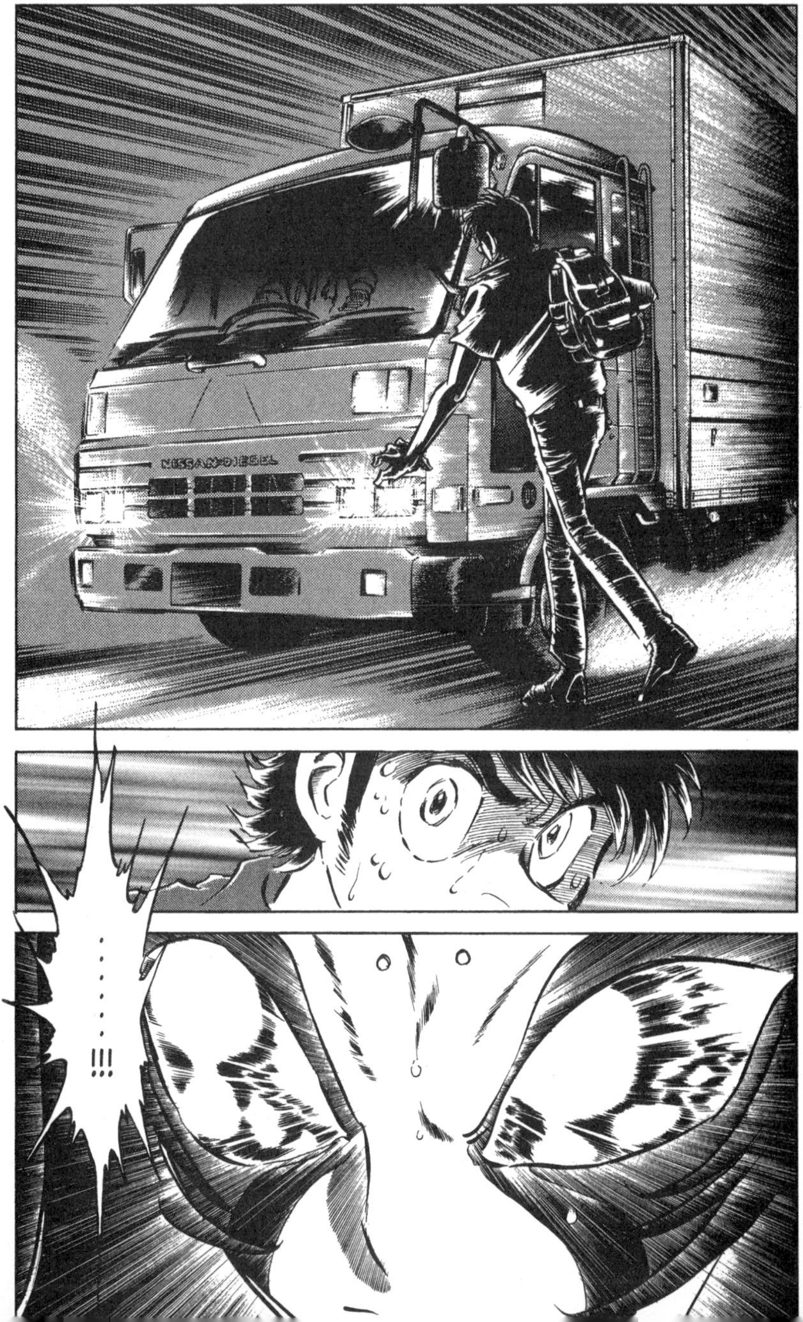
NISSAN DIESEL
......!!!

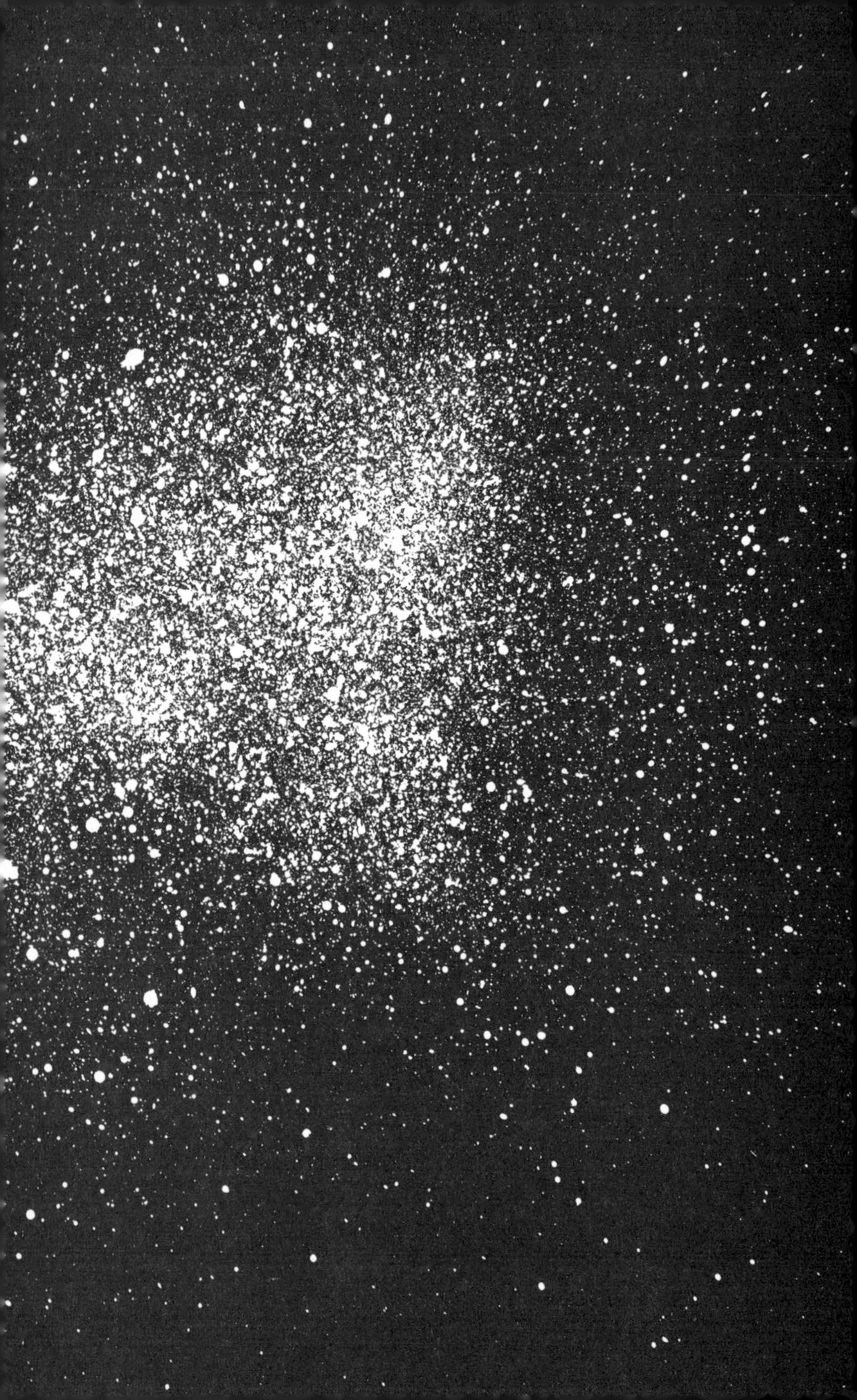

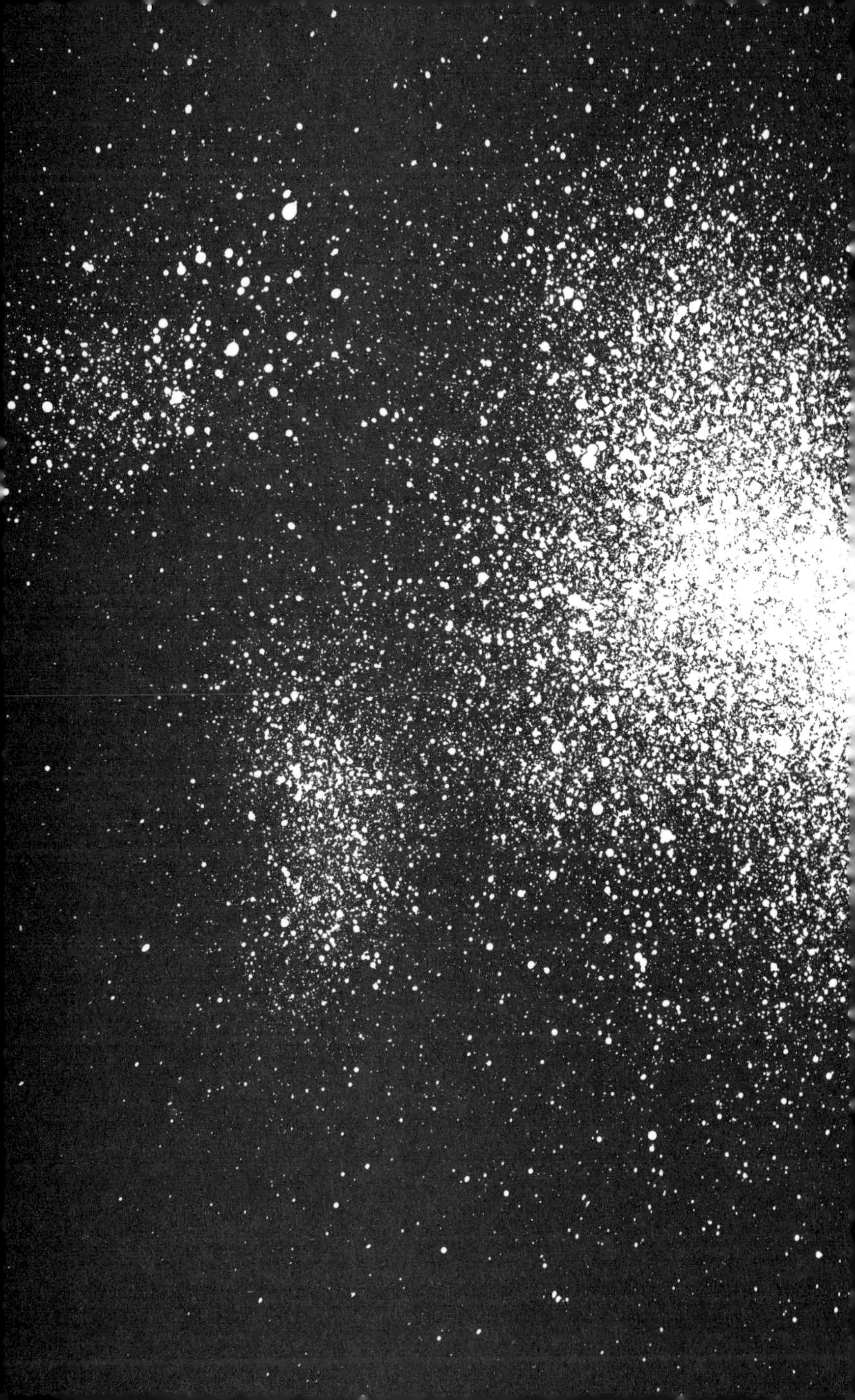

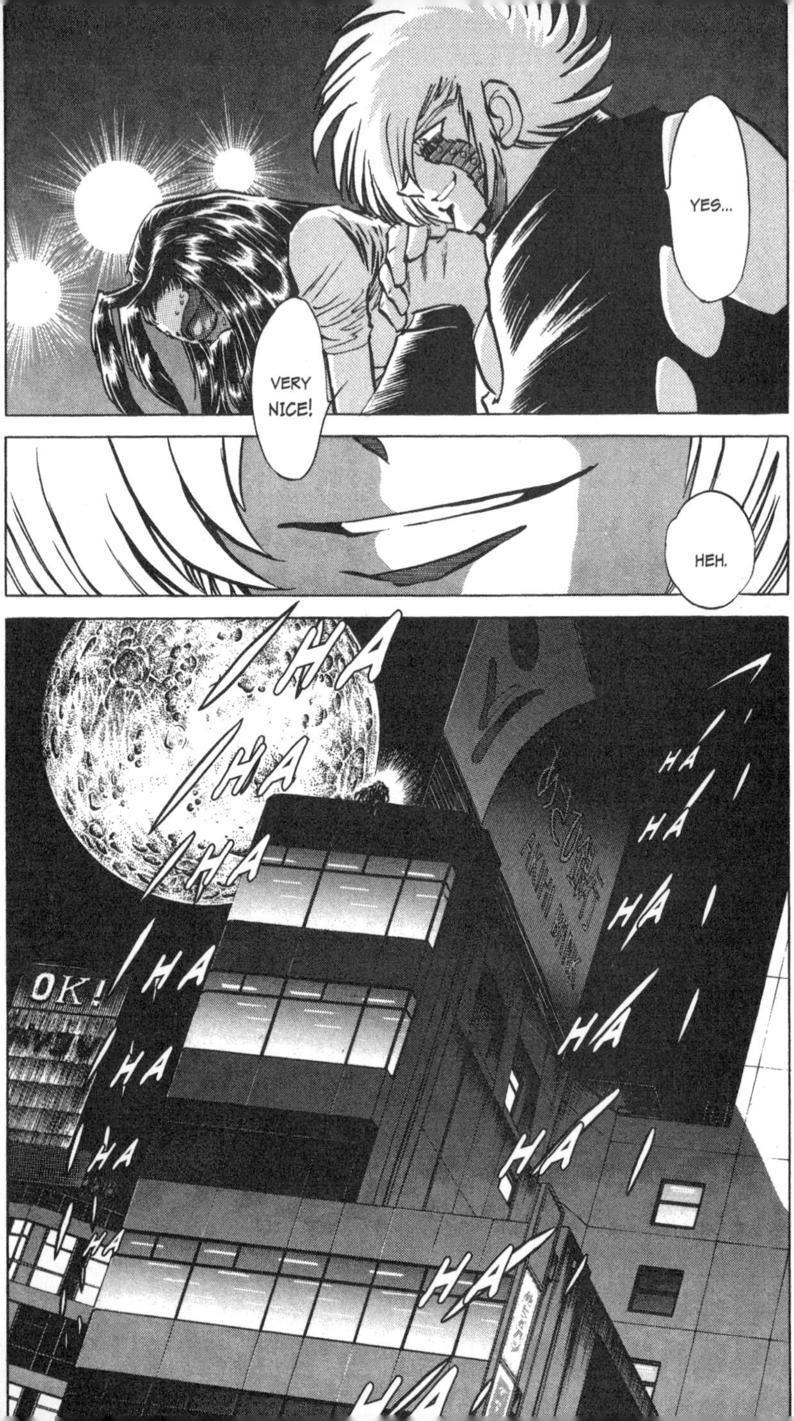
YES...
VERY NICE!
HEH.
HA HA HA HA HA HA HA
HA HA HA
HA HA HA HA
OK!

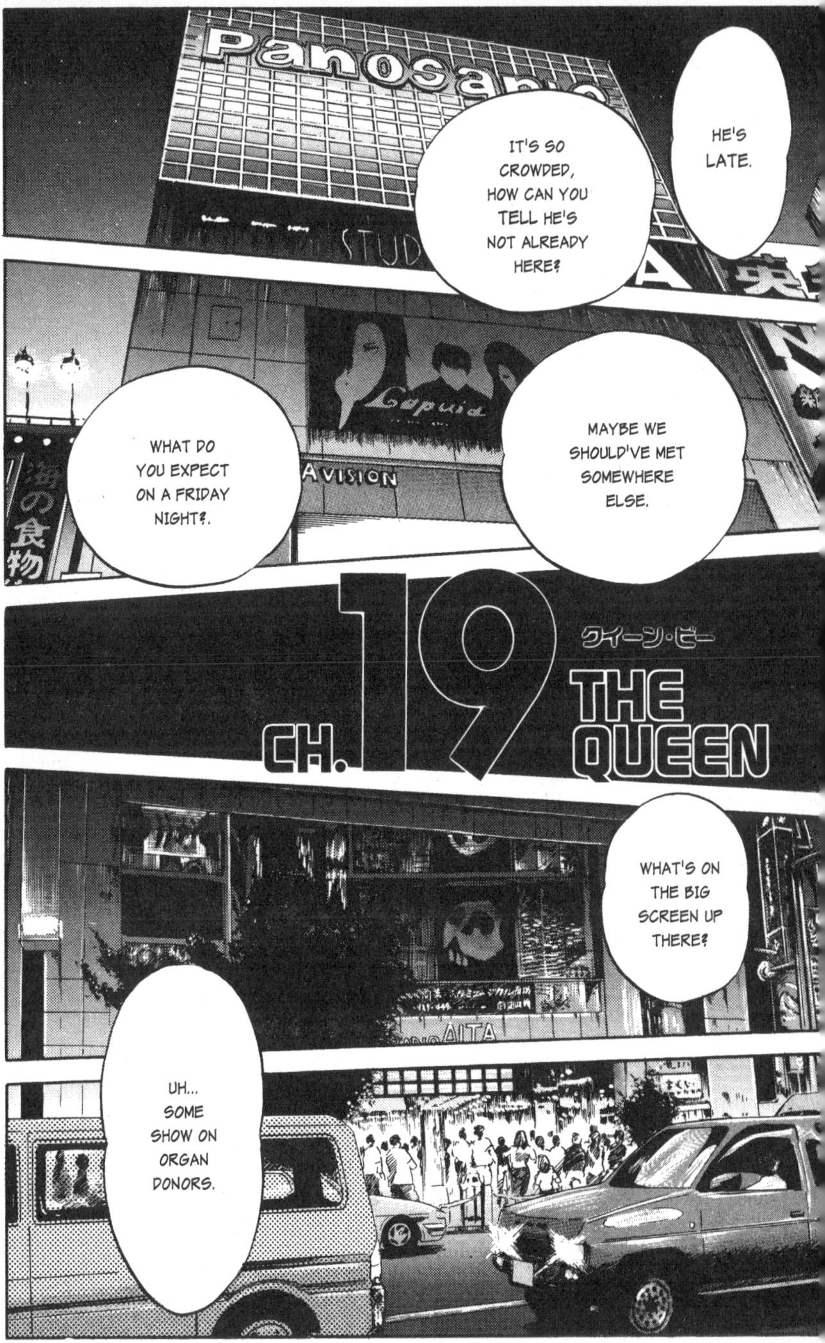
HE'S LATE.
IT'S SO CROWDED, HOW CAN YOU TELL HE'S NOT ALREADY HERE?
MAYBE WE SHOULD'VE MET SOMEWHERE ELSE.
WHAT DO YOU EXPECT ON A FRIDAY NIGHT?.
クイーン・ビー
CH. 19 THE QUEEN
WHAT'S ON THE BIG SCREEN UP THERE?
UH... SOME SHOW ON ORGAN DONORS.

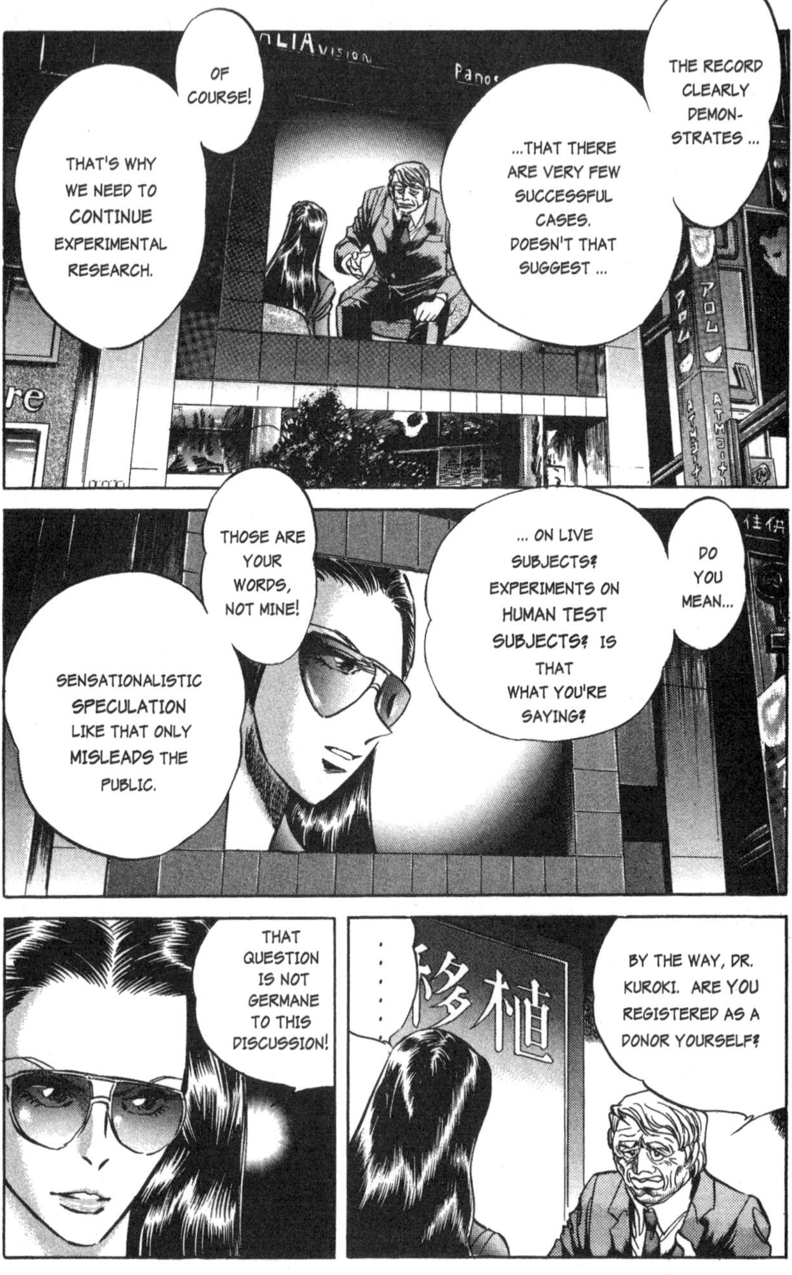
THE RECORD CLEARLY DEMON-STRATES ...
...THAT THERE ARE VERY FEW SUCCESSFUL CASES. DOESN'T THAT SUGGEST ...
OF COURSE!
THAT'S WHY WE NEED TO CONTINUE EXPERIMENTAL RESEARCH.
DO YOU MEAN...
... ON LIVE SUBJECTS? EXPERIMENTS ON HUMAN TEST SUBJECTS? IS THAT WHAT YOU'RE SAYING?
THOSE ARE YOUR WORDS, NOT MINE!
SENSATIONALISTIC SPECULATION LIKE THAT ONLY MISLEADS THE PUBLIC.
BY THE WAY, DR. KUROKI. ARE YOU REGISTERED AS A DONOR YOURSELF?
移植
......
THAT QUESTION IS NOT GERMANE TO THIS DISCUSSION!

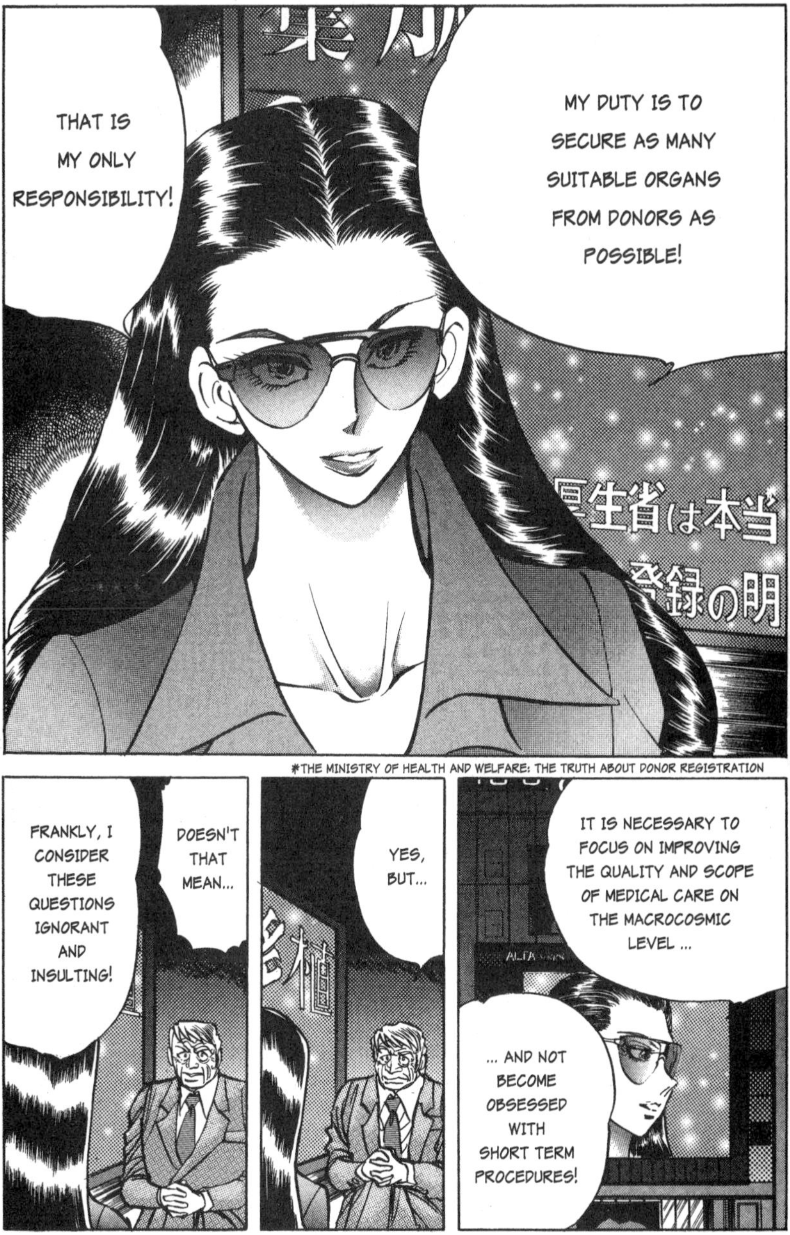
MY DUTY IS TO SECURE AS MANY SUITABLE ORGANS FROM DONORS AS POSSIBLE!
THAT IS MY ONLY RESPONSIBILITY!
*THE MINISTRY OF HEALTH AND WELFARE: THE TRUTH ABOUT DONOR REGISTRATION
IT IS NECESSARY TO FOCUS ON IMPROVING THE QUALITY AND SCOPE OF MEDICAL CARE ON THE MACROCOSMIC LEVEL ...
... AND NOT BECOME OBSESSED WITH SHORT TERM PROCEDURES!
YES, BUT...
DOESN'T THAT MEAN...
FRANKLY, I CONSIDER THESE QUESTIONS IGNORANT AND INSULTING!

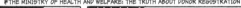

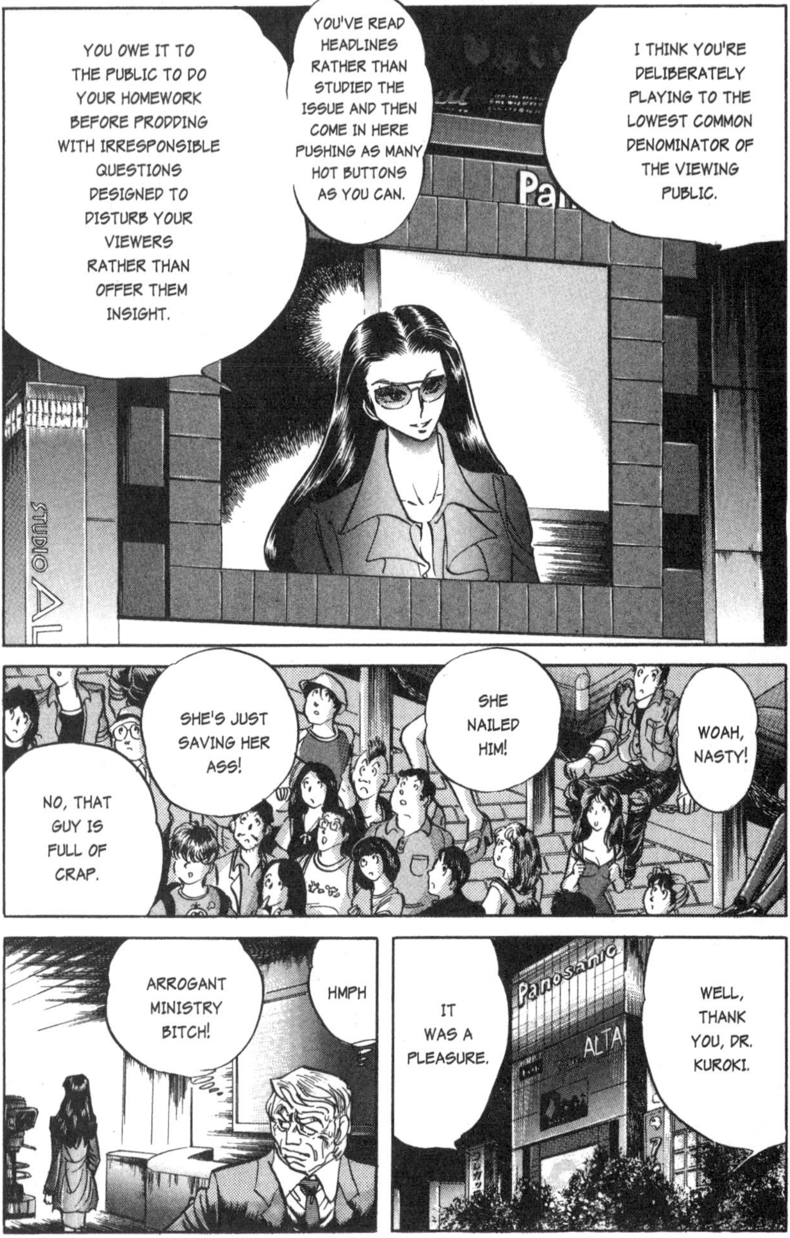
I THINK YOU'RE DELIBERATELY PLAYING TO THE LOWEST COMMON DENOMINATOR OF THE VIEWING PUBLIC.
YOU'VE READ HEADLINES RATHER THAN STUDIED THE ISSUE AND THEN COME IN HERE PUSHING AS MANY HOT BUTTONS AS YOU CAN.
YOU OWE IT TO THE PUBLIC TO DO YOUR HOMEWORK BEFORE PRODDING WITH IRRESPONSIBLE QUESTIONS DESIGNED TO DISTURB YOUR VIEWERS RATHER THAN OFFER THEM INSIGHT.
STUDIO
WOAH, NASTY!
SHE NAILED HIM!
SHE'S JUST SAVING HER ASS!
NO, THAT GUY IS FULL OF CRAP.
WELL, THANK YOU, DR. KUROKI.
IT WAS A PLEASURE.
Panosanic
ALTA
HMPH
ARROGANT MINISTRY BITCH!

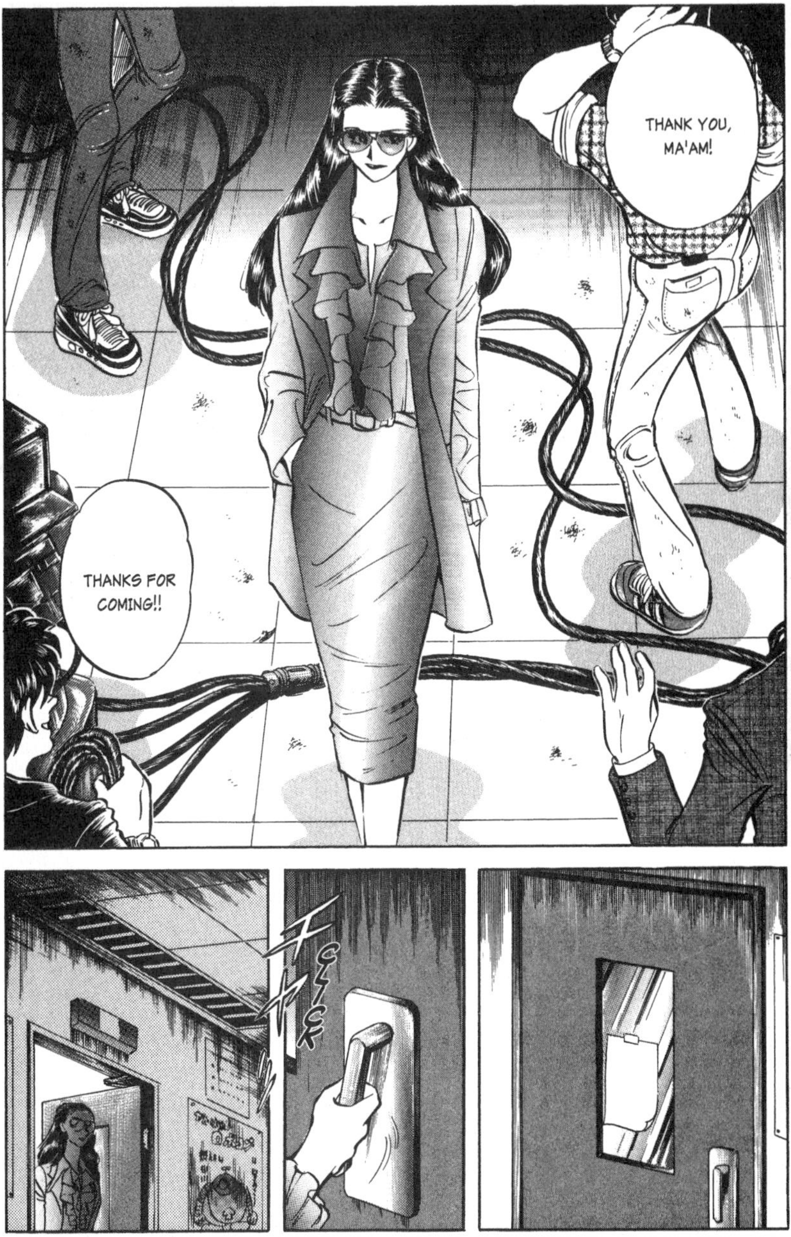
THANK YOU, MA'AM!
THANKS FOR COMING!!
CLICK

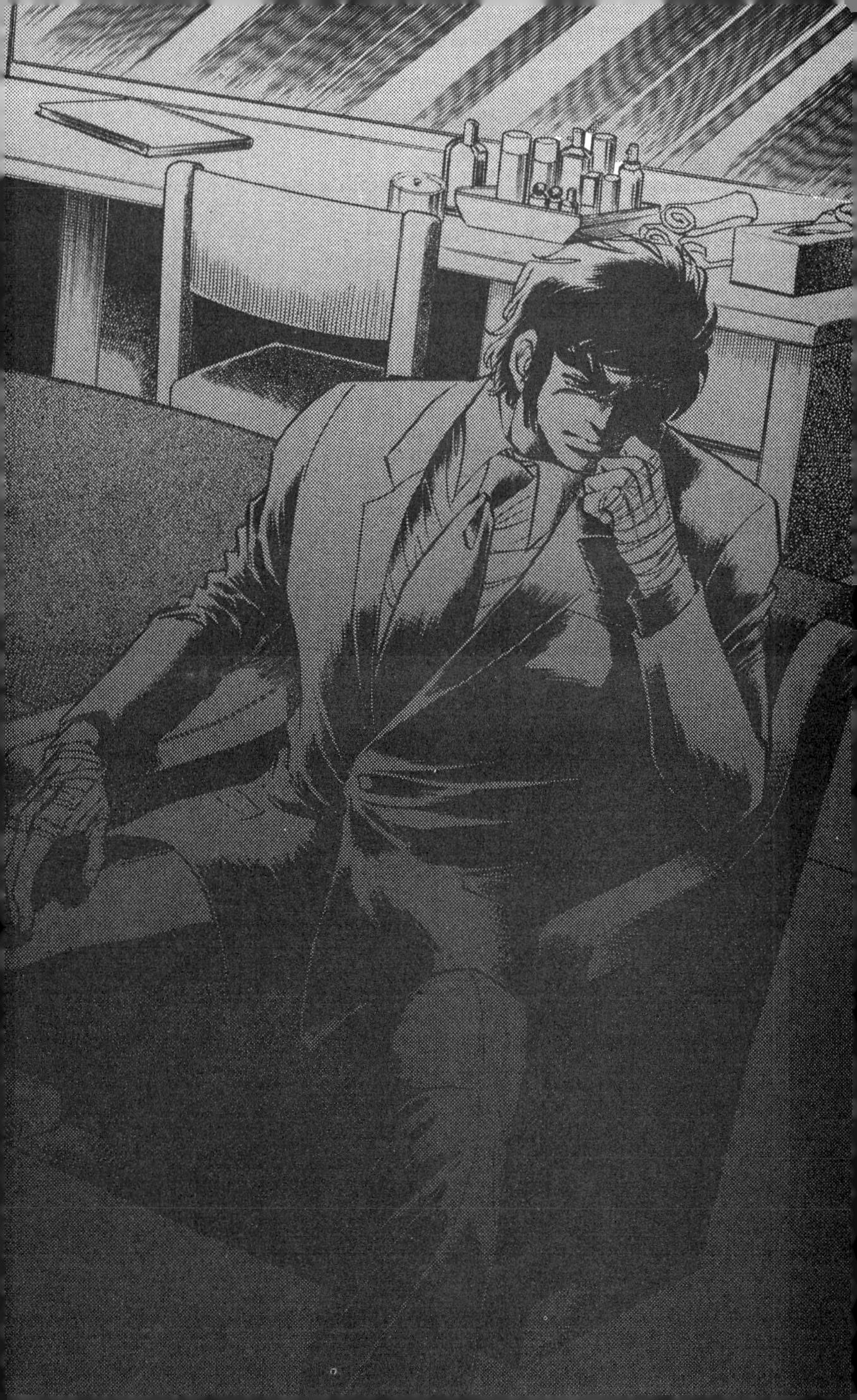

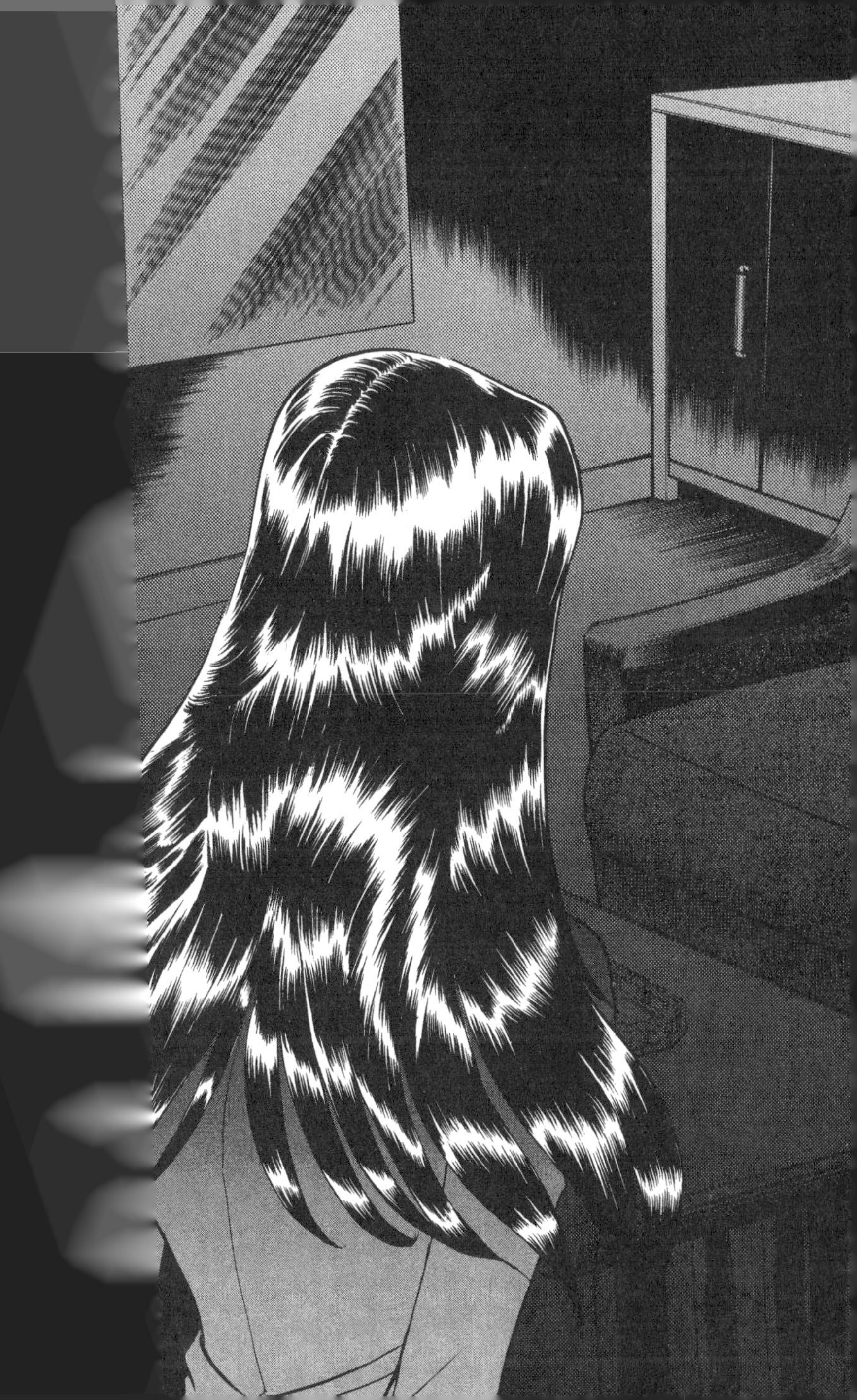

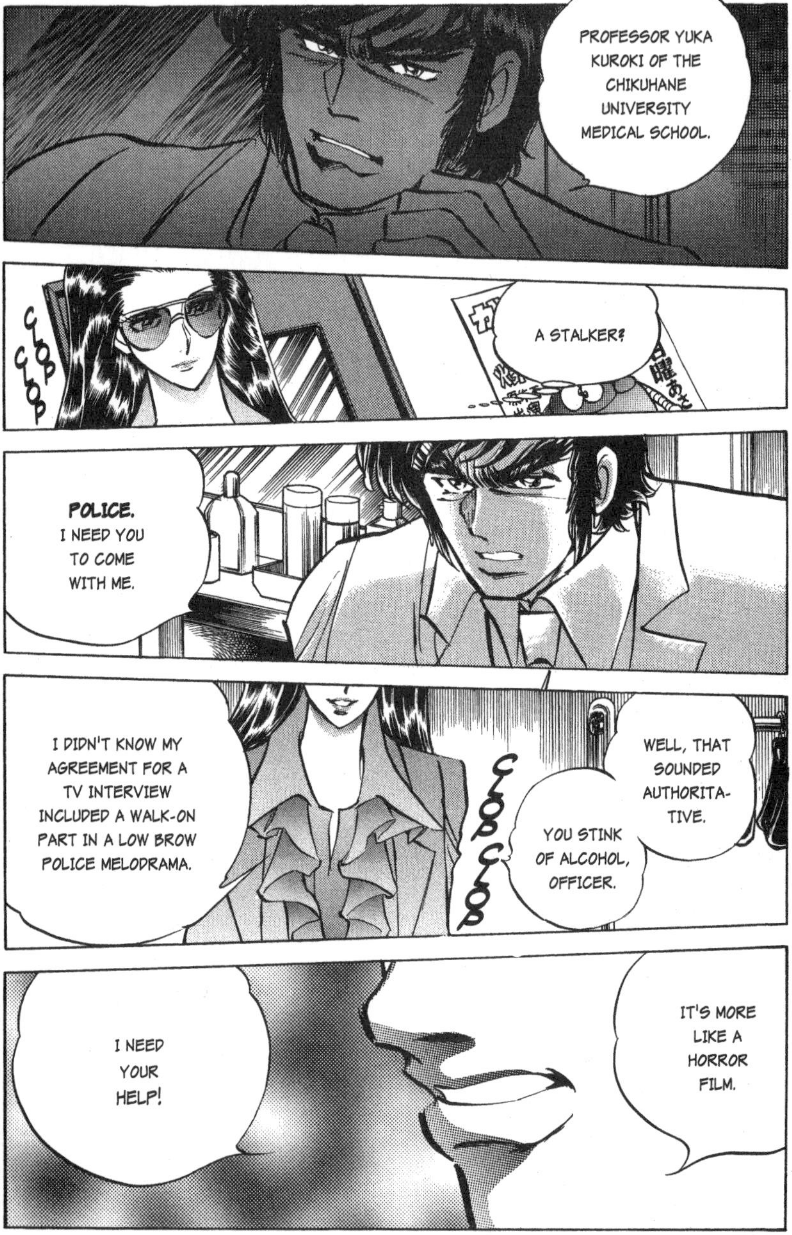
PROFESSOR YUKA KUROKI OF THE CHIKUHANE UNIVERSITY MEDICAL SCHOOL.
A STALKER?
CLOP CLOP
POLICE. I NEED YOU TO COME WITH ME.
WELL, THAT SOUNDED AUTHORITA-TIVE.
YOU STINK OF ALCOHOL, OFFICER.
CLOP CLOP
I DIDN'T KNOW MY AGREEMENT FOR A TV INTERVIEW INCLUDED A WALK-ON PART IN A LOW BROW POLICE MELODRAMA.
IT'S MORE LIKE A HORROR FILM.
I NEED YOUR HELP!

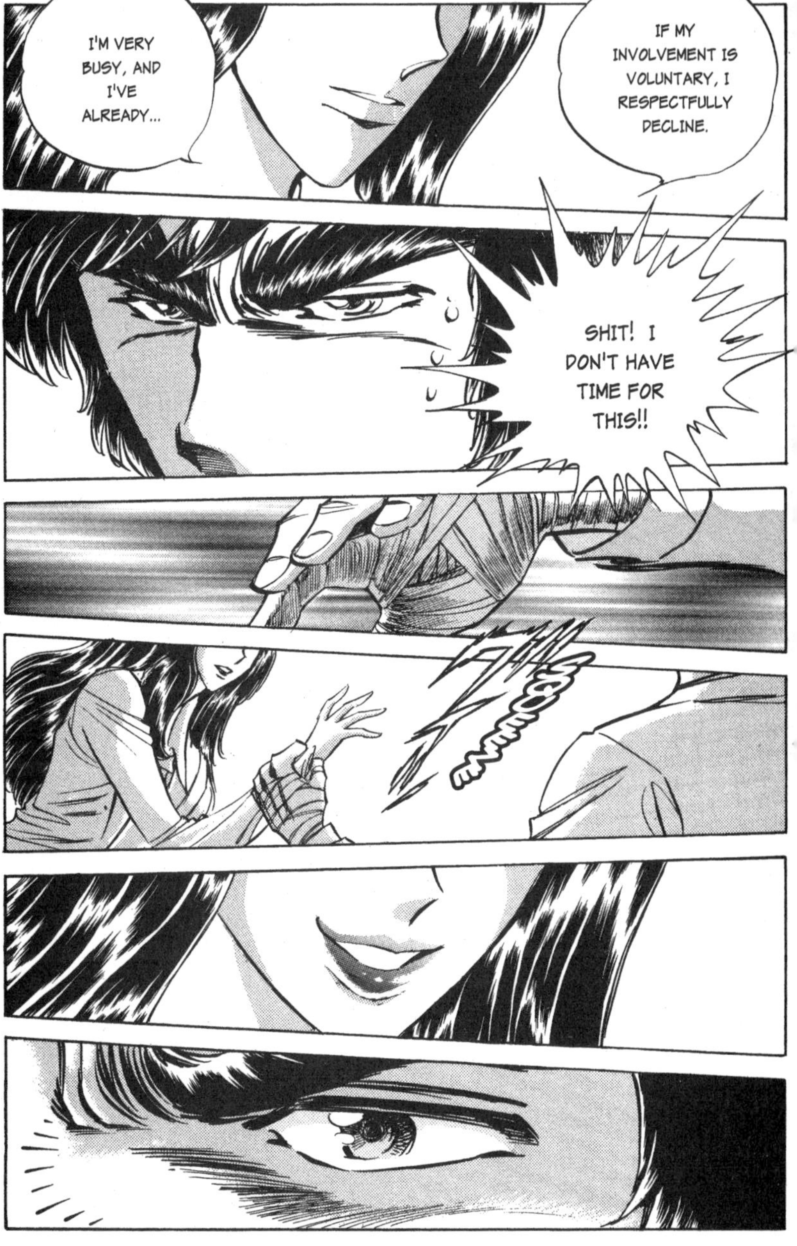
IF MY INVOLVEMENT IS VOLUNTARY, I RESPECTFULLY DECLINE.
I'M VERY BUSY, AND I'VE ALREADY...
SHIT! I DON'T HAVE TIME FOR THIS!!

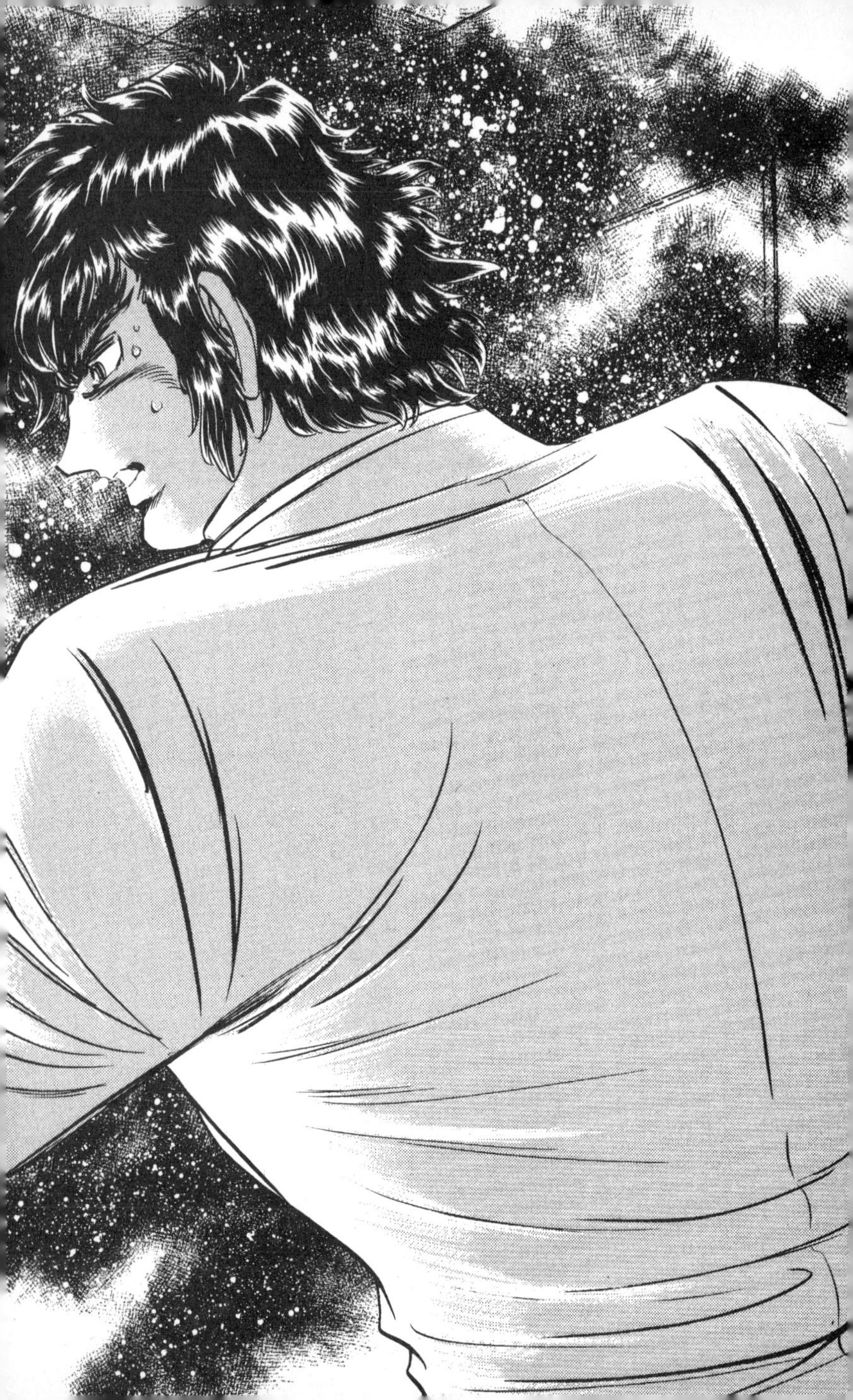

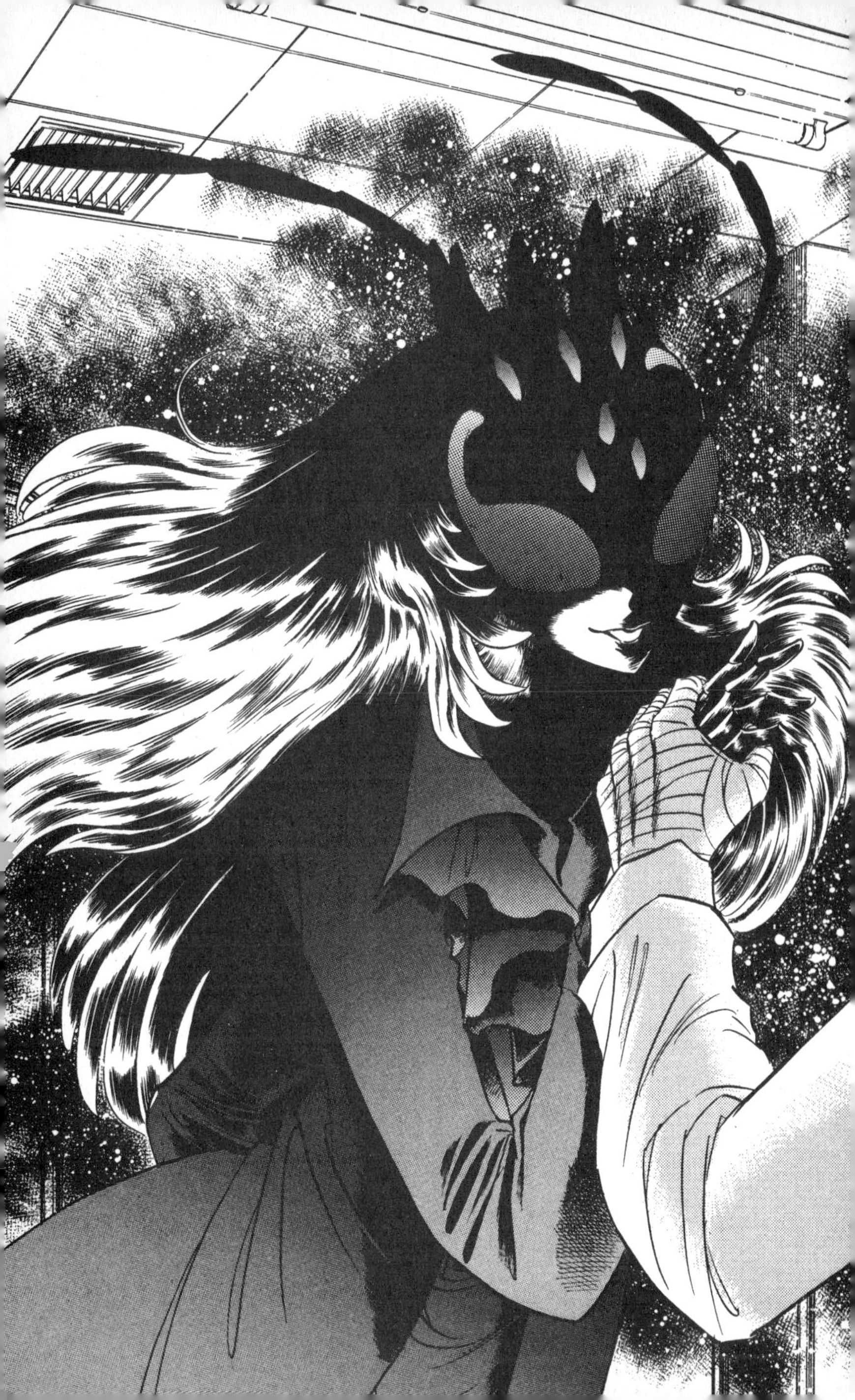

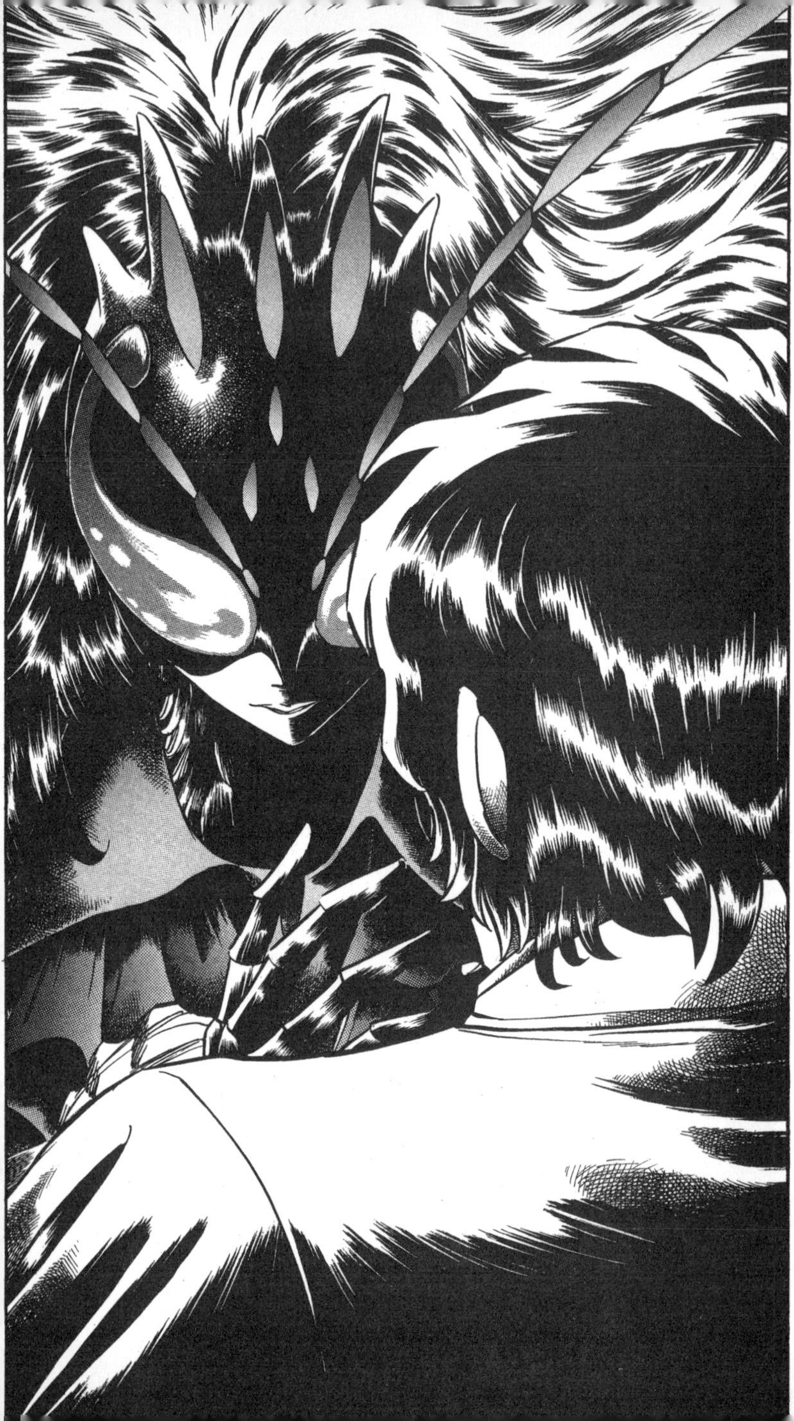

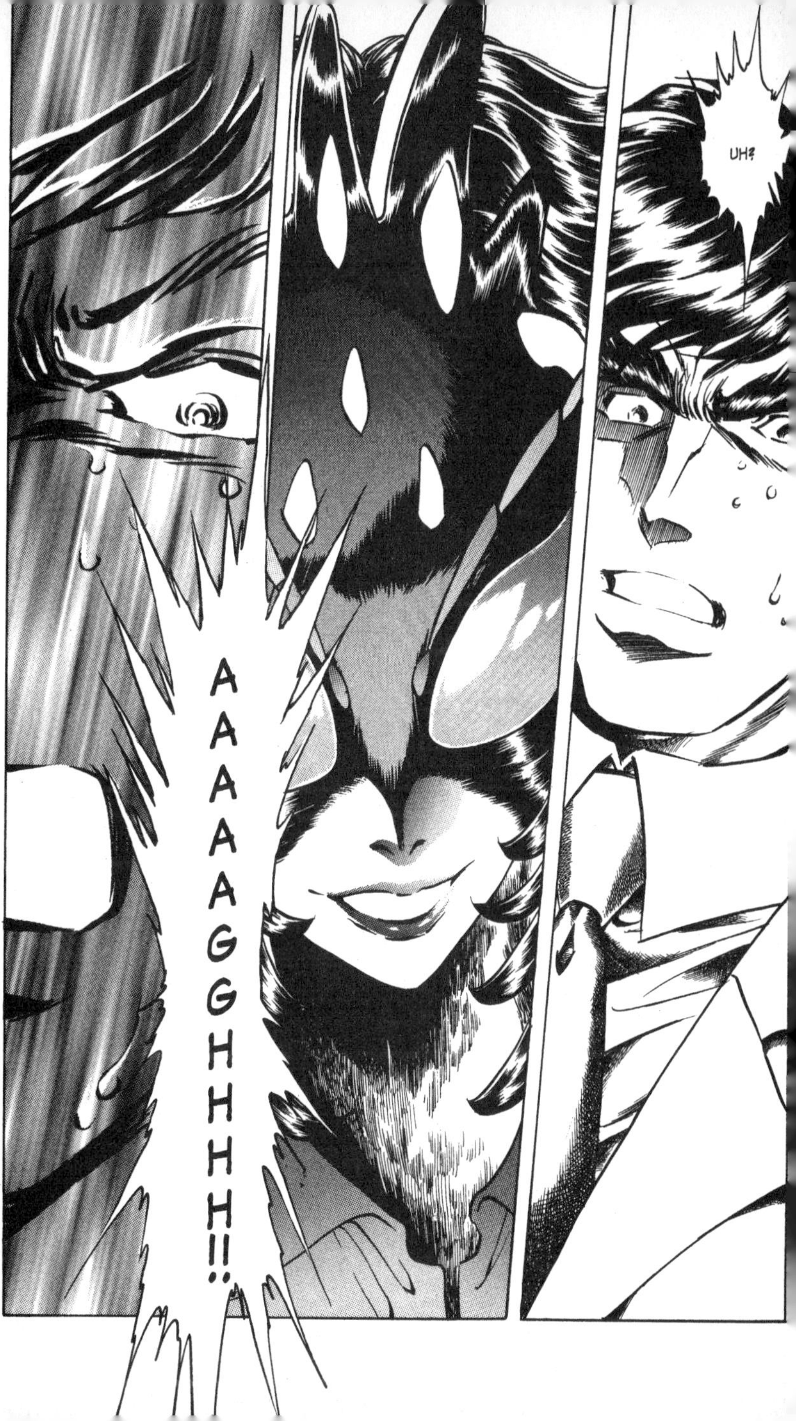
UH?
AAAAAAGGHHHHH!!

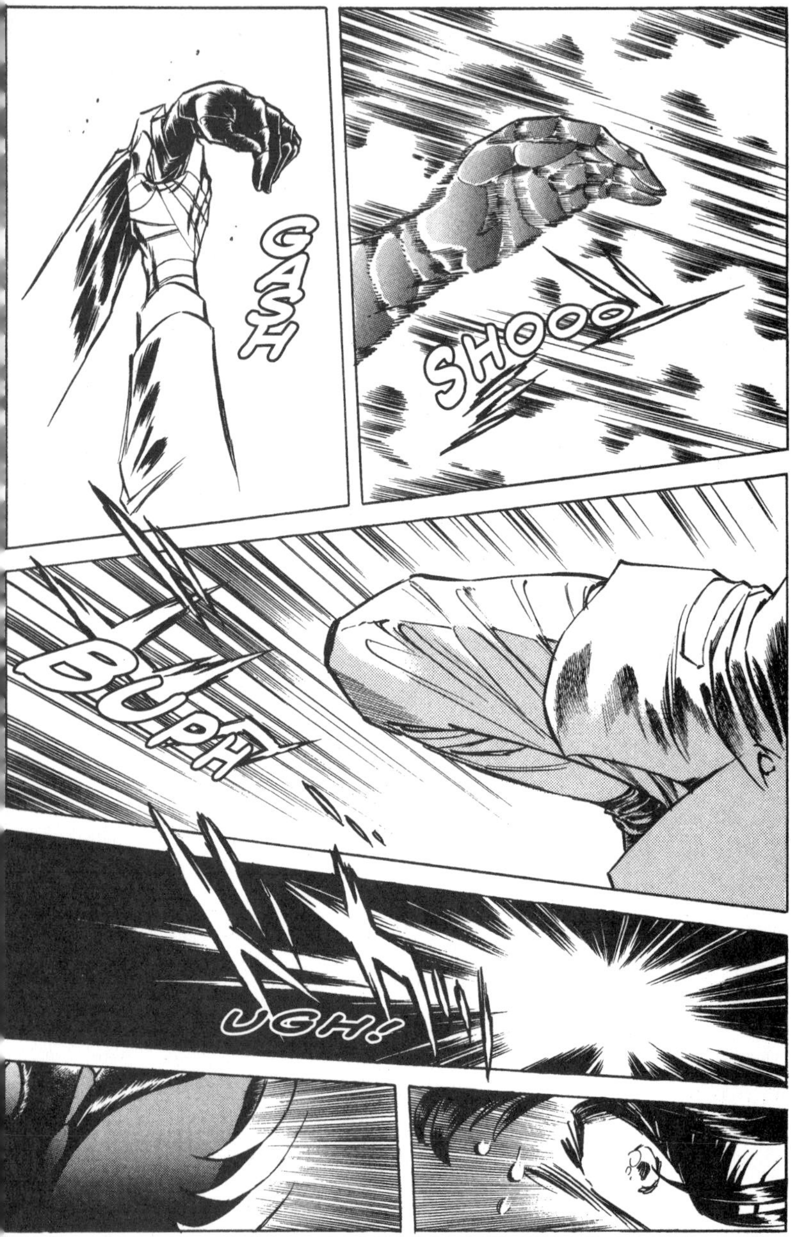
SHOOO
GASH
BUPH
UGH!

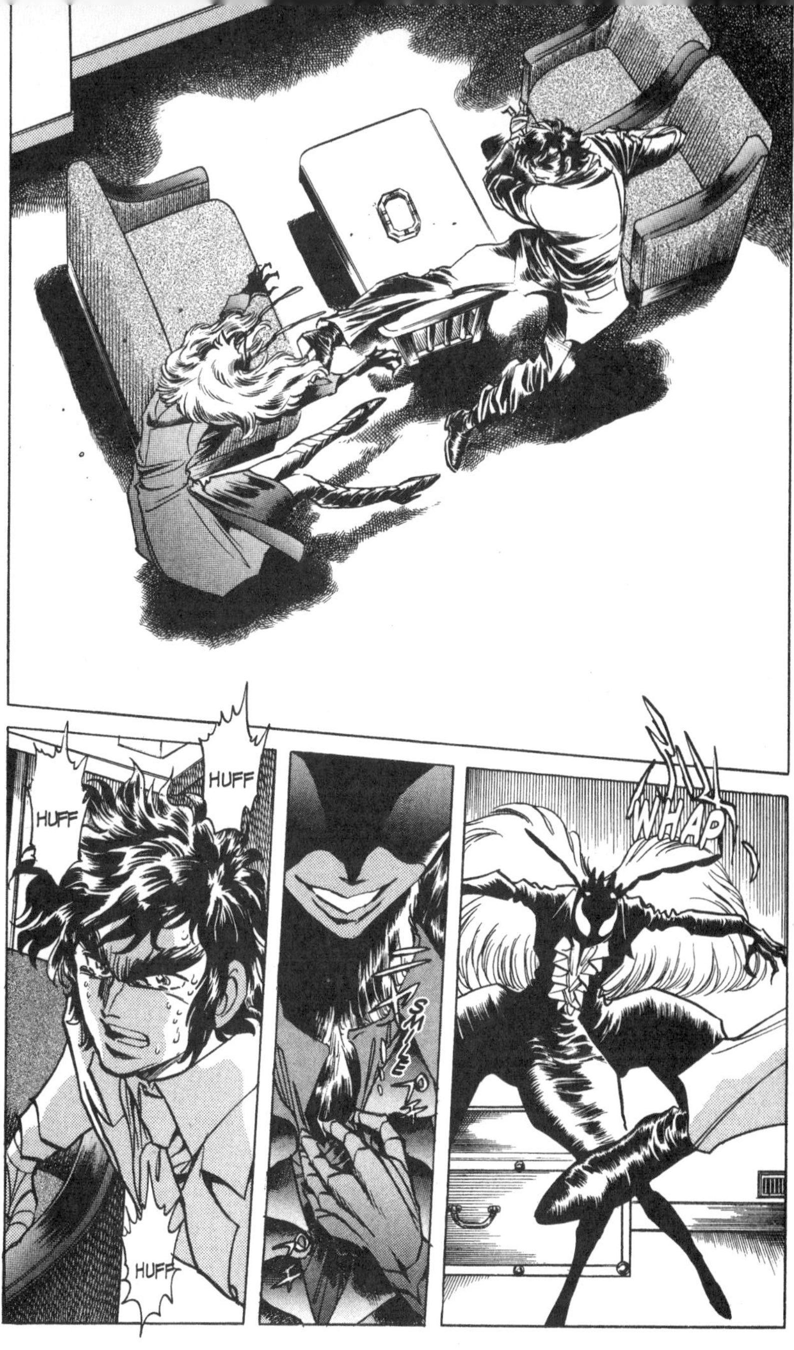

WHAP
SMILE
HUFF
HUFF
HUFF

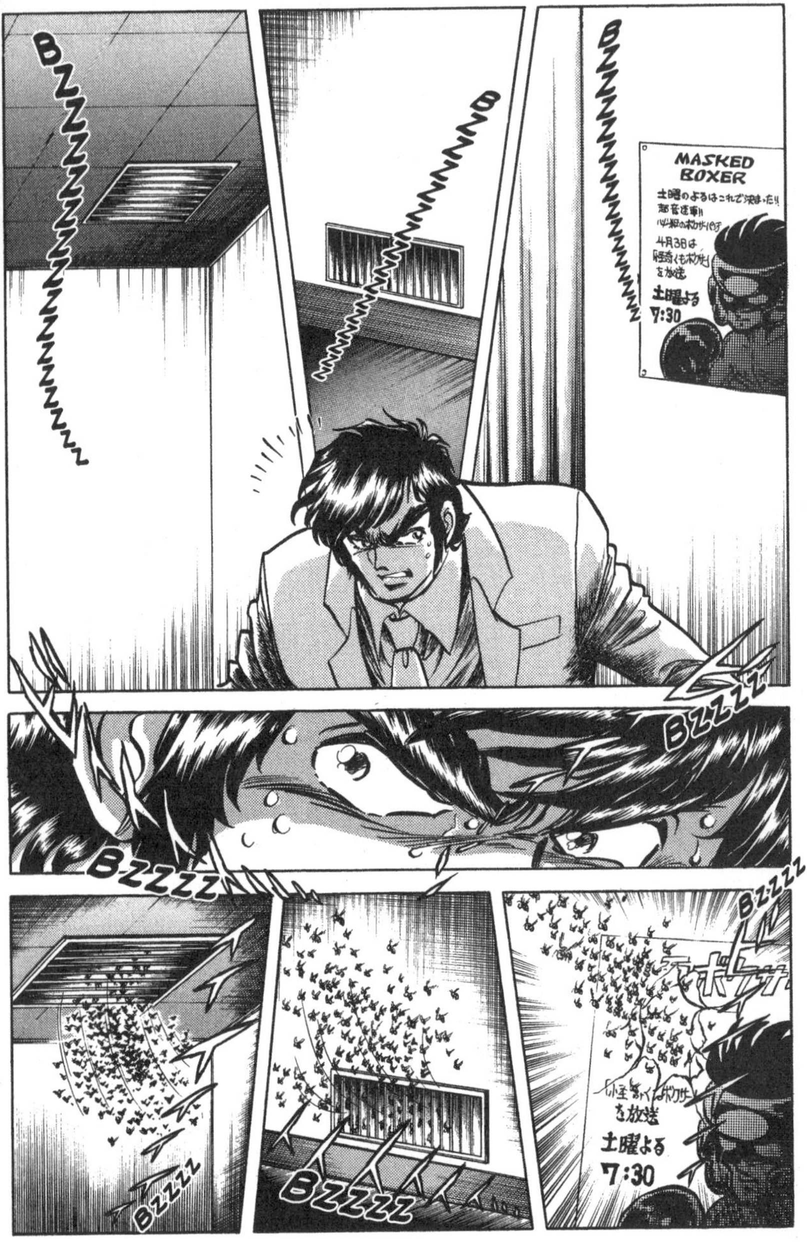

BZZZZZZZZZZZZZZZZZZ
MASKED BOXER
土曜のよるはこれで決まった!!
4月3日は
「怪奇くもボクサー」
を放送
土曜よる
7:30
BZZZZZZZZZZZZZZZZZ
BZZZZZZZZZZZZZZZZ
BZZZZ
BZZZZZ
BZZZZ
BZZZZZ
土曜よる
7:30
BZZZZZ
BZZZZ

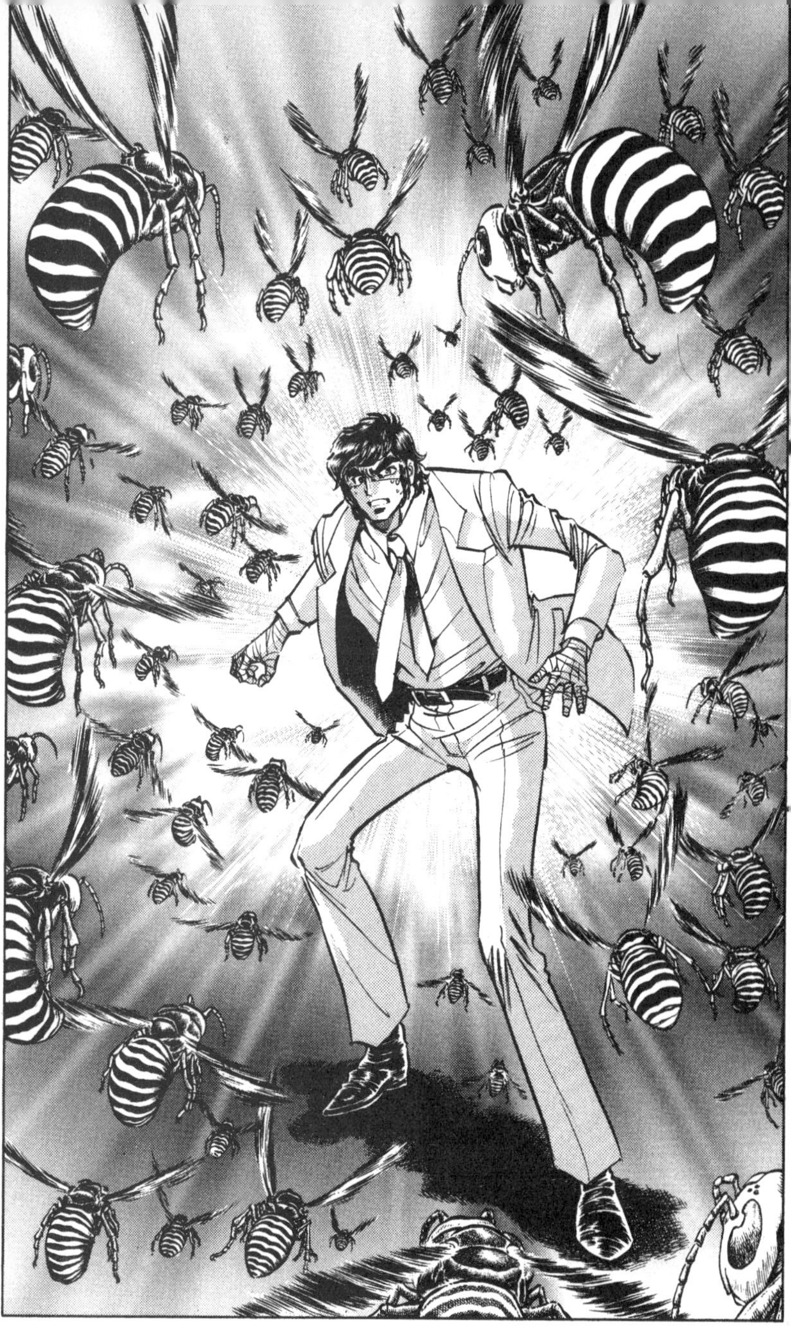

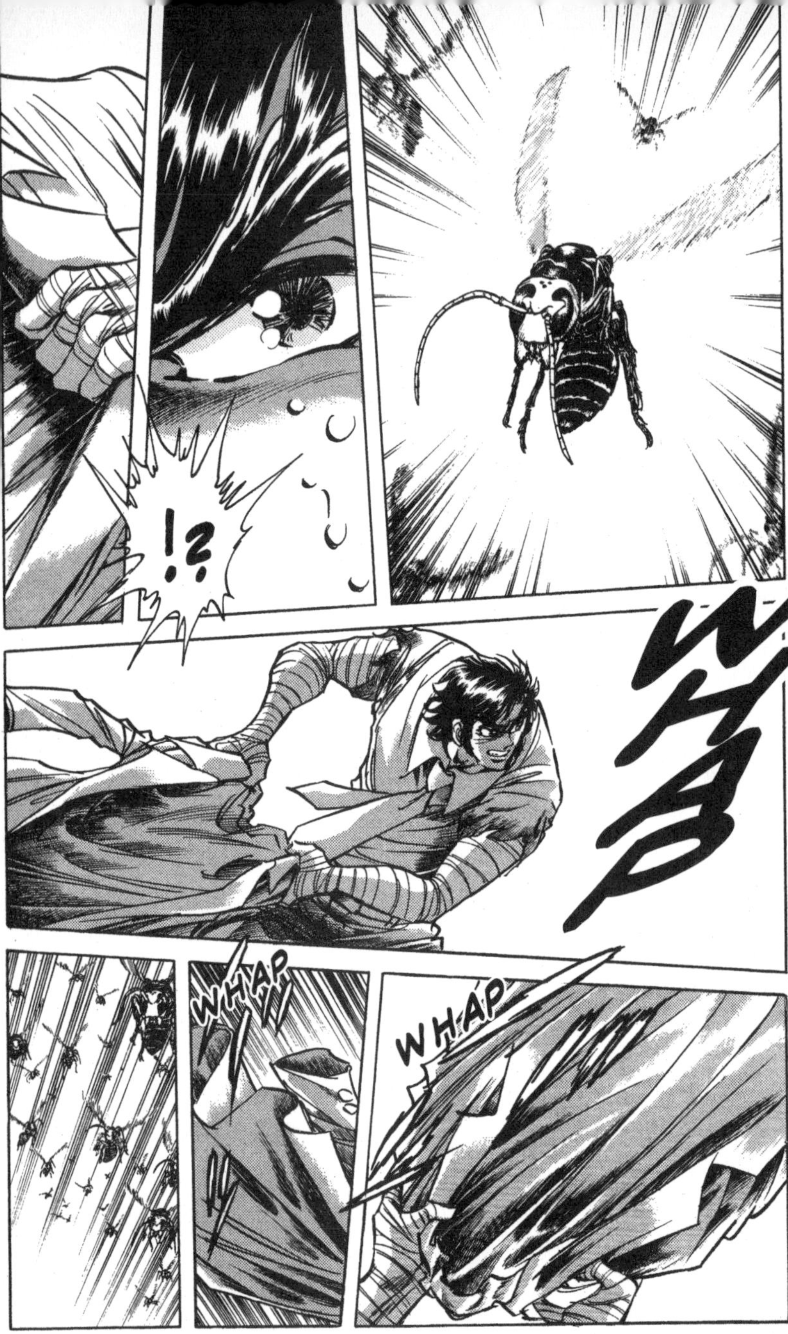
!?
WHAP
WHAP
WHAP

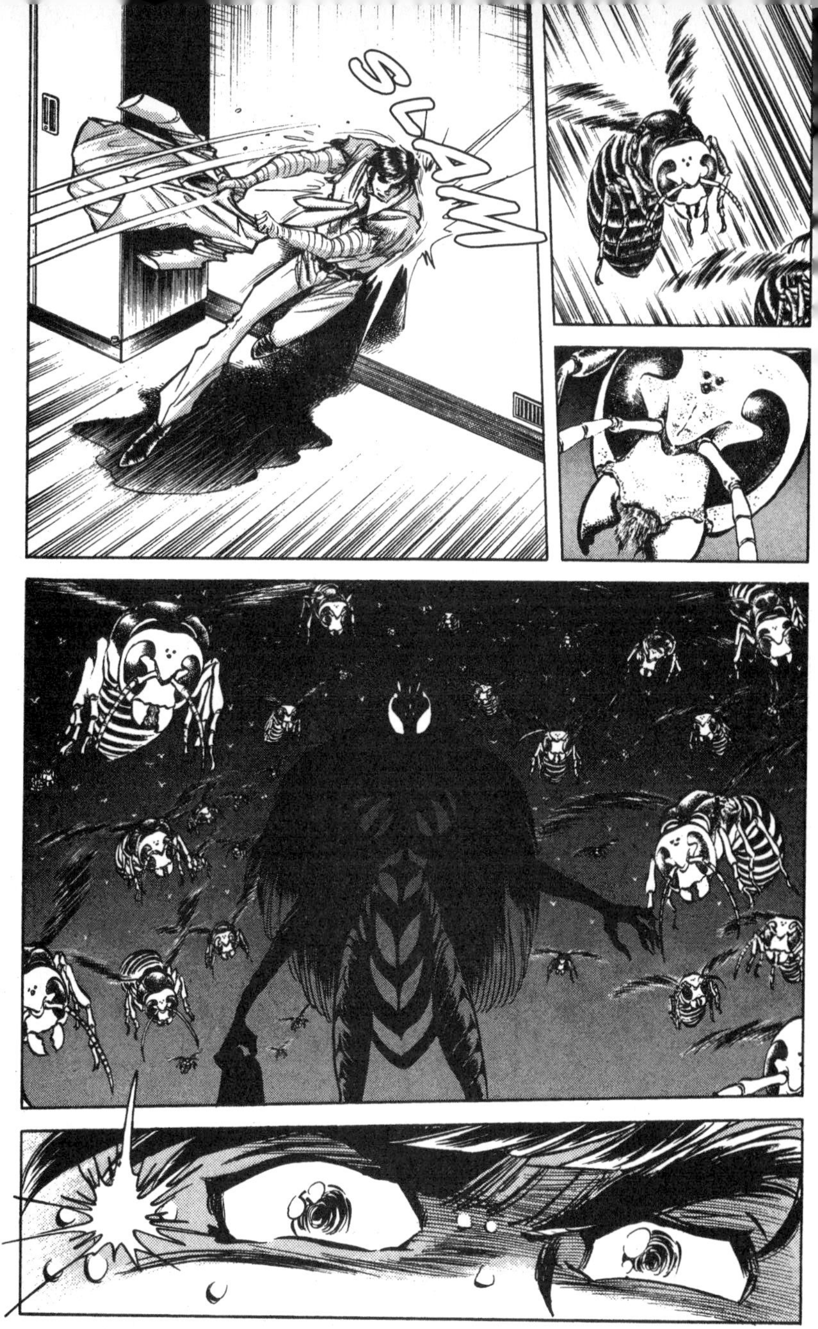
SLAM

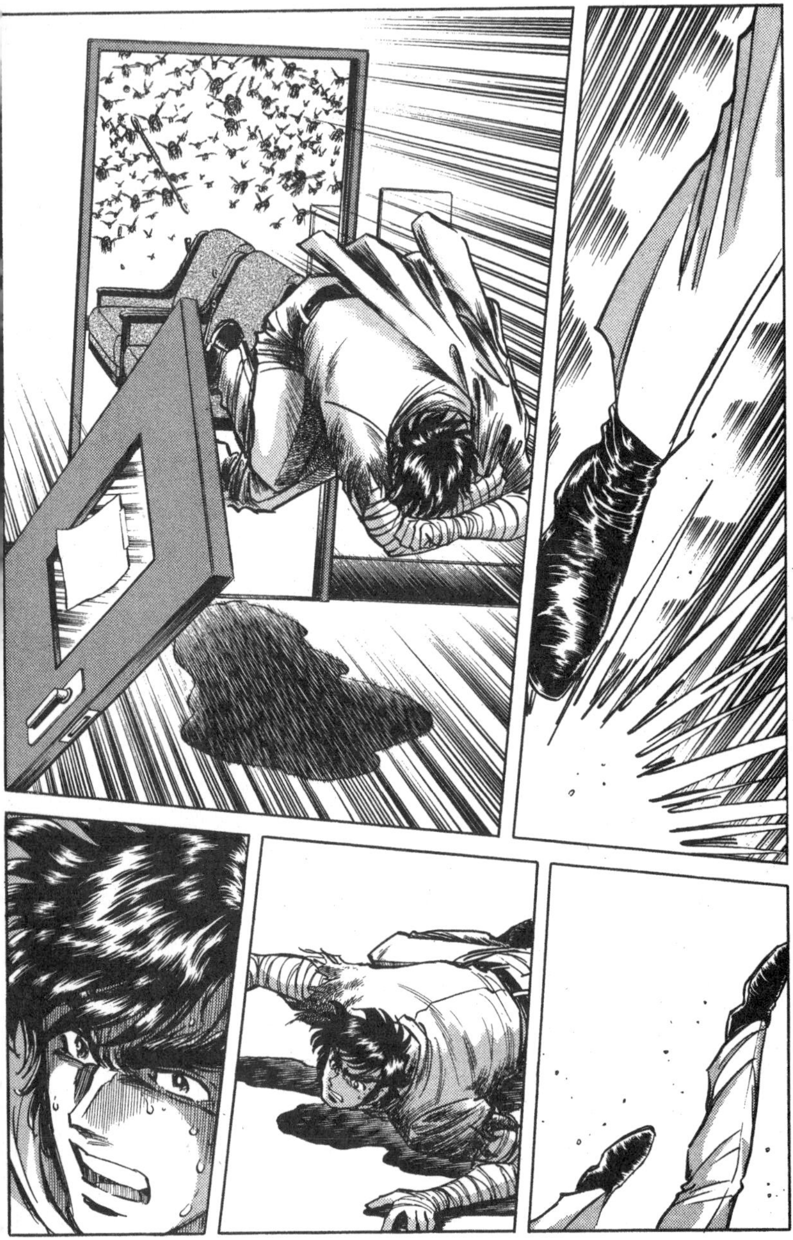

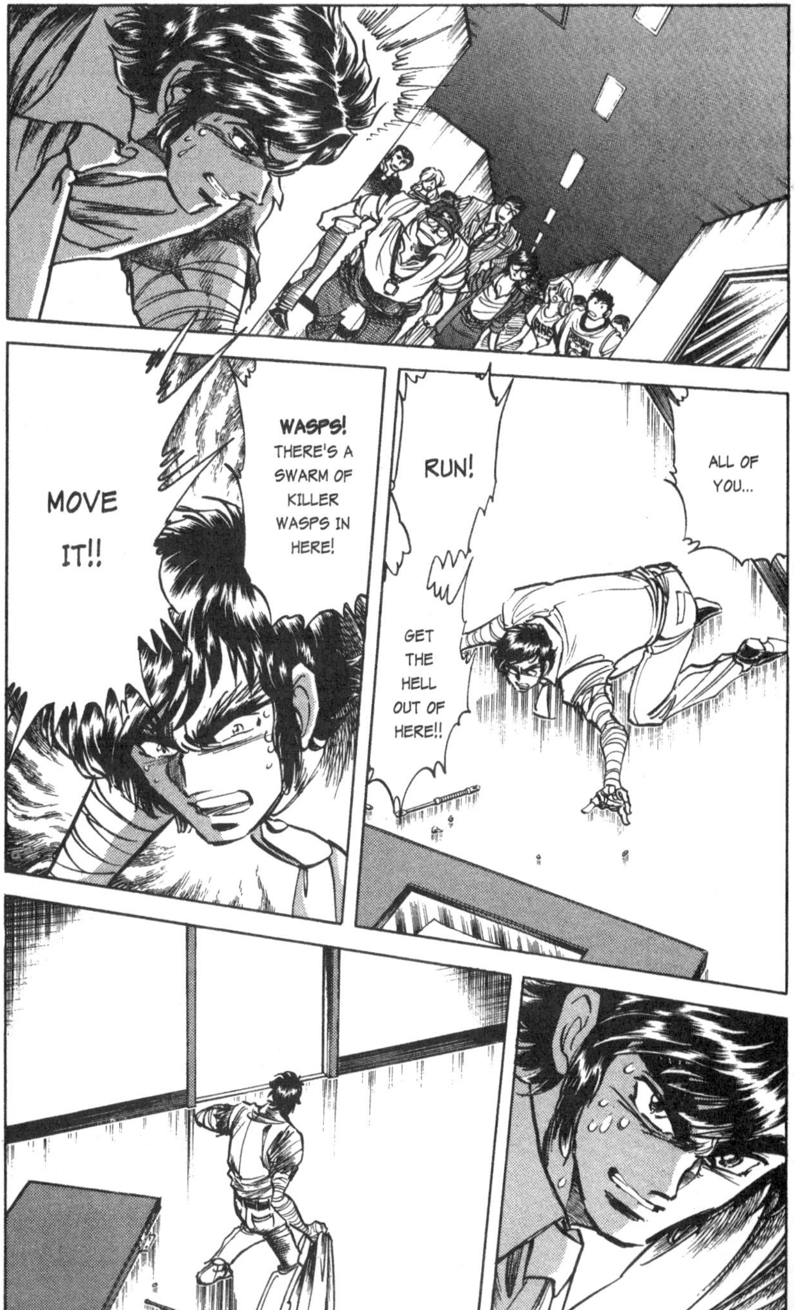
ALL OF YOU...
RUN!
GET THE HELL OUT OF HERE!!
WASPS! THERE'S A SWARM OF KILLER WASPS IN HERE!
MOVE IT!!

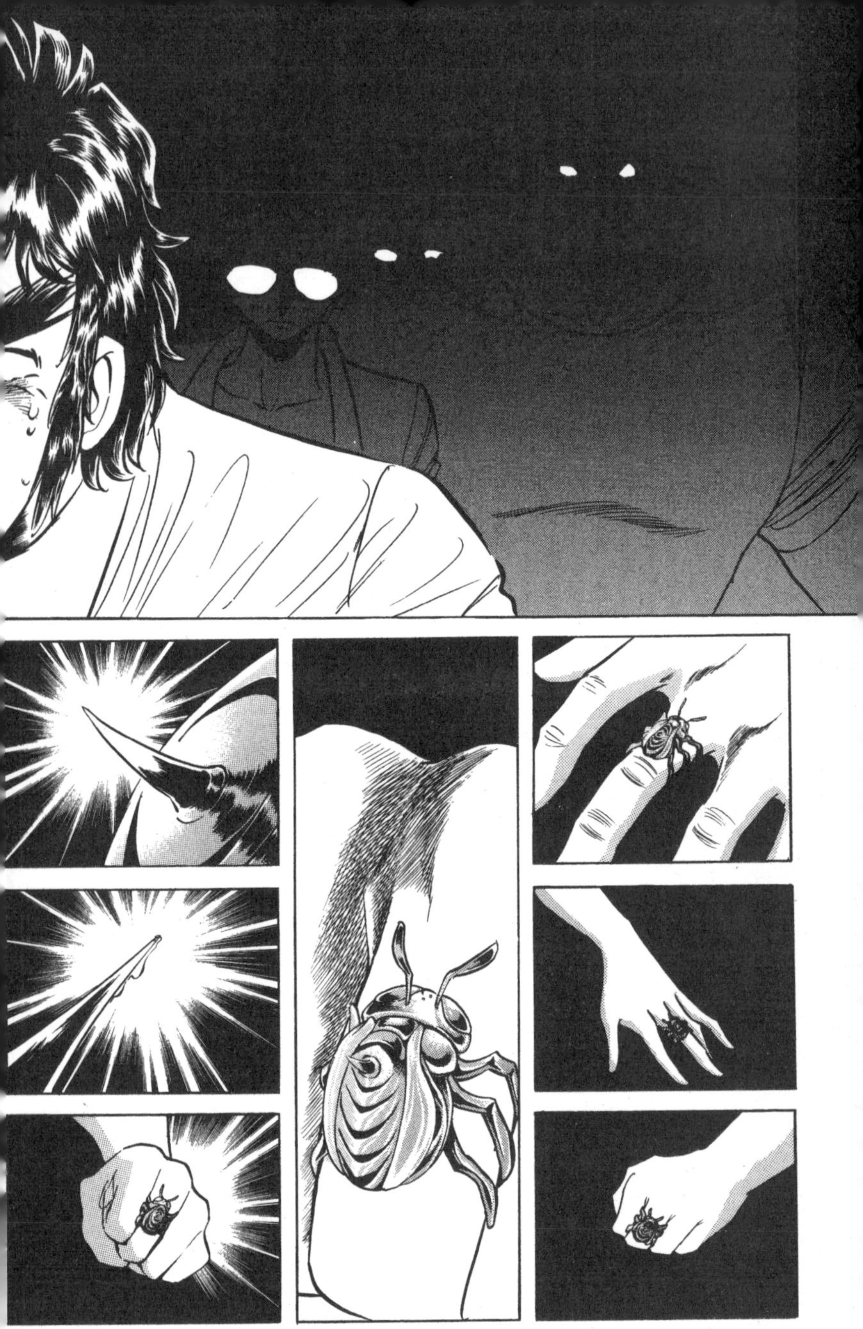

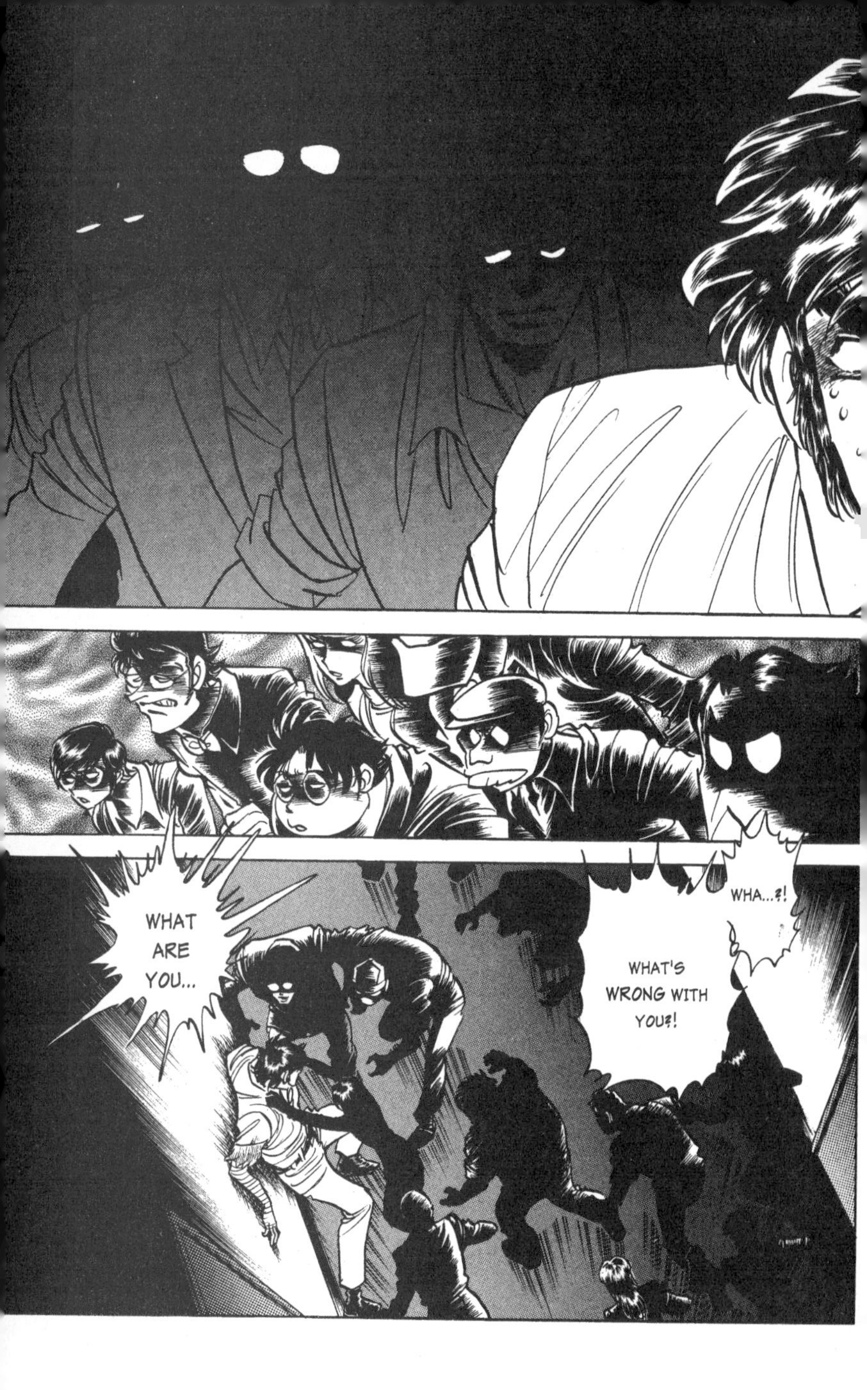
WHA...?!
WHAT'S WRONG WITH YOU?!
WHAT ARE YOU...

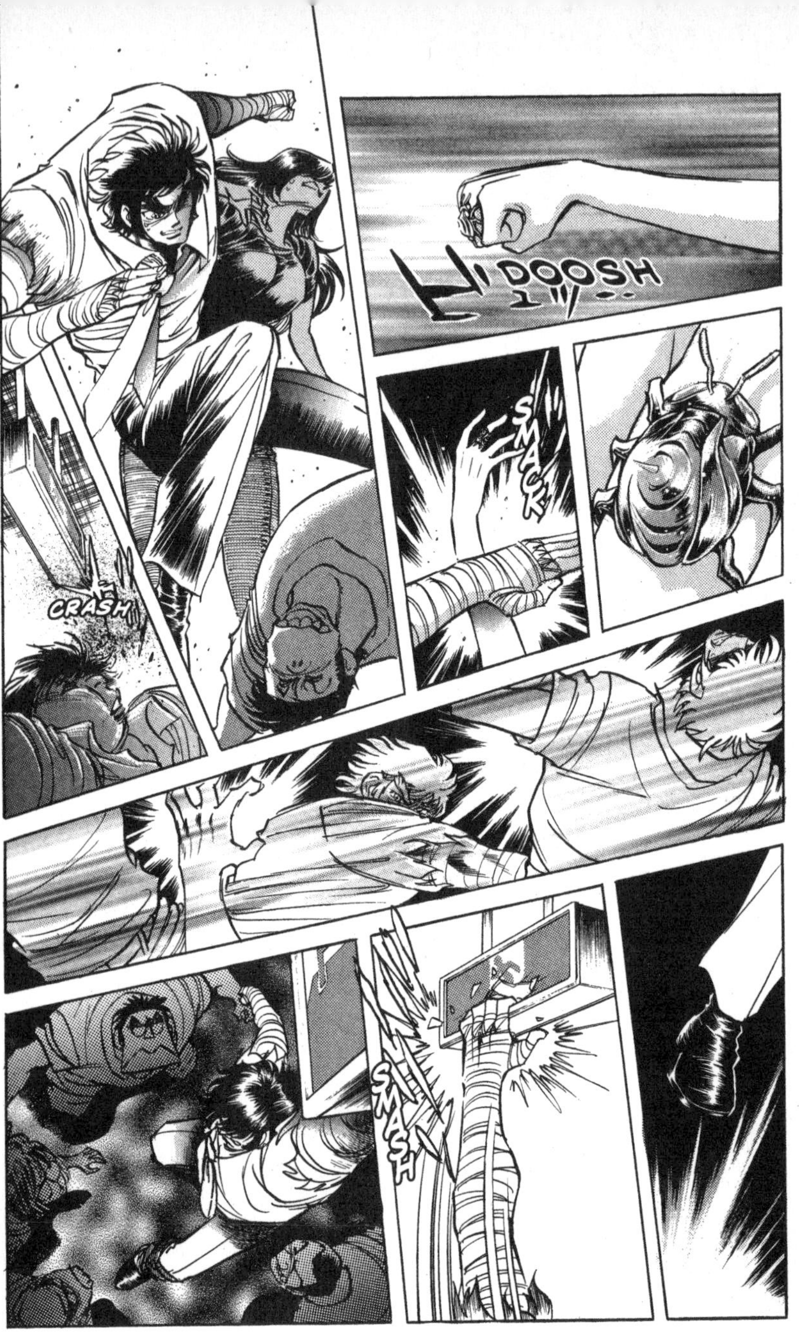
DOOSH
SMACK
CRASH
SMASH

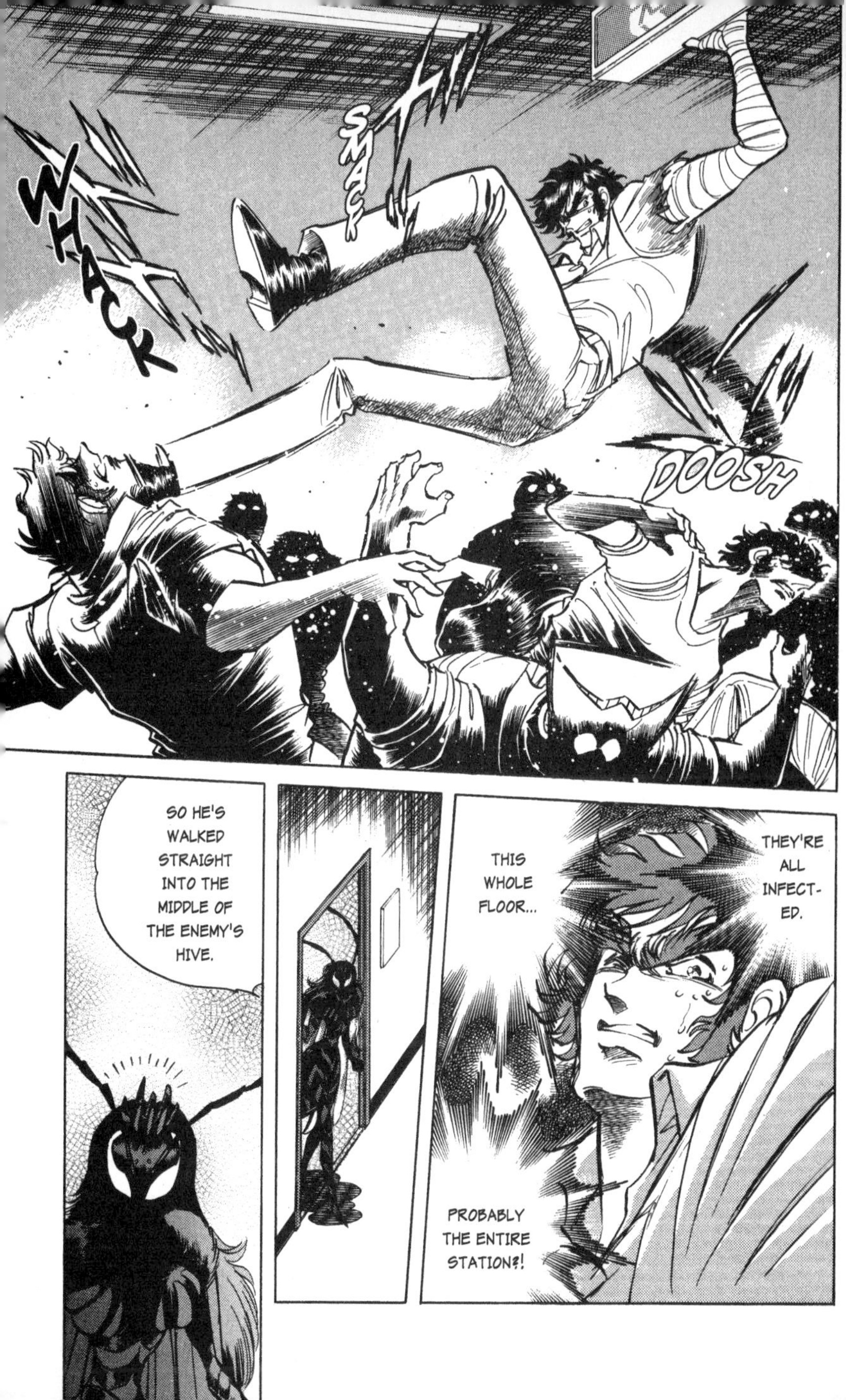
SMACK
WHACK
DOOSH
THEY'RE ALL INFECTED.
THIS WHOLE FLOOR...
PROBABLY THE ENTIRE STATION?!
SO HE'S WALKED STRAIGHT INTO THE MIDDLE OF THE ENEMY'S HIVE.

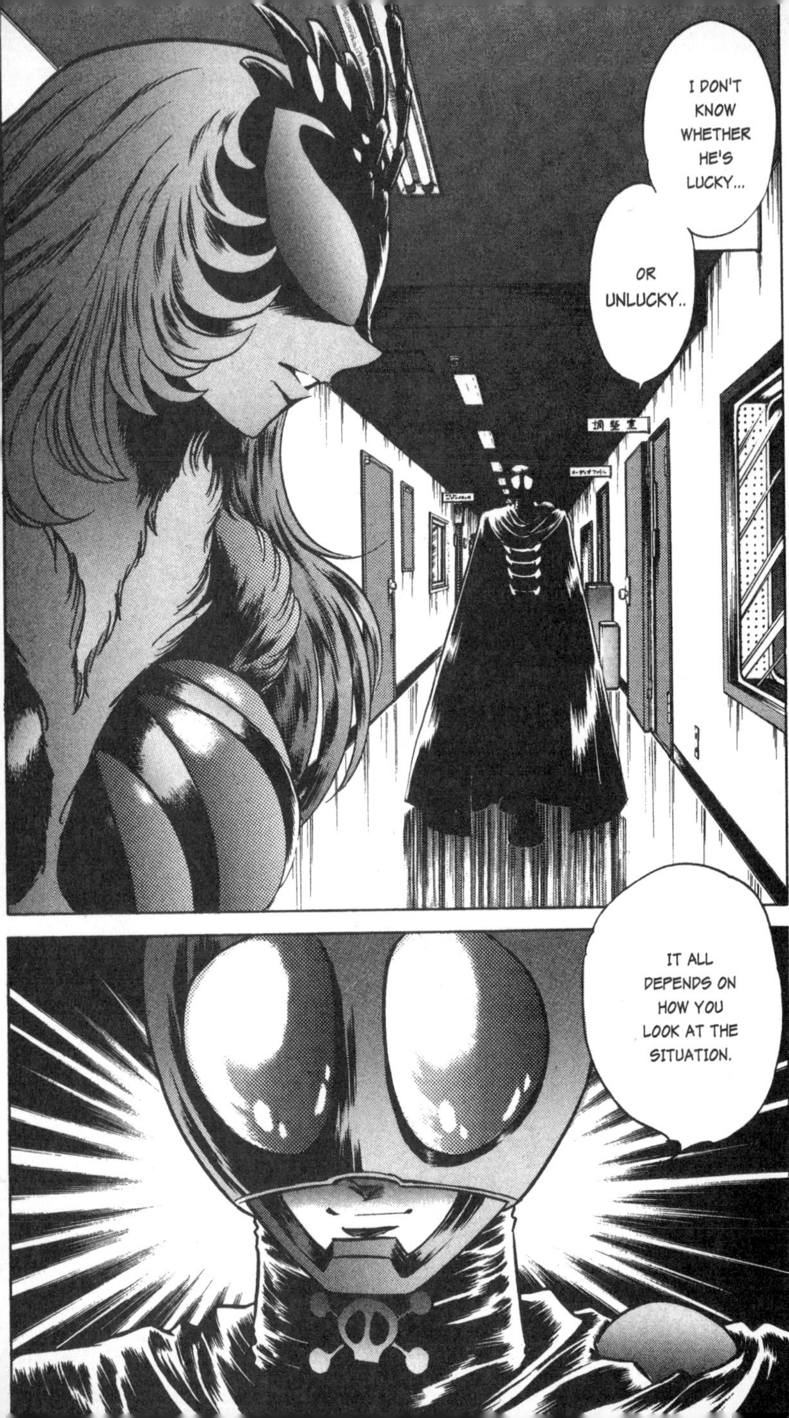
I DON'T KNOW WHETHER HE'S LUCKY...
OR UNLUCKY..
IT ALL DEPENDS ON HOW YOU LOOK AT THE SITUATION.

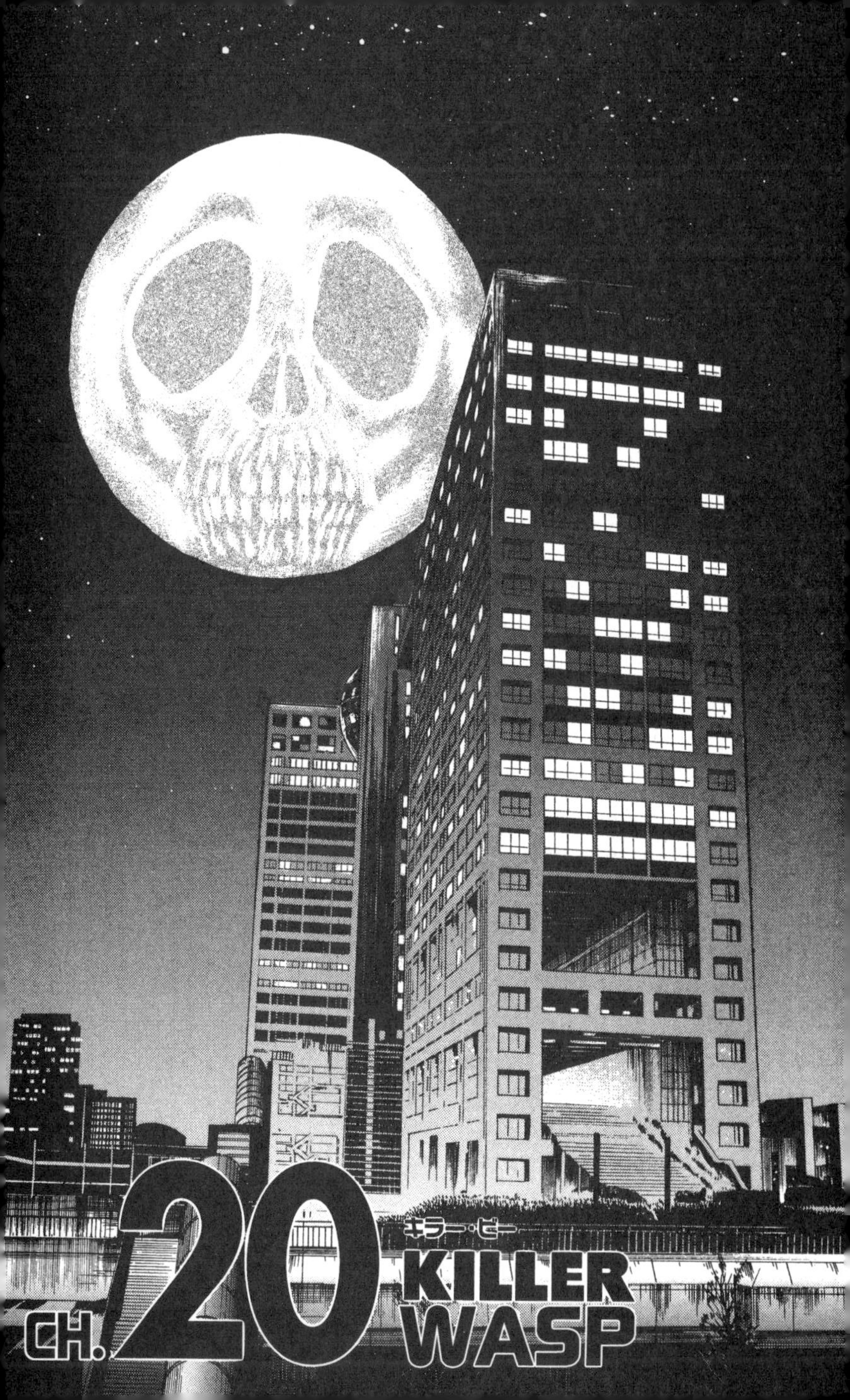
CH. 20
キラー・ビー
KILLER WASP

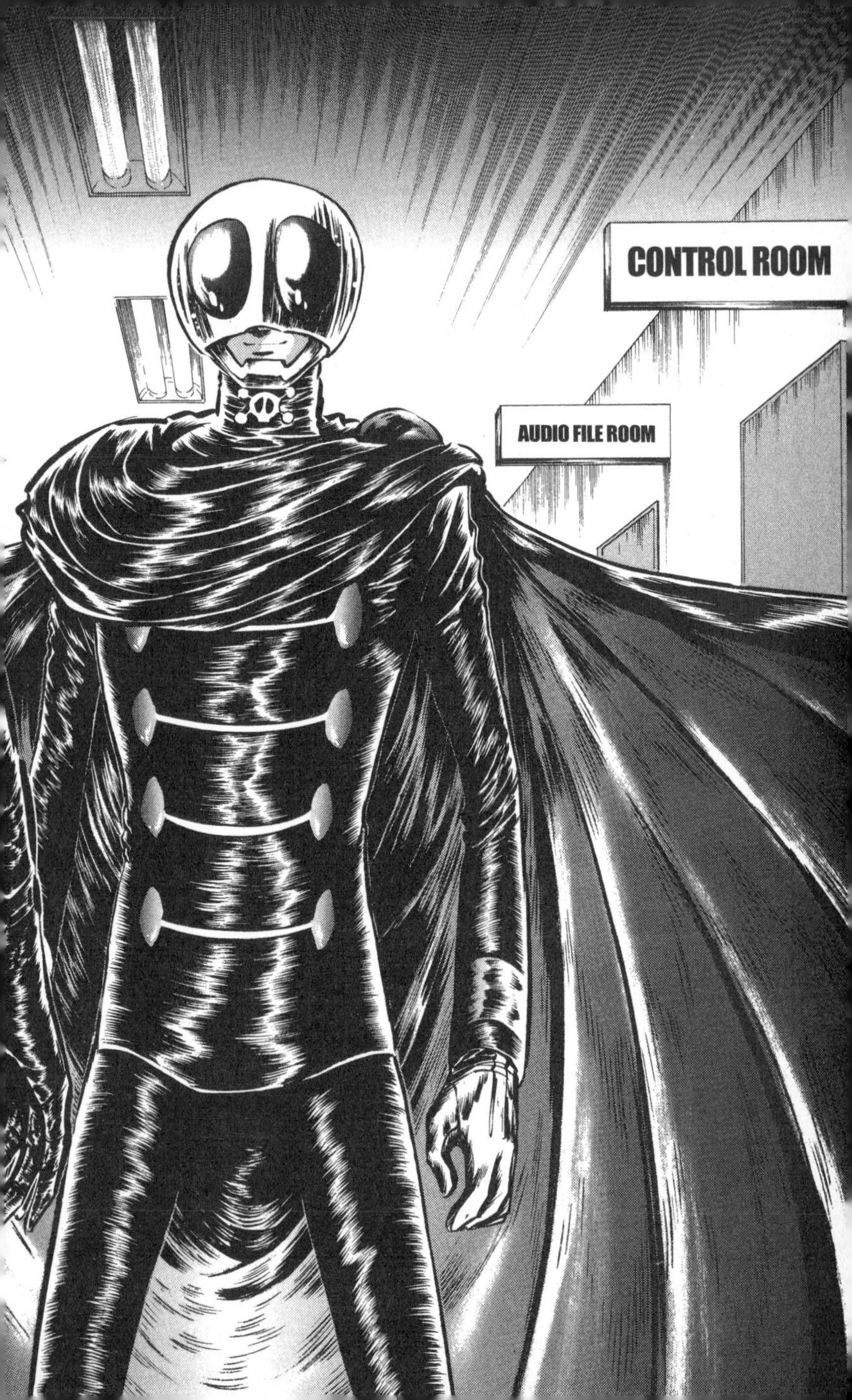
CONTROL ROOM
AUDIO FILE ROOM

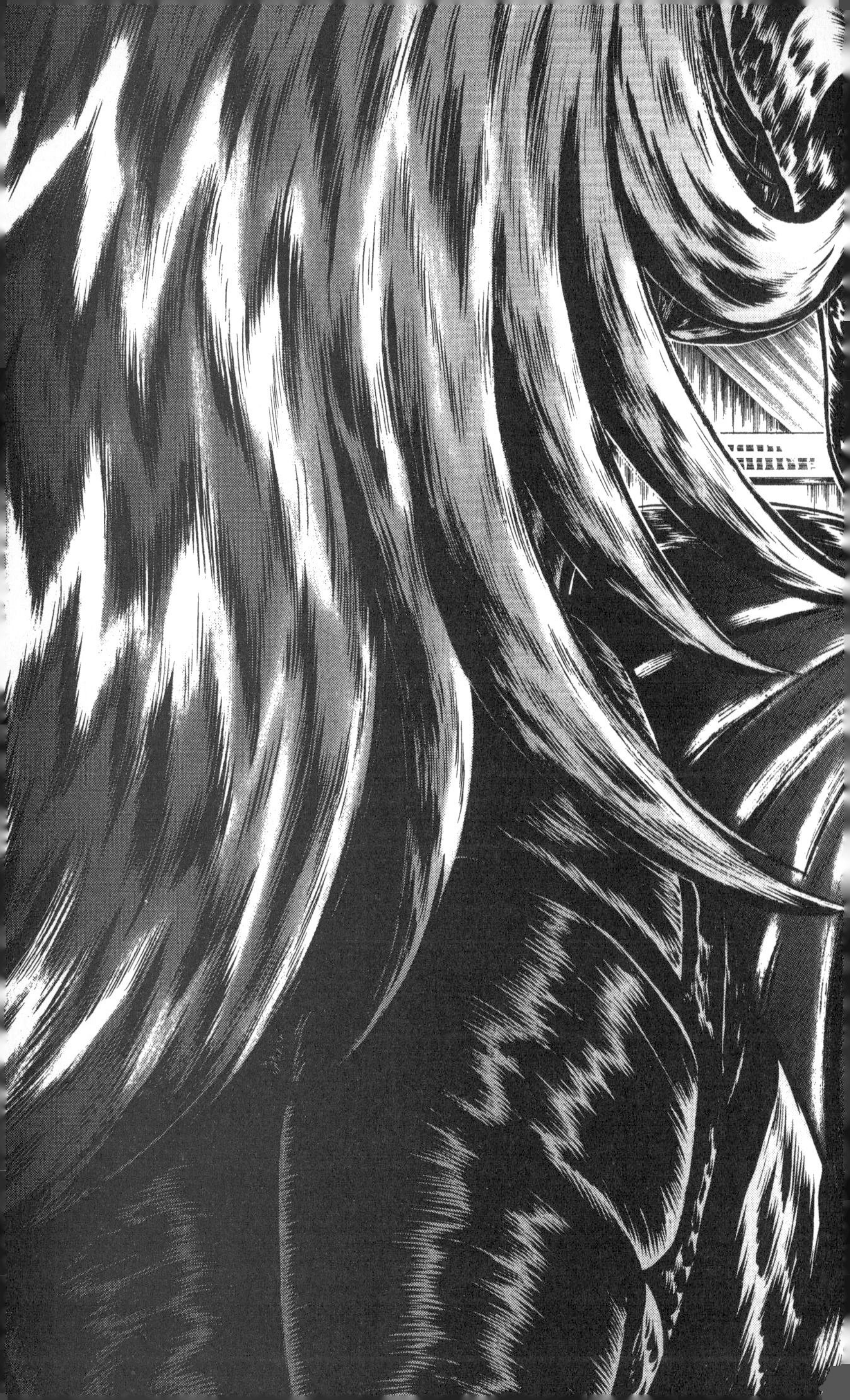

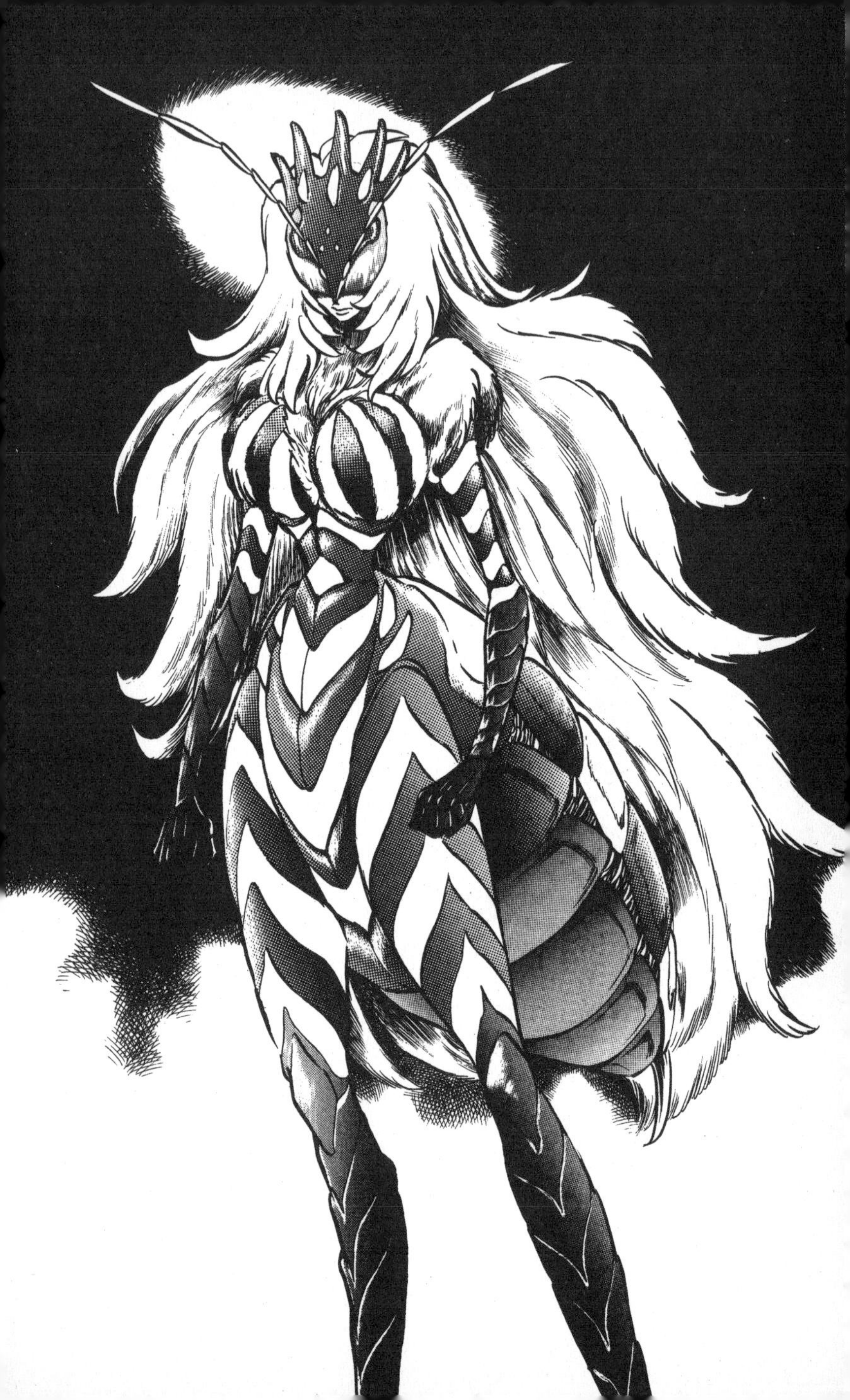

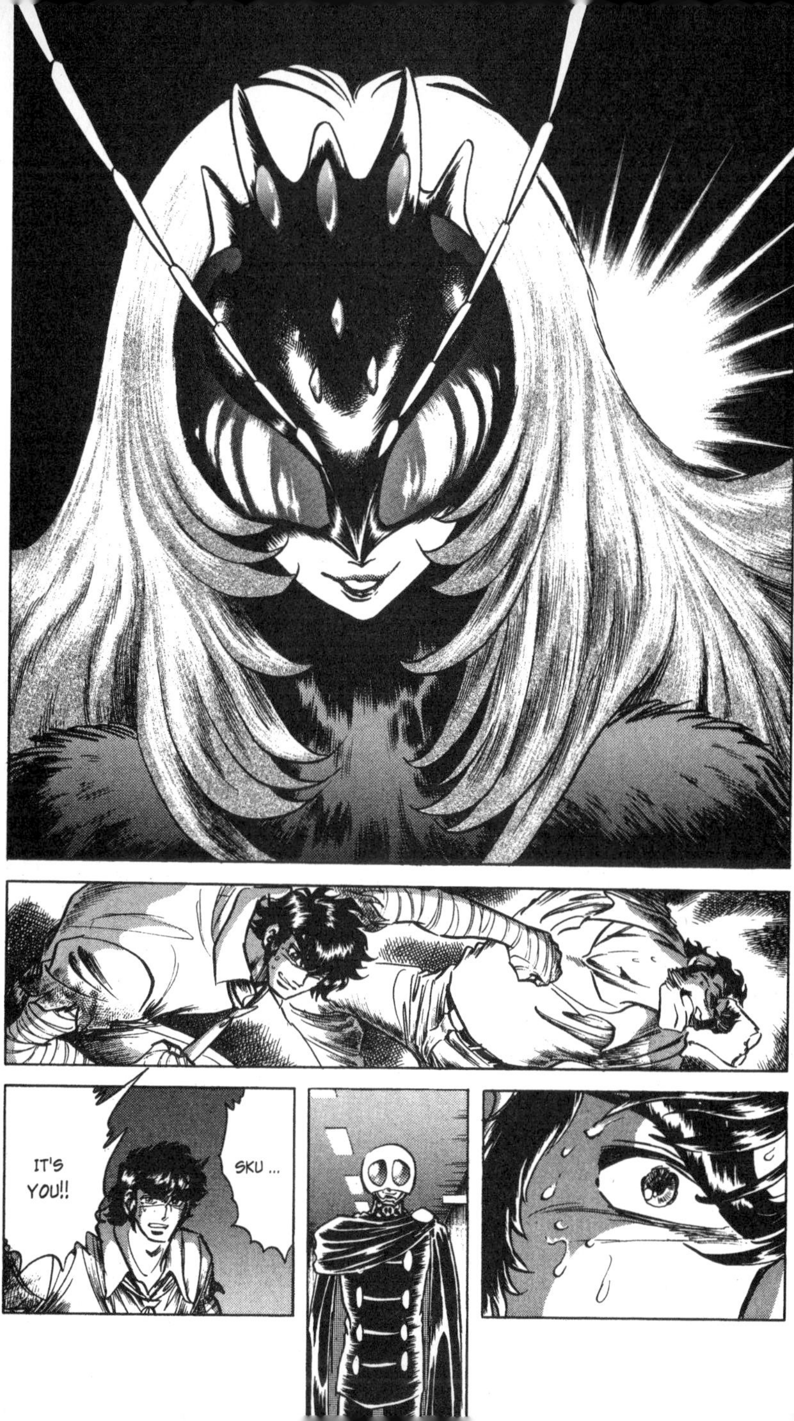
SKU ...
IT'S YOU!!

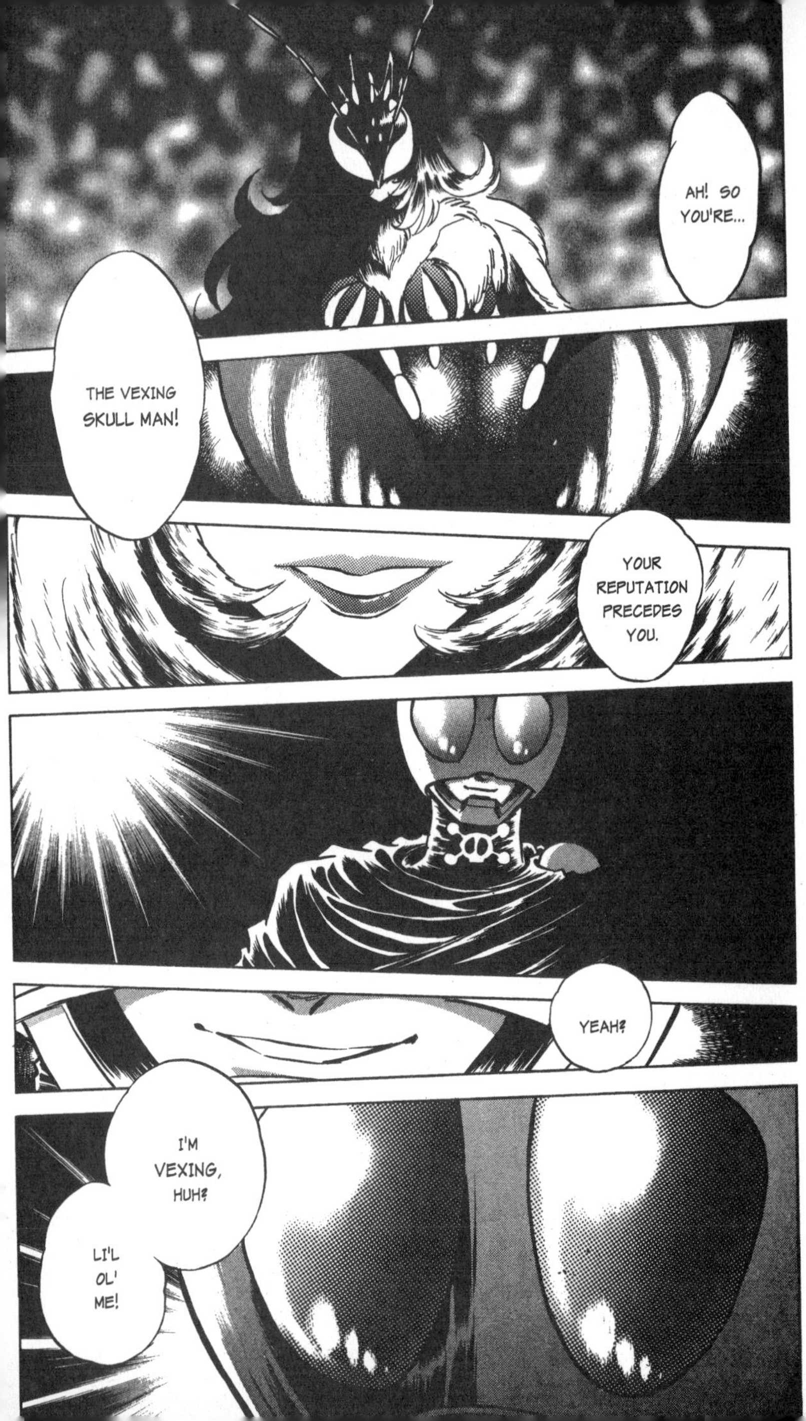
AH! SO YOU'RE...
THE VEXING SKULL MAN!
YOUR REPUTATION PRECEDES YOU.
YEAH?
I'M VEXING, HUH?
LI'L OL' ME!

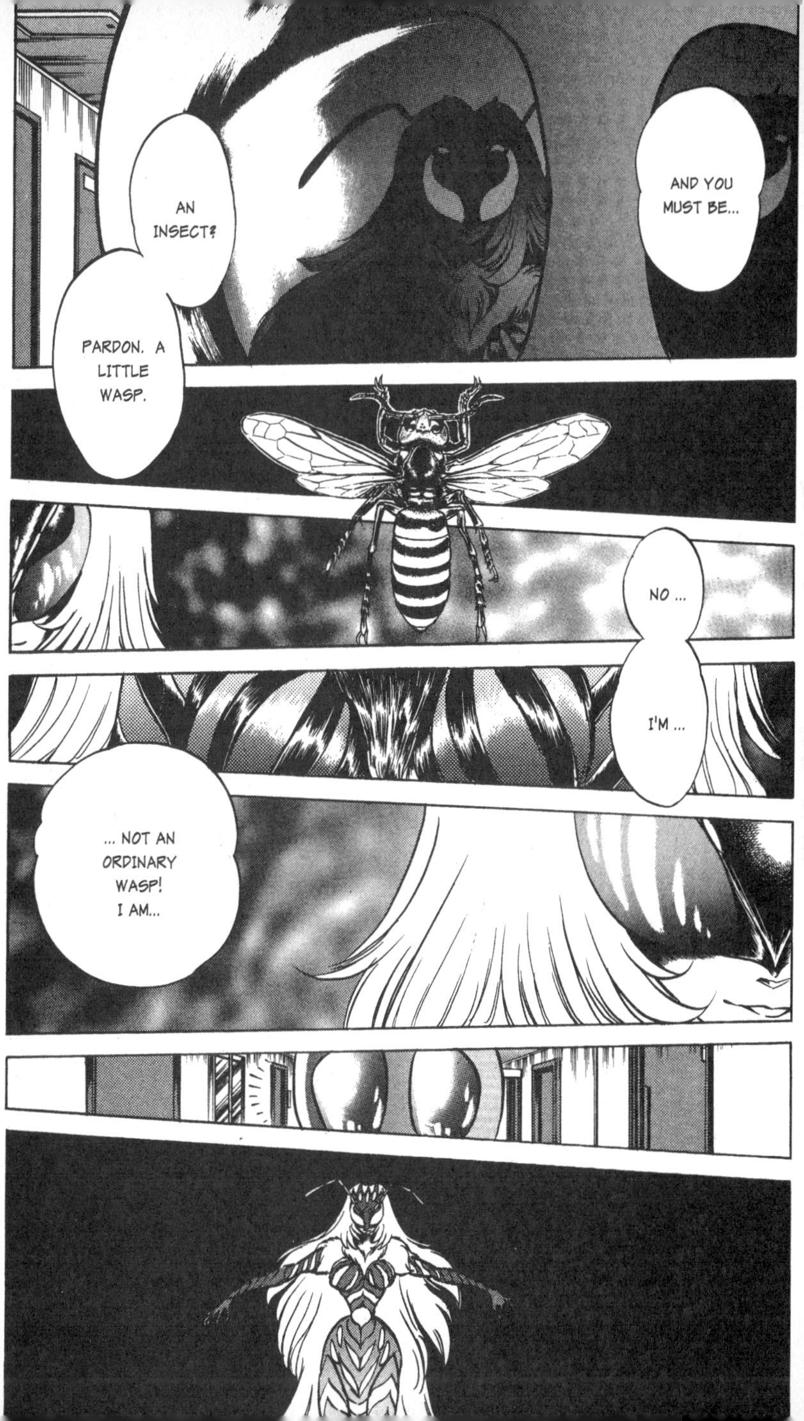
AND YOU MUST BE...
AN INSECT?
PARDON. A LITTLE WASP.
NO ...
I'M ...
... NOT AN ORDINARY WASP! I AM...

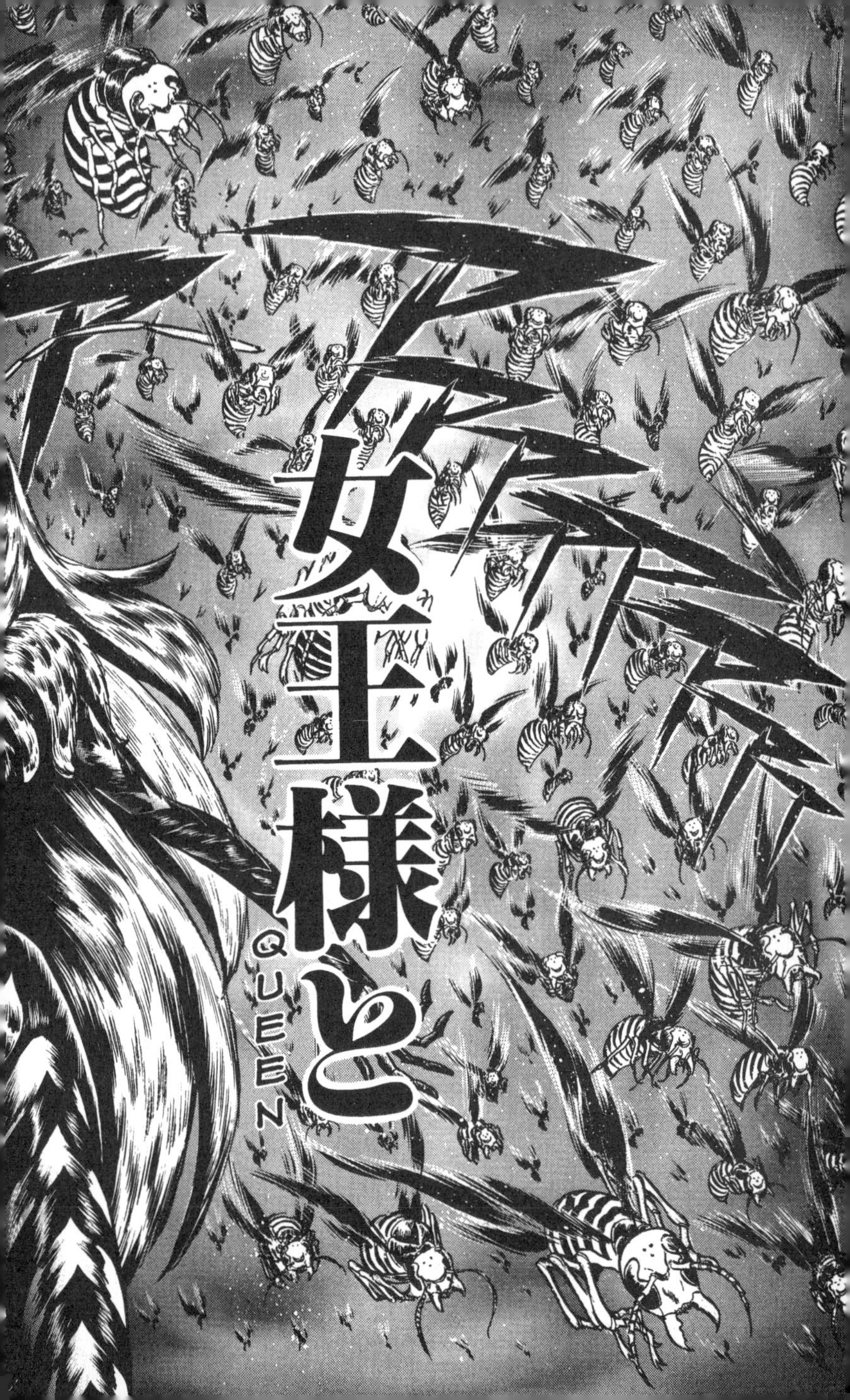
女王様と
QUEEN

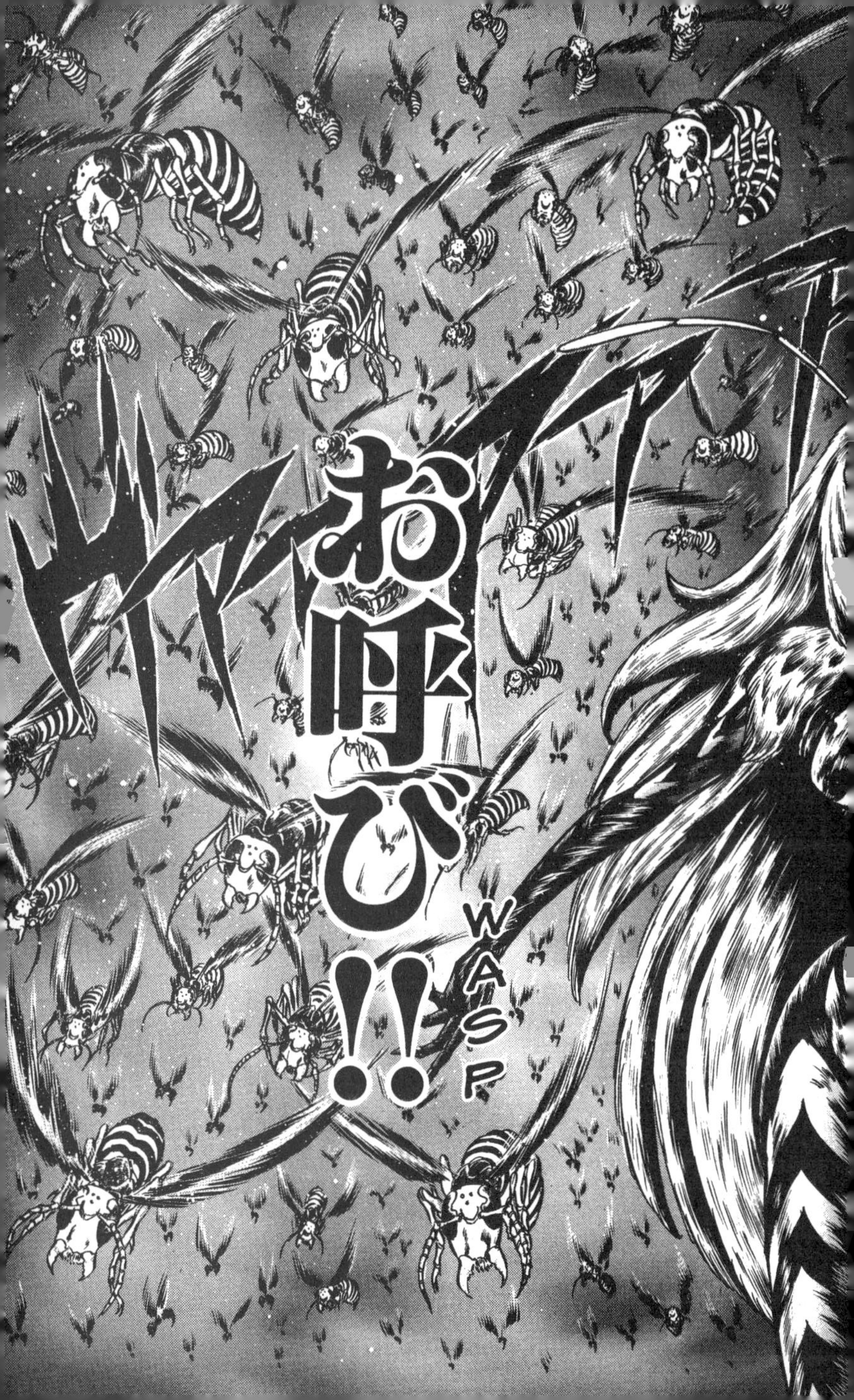
お呼び!!
WASP

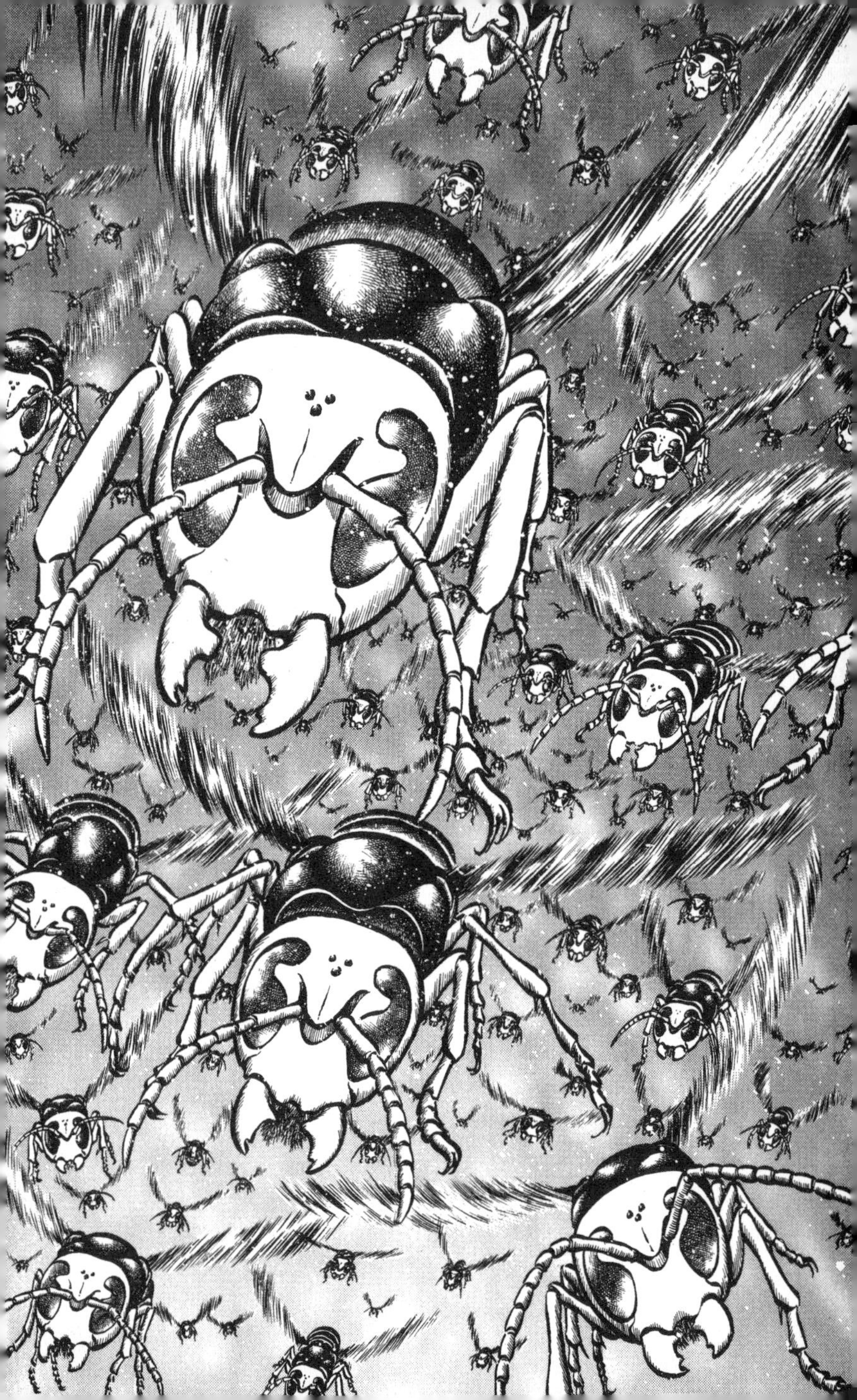

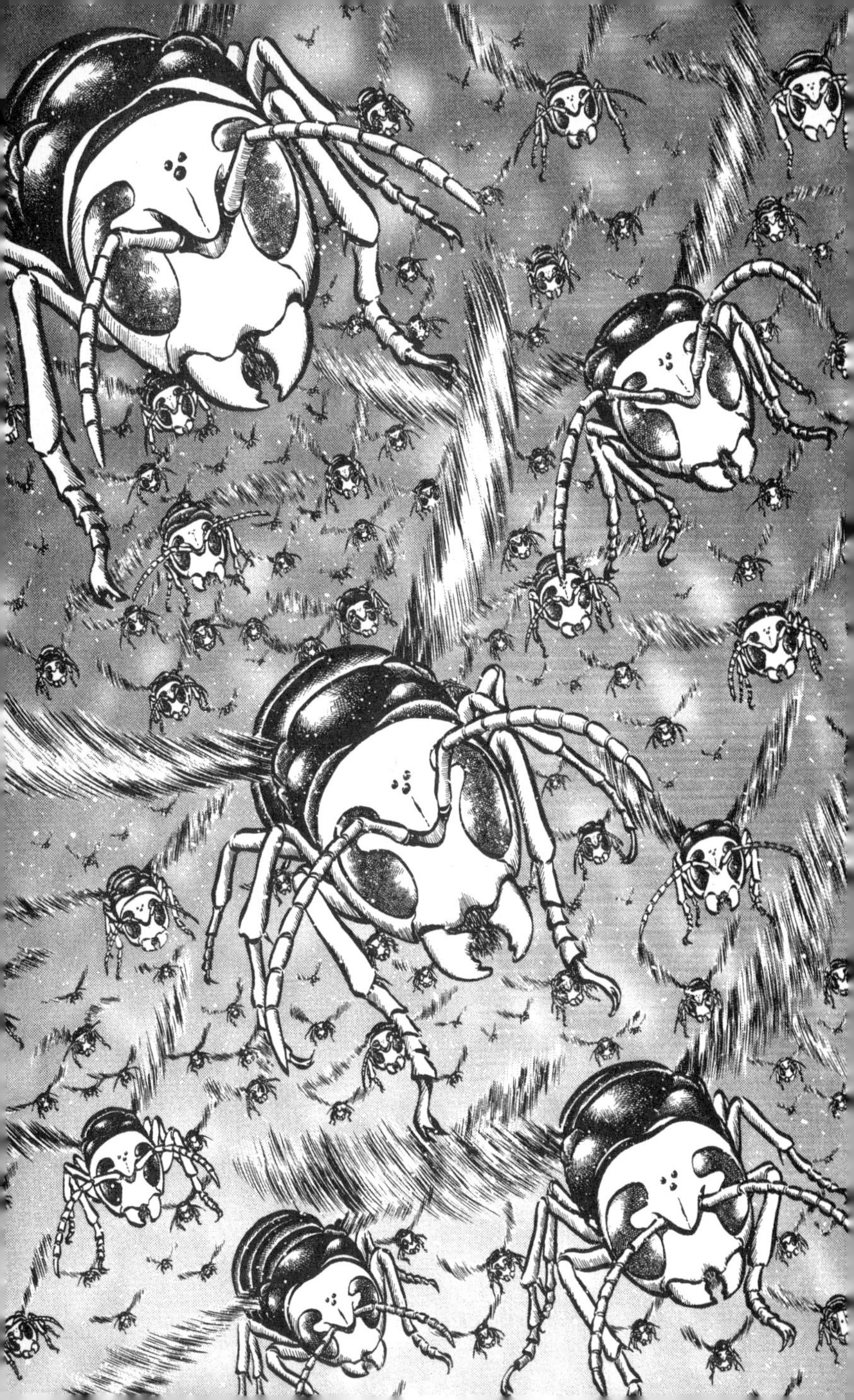

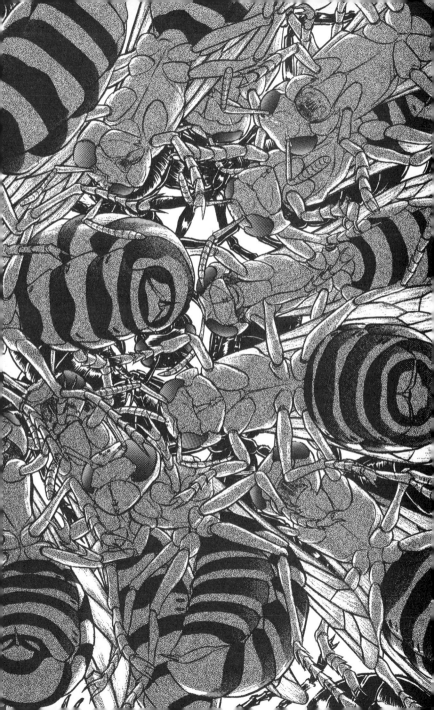

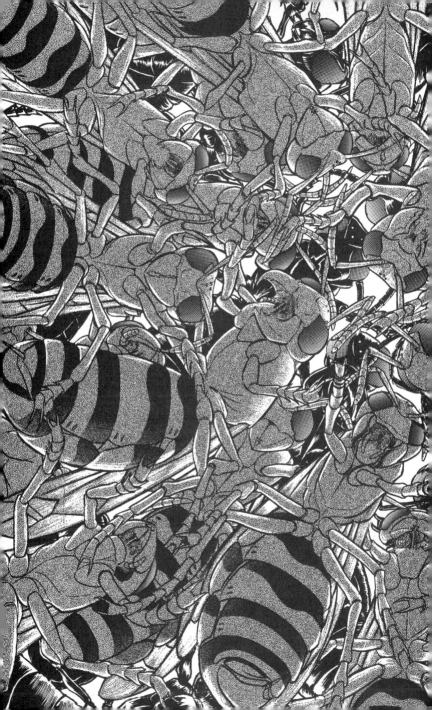

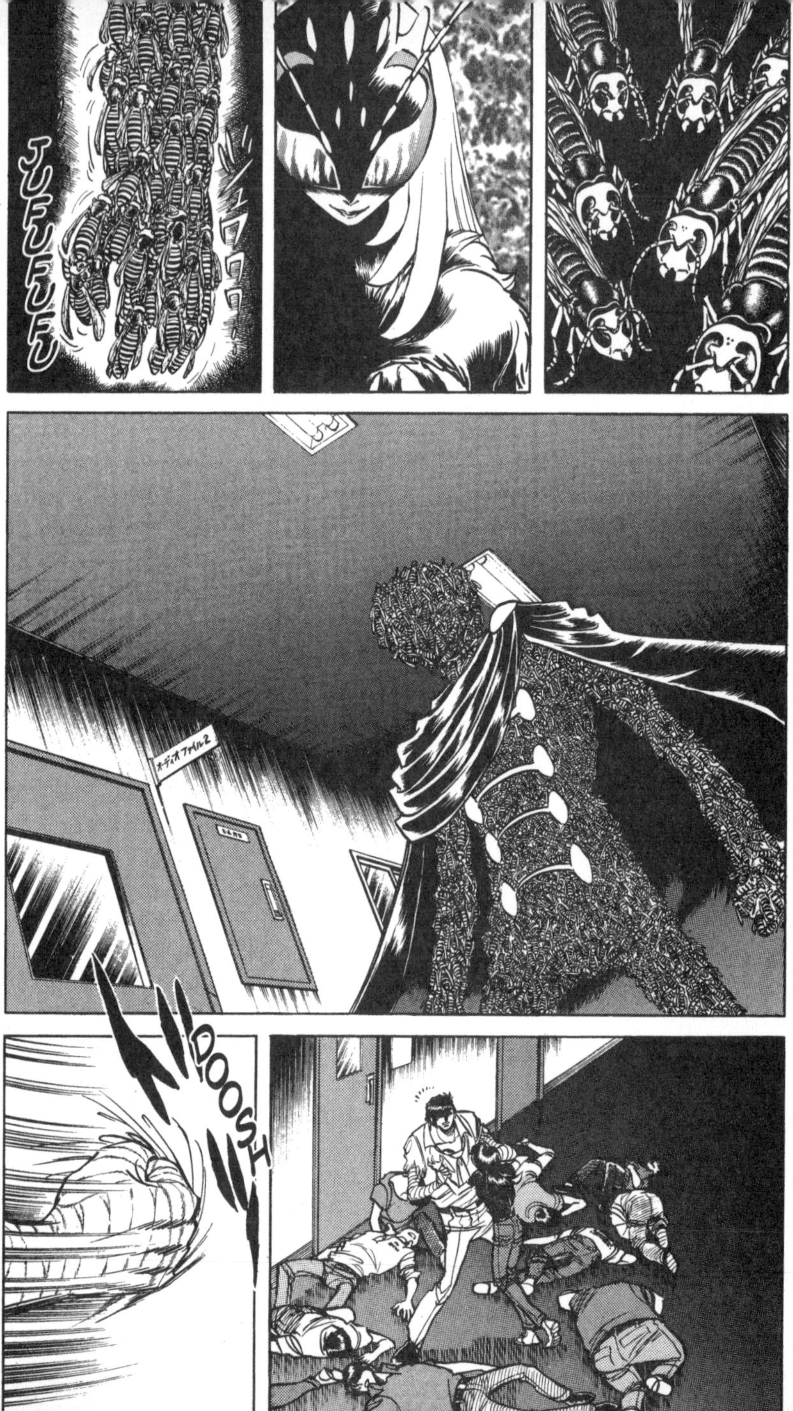
JUFUFUFU
オーディオファイル2
DOOSH

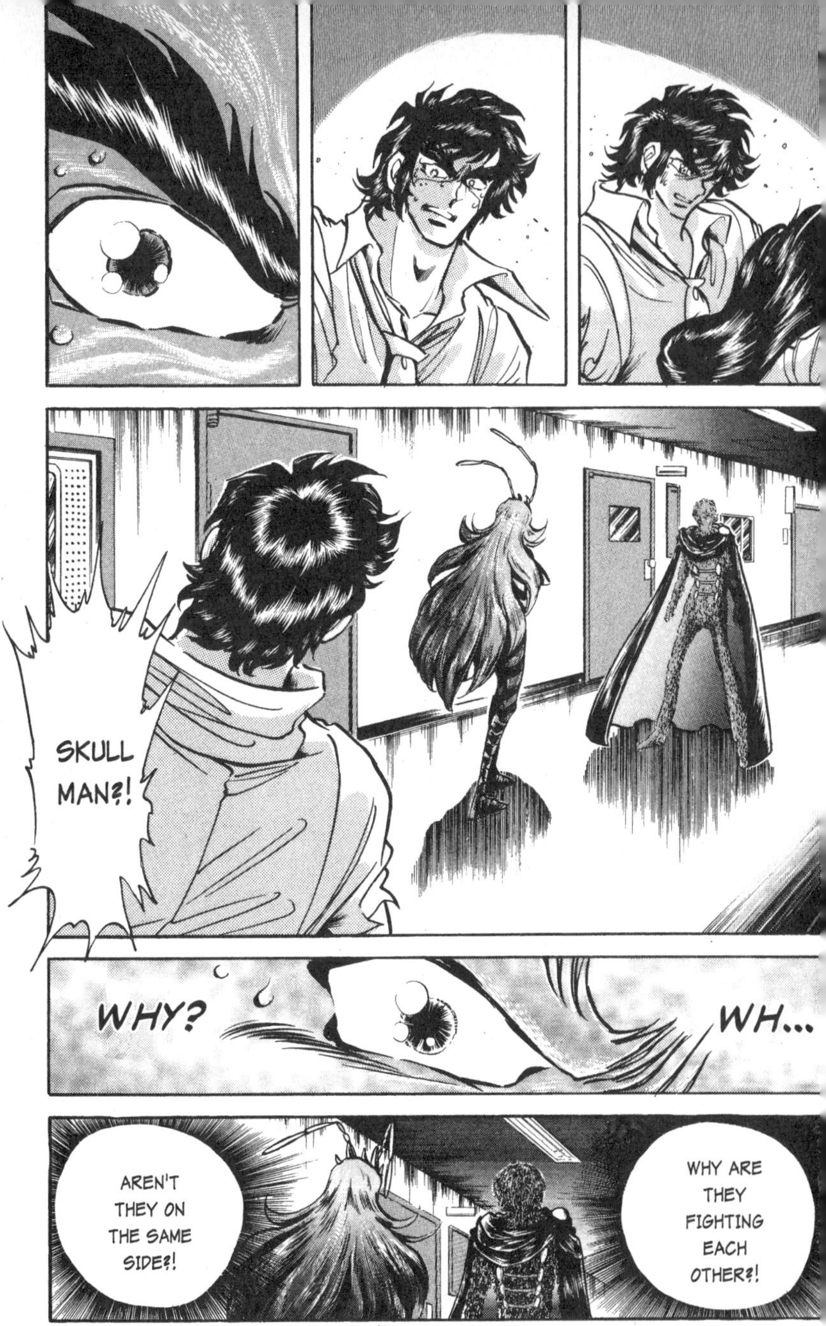
SKULL MAN?!
WH...
WHY?
WHY ARE THEY FIGHTING EACH OTHER?!
AREN'T THEY ON THE SAME SIDE?!

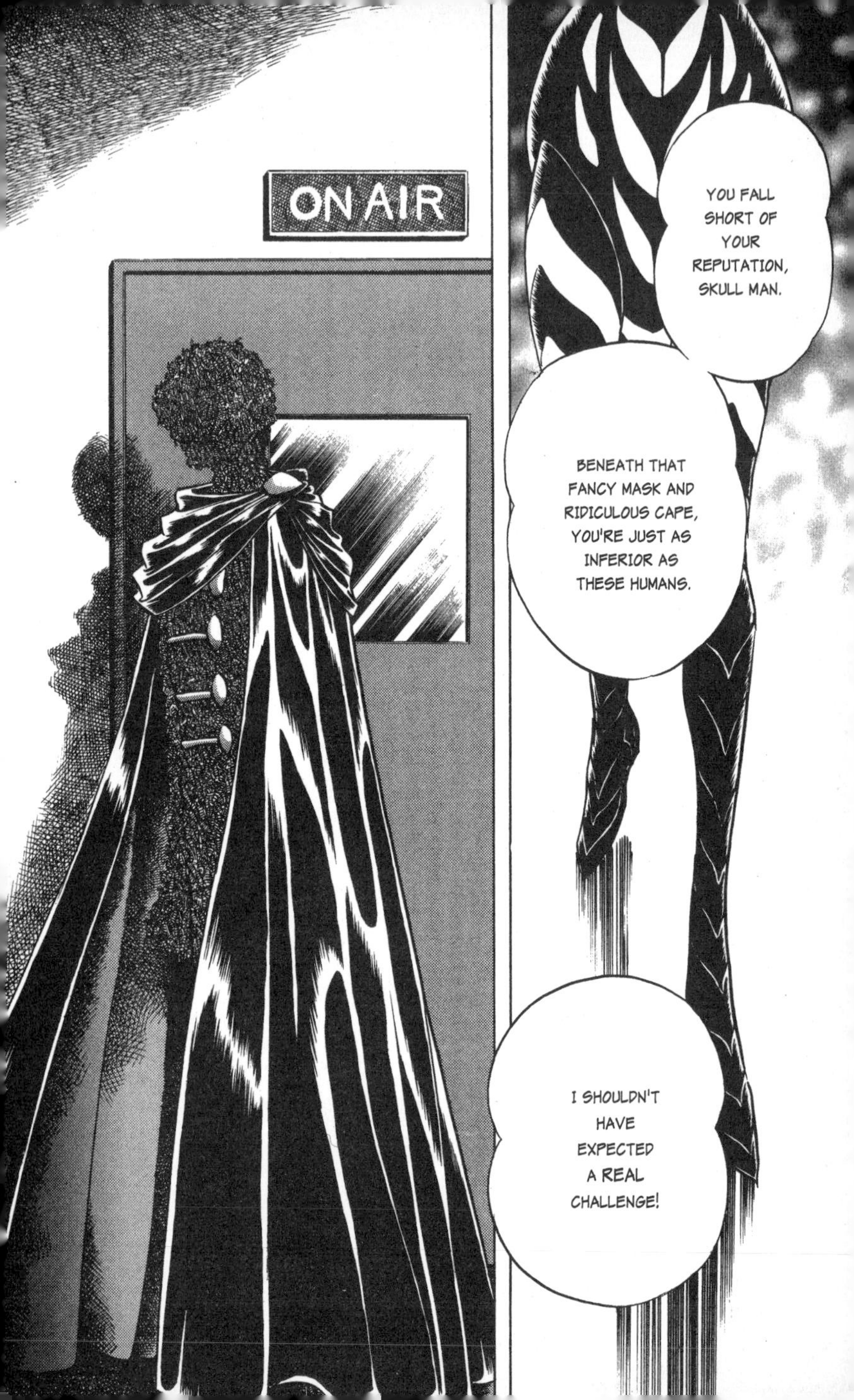
YOU FALL SHORT OF YOUR REPUTATION, SKULL MAN.
BENEATH THAT FANCY MASK AND RIDICULOUS CAPE, YOU'RE JUST AS INFERIOR AS THESE HUMANS.
I SHOULDN'T HAVE EXPECTED A REAL CHALLENGE!
ON AIR

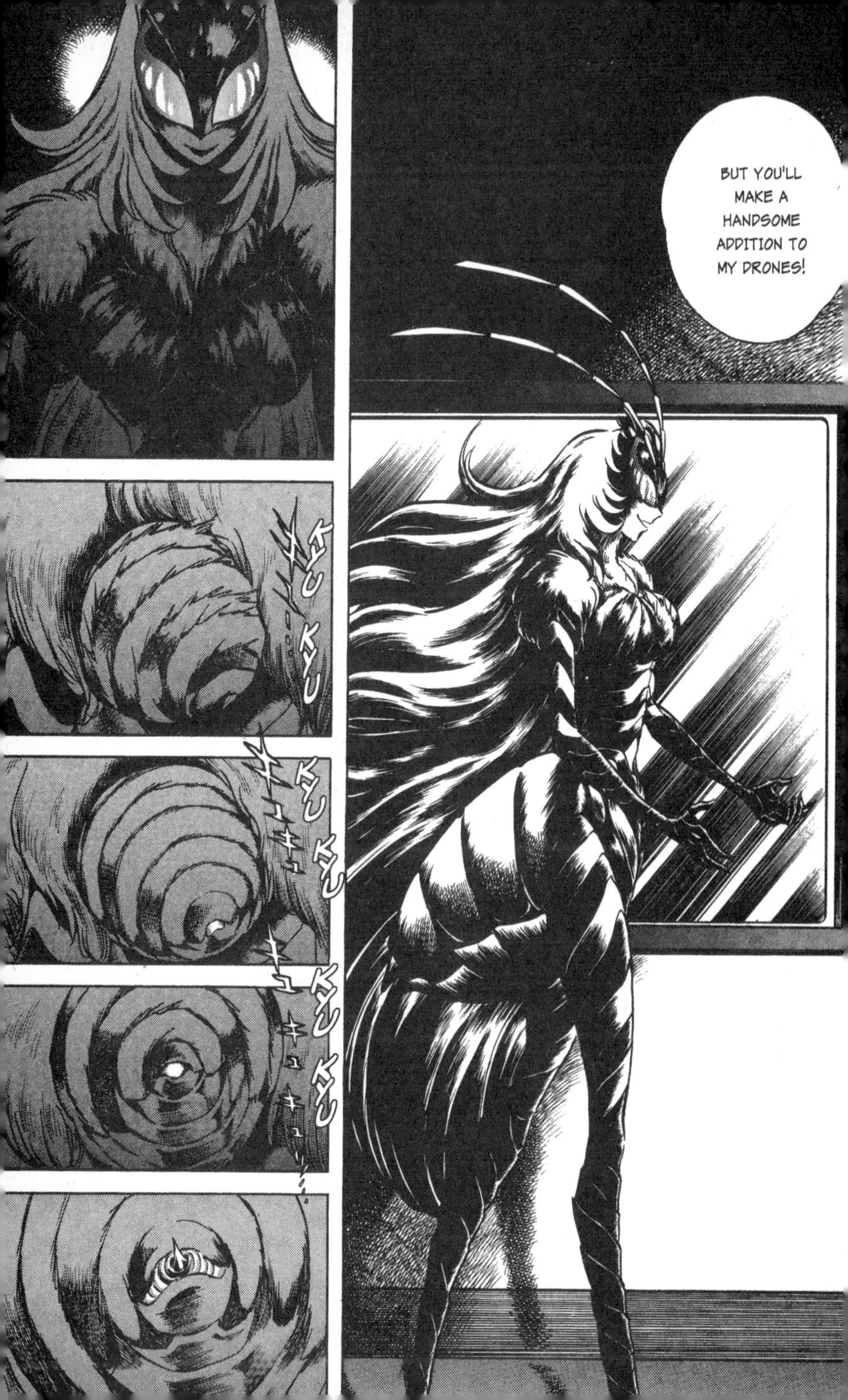
BUT YOU'LL MAKE A HANDSOME ADDITION TO MY DRONES!
KYU KYU
KYU KYU
KYU KYU KYU

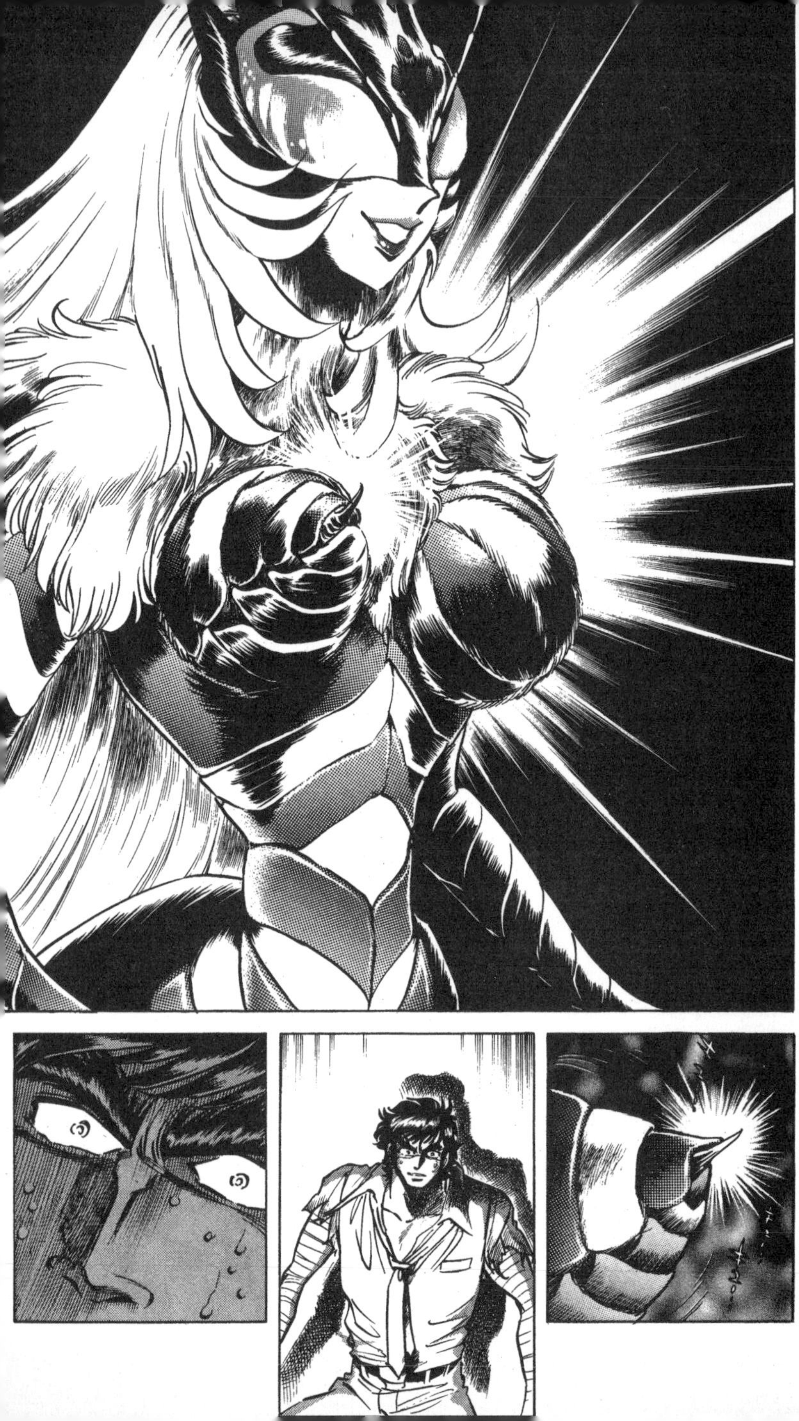

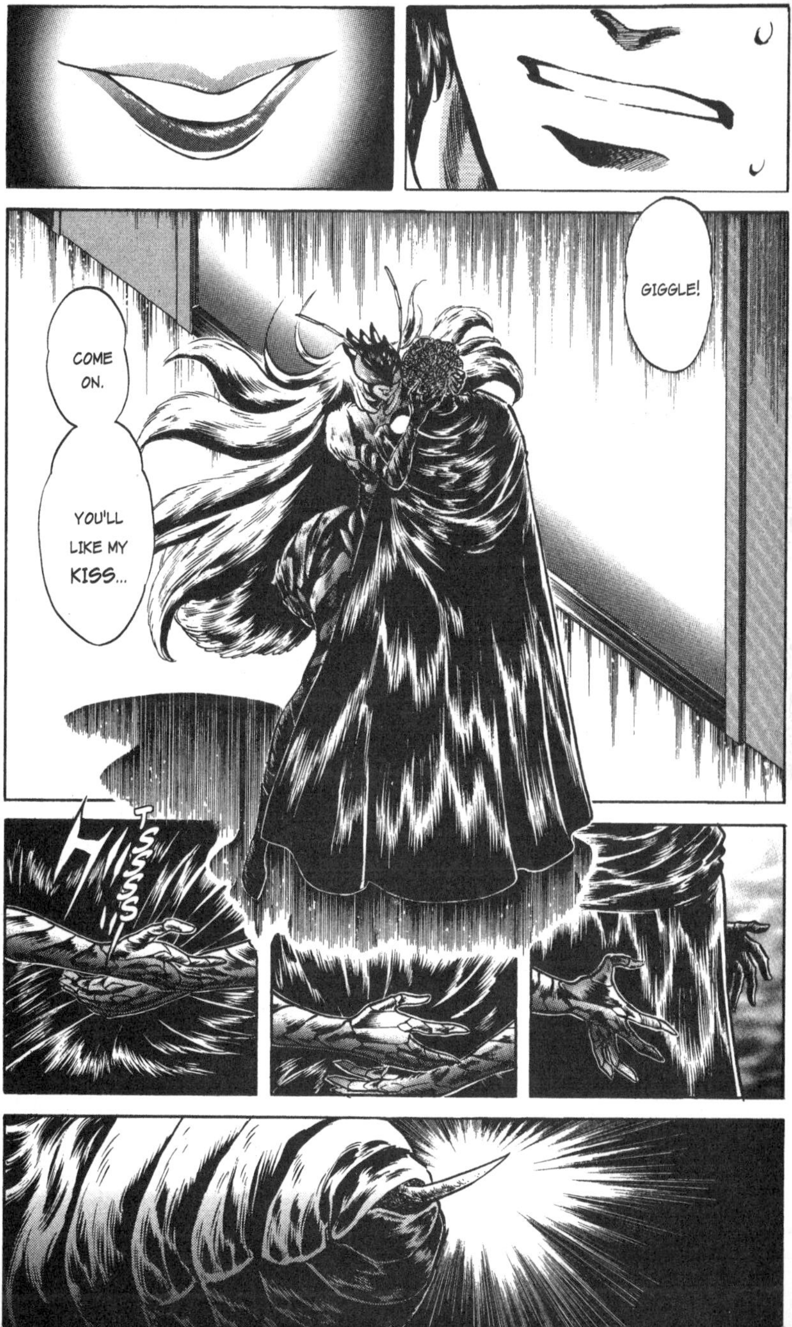
GIGGLE!
COME ON.
YOU'LL LIKE MY KISS...
TSSSSS
HISS

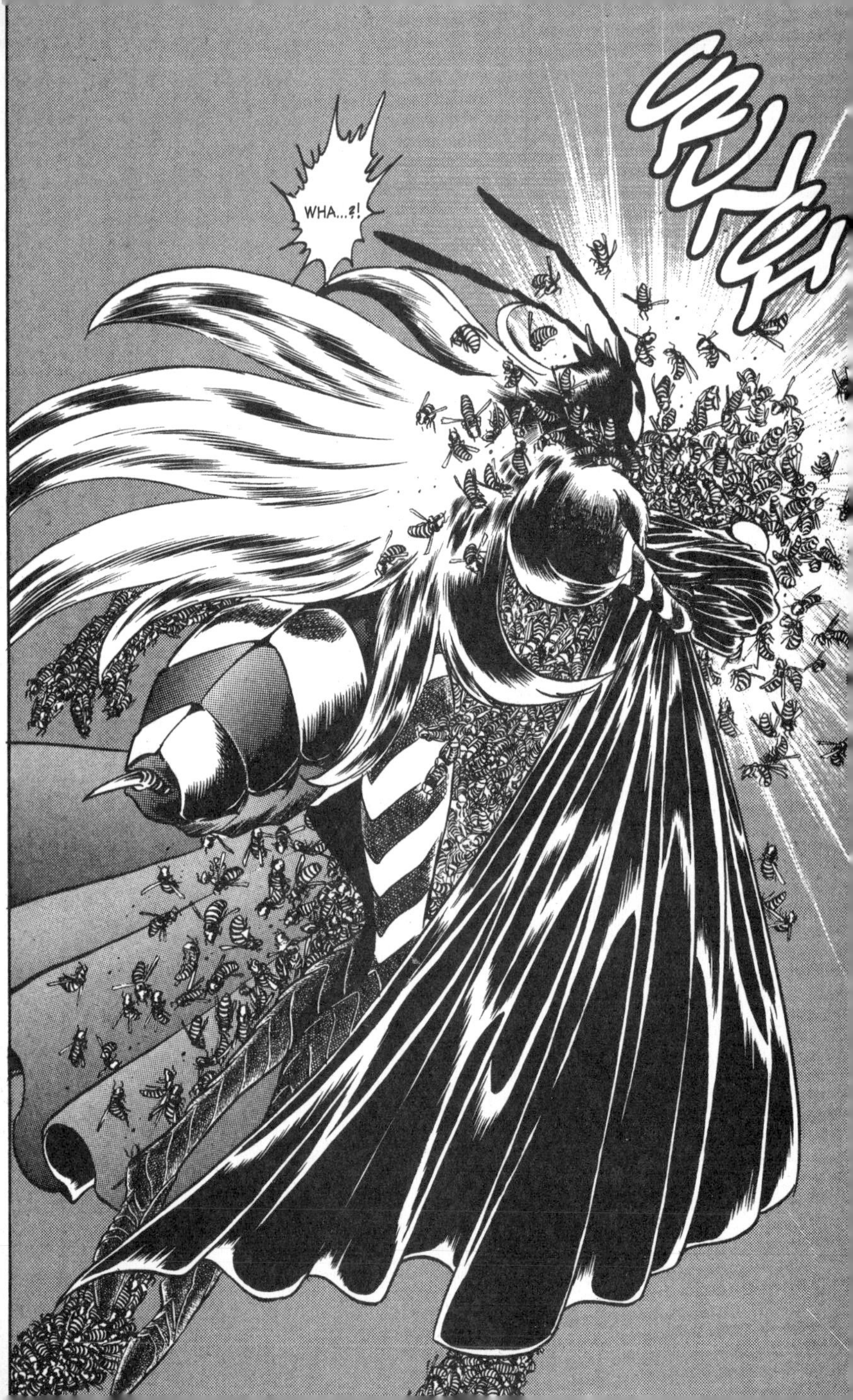
WHA...?!

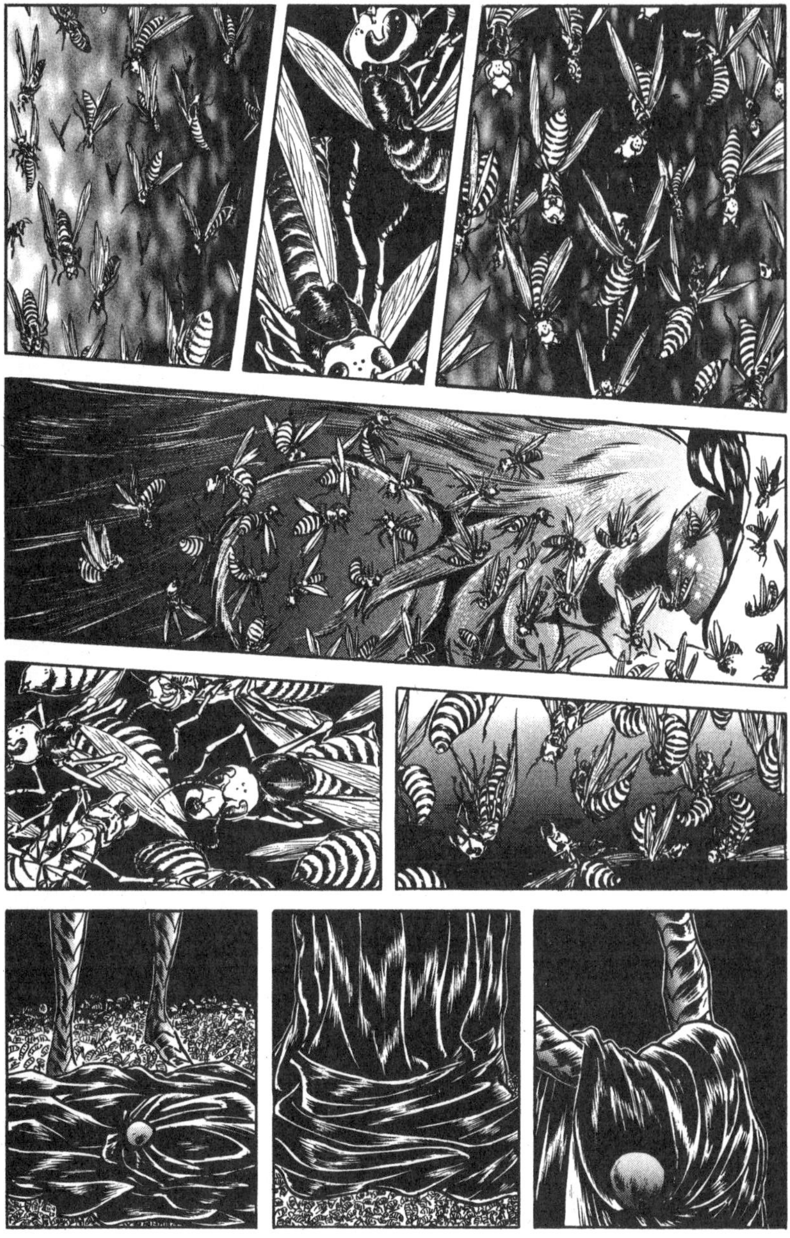

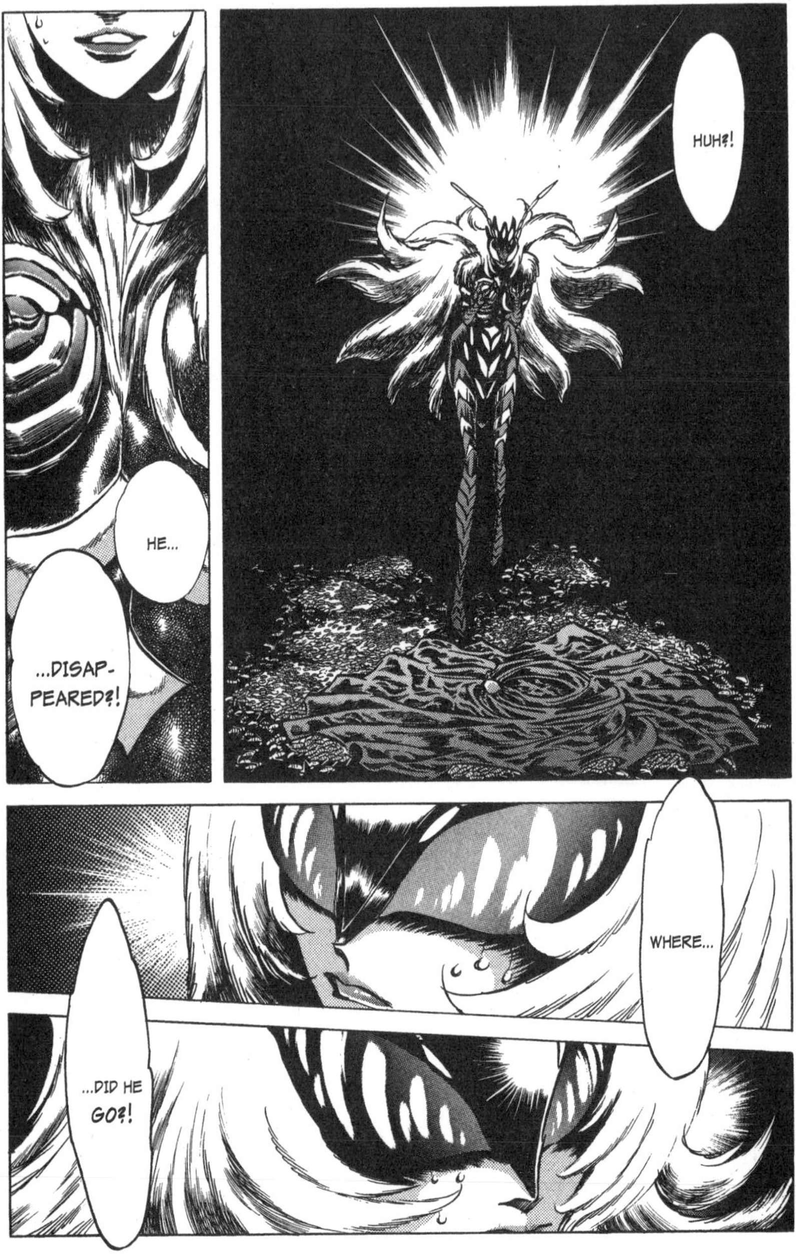
HUH?!
HE...
...DISAP-PEARED?!
WHERE...
...DID HE GO?!

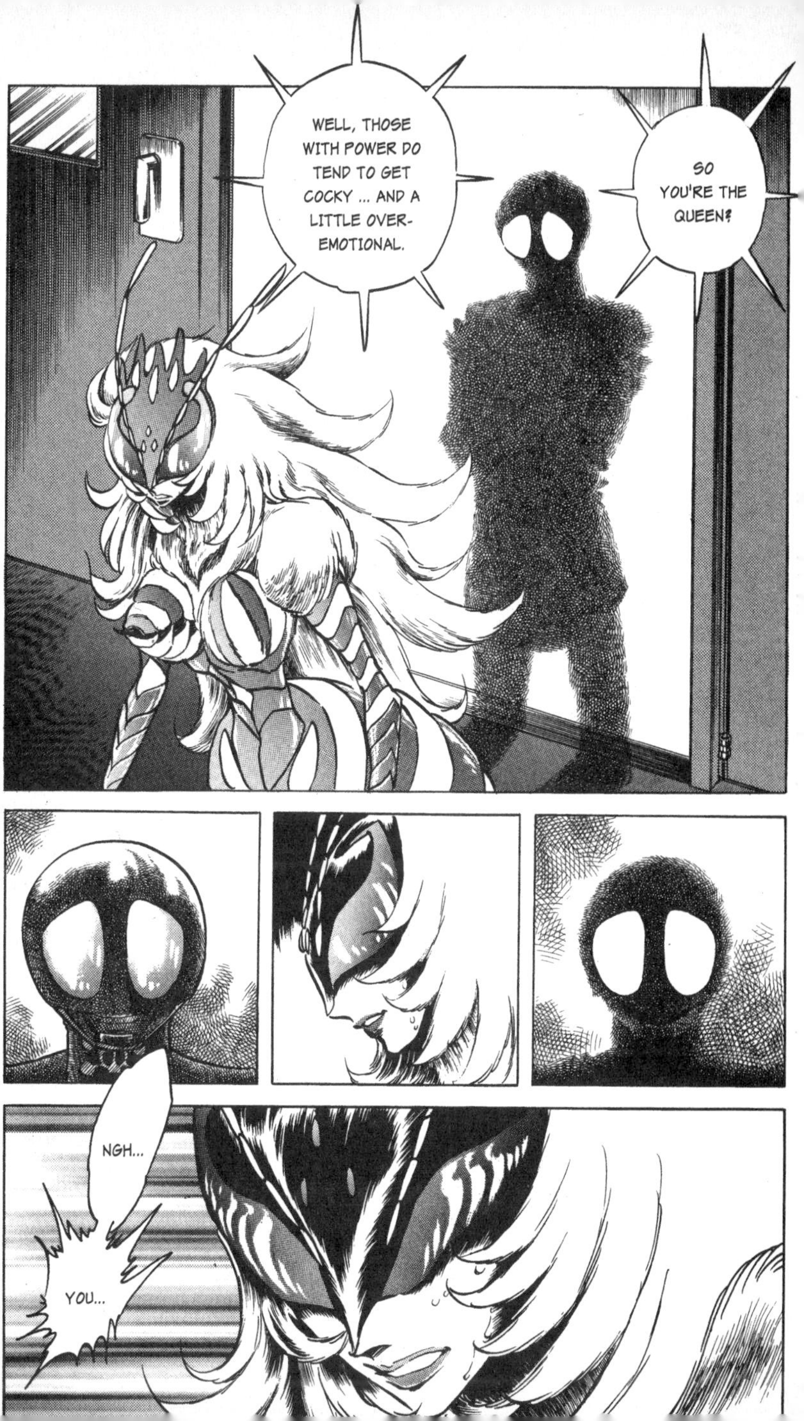
SO YOU'RE THE QUEEN?
WELL, THOSE WITH POWER DO TEND TO GET COCKY ... AND A LITTLE OVER-EMOTIONAL.
NGH...
YOU...

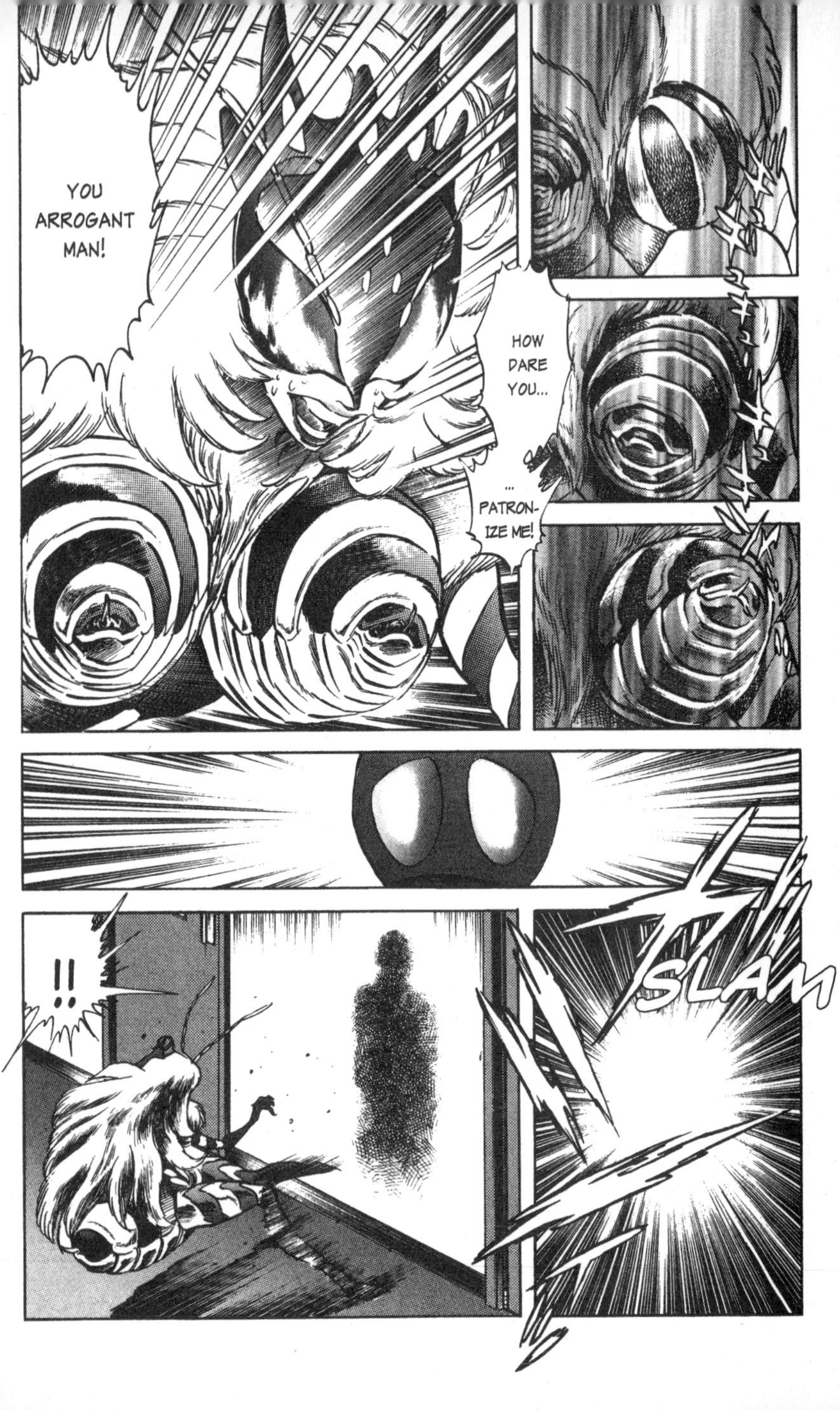
HOW DARE YOU...
... PATRON-IZE ME!
YOU ARROGANT MAN!
SLAM
!!

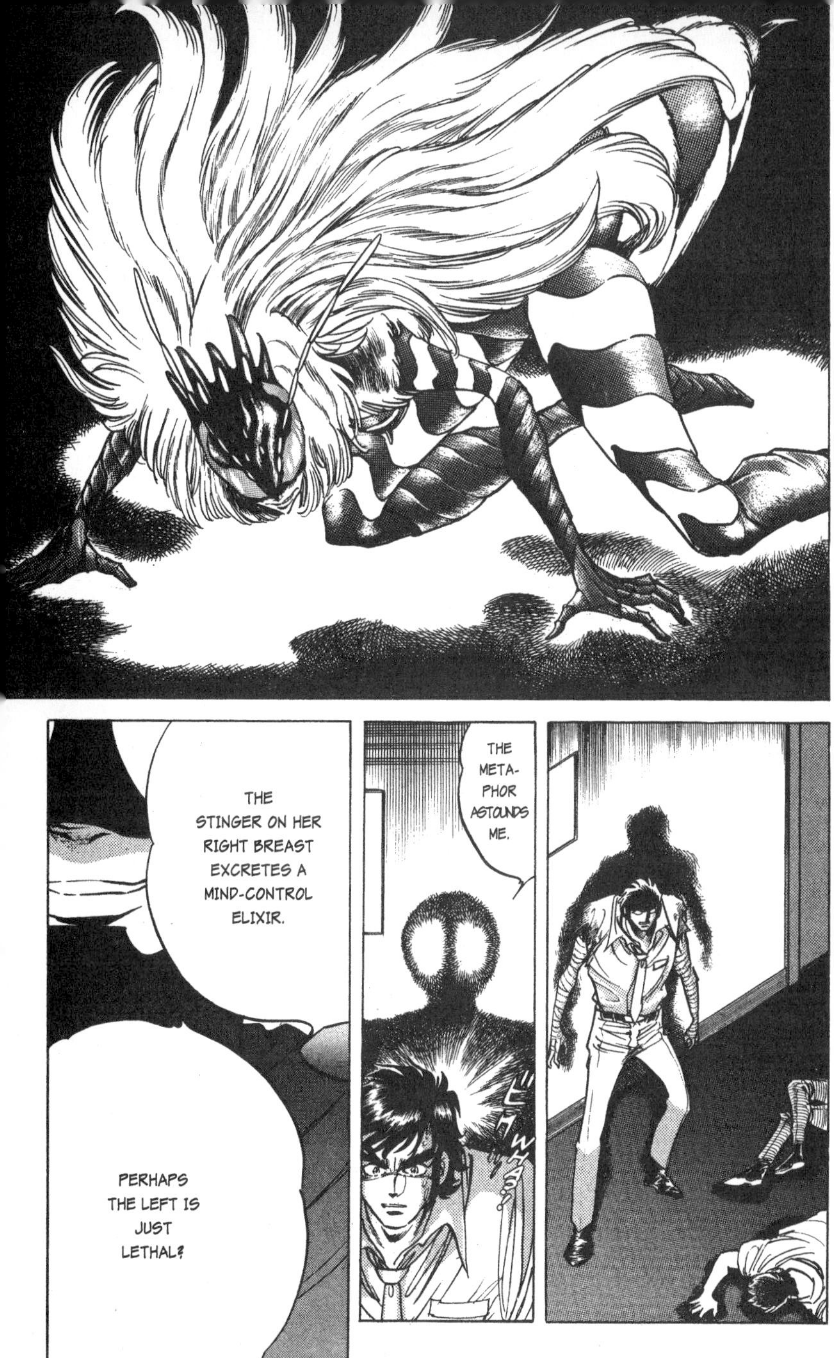
THE META-PHOR ASTOUNDS ME.
THE STINGER ON HER RIGHT BREAST EXCRETES A MIND-CONTROL ELIXIR.
PERHAPS THE LEFT IS JUST LETHAL?

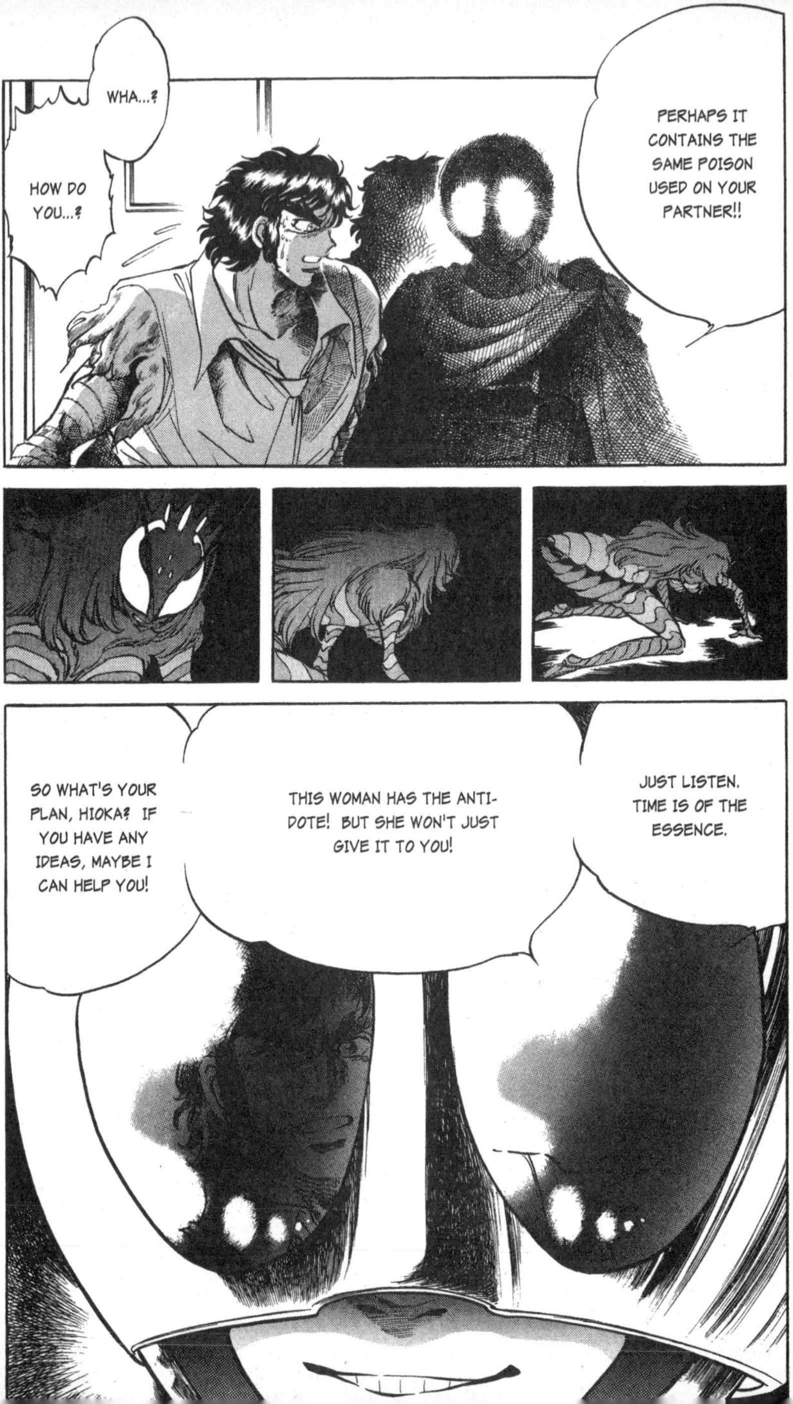
PERHAPS IT CONTAINS THE SAME POISON USED ON YOUR PARTNER!!
WHA...?
HOW DO YOU...?
JUST LISTEN. TIME IS OF THE ESSENCE.
THIS WOMAN HAS THE ANTI-DOTE! BUT SHE WON'T JUST GIVE IT TO YOU!
SO WHAT'S YOUR PLAN, HIOKA? IF YOU HAVE ANY IDEAS, MAYBE I CAN HELP YOU!

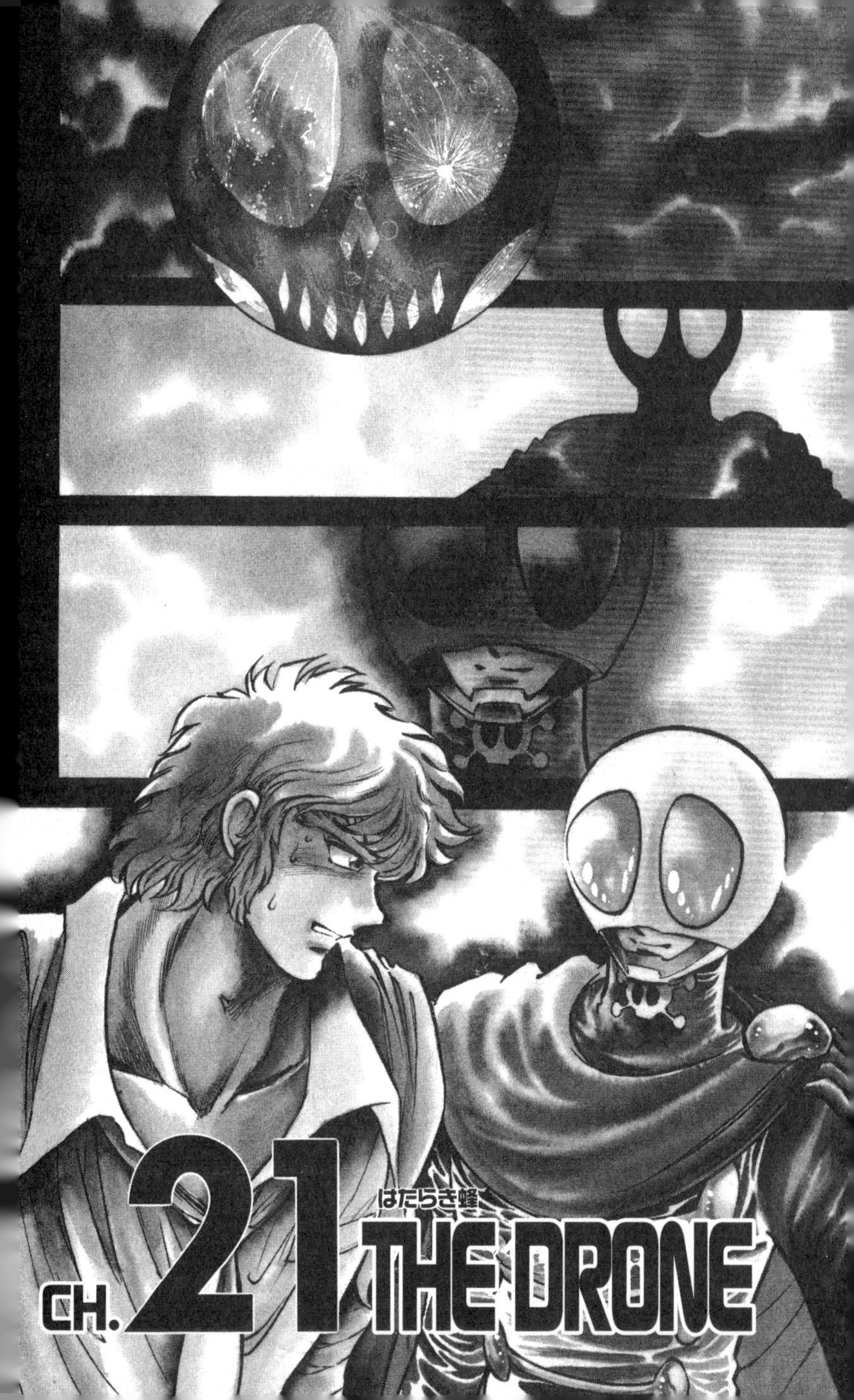
はたらき蜂
CH. 21 THE DRONE

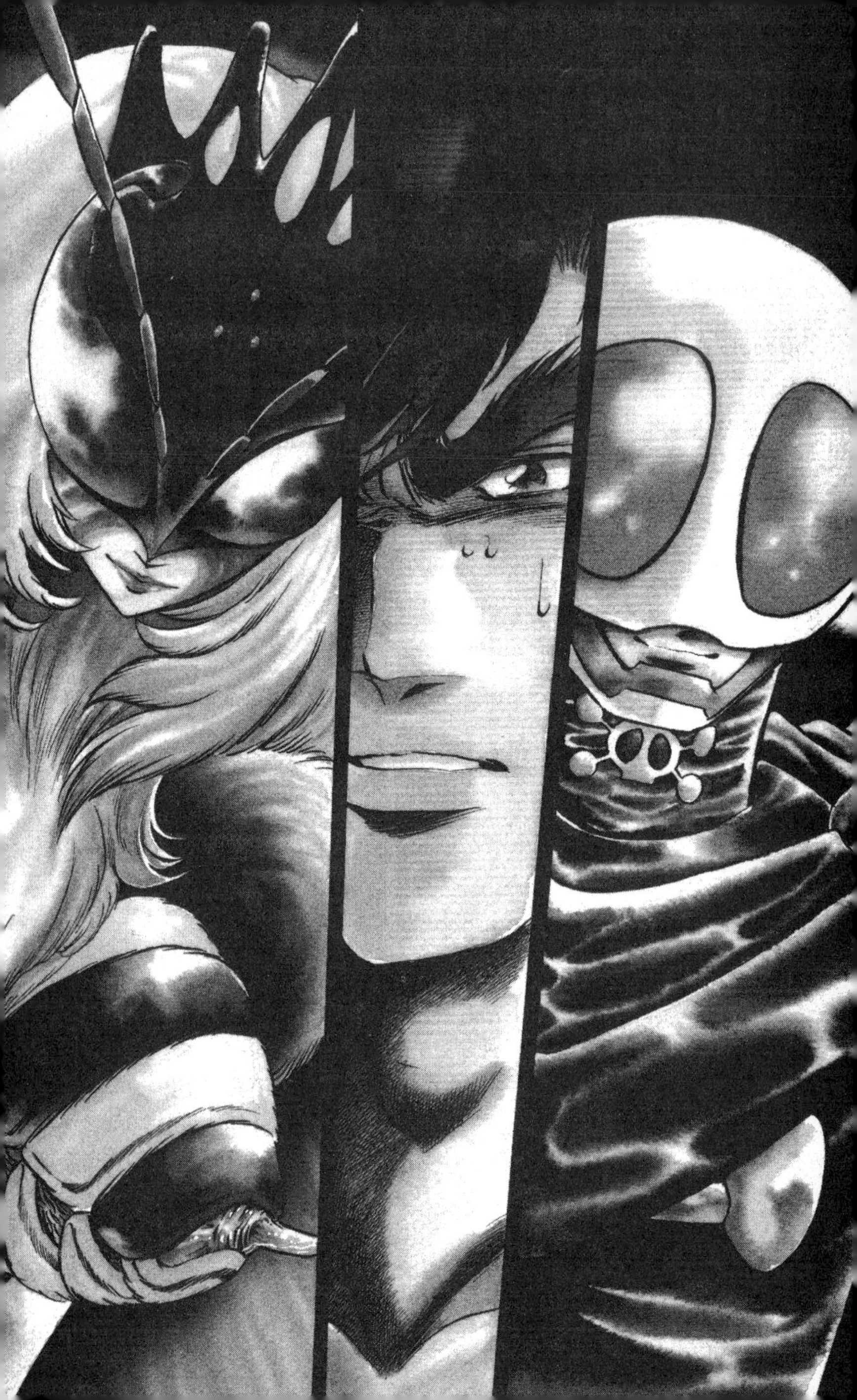

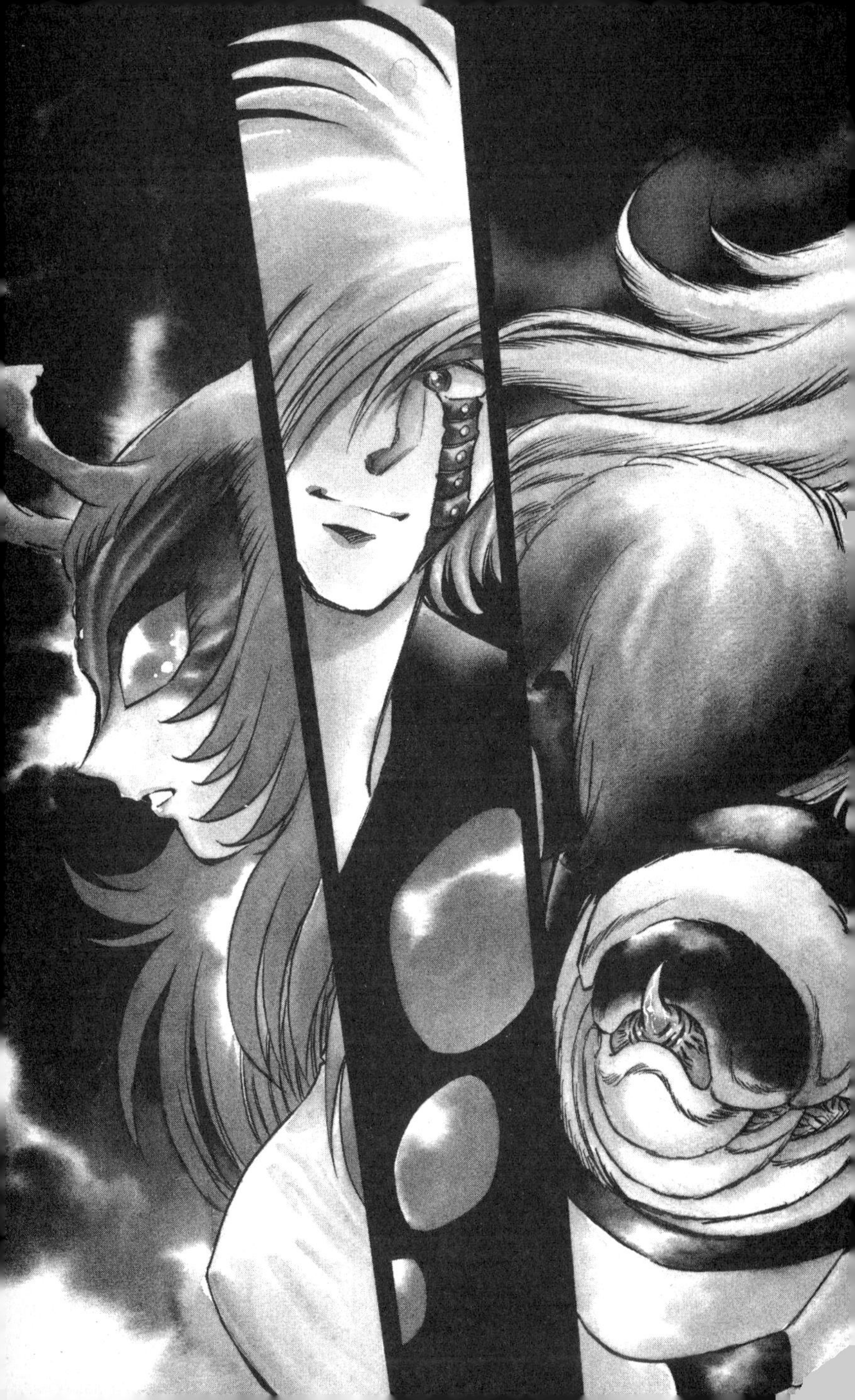

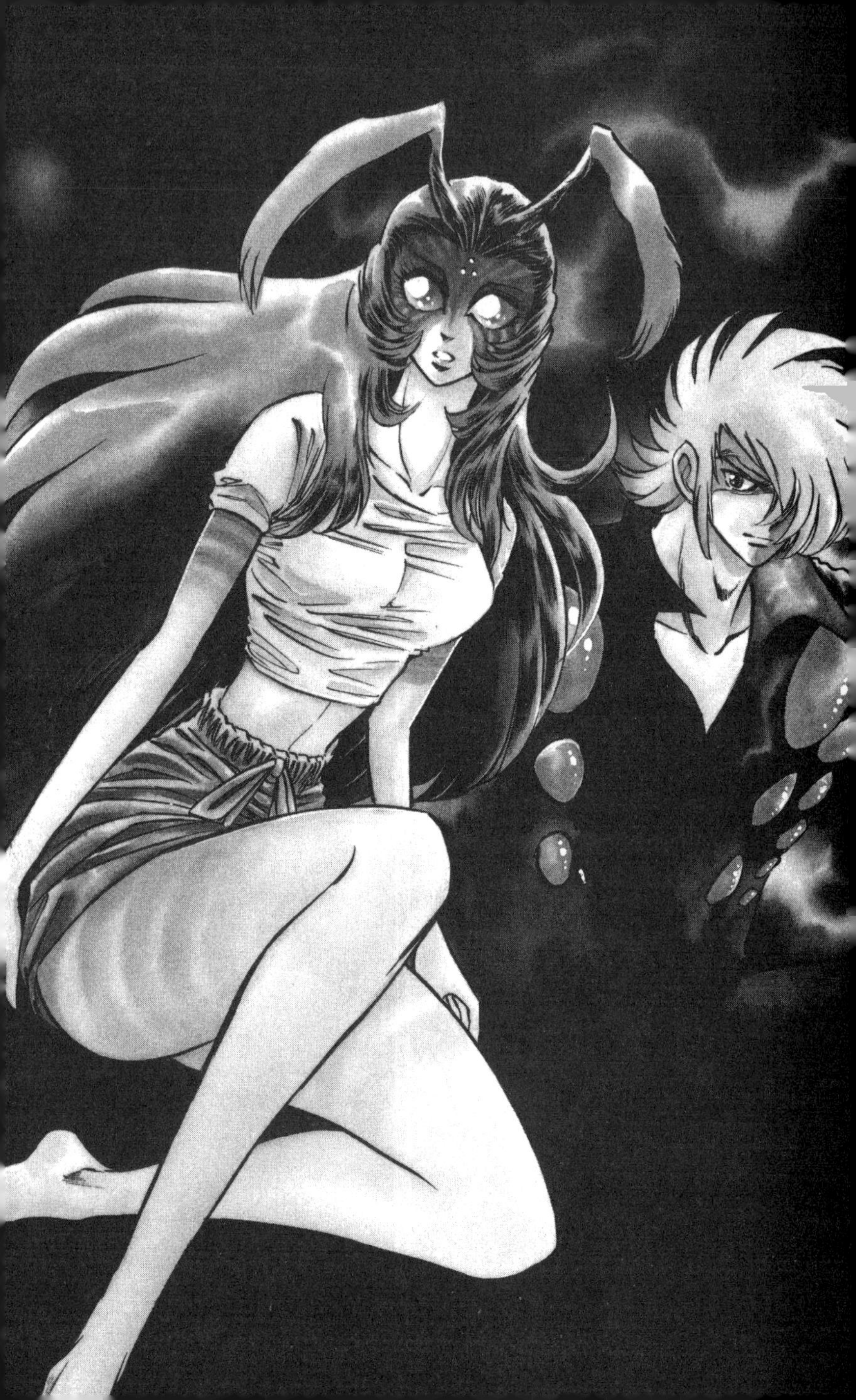

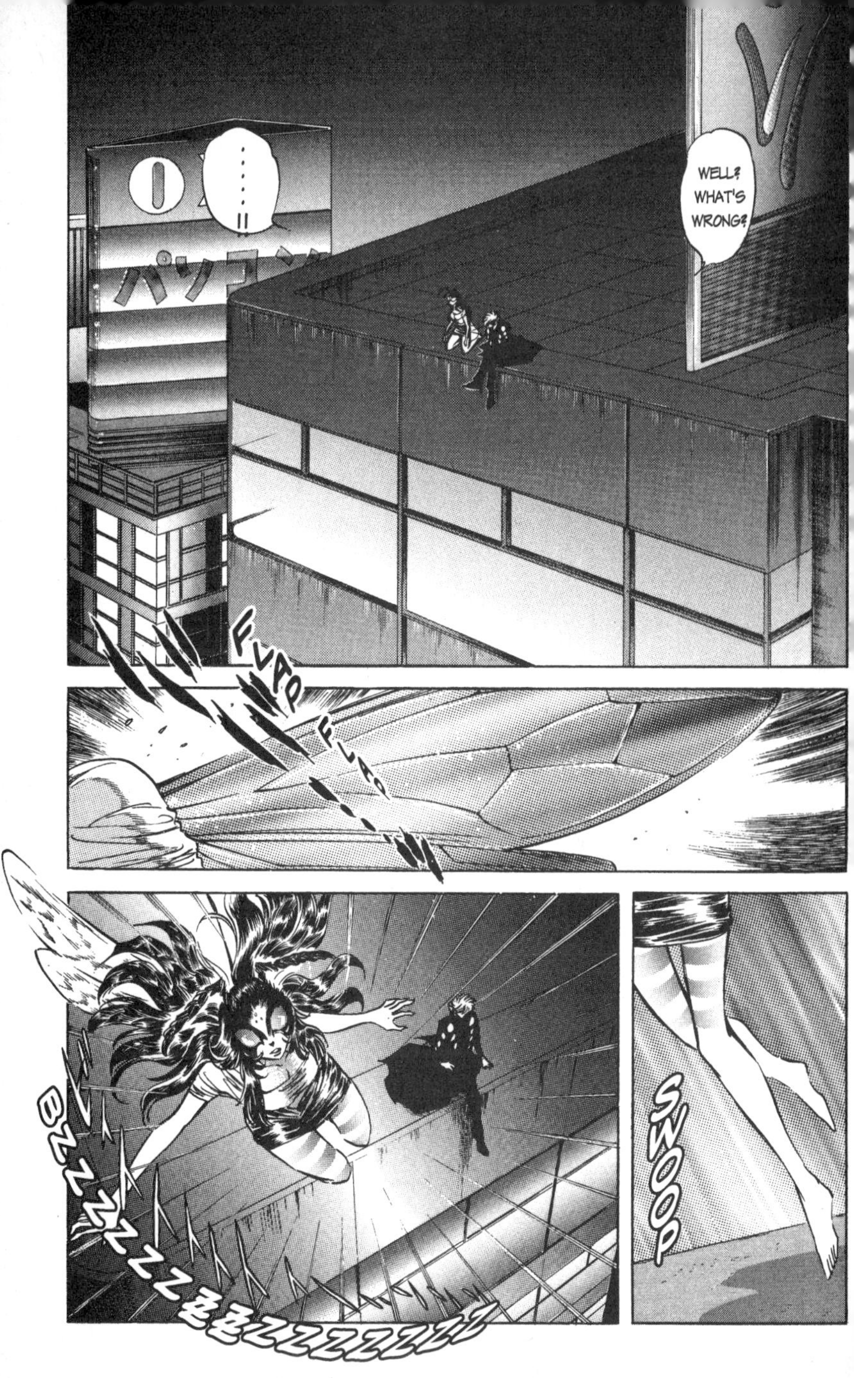
WELL? WHAT'S WRONG?
......!!
FVPP
FVPP
SWOOP
BZZZZZZZZZZZZZZZZZZ

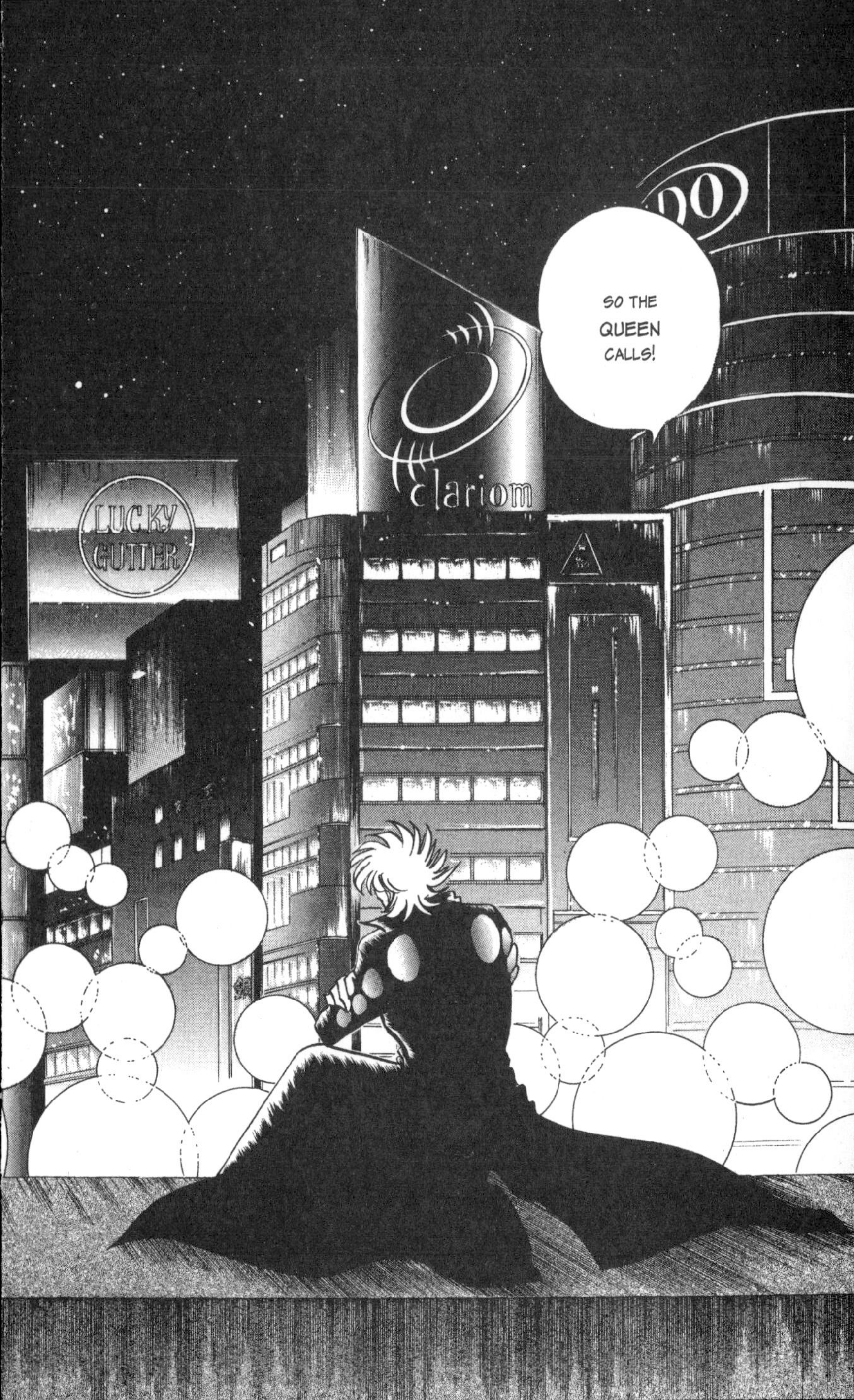
SO THE QUEEN CALLS!
LUCKY GUTTER
clariom
DO

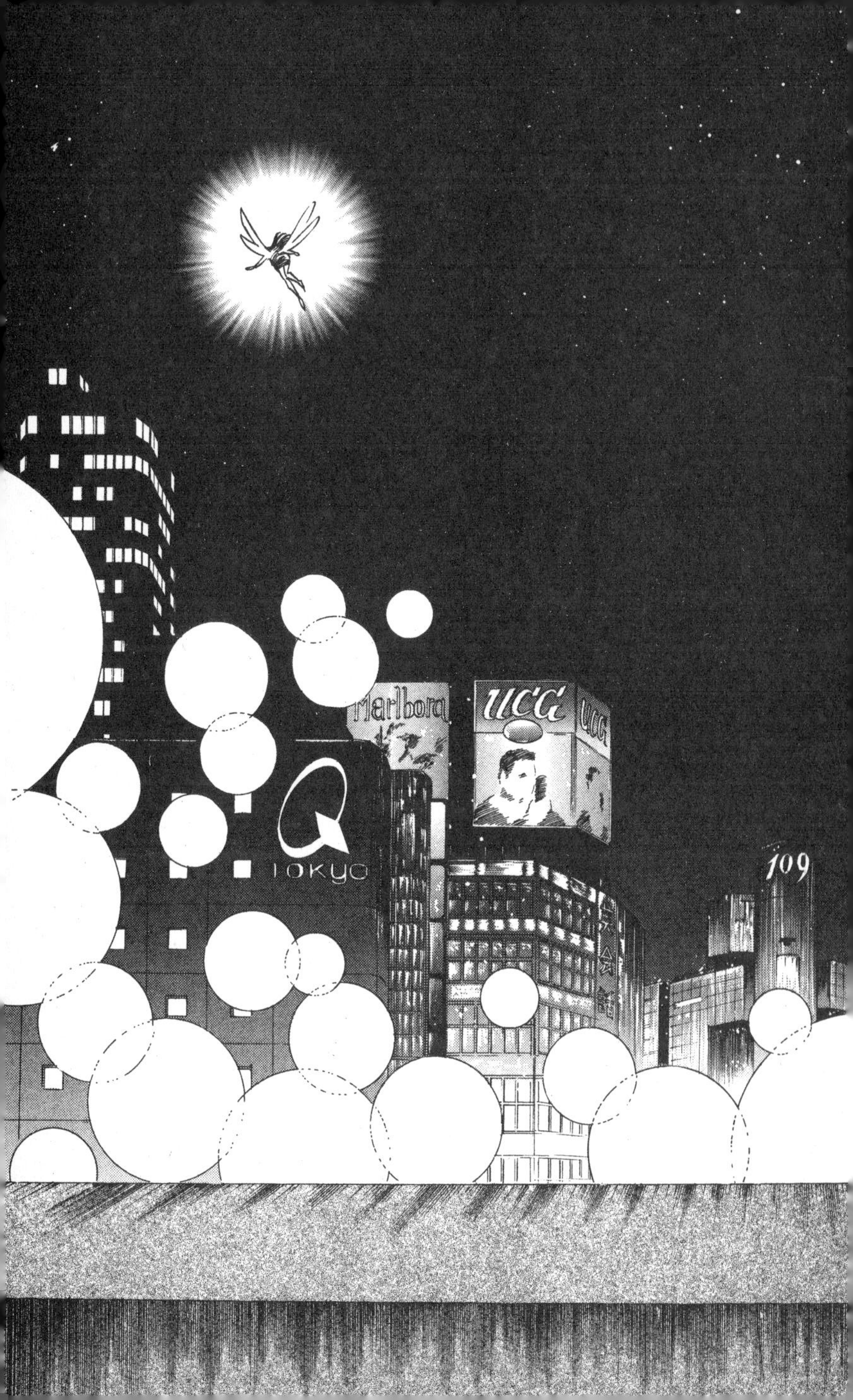
Marlboro
UCC
UCC
TOKYO
109

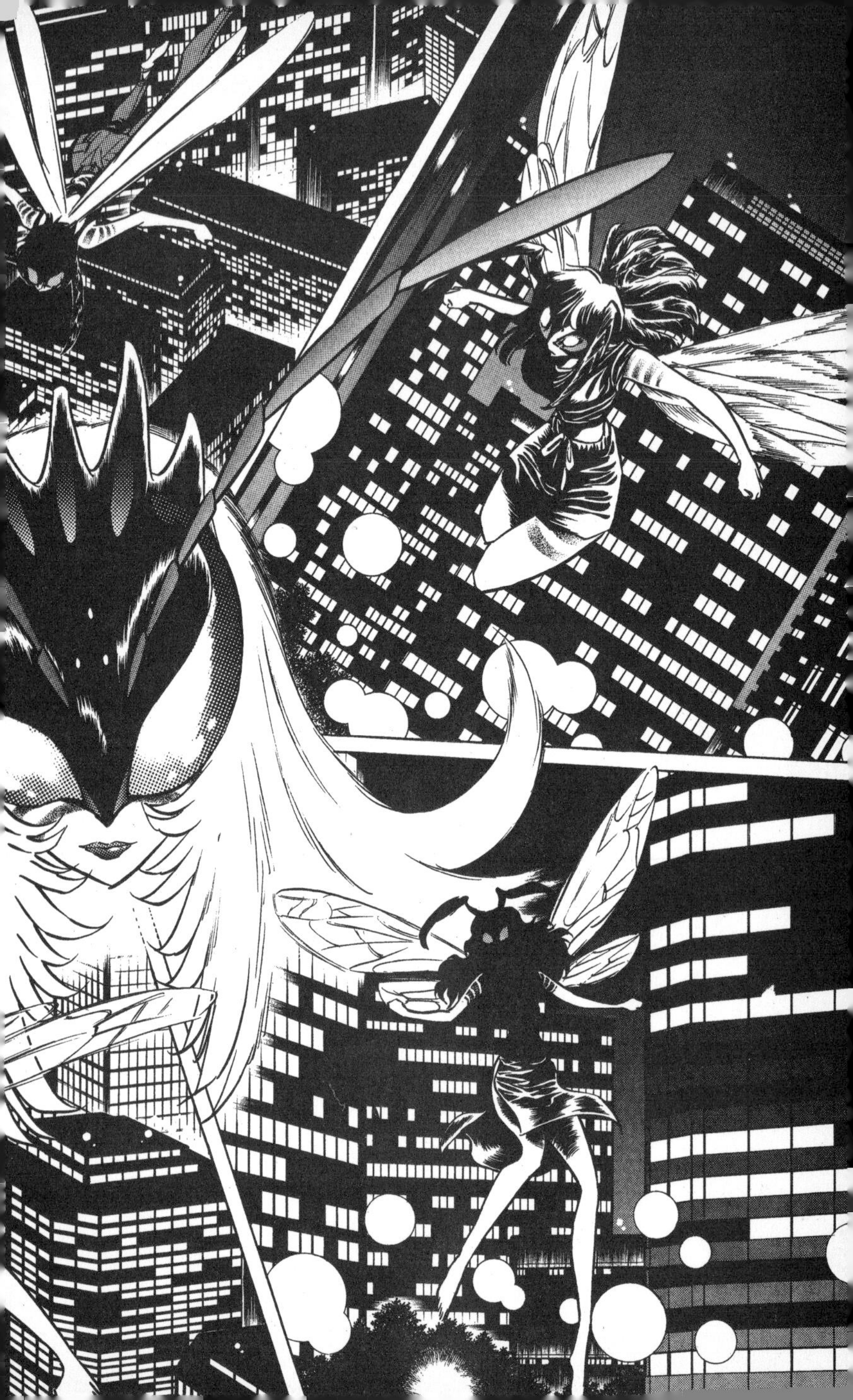

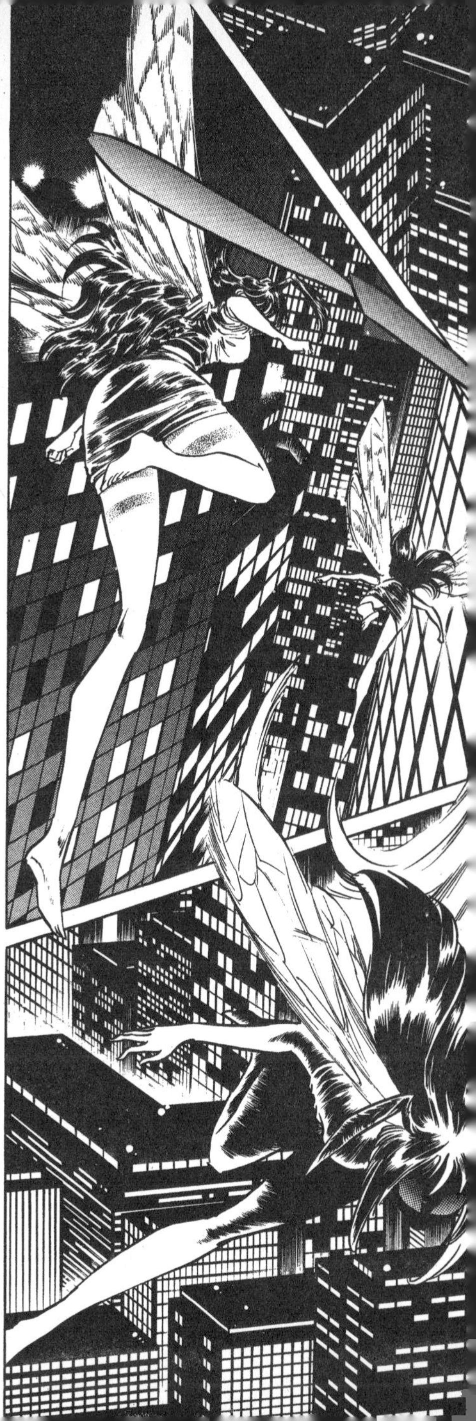
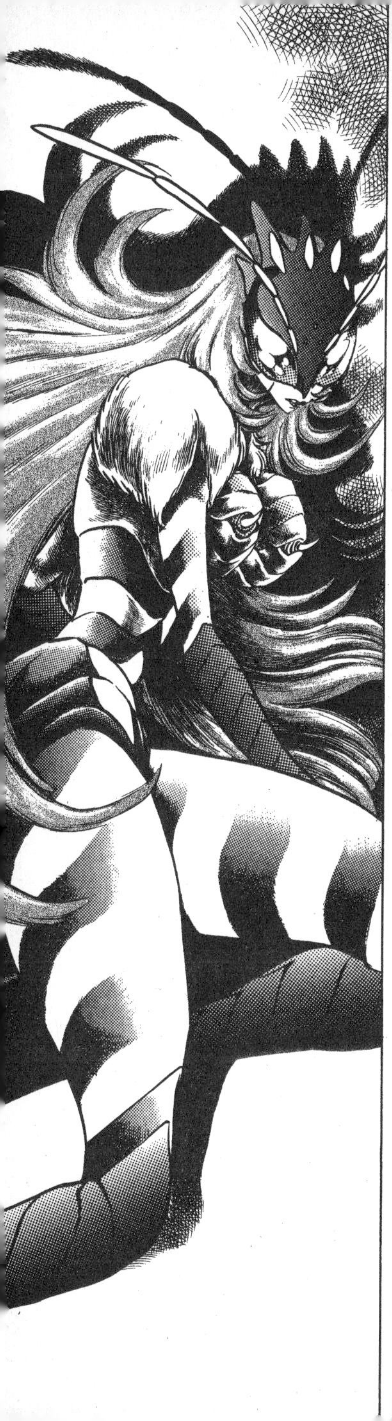

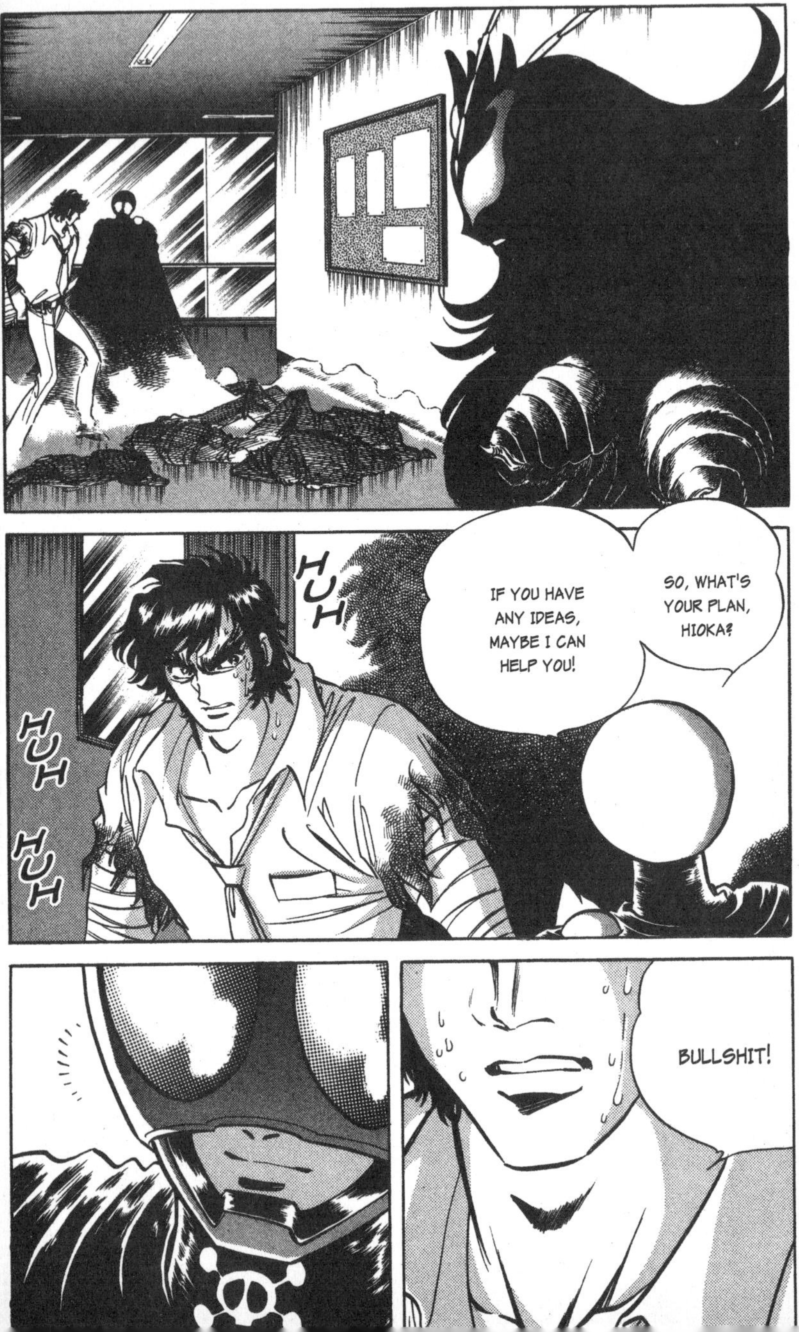
SO, WHAT'S YOUR PLAN, HIOKA?
IF YOU HAVE ANY IDEAS, MAYBE I CAN HELP YOU!
HUH
HUH HUH
HUH HUH
BULLSHIT!

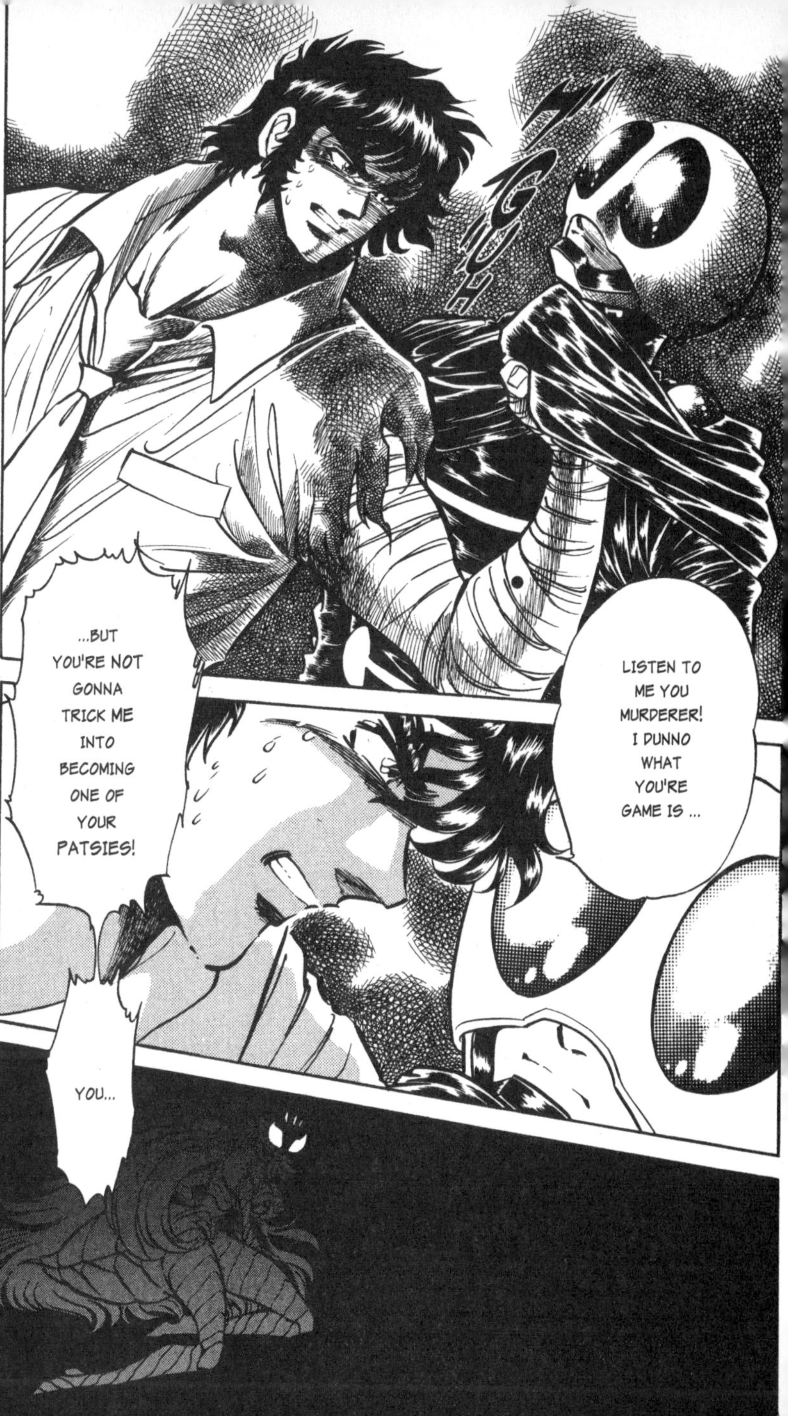
HGUH
LISTEN TO ME YOU MURDERER! I DUNNO WHAT YOU'RE GAME IS ...
...BUT YOU'RE NOT GONNA TRICK ME INTO BECOMING ONE OF YOUR PATSIES!
YOU...

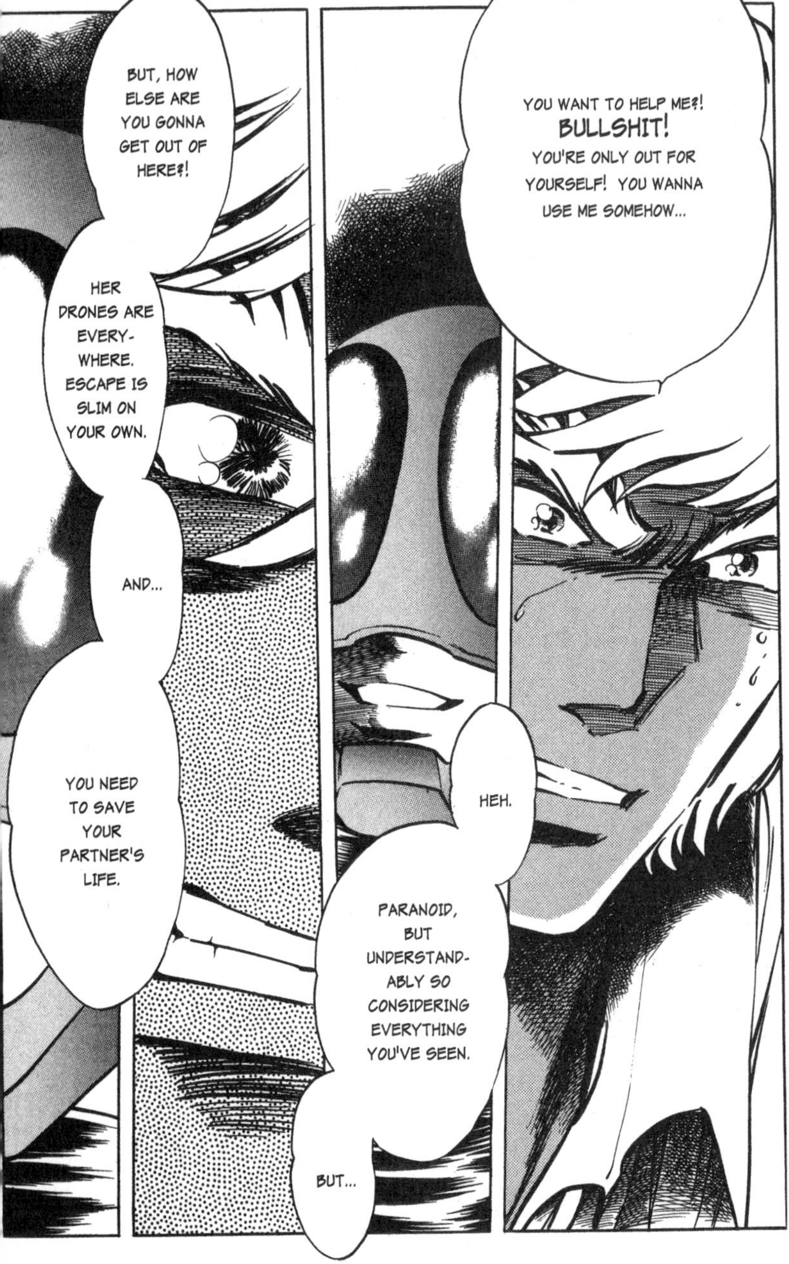
YOU WANT TO HELP ME?! BULLSHIT! YOU'RE ONLY OUT FOR YOURSELF! YOU WANNA USE ME SOMEHOW...
HEH.
PARANOID, BUT UNDERSTAND-ABLY SO CONSIDERING EVERYTHING YOU'VE SEEN.
BUT...
BUT, HOW ELSE ARE YOU GONNA GET OUT OF HERE?!
HER DRONES ARE EVERY-WHERE. ESCAPE IS SLIM ON YOUR OWN.
AND...
YOU NEED TO SAVE YOUR PARTNER'S LIFE.

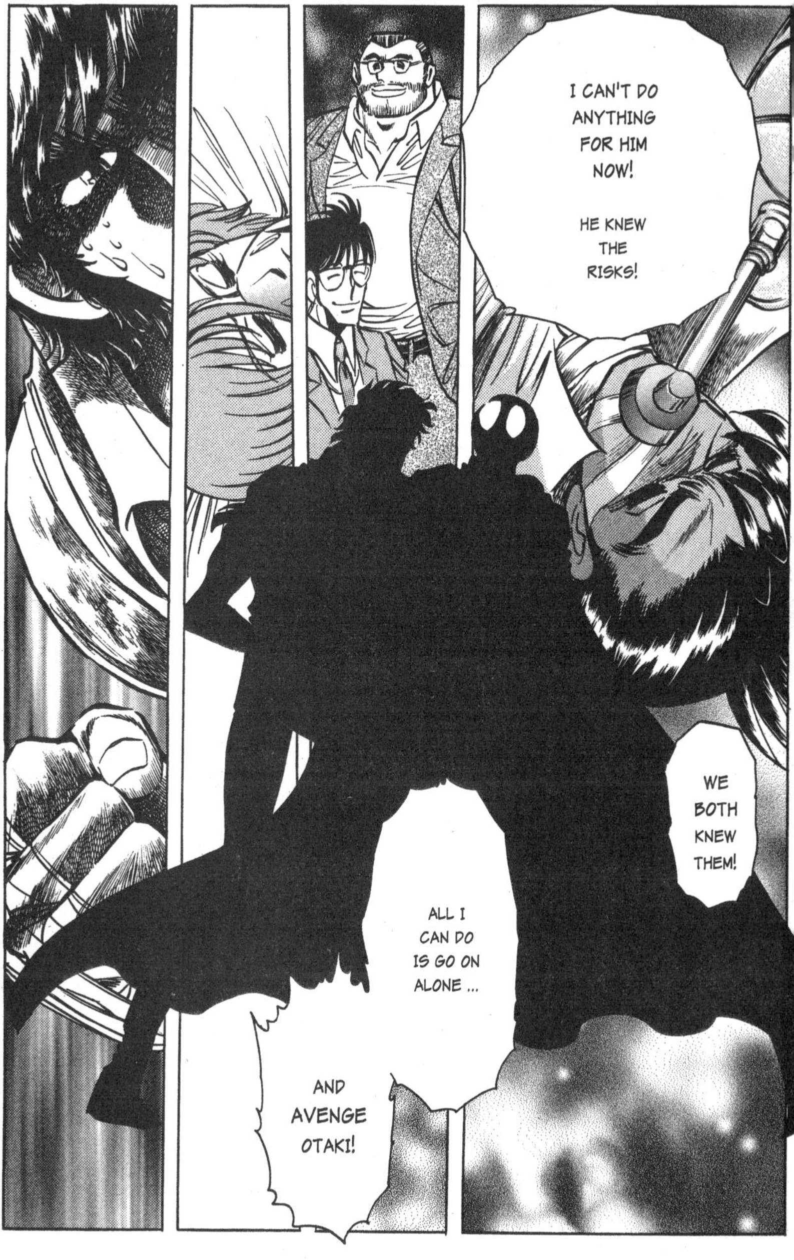

I CAN'T DO ANYTHING FOR HIM NOW!
HE KNEW THE RISKS!
WE BOTH KNEW THEM!
ALL I CAN DO IS GO ON ALONE ...
AND AVENGE OTAKI!

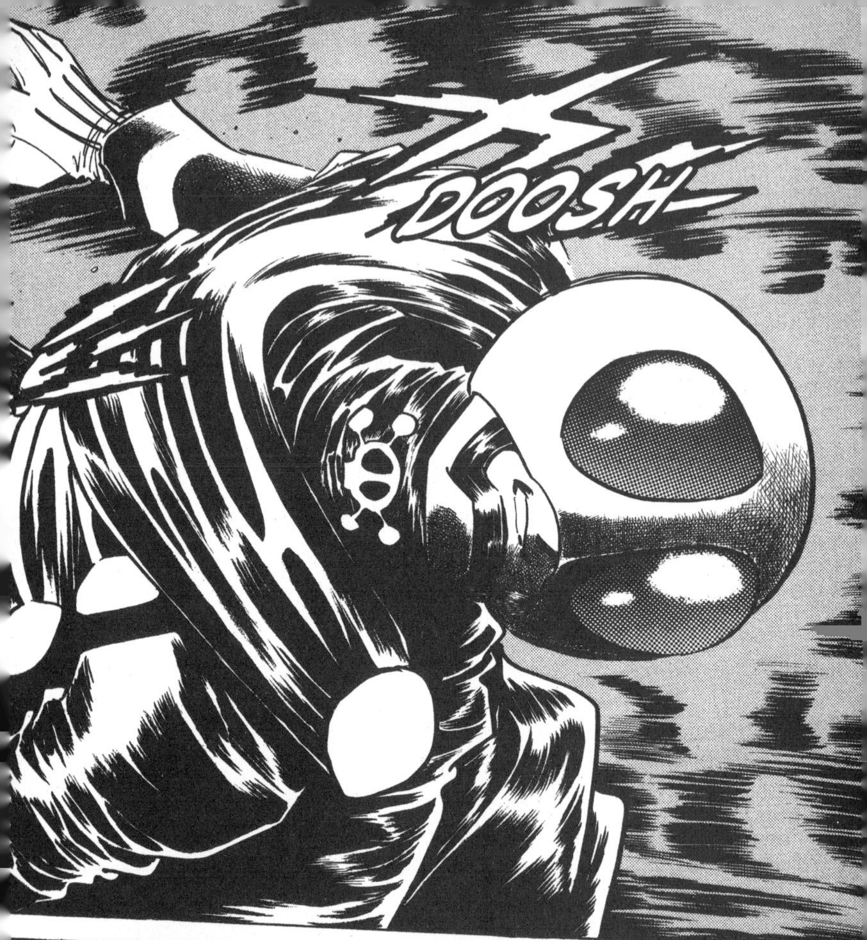
DOOSH
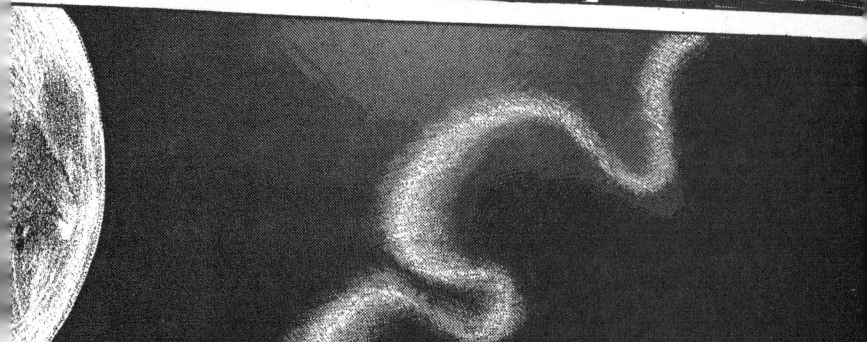

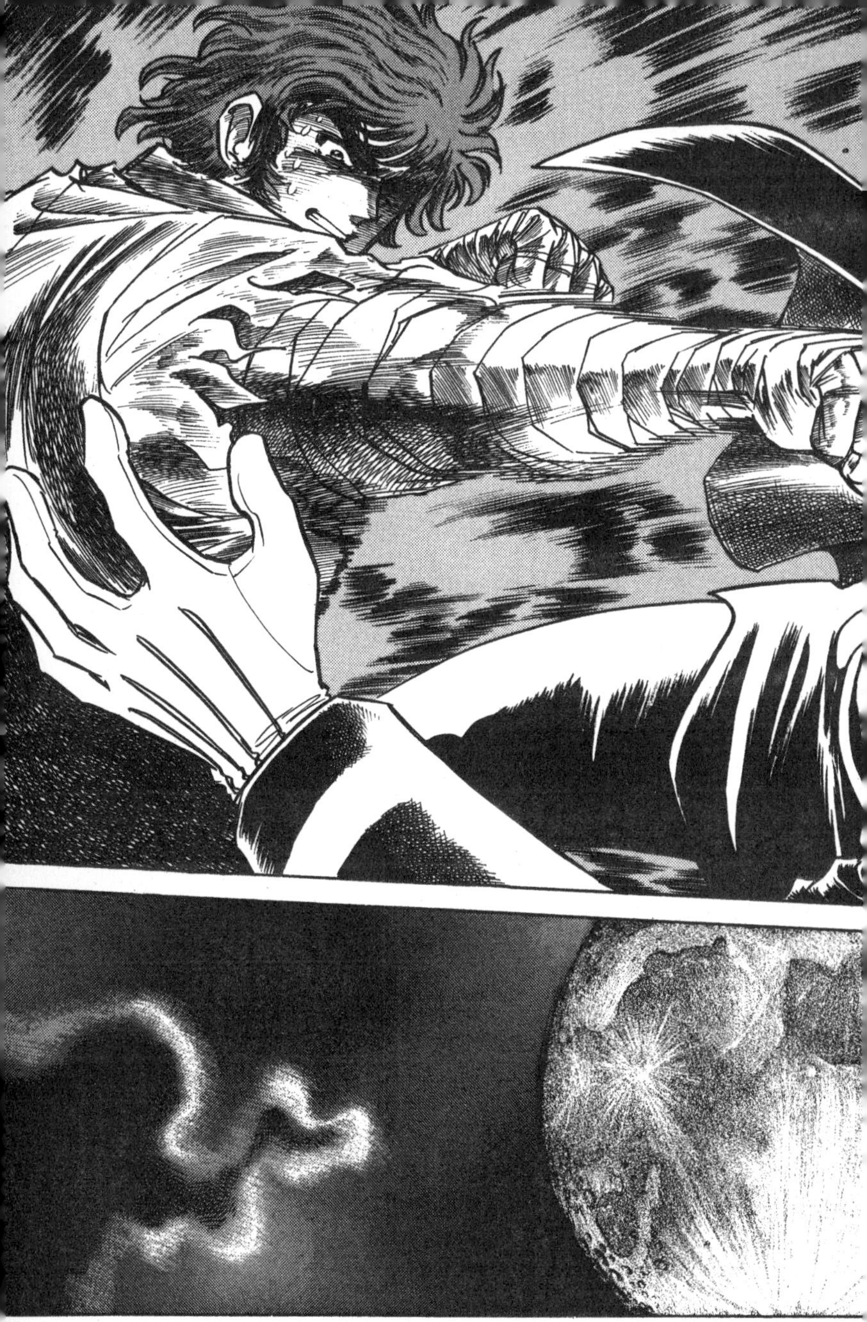

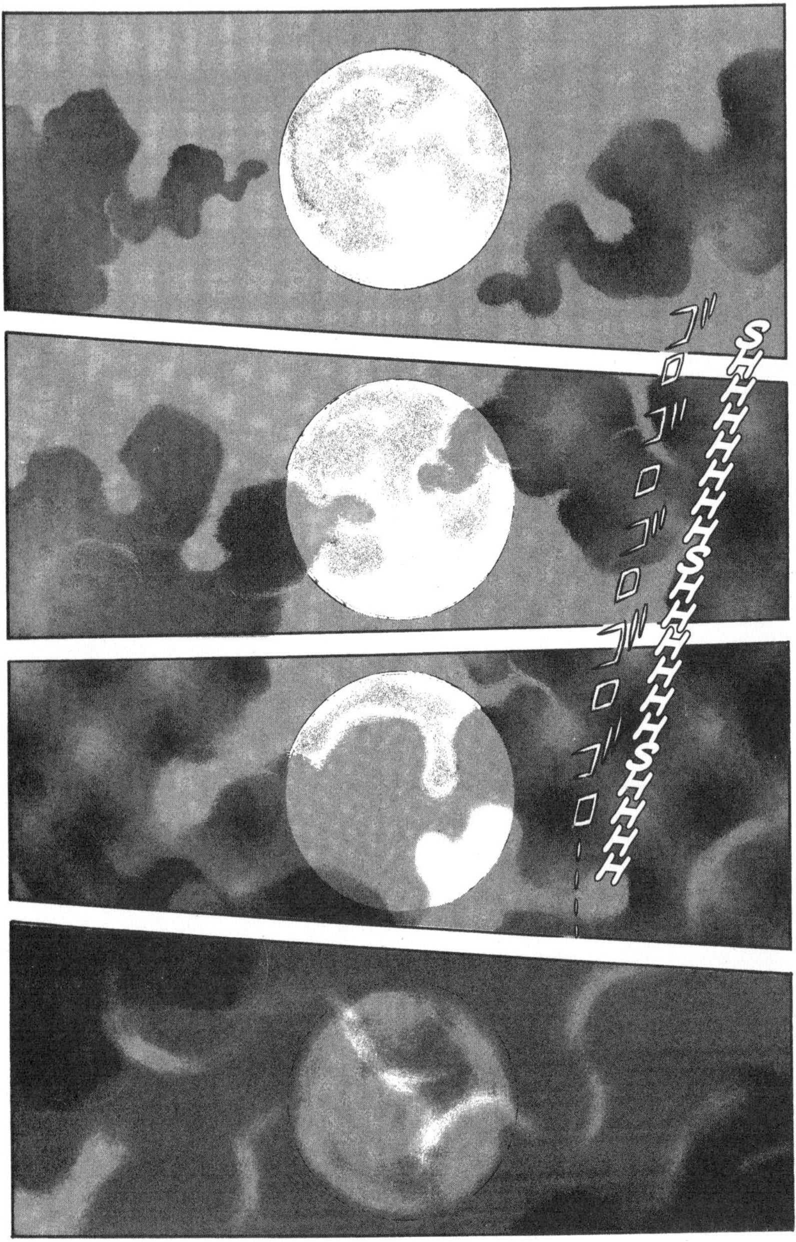
SHHHHHHHSHHHHHHSHHHH
ゴロゴロゴロゴロゴロ……

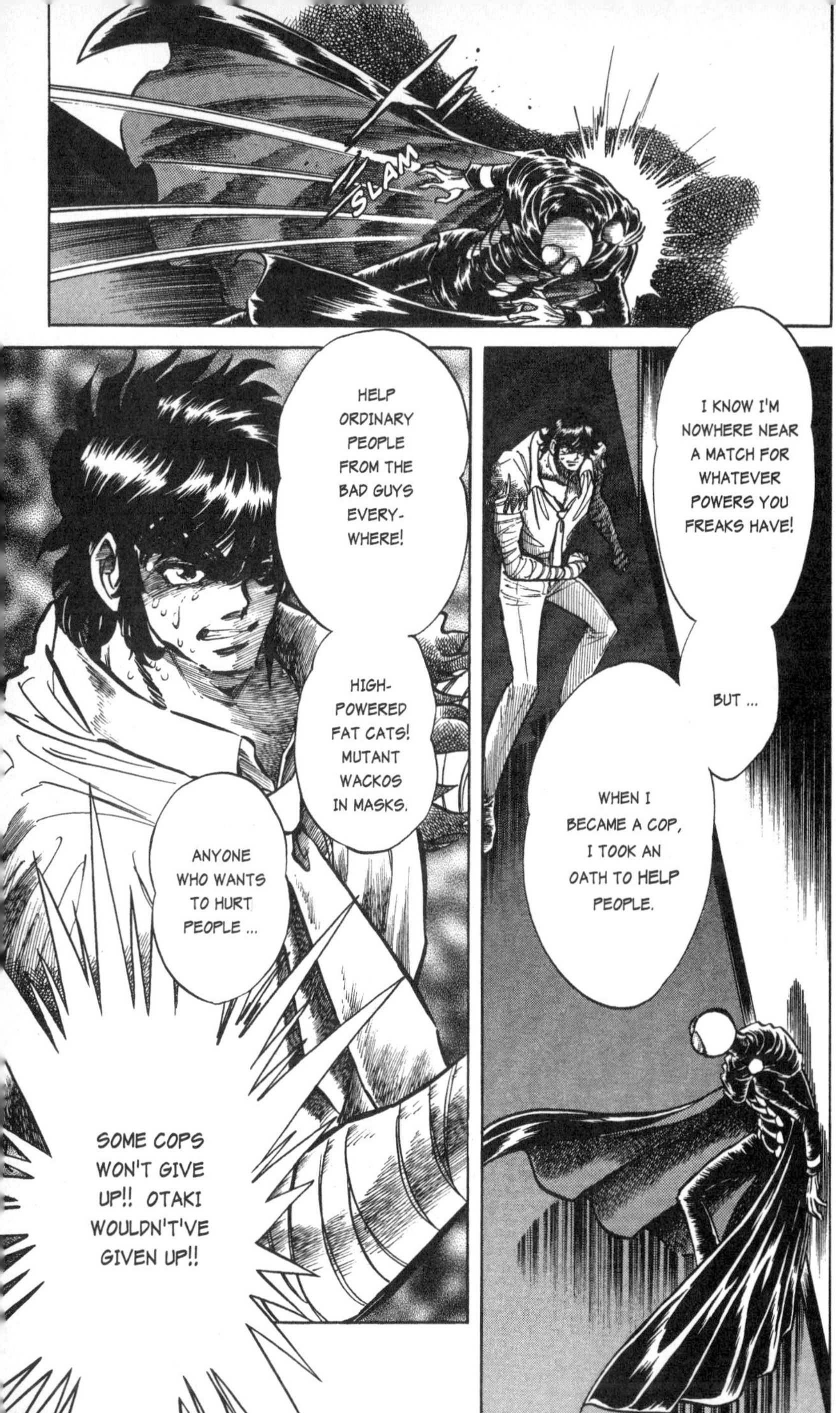
SLAM
I KNOW I'M NOWHERE NEAR A MATCH FOR WHATEVER POWERS YOU FREAKS HAVE!
BUT ...
WHEN I BECAME A COP, I TOOK AN OATH TO HELP PEOPLE.
HELP ORDINARY PEOPLE FROM THE BAD GUYS EVERY-WHERE!
HIGH-POWERED FAT CATS! MUTANT WACKOS IN MASKS.
ANYONE WHO WANTS TO HURT PEOPLE ...
SOME COPS WON'T GIVE UP!! OTAKI WOULDN'T'VE GIVEN UP!!

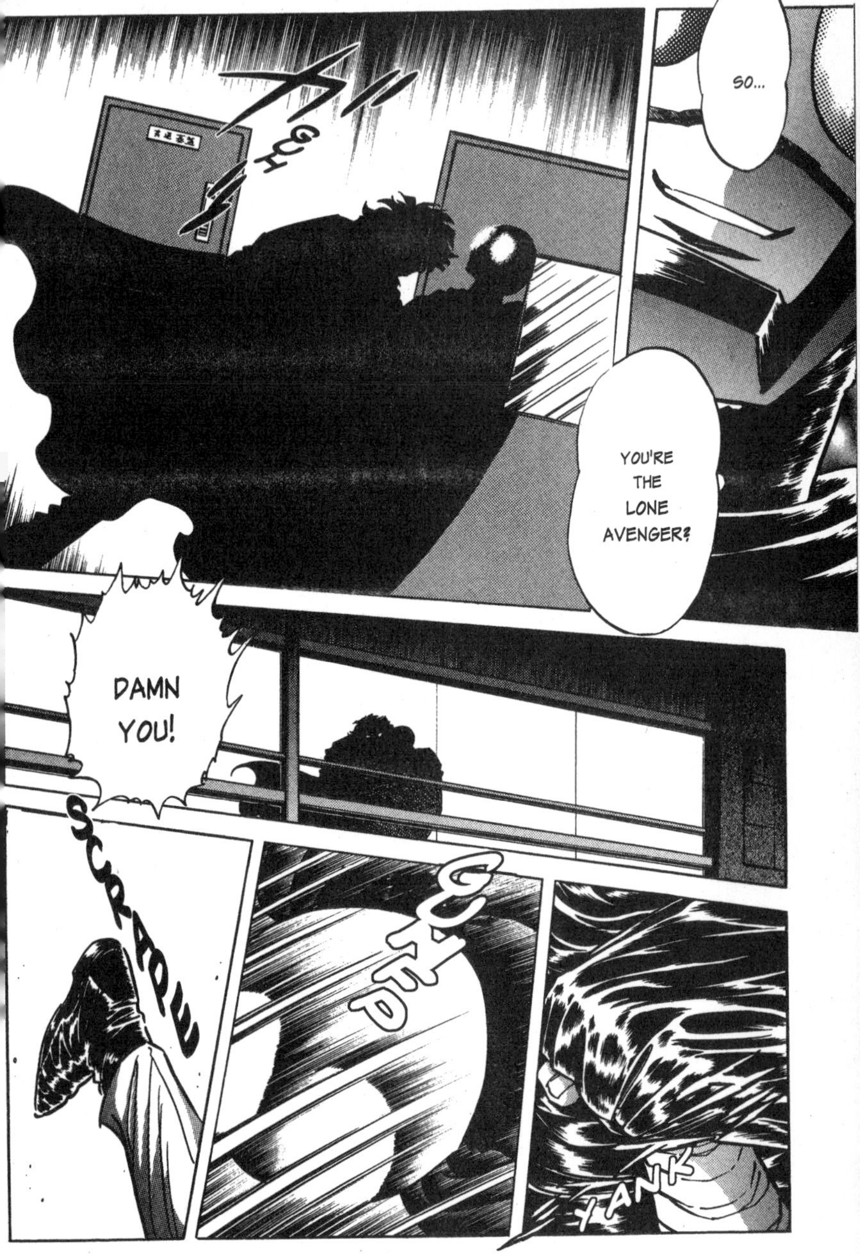
SO...
YOU'RE THE LONE AVENGER?
GUH
DAMN YOU!
YANK
GUHP
SCRAPE

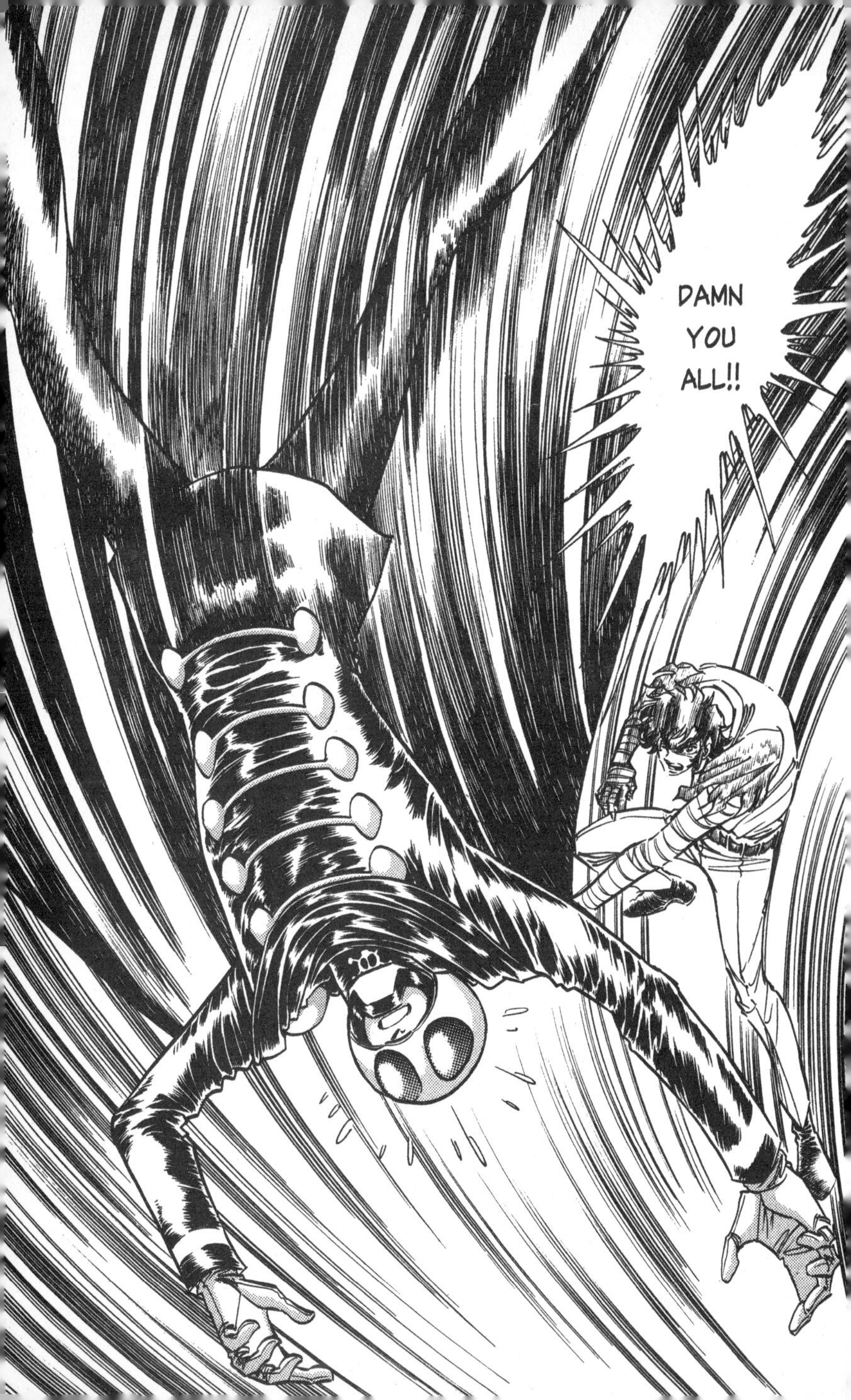
DAMN YOU ALL!!

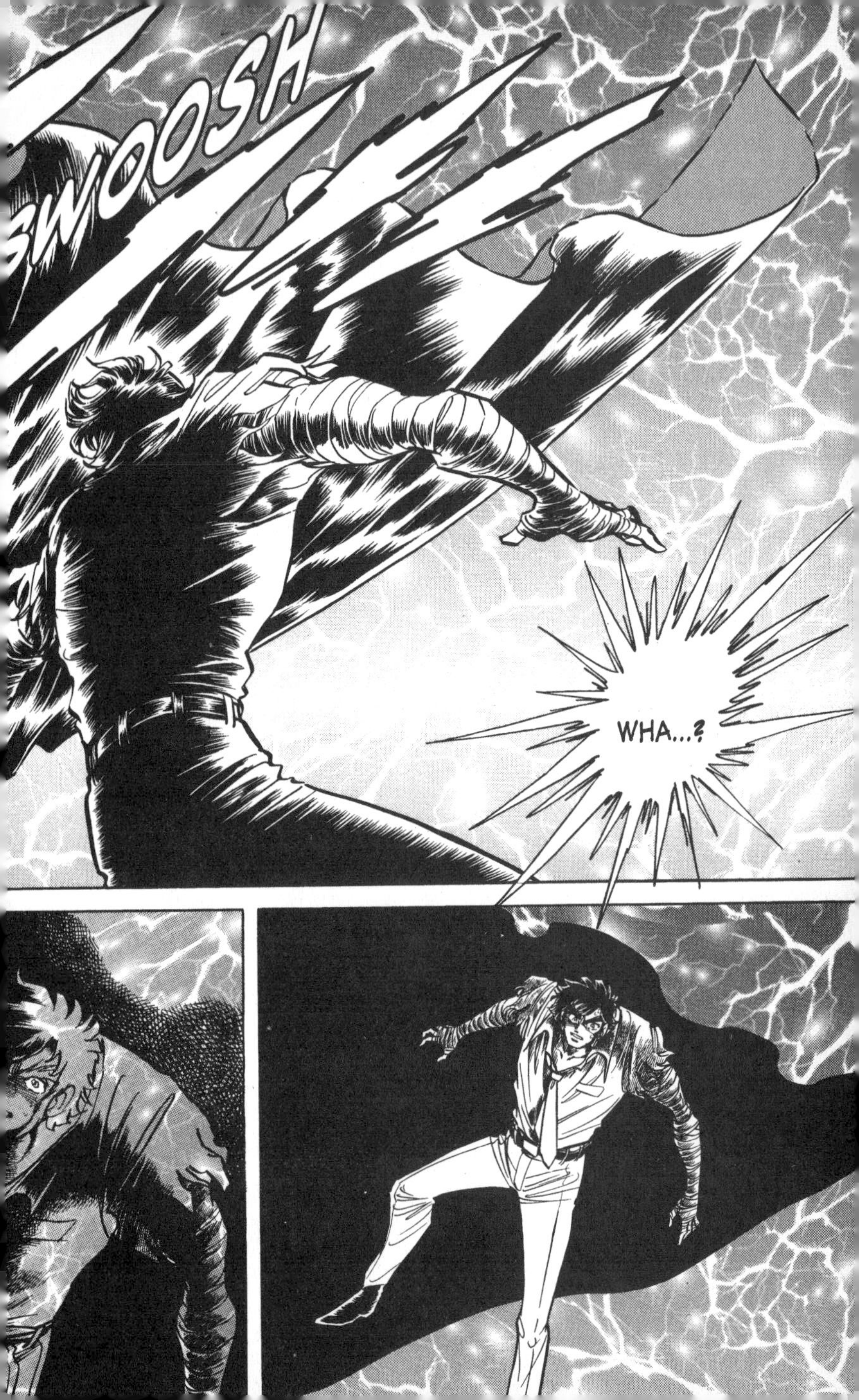
SWOOSH
WHA...?

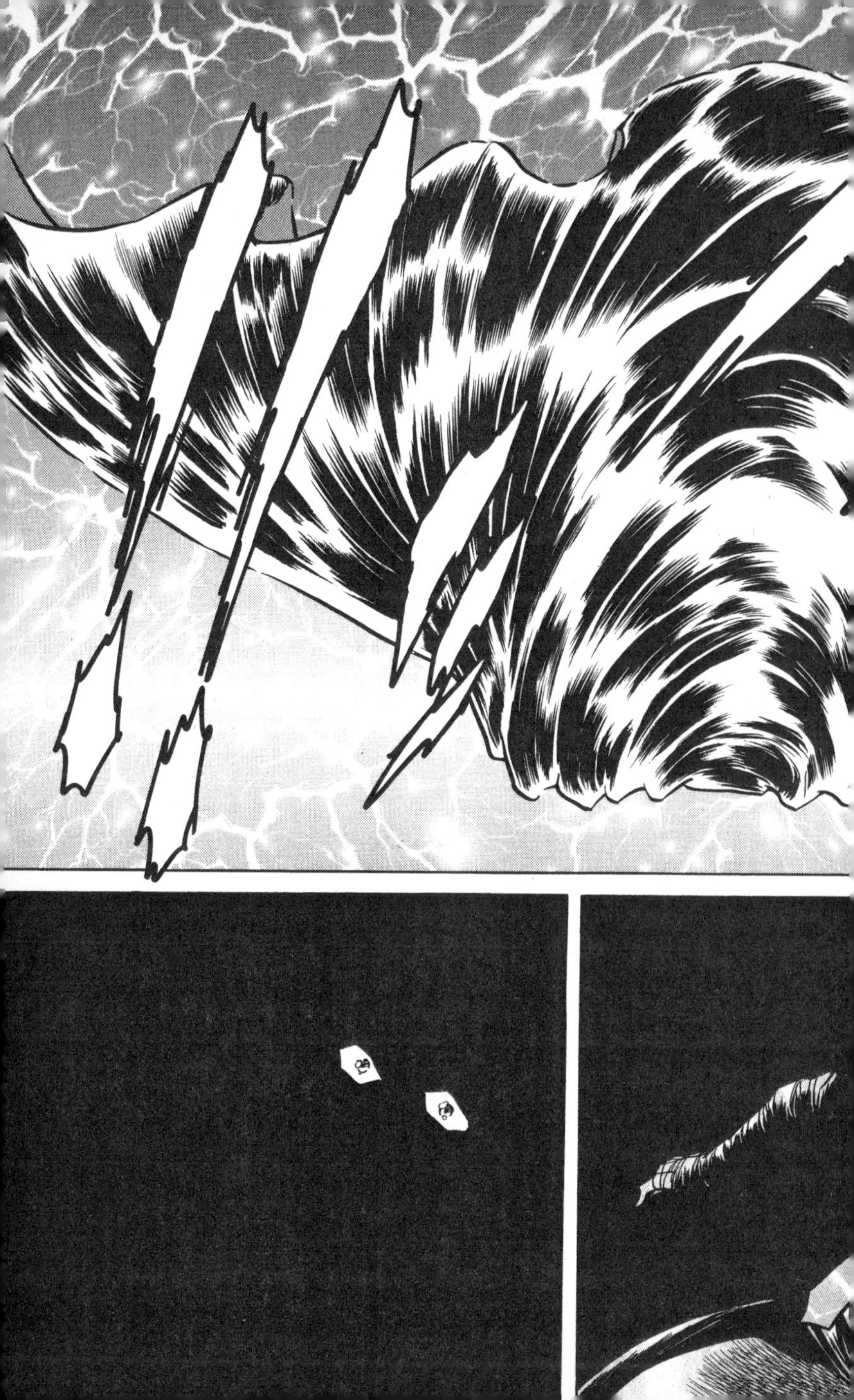

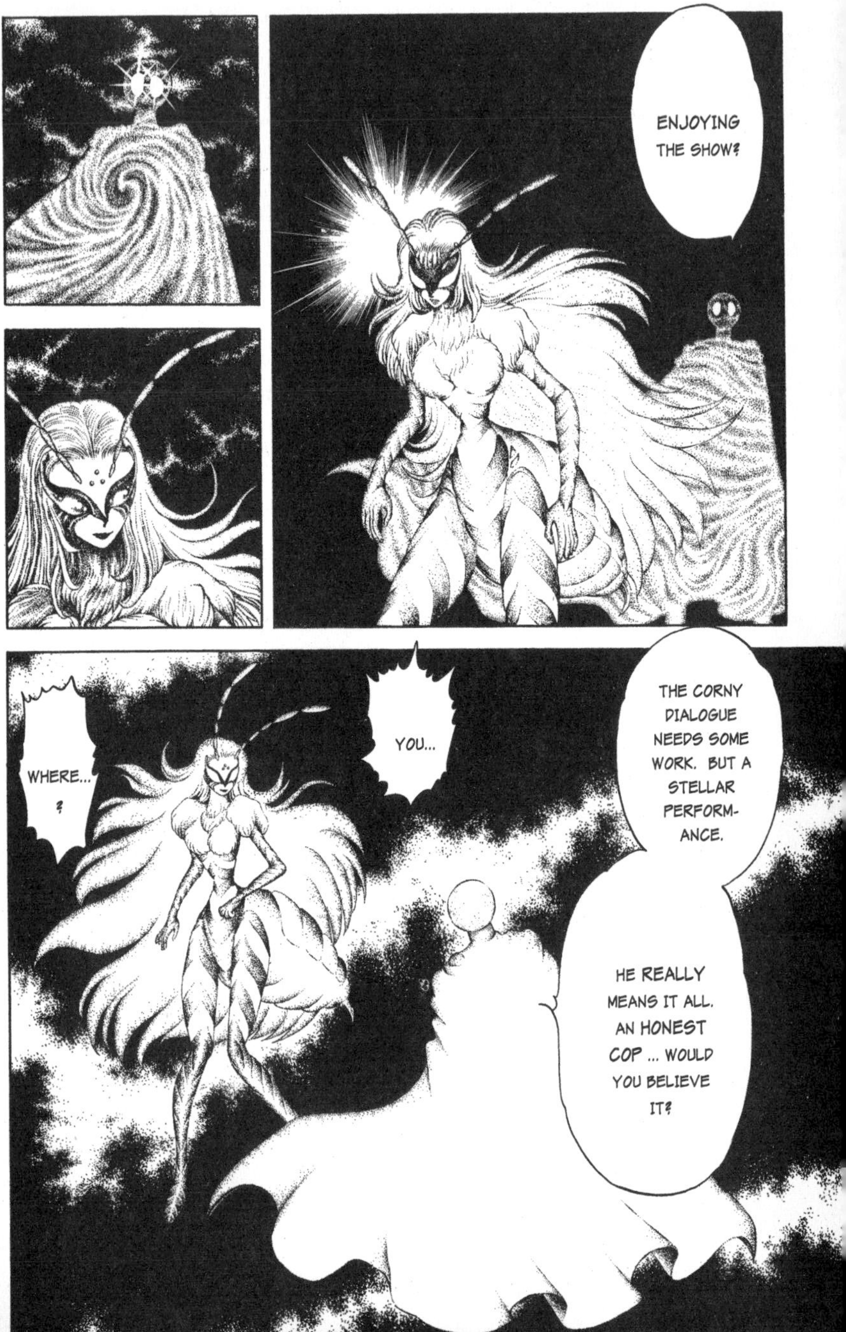
ENJOYING THE SHOW?
THE CORNY DIALOGUE NEEDS SOME WORK. BUT A STELLAR PERFORM-ANCE.
HE REALLY MEANS IT ALL. AN HONEST COP ... WOULD YOU BELIEVE IT?
YOU...
WHERE... ?

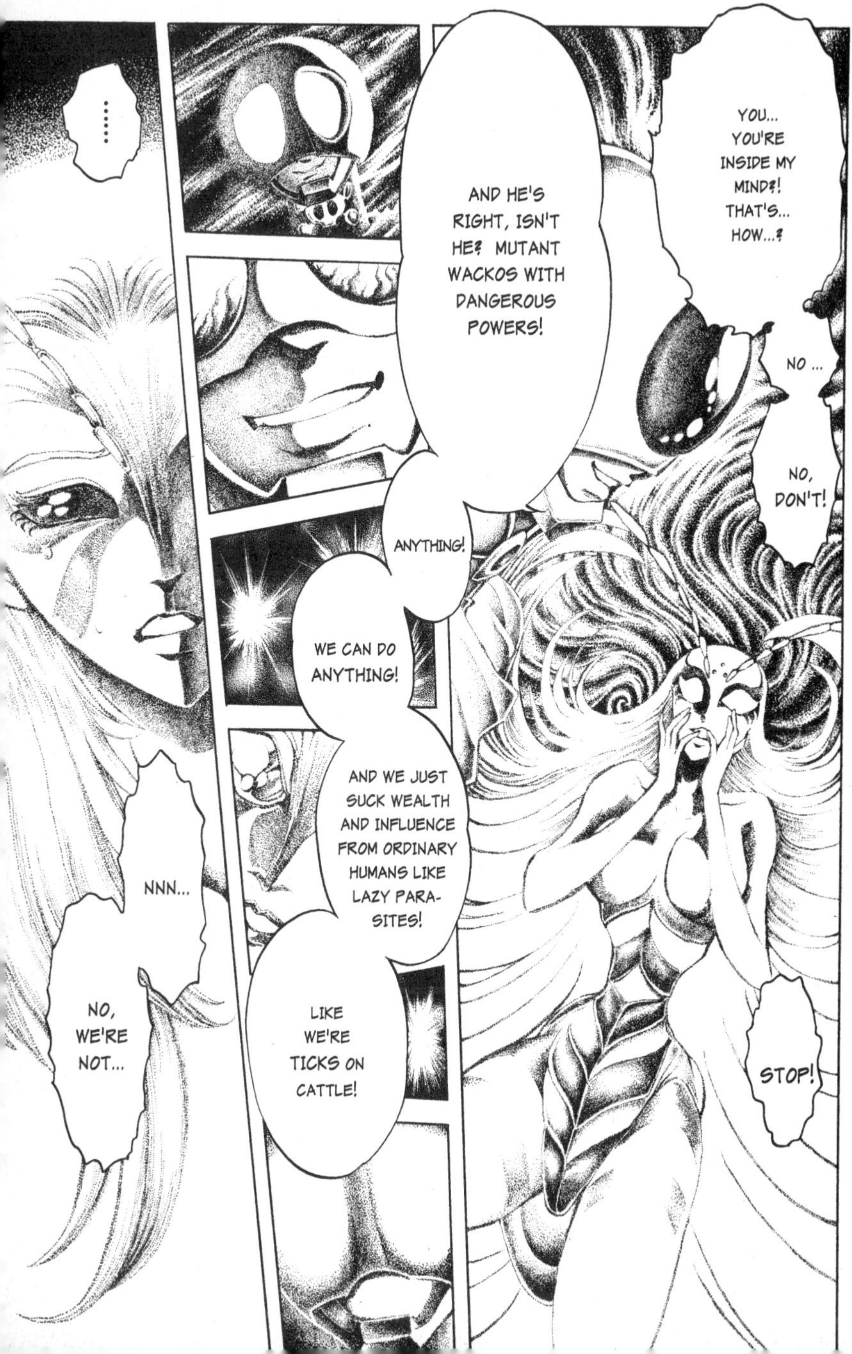
YOU... YOU'RE INSIDE MY MIND?! THAT'S... HOW...?
AND HE'S RIGHT, ISN'T HE? MUTANT WACKOS WITH DANGEROUS POWERS!
NO ...
NO, DON'T!
ANYTHING!
WE CAN DO ANYTHING!
AND WE JUST SUCK WEALTH AND INFLUENCE FROM ORDINARY HUMANS LIKE LAZY PARA-SITES!
LIKE WE'RE TICKS ON CATTLE!
STOP!
......
NNN...
NO, WE'RE NOT...

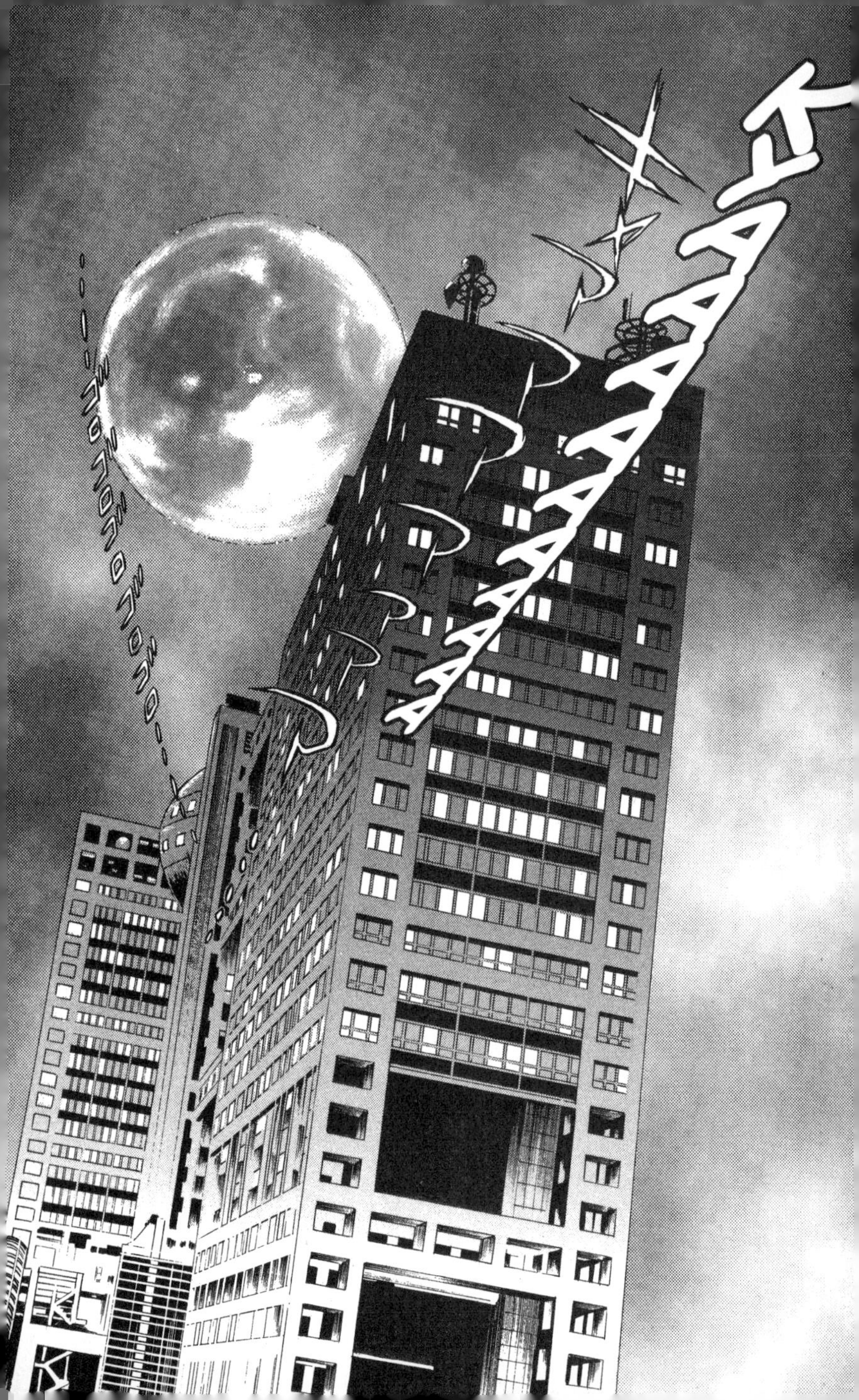
KYAAAAAAAAAAA
ーーーゴロゴロゴロゴロー

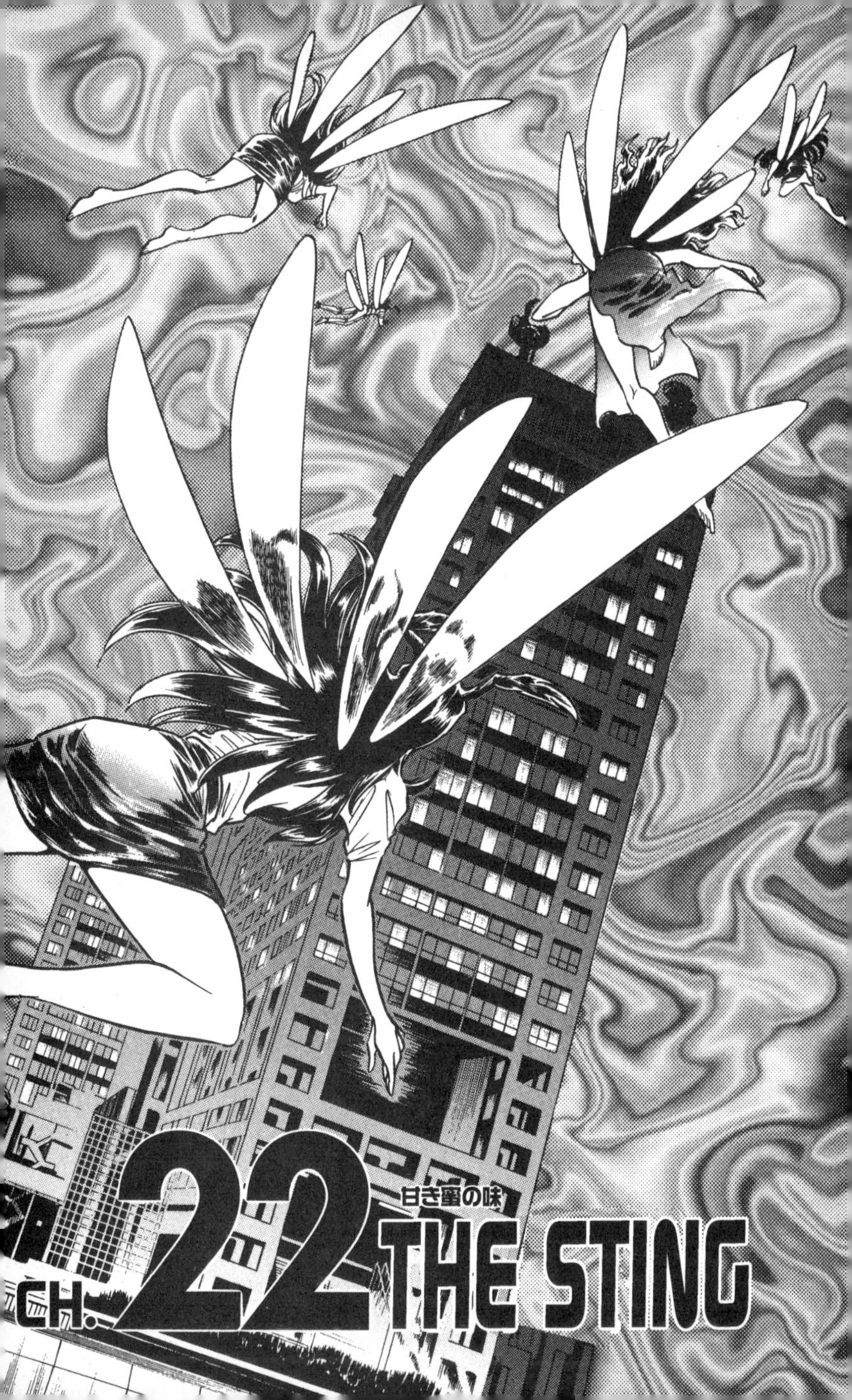
CH. 22
甘き蜜の味
THE STING

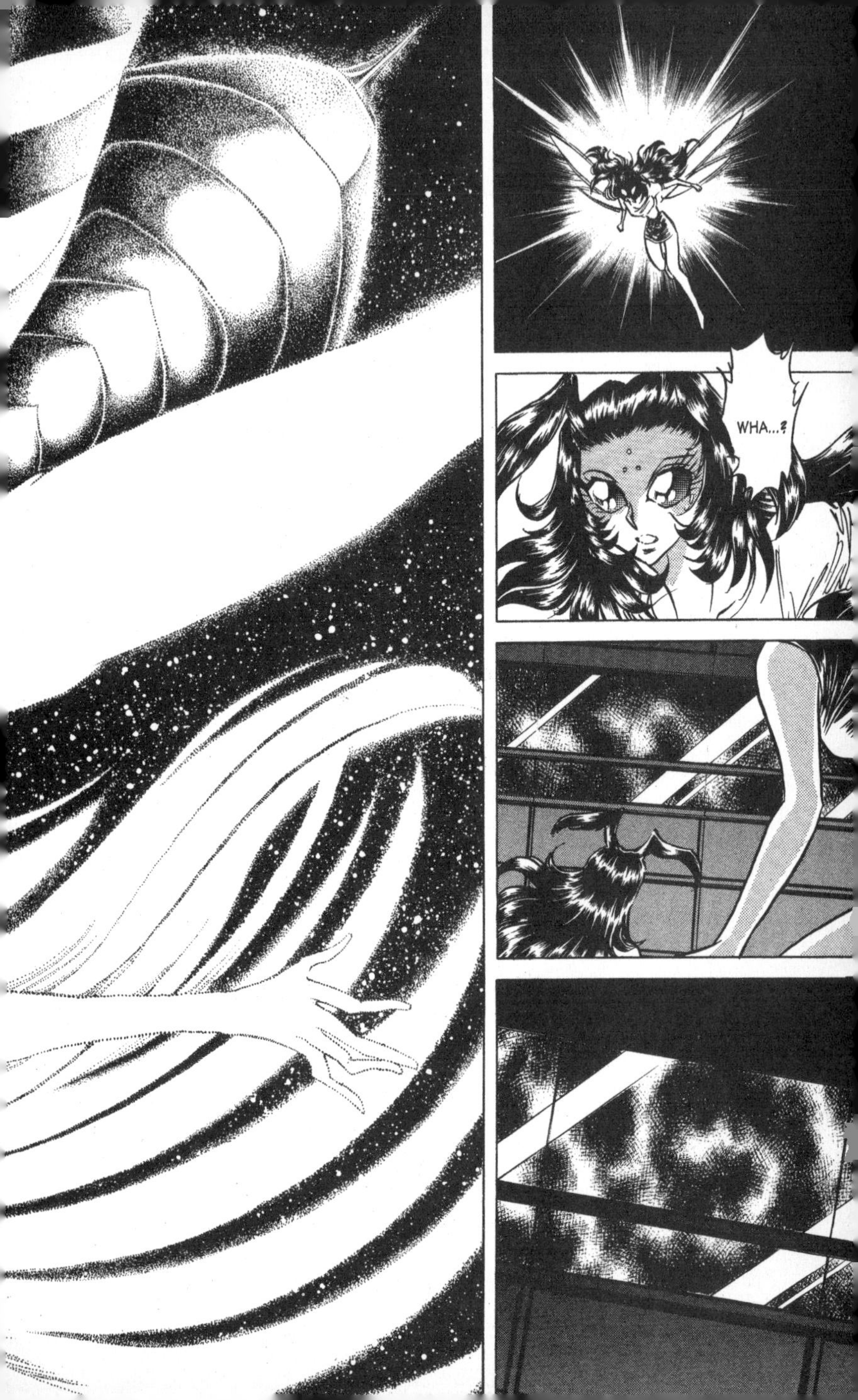
WHA...?

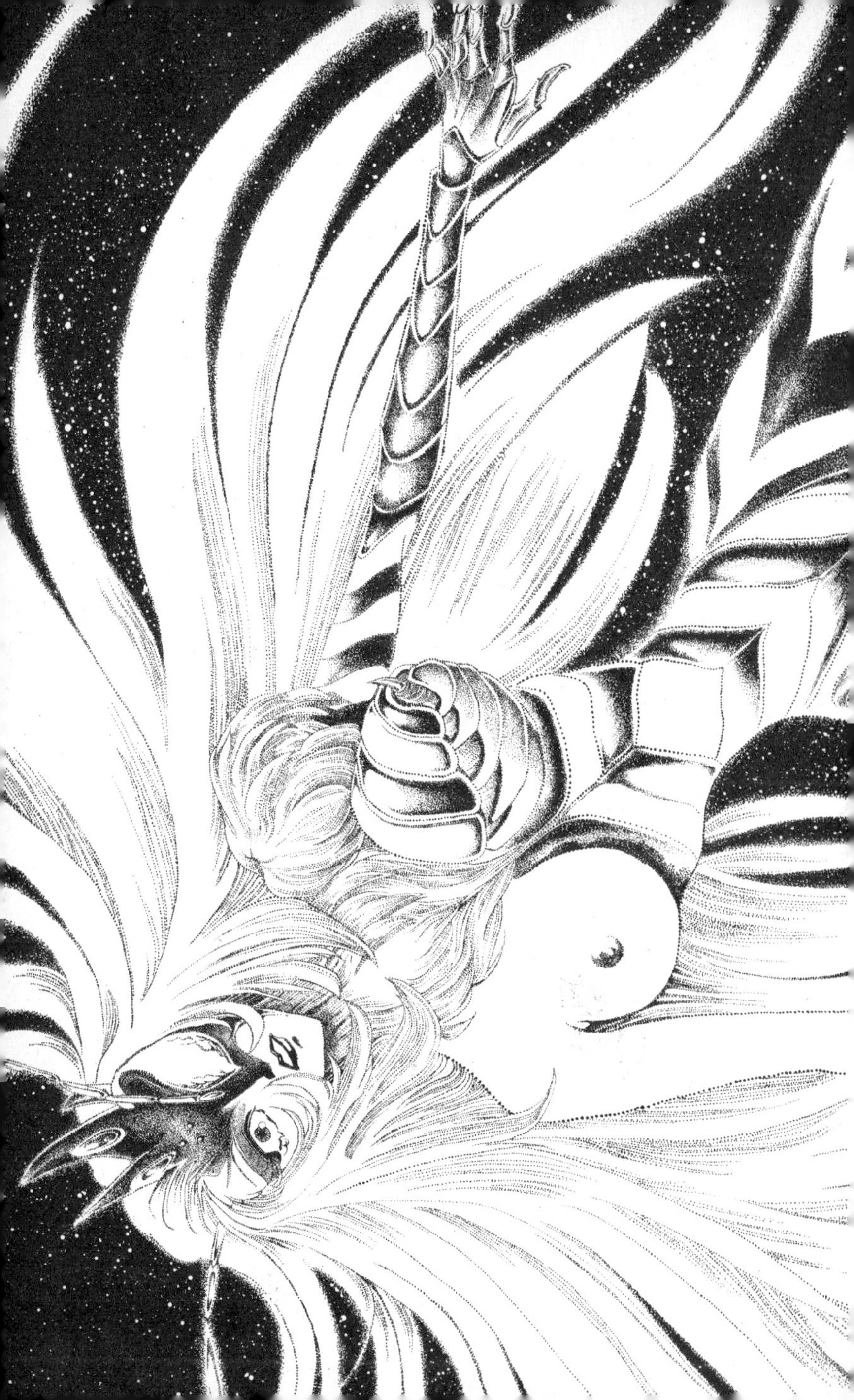

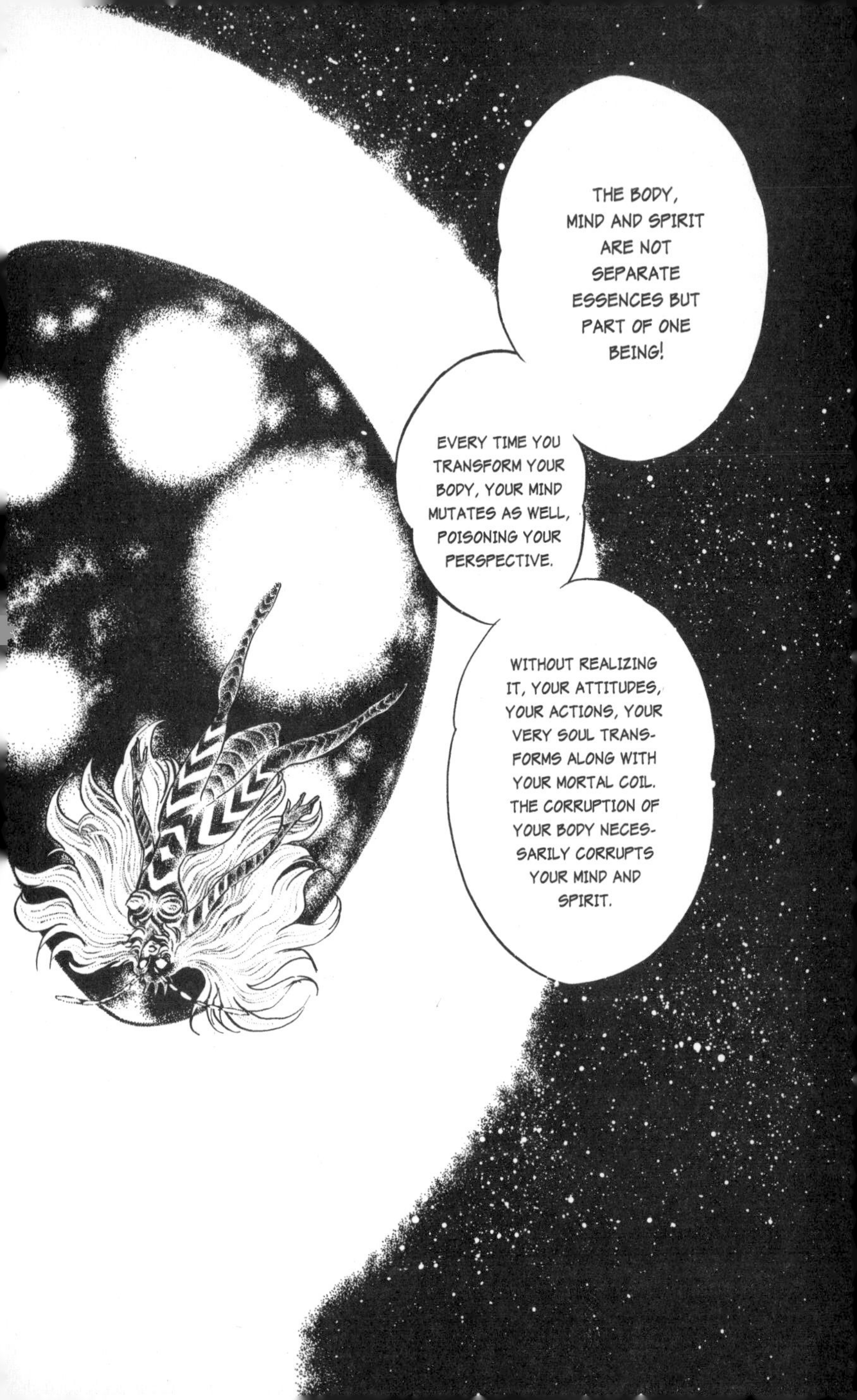
THE BODY, MIND AND SPIRIT ARE NOT SEPARATE ESSENCES BUT PART OF ONE BEING!
EVERY TIME YOU TRANSFORM YOUR BODY, YOUR MIND MUTATES AS WELL, POISONING YOUR PERSPECTIVE.
WITHOUT REALIZING IT, YOUR ATTITUDES, YOUR ACTIONS, YOUR VERY SOUL TRANS-FORMS ALONG WITH YOUR MORTAL COIL. THE CORRUPTION OF YOUR BODY NECES-SARILY CORRUPTS YOUR MIND AND SPIRIT.

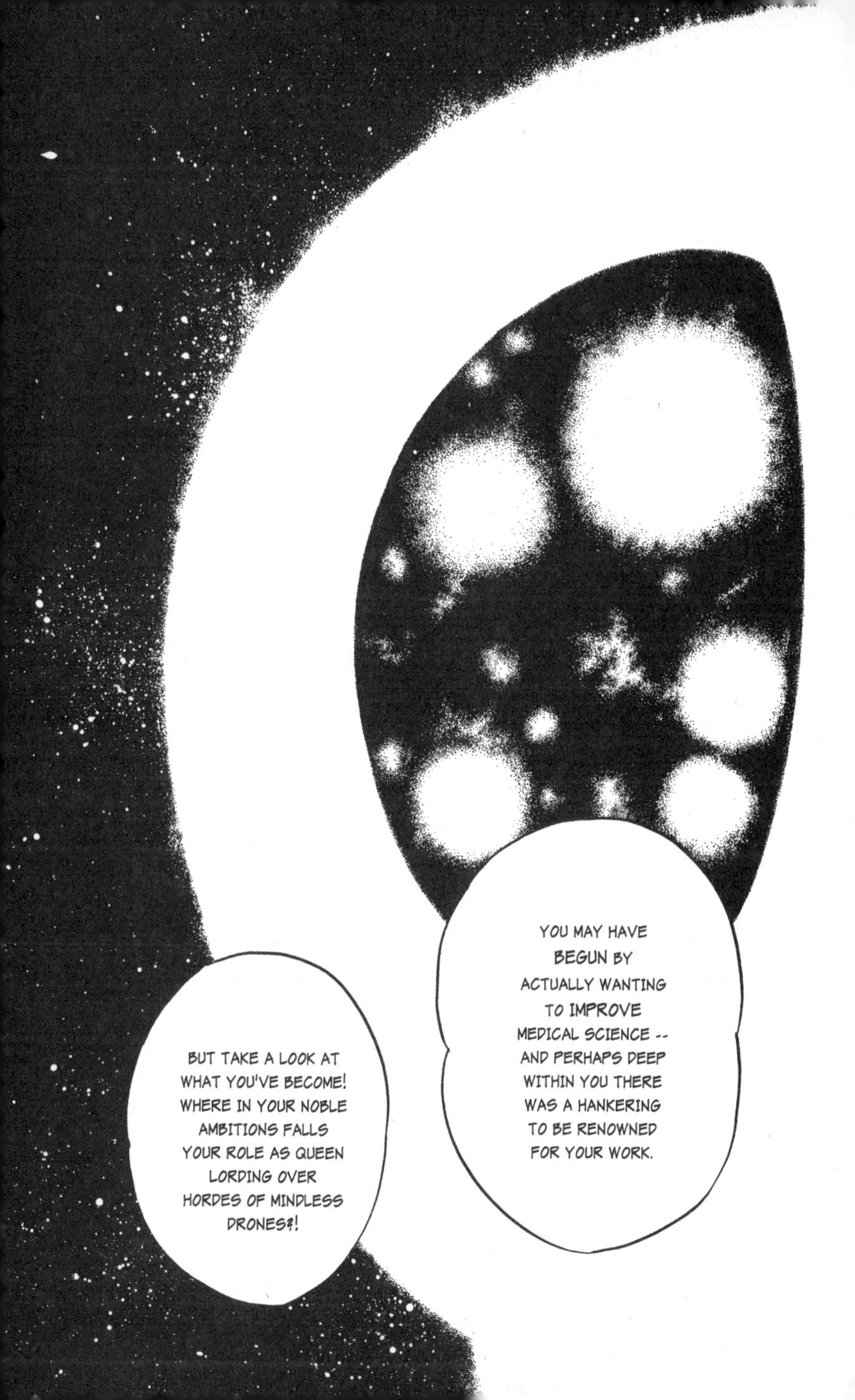
YOU MAY HAVE BEGUN BY ACTUALLY WANTING TO IMPROVE MEDICAL SCIENCE -- AND PERHAPS DEEP WITHIN YOU THERE WAS A HANKERING TO BE RENOWNED FOR YOUR WORK.
BUT TAKE A LOOK AT WHAT YOU'VE BECOME! WHERE IN YOUR NOBLE AMBITIONS FALLS YOUR ROLE AS QUEEN LORDING OVER HORDES OF MINDLESS DRONES?!

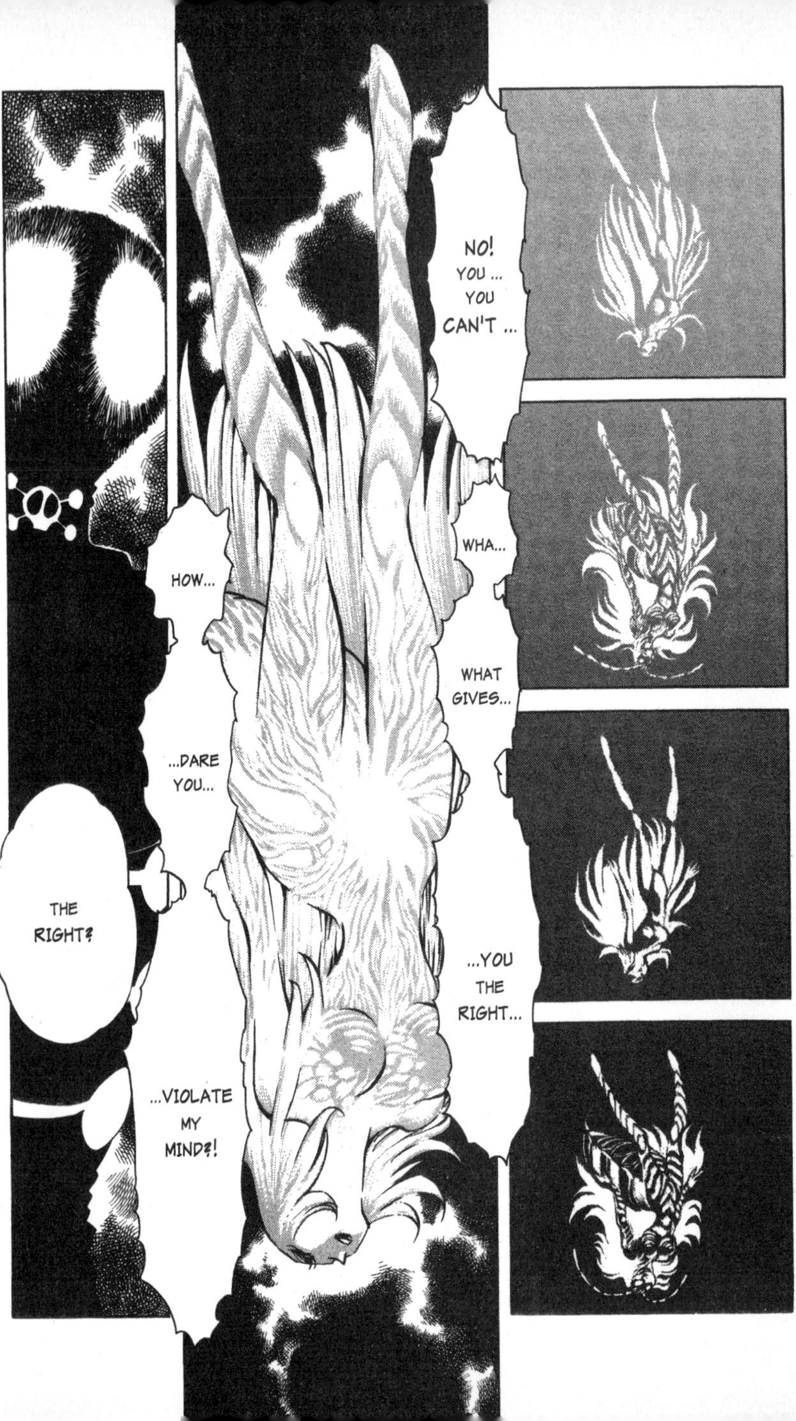
NO! YOU ... YOU CAN'T ...
WHA...
WHAT GIVES...
...YOU THE RIGHT...
HOW...
...DARE YOU...
...VIOLATE MY MIND?!
THE RIGHT?

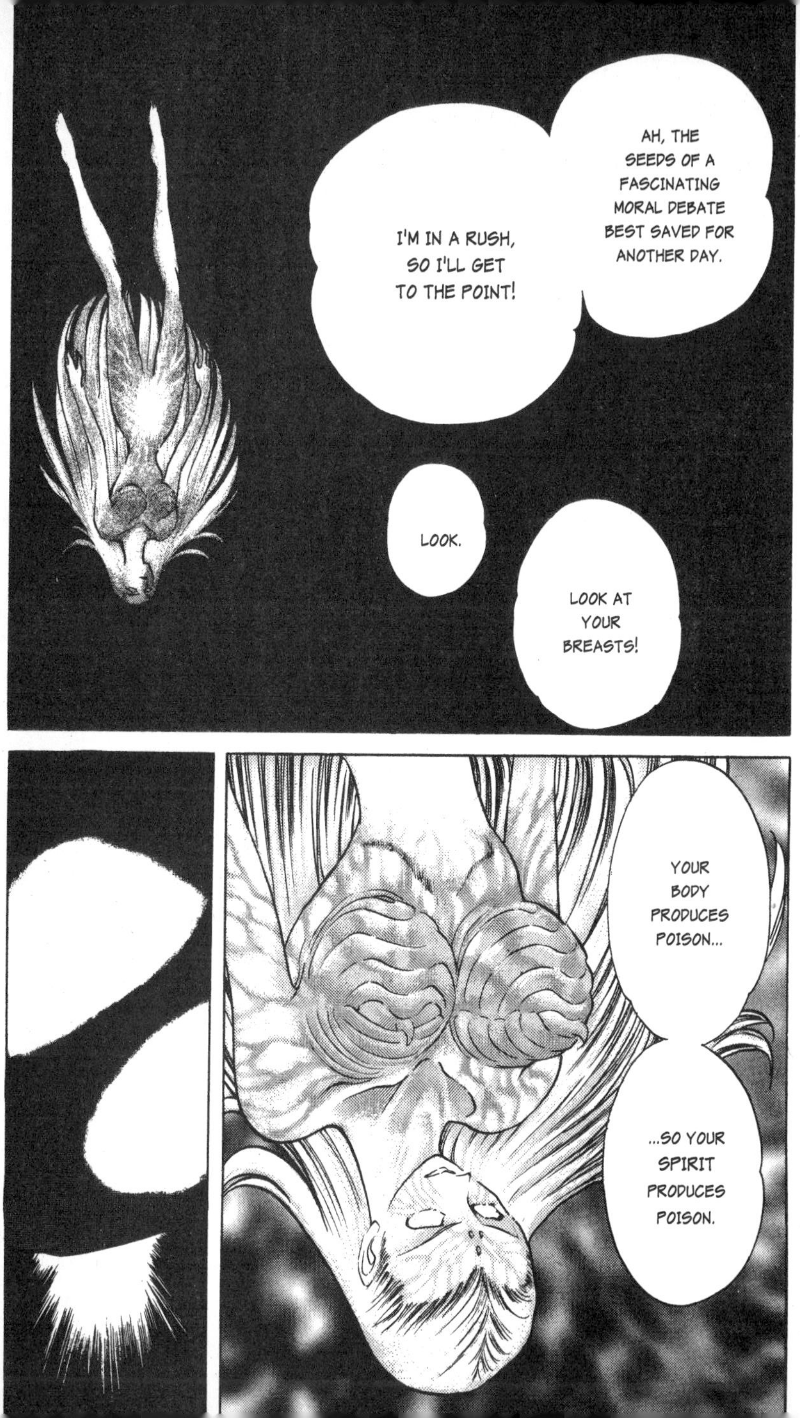
AH, THE SEEDS OF A FASCINATING MORAL DEBATE BEST SAVED FOR ANOTHER DAY.
I'M IN A RUSH, SO I'LL GET TO THE POINT!
LOOK.
LOOK AT YOUR BREASTS!
YOUR BODY PRODUCES POISON...
...SO YOUR SPIRIT PRODUCES POISON.

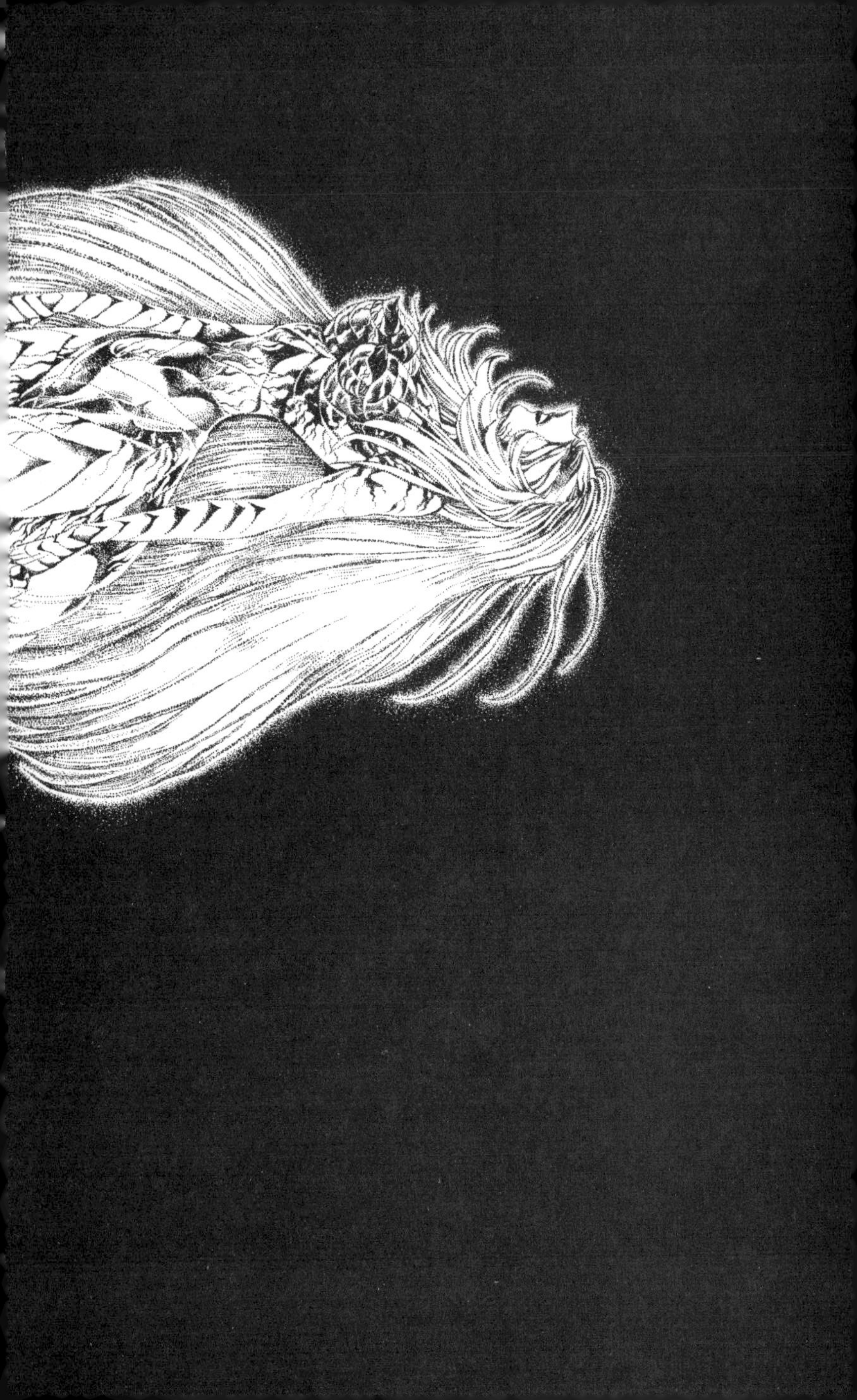

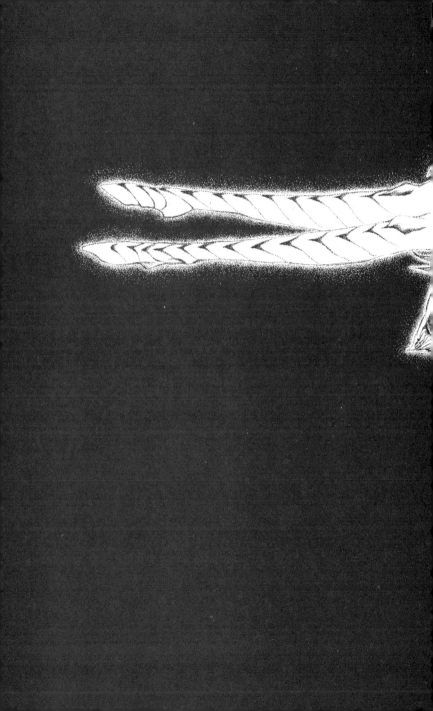

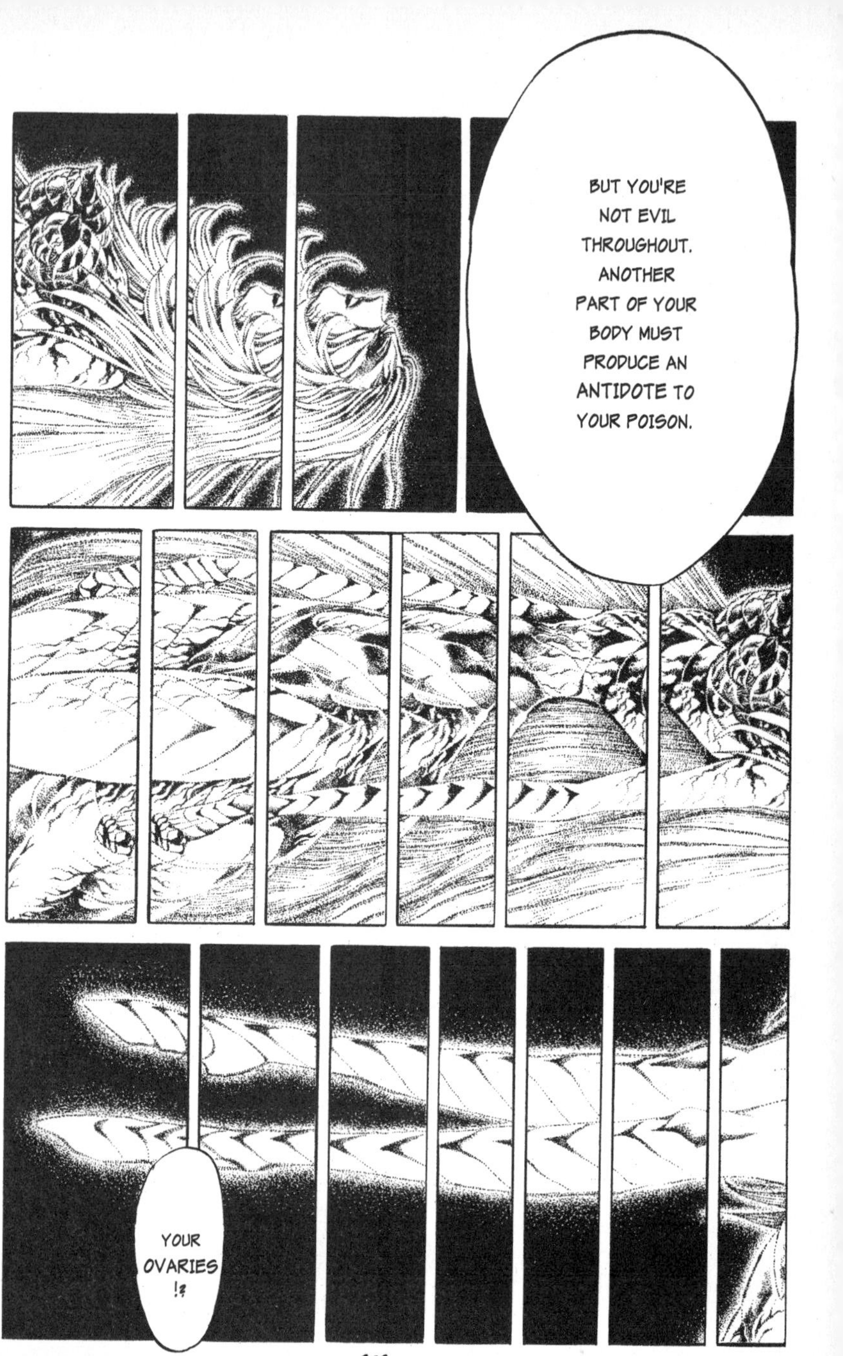
BUT YOU'RE NOT EVIL THROUGHOUT. ANOTHER PART OF YOUR BODY MUST PRODUCE AN ANTIDOTE TO YOUR POISON.
YOUR OVARIES !?

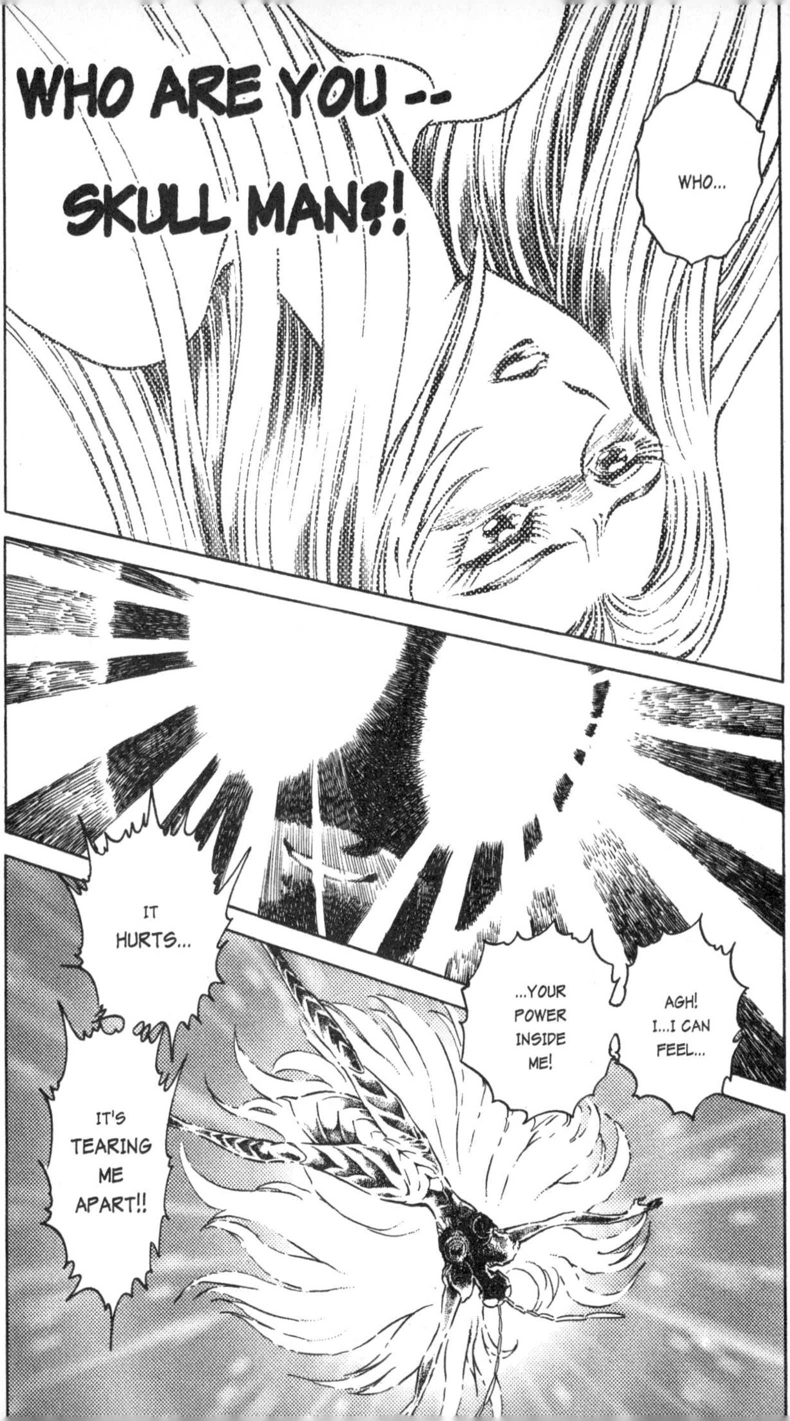
WHO...
WHO ARE YOU -- SKULL MAN?!
AGH! I...I CAN FEEL...
...YOUR POWER INSIDE ME!
IT HURTS...
IT'S TEARING ME APART!!

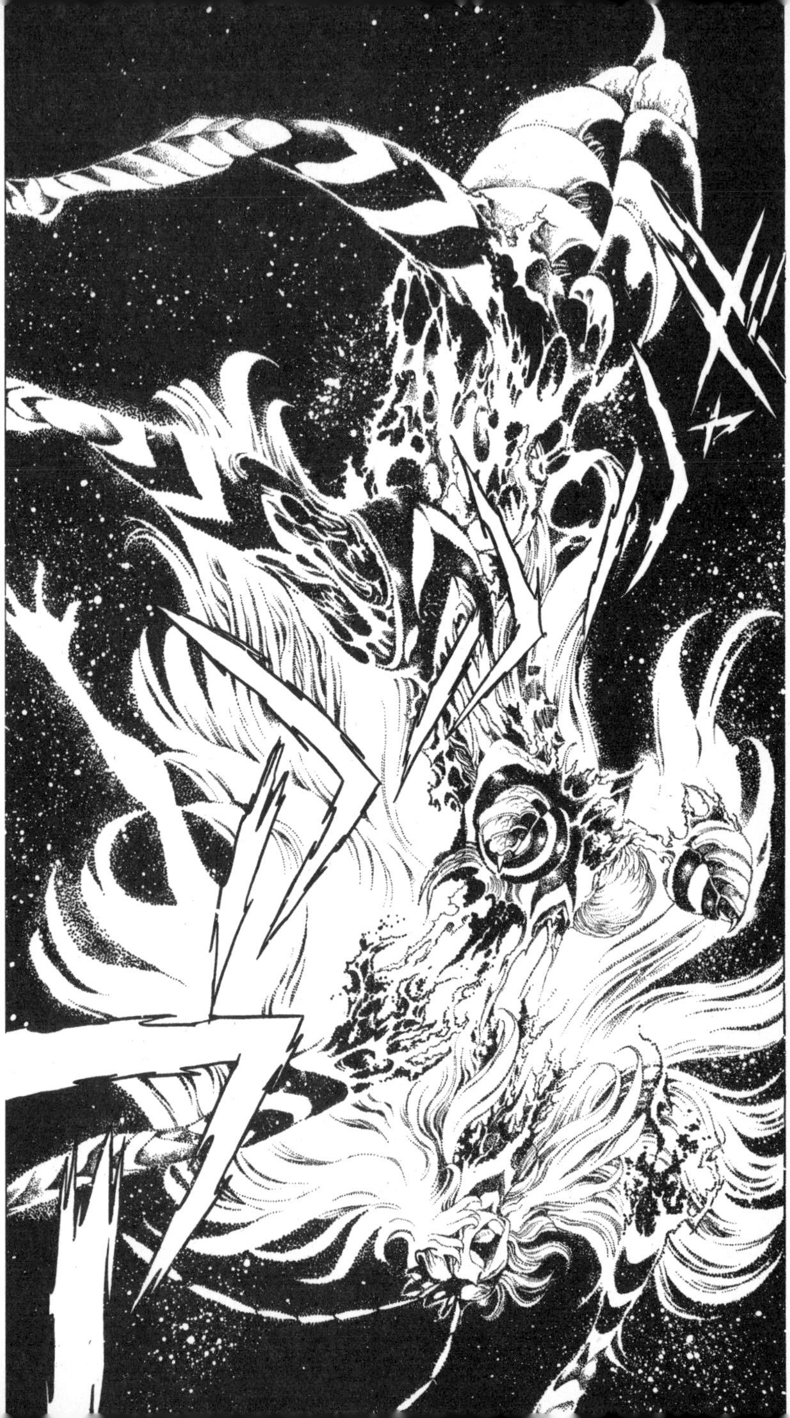

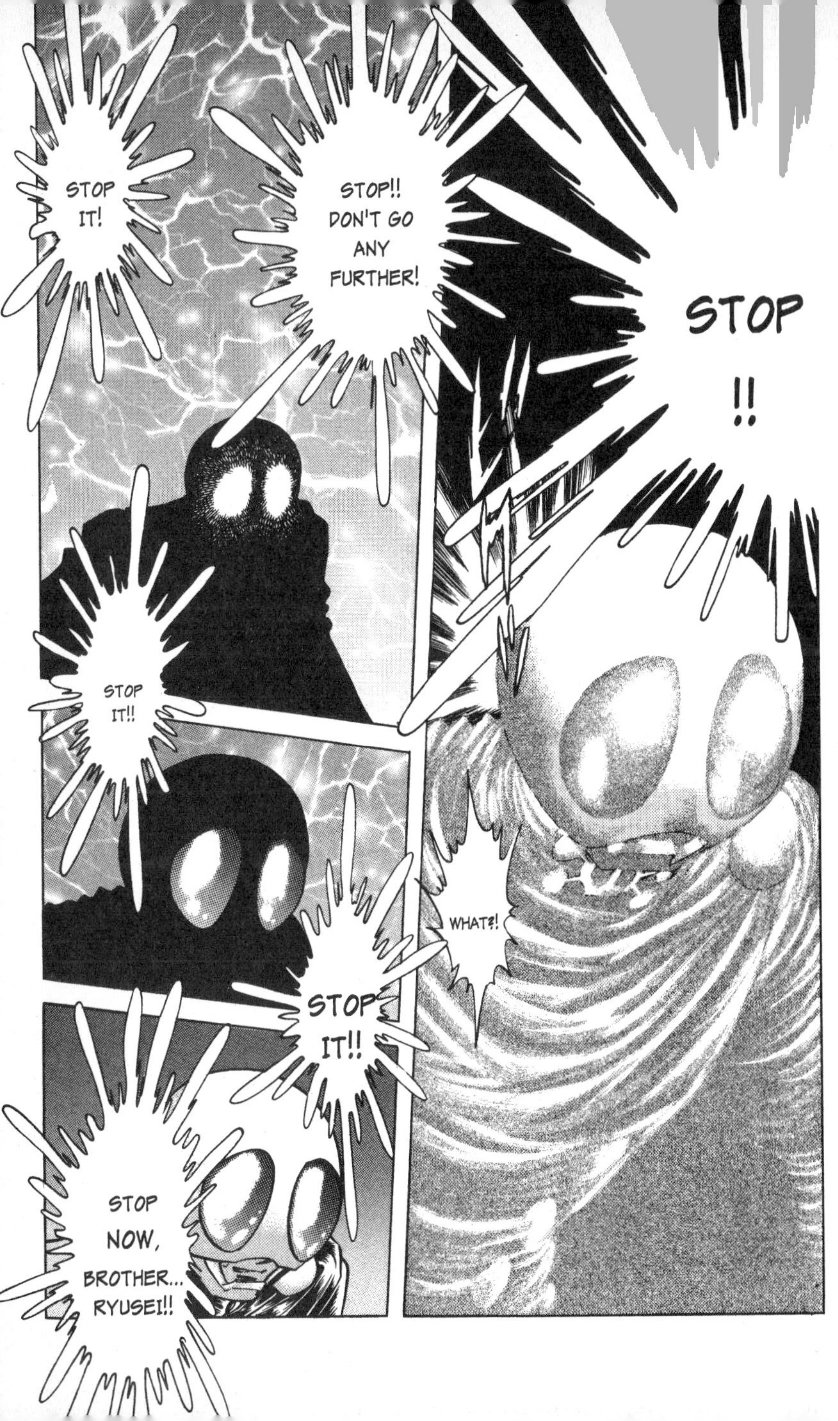
STOP !!
WHAT?!
STOP!! DON'T GO ANY FURTHER!
STOP IT!
STOP IT!!
STOP IT!!
STOP NOW, BROTHER... RYUSEI!!

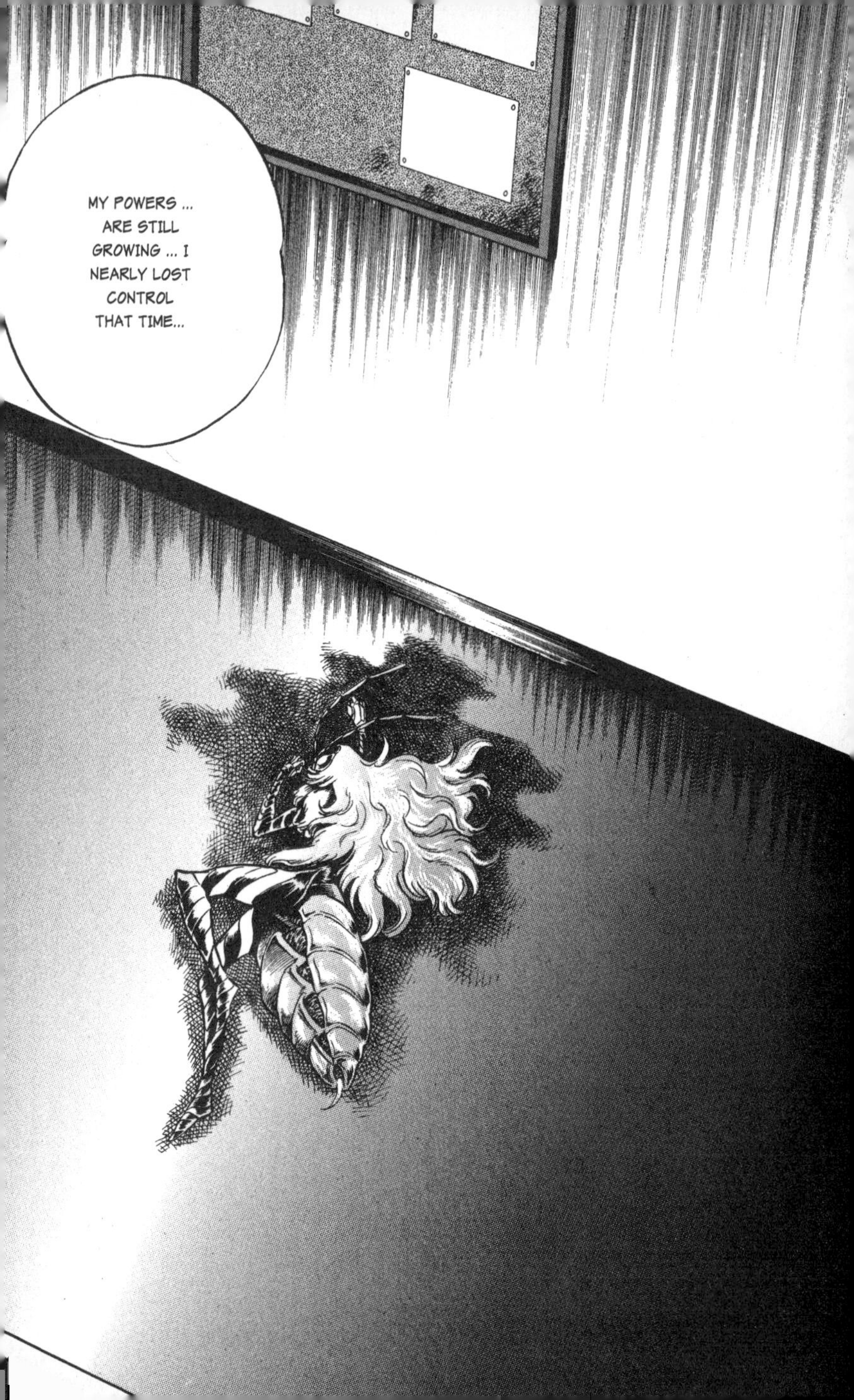
MY POWERS ... ARE STILL GROWING ... I NEARLY LOST CONTROL THAT TIME...

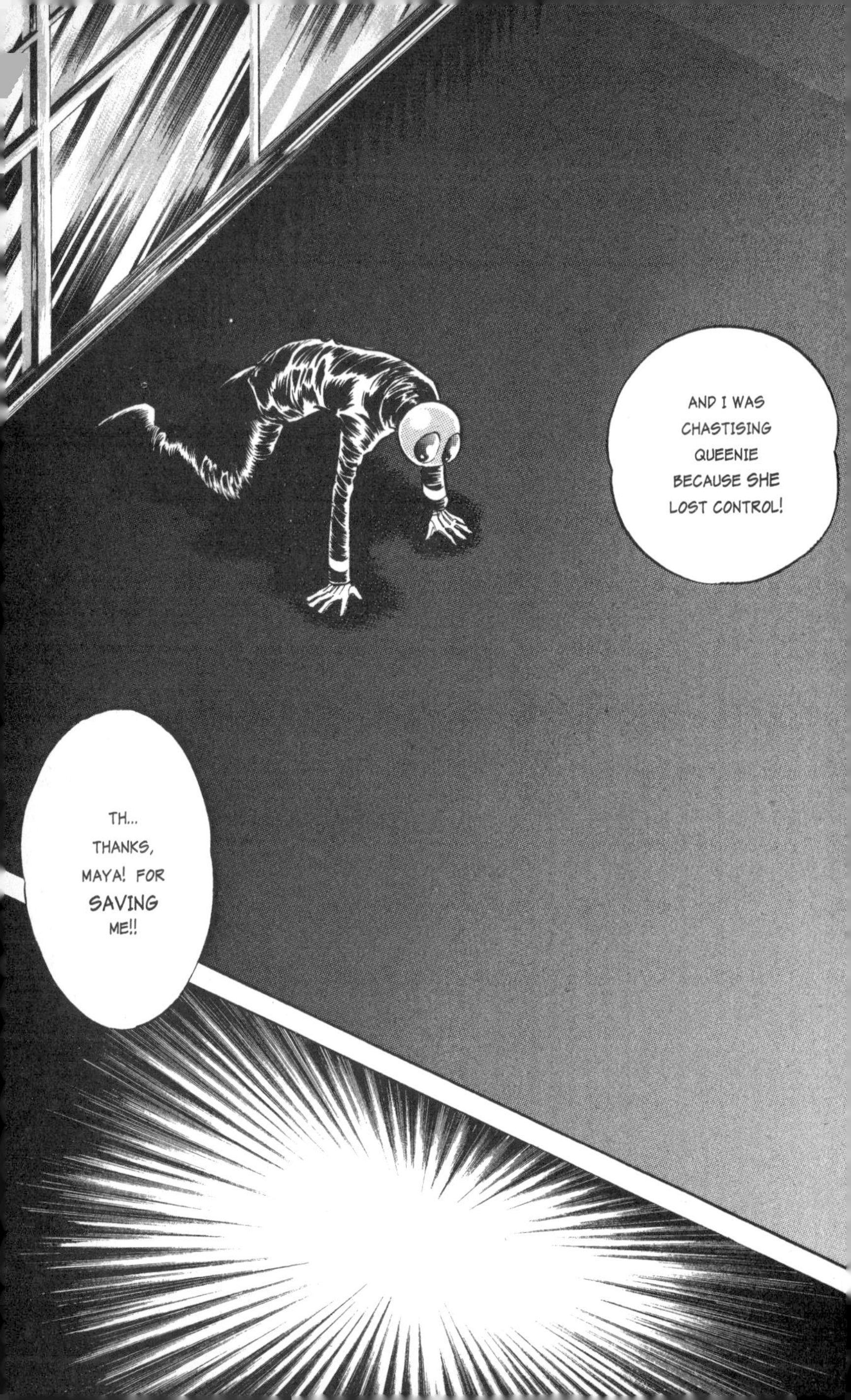
AND I WAS CHASTISING QUEENIE BECAUSE SHE LOST CONTROL!
TH... THANKS, MAYA! FOR SAVING ME!!

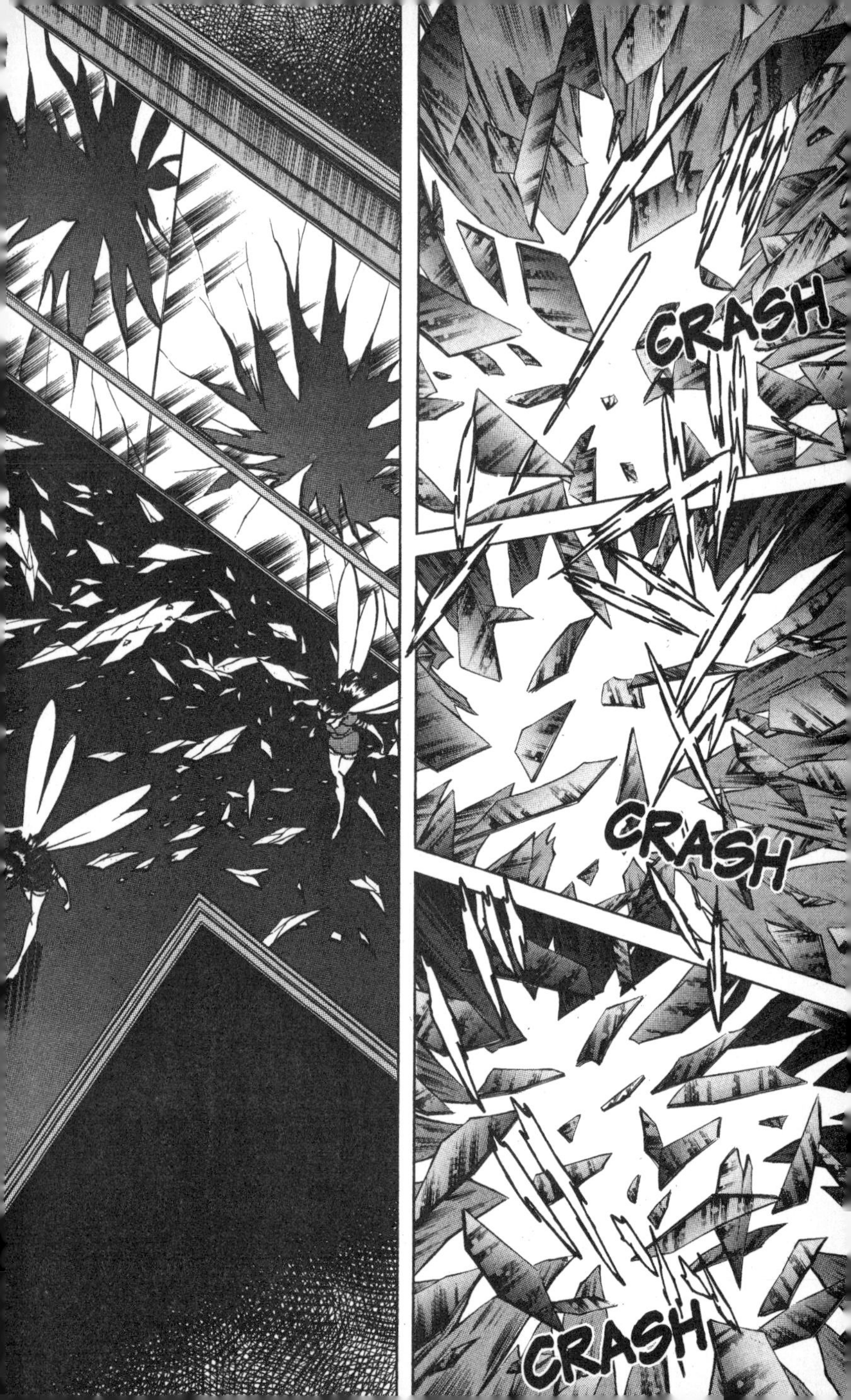
CRASH
CRASH
CRASH

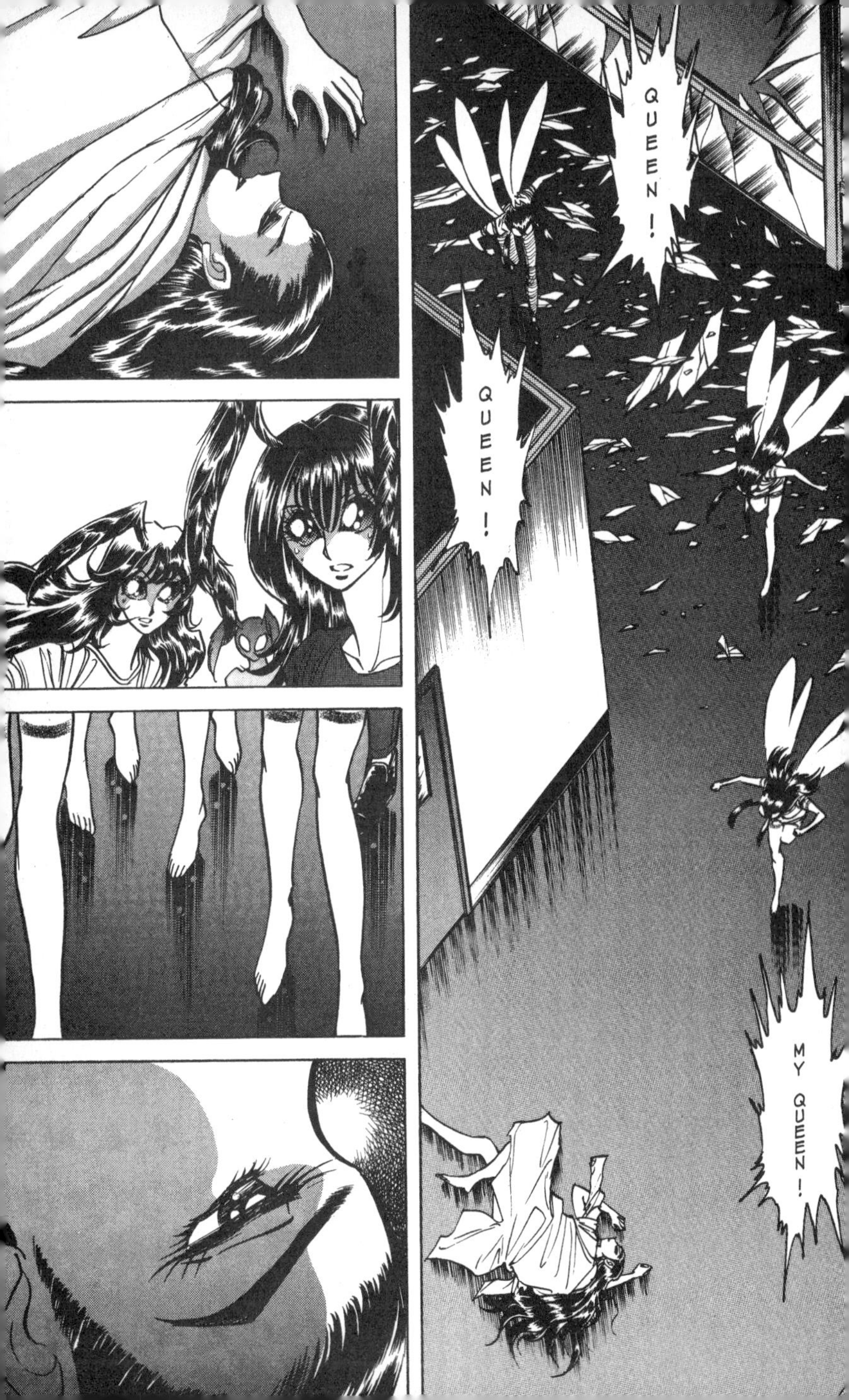
QUEEN!
QUEEN!
MY QUEEN!

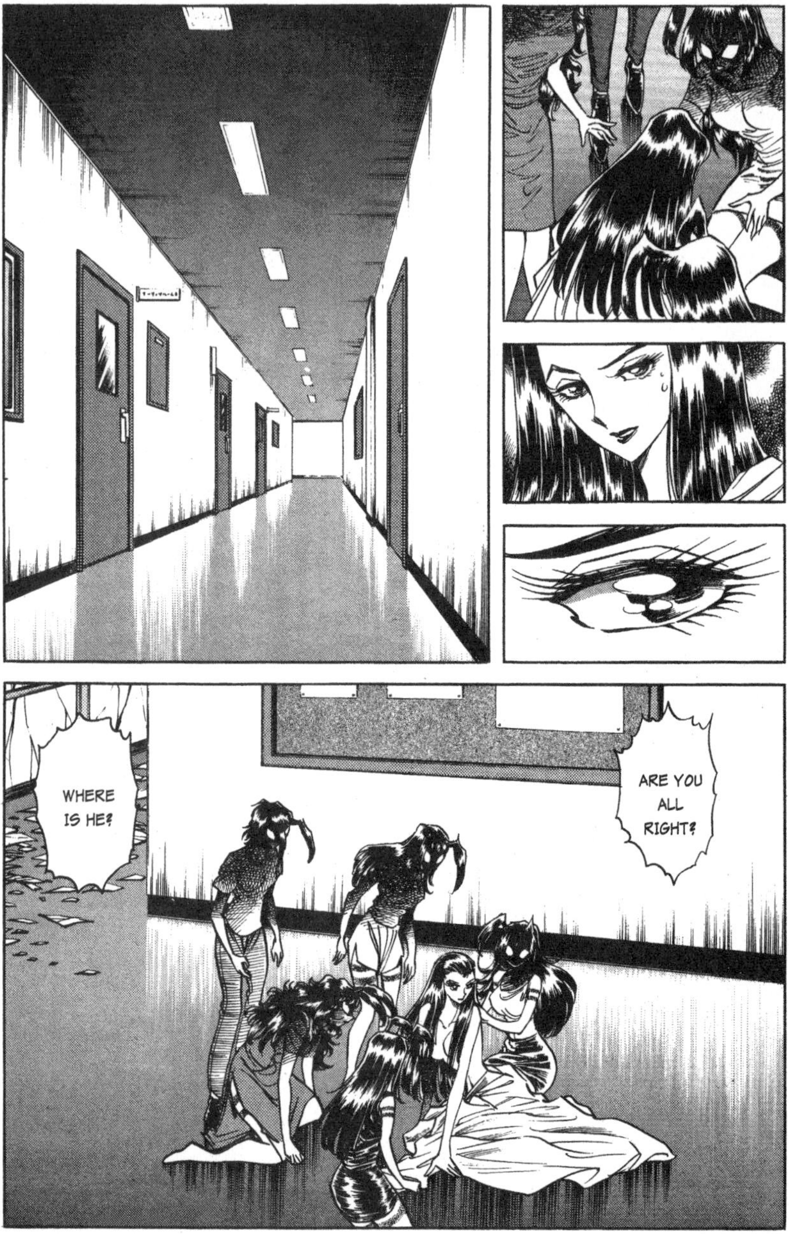

ARE YOU ALL RIGHT?
WHERE IS HE?

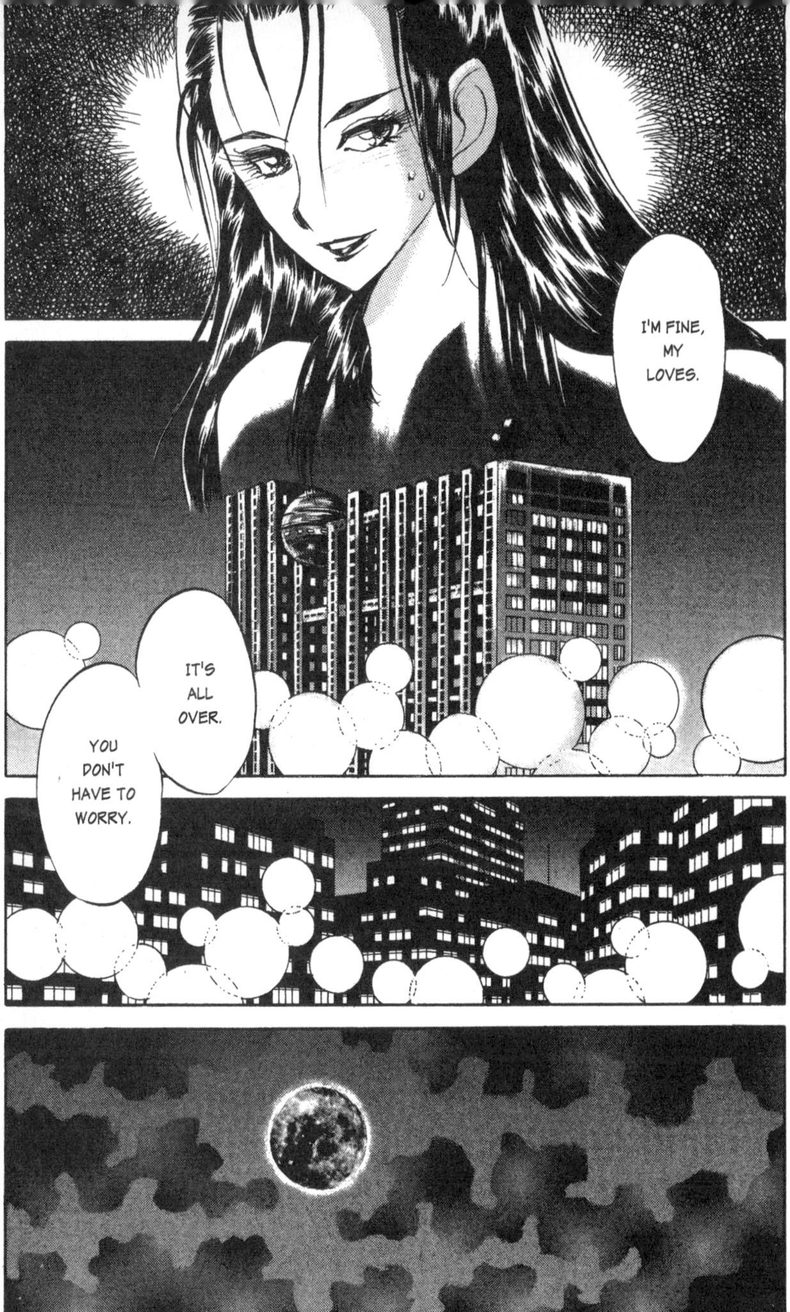
I'M FINE, MY LOVES.
IT'S ALL OVER.
YOU DON'T HAVE TO WORRY.

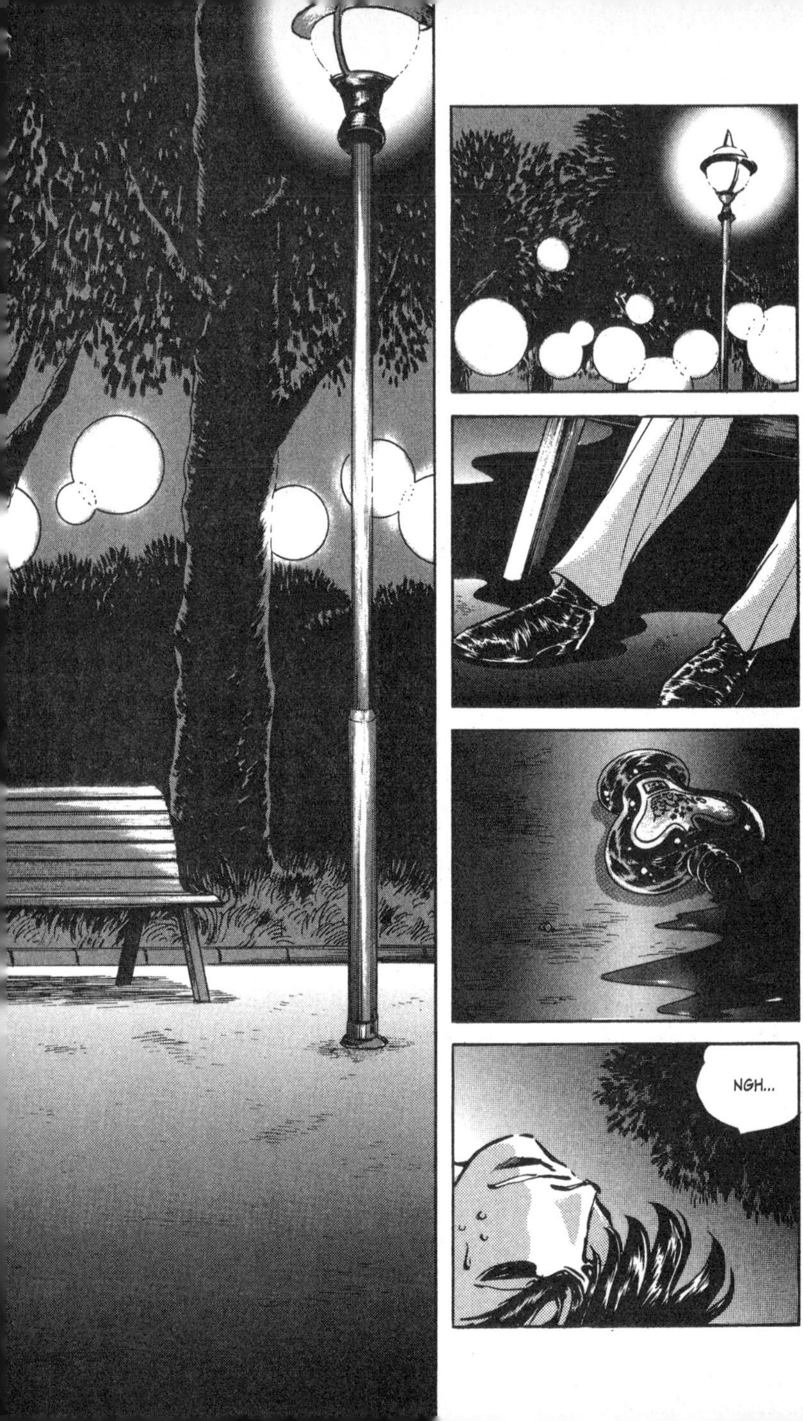
NGH...

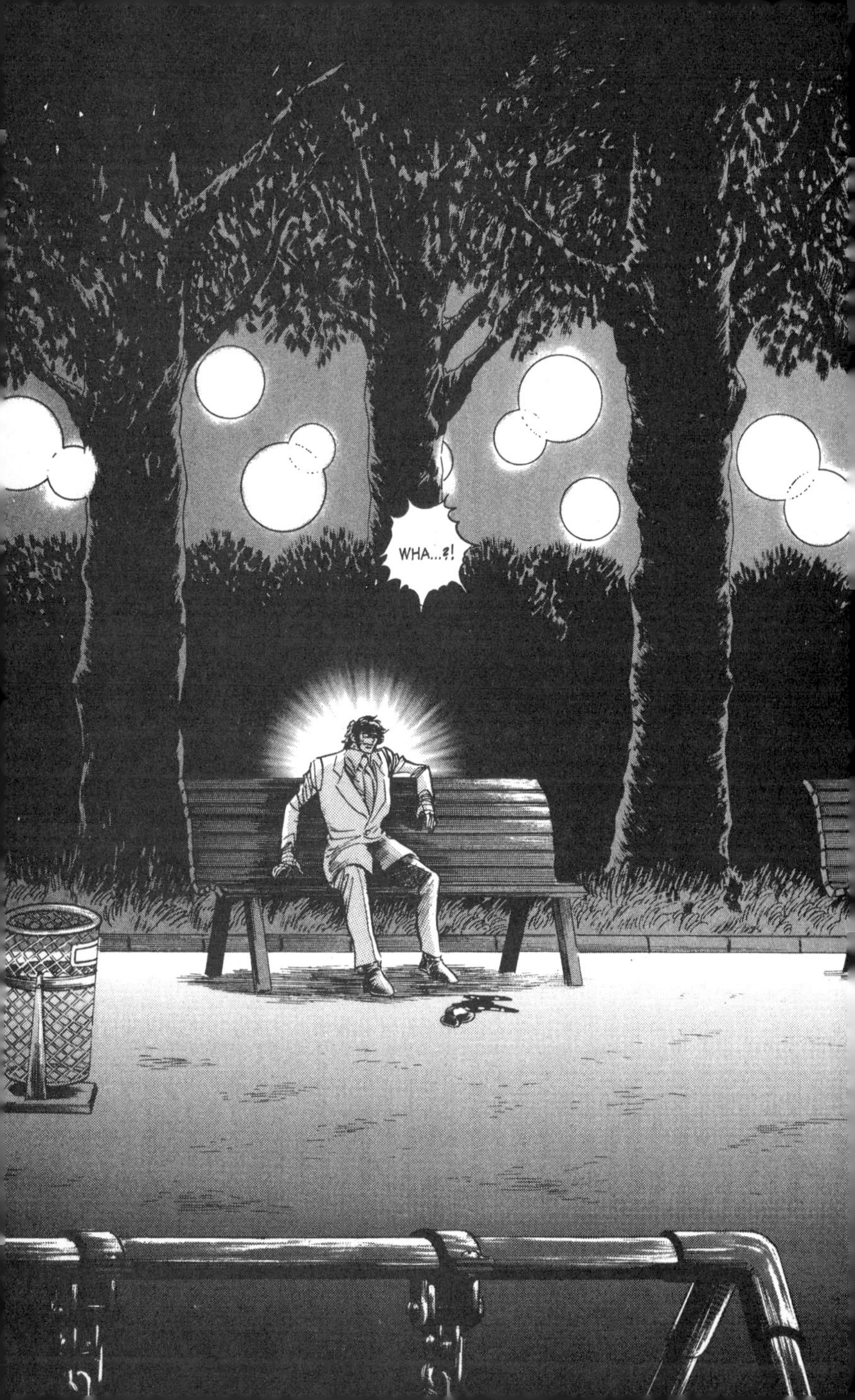
WHA...?!

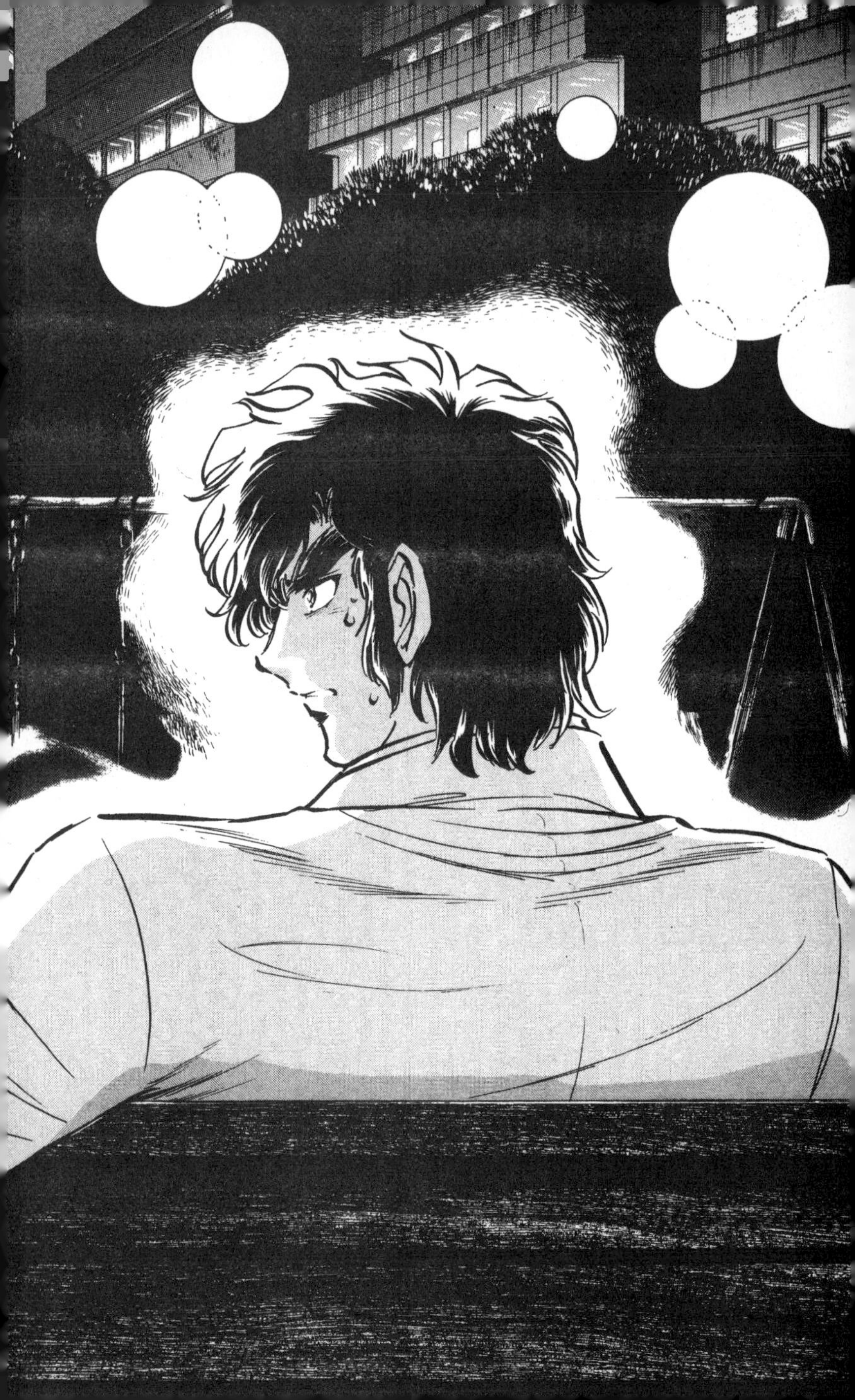

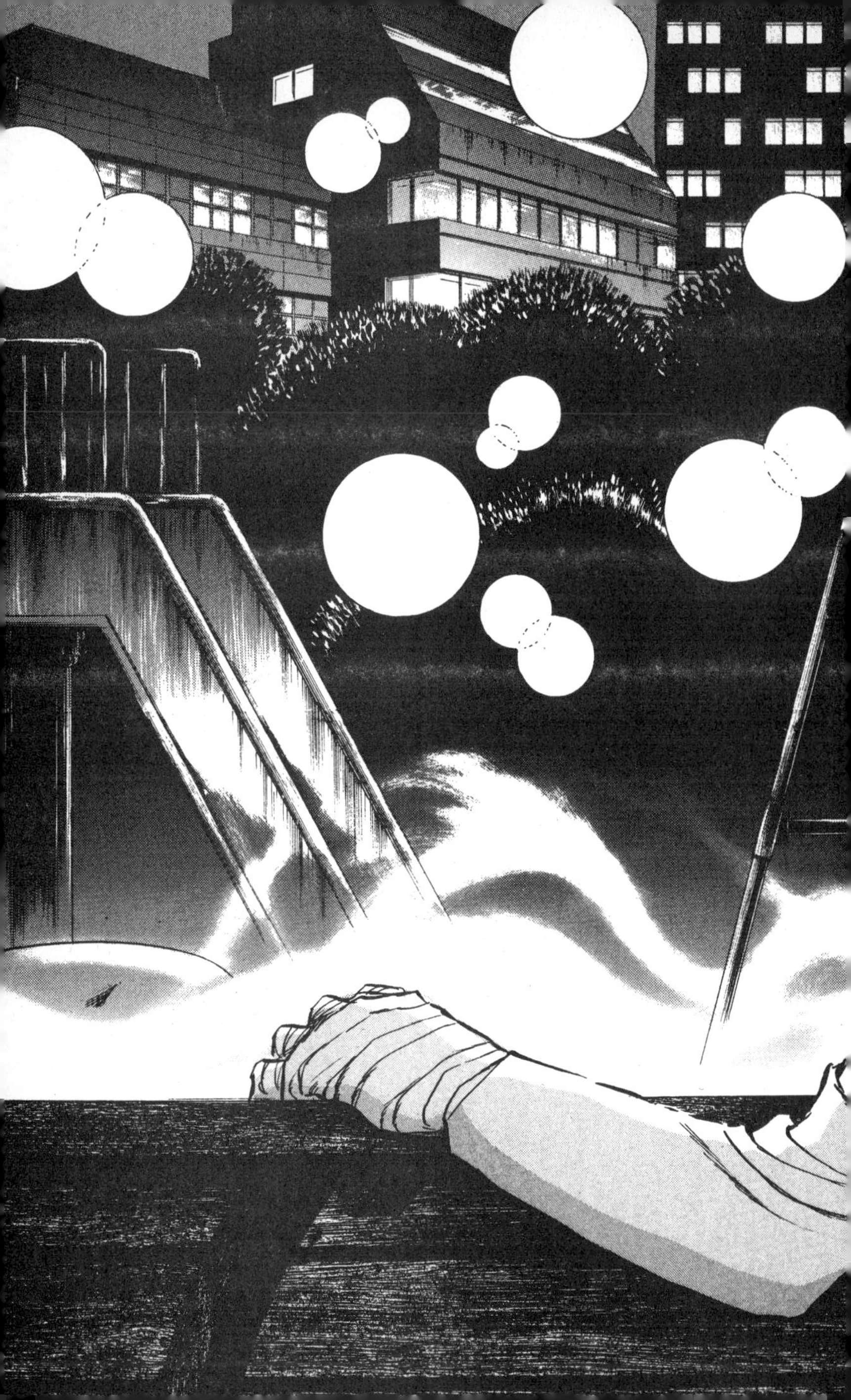

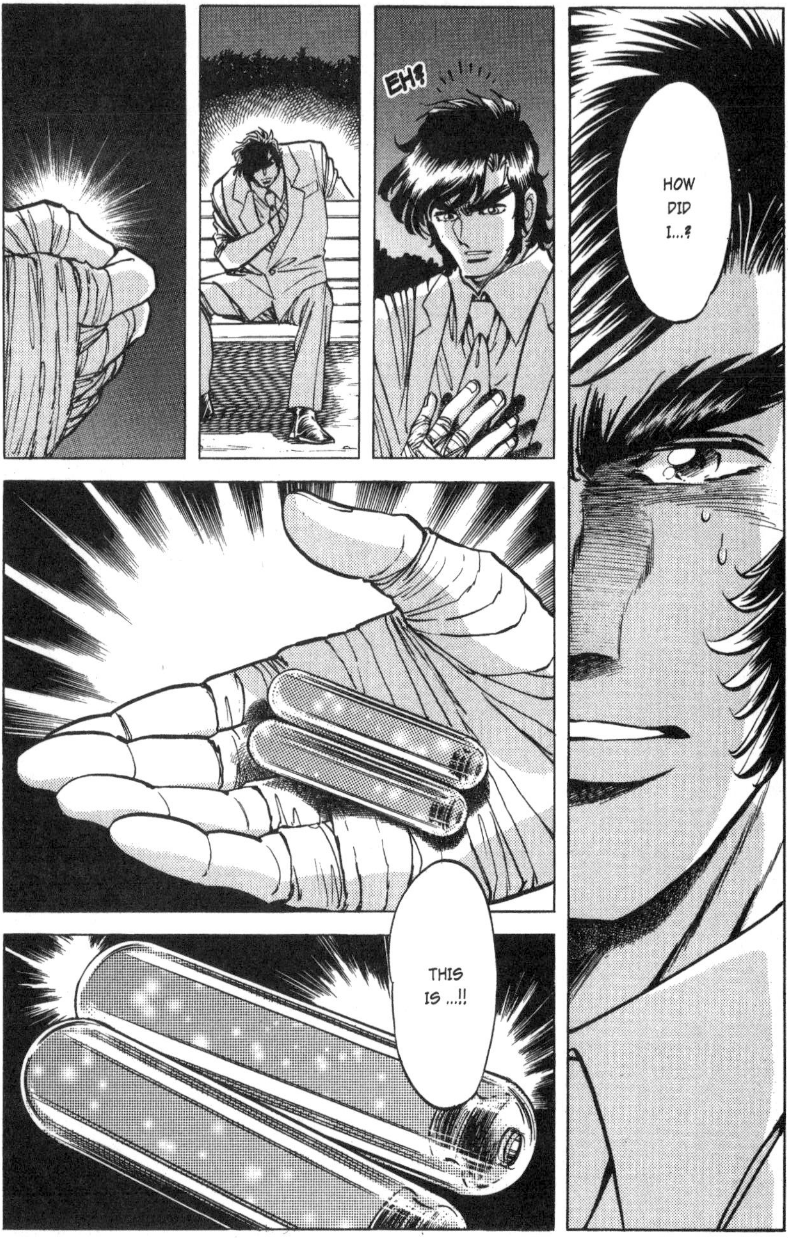
HOW DID I...?
EH?
THIS IS ...!!

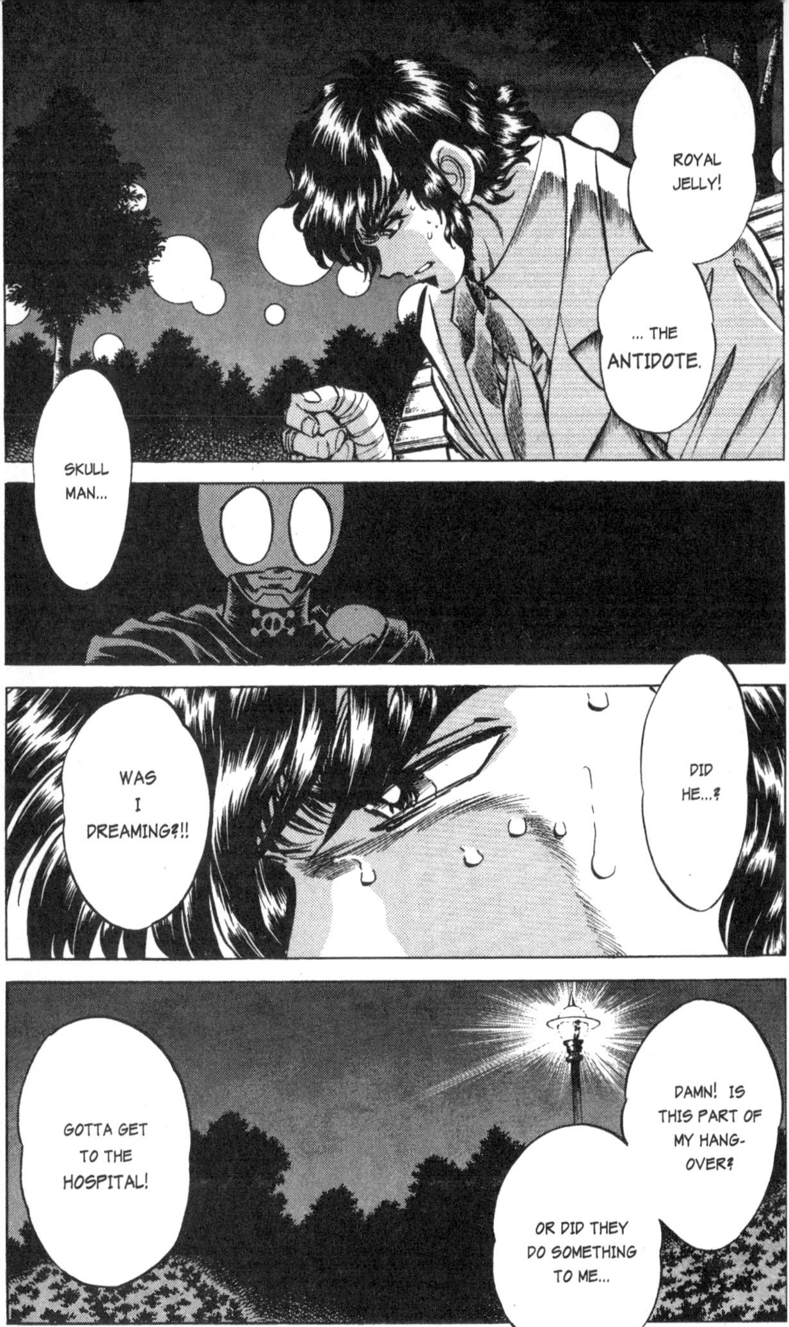
ROYAL JELLY!
... THE ANTIDOTE.
SKULL MAN...
DID HE...?
WAS I DREAMING?!!
DAMN! IS THIS PART OF MY HANG-OVER?
OR DID THEY DO SOMETHING TO ME...
GOTTA GET TO THE HOSPITAL!

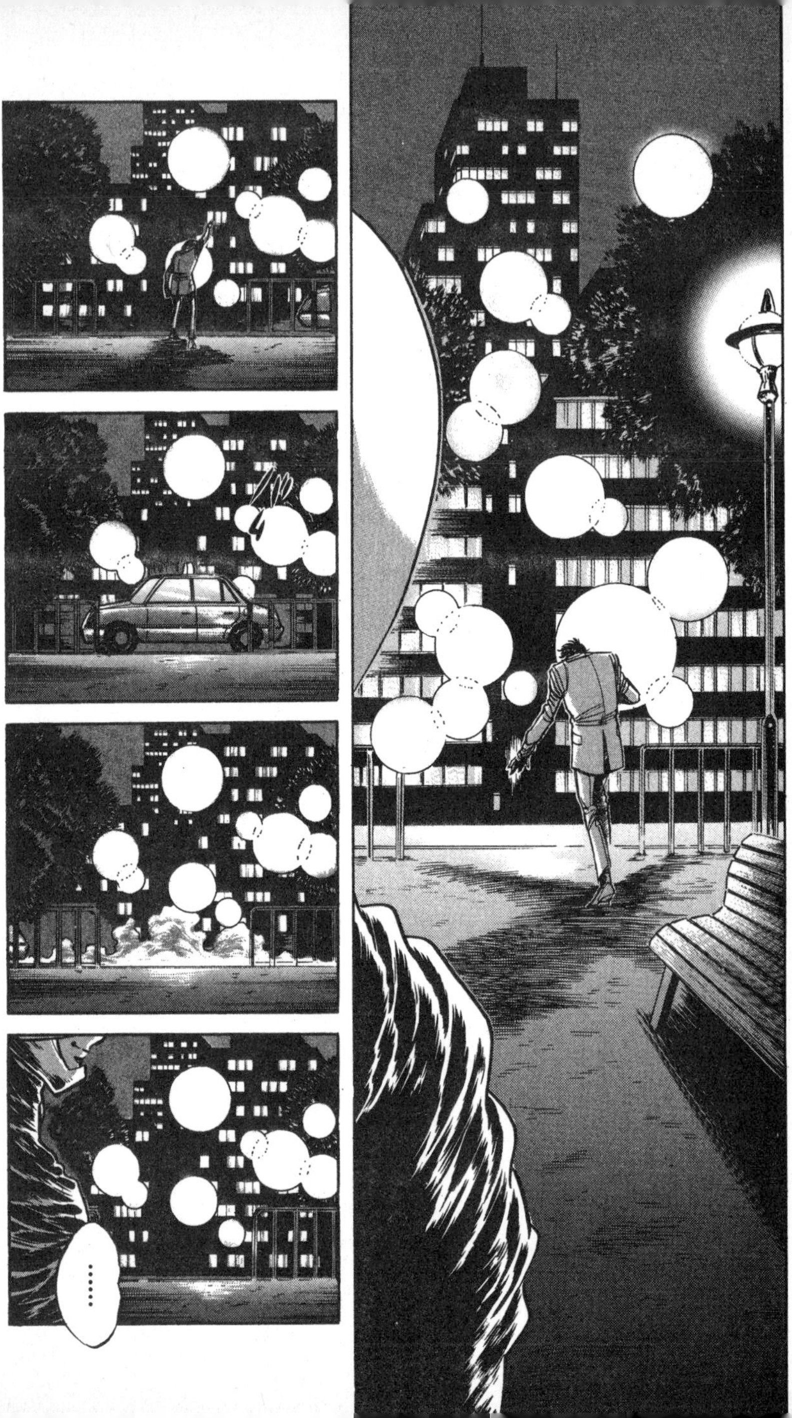
……

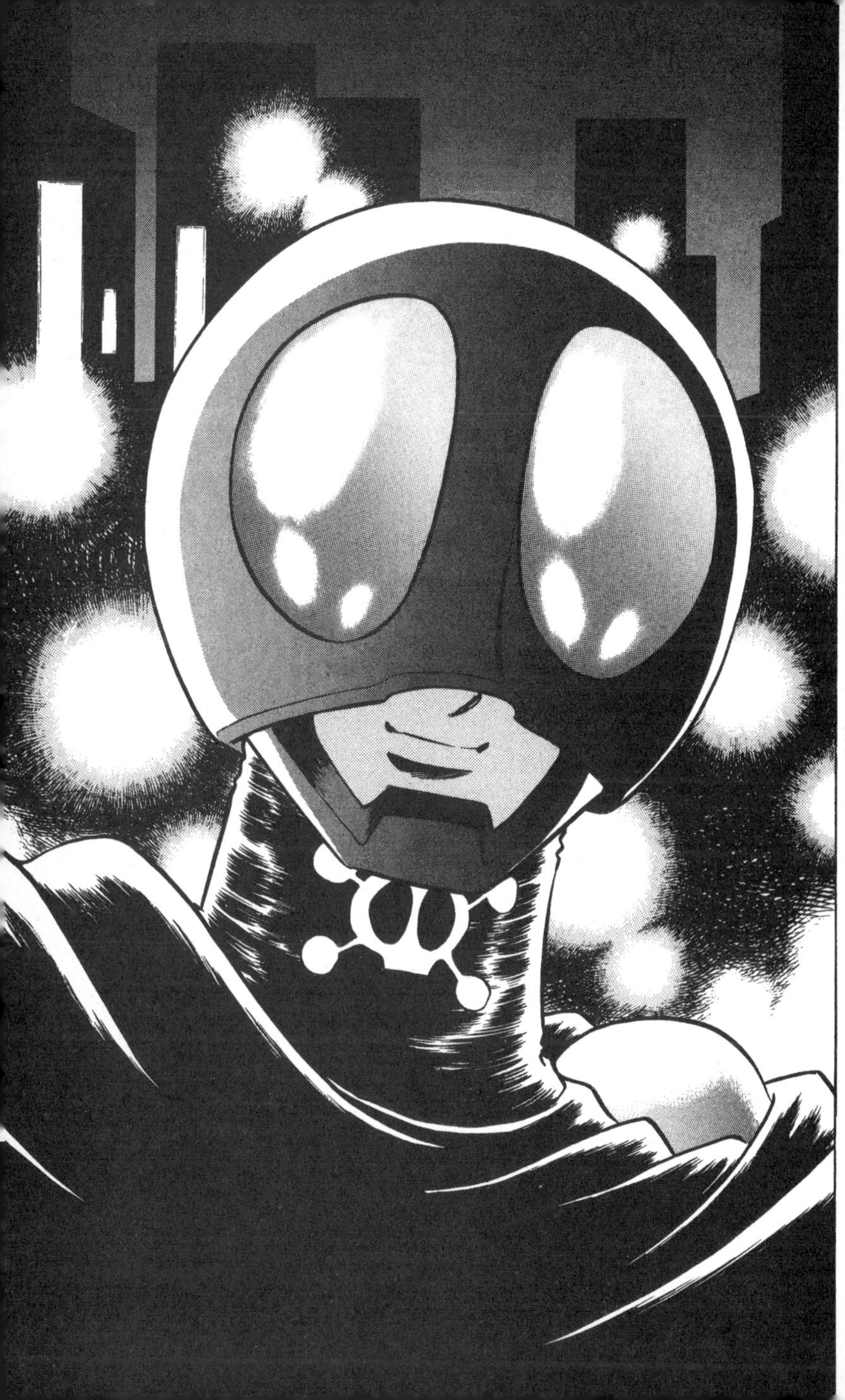

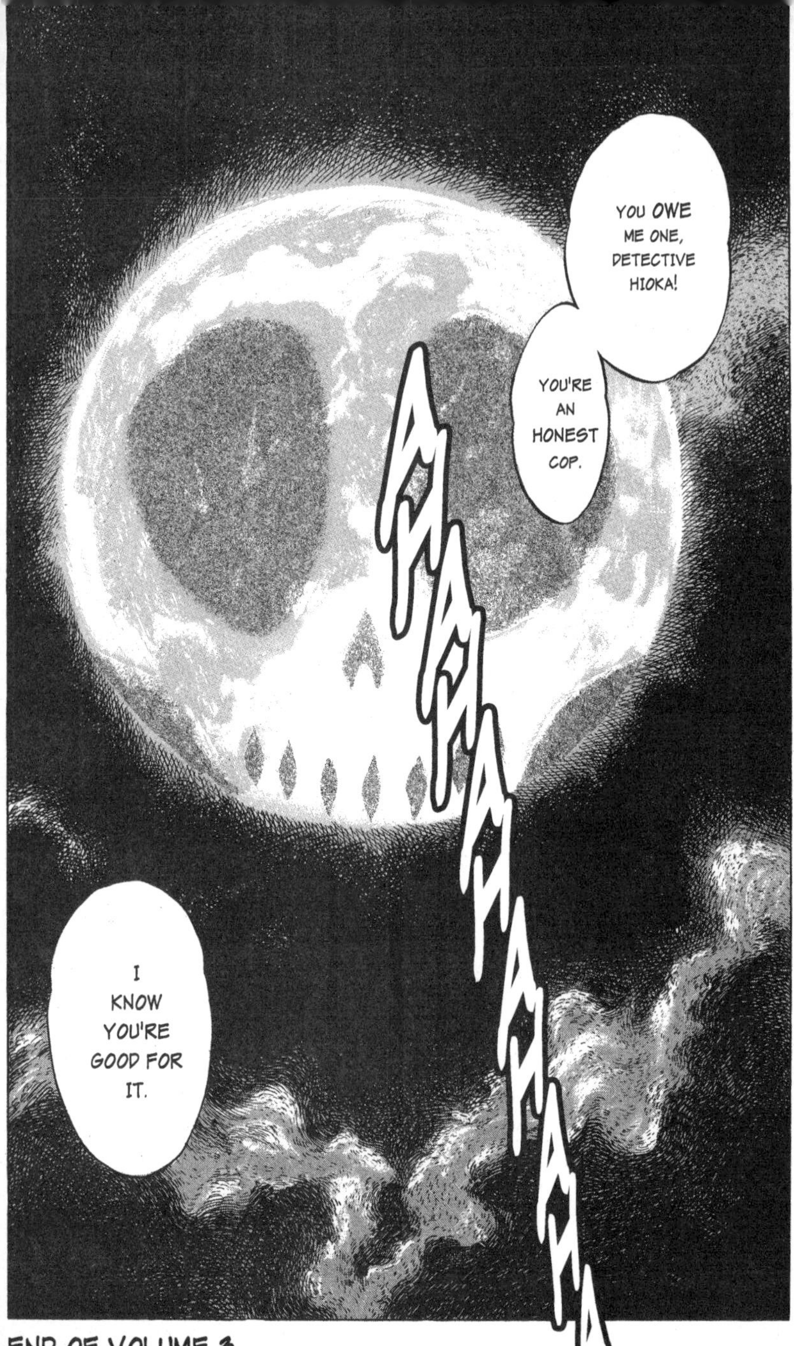
YOU OWE ME ONE, DETECTIVE HIOKA!
YOU'RE AN HONEST COP.
I KNOW YOU'RE GOOD FOR IT.

END OF VOLUME 3

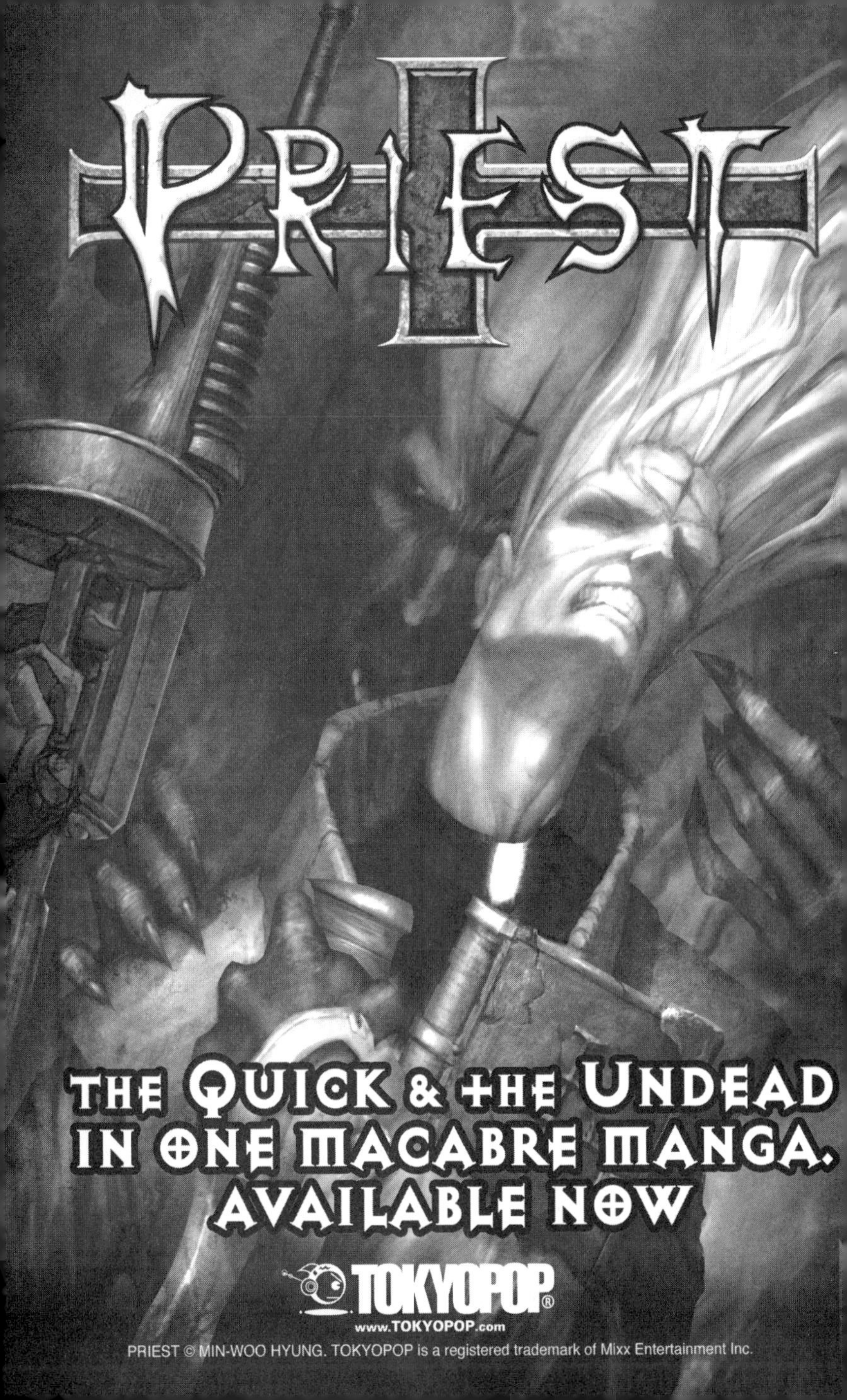
PRIEST
THE QUICK & THE UNDEAD
IN ONE MACABRE MANGA.
AVAILABLE NOW
TOKYOPOP®
www.TOKYOPOP.com
PRIEST © MIN-WOO HYUNG. TOKYOPOP is a registered trademark of Mixx Entertainment Inc.

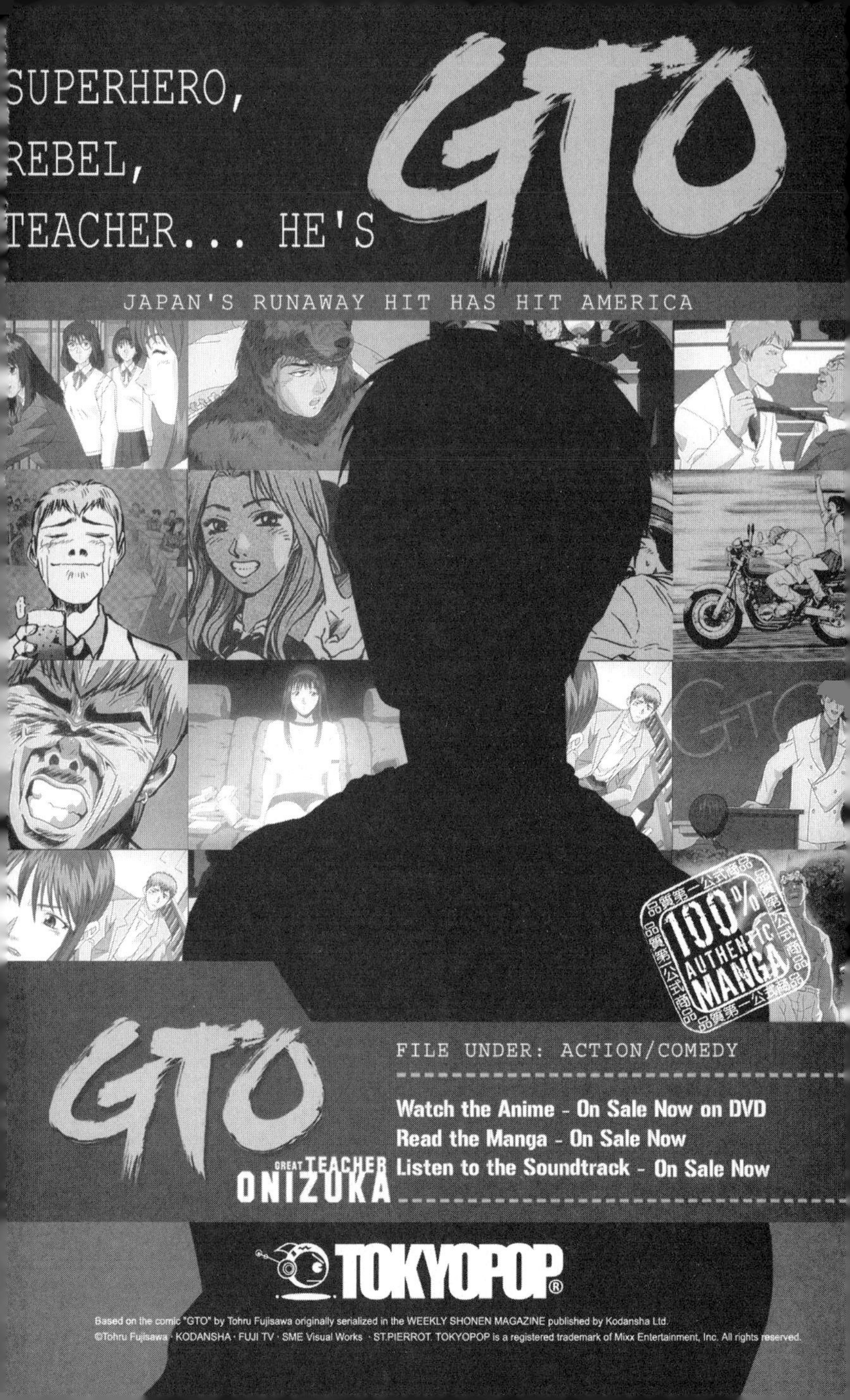

YA-G
SHI

STOP!

This is the back of the book.
You wouldn't want to spoil a great ending!

This book is printed "manga-style," in the authentic Japanese right-to-left format. Since none of the artwork has been flipped or altered, readers get to experience the story just as the creator intended. You've been asking for it, so TOKYOPOP® delivered: authentic, hot-off-the-press, and far more fun!

DIRECTIONS

If this is your first time reading manga-style, here's a quick guide to help you understand how it works.

It's easy... just start in the top right panel and follow the numbers. Have fun, and look for more 100% authentic manga from TOKYOPOP®!